# FEDERALISM AND CONSTITUTIONAL CHANGE

# FEDERALISM AND CONSTITUTIONAL CHANGE

BY

WILLIAM S. LIVINGSTON



GREENWOOD PRESS, PUBLISHERS
WESTPORT, CONNECTICUT

**Library of Congress Cataloging in Publication Data**

Livingston, William S
Federalism and constitutional change.

Originally submitted as a doctoral thesis at Yale University.
Reprint of the 1956 ed. published at the Clarendon Press, Oxford.
Bibliography: p.
1. Constitutional amendments. 2. Federal government
I. Title.
Law 342.03 74-9226
ISBN 0-8371-7623-9

'Federal governments are not the offspring of political science; they are the product of economic and social pressures.'

FELIX FRANKFURTER

'Every state is something of a federal society and contains different national groups, different churches, different economic organizations, each exercising its measure of control over its members.'

SIR ERNEST BARKER

Originally published in 1956 by the Clarendon Press, Oxford

This reprint has been authorized by the Clarendon Press, Oxford

Reprinted in 1974 by Greenwood Press,
a division of Williamhouse-Regency Inc.

Library of Congress Catalog Card Number 74-9226

ISBN 0-8371-7623-9

Printed in the United States of America

# PREFACE

THIS study is conceived as an attempt to view the federal system in a somewhat different light from that in which it is ordinarily displayed. That federalism is a legal concept and poses vast problems of a legal nature is not to be denied; but it has appeared to me that a better understanding of the nature of federal government can be secured by trying to picture its workings as a process in which the diversified elements that compose a federal state integrate and compromise their differences, rather than as a set of institutions and procedures whose operation is wholly determined by the legal norms and structures. That a complete examination of federalism from this point of view would require much more than a single volume is obvious; I have therefore tried to interpret it through the single medium of constitutional amendment. No one realizes more than I that this limits the validity of the exercise to a single aspect of the problem. But if the book suggests a different (and, I think, more realistic) approach to the problem and provides an example for further studies by others, it will have been of value. It is my hope that the present study may stimulate examination from a similar point of view of some of the other instrumentalities of federalism.

In the course of its preparation the volume has undergone what at times seemed an endless series of revisions, and now bears but little resemblance to the original form in which it was submitted as a doctoral thesis at Yale University. Both at New Haven and at Austin I have benefited from the counsel and assistance of several persons to whom I gladly make acknowledgement. I should like to extend my thanks in some better way than this to the following: to Hans Bronner, J. Lloyd Mecham, O. Douglas Weeks, and Willmoore Kendall for assisting me at difficult points and for reading portions of the manuscript; to the following for supplying me with needed information at the expense of much time and effort: the Legal Adviser of the State Department at Washington, the Deputy Attorney-General at Ottawa, the staffs of the Canadian Information Service, the Australian News and

Information Service, and the Consulate-General of Switzerland, all in New York; to the Regents and the University Research Council of the University of Texas for a grant that furthered the project; to the editors of the *Political Science Quarterly* and the *American Political Science Review* for permission to reproduce material that has appeared in a somewhat different form in those journals; to Fred V. Cahill and K. C. Wheare for reading the entire manuscript and giving me detailed criticisms and suggestions for its betterment; and most especially to C. H. Driver, who guided the original research, who provided the indispensable counsel and assistance, and who, by his example and unfailing encouragement, moved me to the completion of the task.

Needless to say, none of these persons is in any way responsible for the errors in the book, of which I have no doubt there are many. I have received much help and many suggestions, all most welcome. Some suggestions have, of course, not been accepted, and to their authors I tender my apologies; but these suggestions, too, have been gratefully received.

Finally, I am grateful to my wife, who has endured it all. A completed book or a word of thanks is little recompense for a thousand grumpy replies and a long series of lonely evenings.

W. S. L.

# CONTENTS

# LIST OF TABLES

# 1

# THE CHARACTER OF FEDERALISM

## *The Sociology of Federalism*

NEARLY every discussion of federal government and its problems has begun with the assumption that the problem here concerned is one of legal formalism and formal jurisprudence. The analysis is usually a legal analysis and political questions are usually subordinated to the principles of constitutional law.

This is assuredly a convenient method of approaching the problem, and in many instances it is the only possible one. But it is not the only one. If a question arises that requires a legal answer, it can be solved only in legal terms. But the validity of such an answer is limited to the frame of reference within which the question is posed. Legal answers are of value only in the solution of legal problems. And federalism is concerned with many other problems than those of a legal nature.

The essential nature of federalism is to be sought for, not in the shadings of legal and constitutional terminology, but in the forces—economic, social, political, cultural—that have made the outward forms of federalism necessary. Federalism, like most institutional forms, is a solution of, or an attempt to solve, a certain kind of problem of political organization. Federal governments and federal constitutions do not grow simply by accident. They arise in response to certain stimuli; a federal system is consciously adopted as a means of solving the problems represented by these stimuli.

But whether the operating constitution of a country may properly be called federal depends not so much on the arrangement of the institutions within it as it does on the manner in which these institutions are employed. Institutions have a habit of serving purposes other than those for which they are designed. The passage of time produces changes in the purposes of any society and these new purposes are reflected in new modes of operating old institutions which frequently retain their original forms. Thus a society may possess institutions that are 'federal' in appearance but may operate them as though they were something else; and, what is more likely, it may possess a unitary set of institutions and employ them as though they were federal in nature. The institutions themselves do not provide an accurate index of the federal nature of the society that subtends them; they are only the surface manifestations of the deeper federal quality of the society that lies beneath the surface. The essence of federalism lies not in the constitutional or institutional structure but in the society itself. Federal government is a device by which the federal qualities of the society are articulated and protected.

Every society, every nation if you will, is more or less closely integrated in accordance with its own peculiar historical, cultural, economic, political, and other determinants. Each is composed of elements that feel themselves to be different from the other elements in varying degrees and that demand in varying degrees a means of self-expression. These diversities may turn on all sorts of questions—economic, religious, racial, historical, for example; any of these can produce in a group within the population a demand for such self-expression. Furthermore the diversities may be distributed through the members of the society in such a way that certain attitudes are found in particular territorial areas, or they may be scattered widely throughout the whole of the society. If they are grouped territorially, i.e. geographically, then the result may be a society that is federal. If they are not grouped territorially, then the society cannot be said to be federal. In either case coherence in the society may depend on the devolution upon these groups of the exercise of functions appropriate to the diversities that they represent. But in the first case only can this take the form of federalism or federal government. In the latter case, it becomes functionalism, pluralism, or some form of corporativism.

I am aware that many students have discerned federal elements in the various forms of pluralism, such as feudalism or corporativism. But I suggest that such students have added a meaning that was not there before and one that introduces confusion into the term. No government has ever been called federal that has been organized on any but the territorial basis; when organized on any other it has gone by another name.

It is true that the geographical diversities may not always follow the boundary lines of the component units. In many countries, and particularly in the United States, the operation of the federal system has displayed diversities of opinion or habit that are more nearly associated with regions or groups of states rather than with the individual states themselves. This is readily understood. Federalism embraces not merely a diversity of opinion on one issue but a great series of diversities on a number of issues. It can scarcely be expected that state boundary lines will be adequate to mark off areas in which opinions differ on all possible questions. But regionalism in this sense is a valid manifestation of the federal principle. It conforms to the criterion suggested above, namely, that the diversities in the society be grouped territorially. It should be noted, moreover, that regionalism in the politics of a federal country is made possible only by the federal allocation of functions to the states. The fact that several states have similar opinions on a particular issue and hence unite on that issue does not detract from the importance of the states as the basic units of the federal system.

On the other hand, federalism becomes nothing if it is held to embrace diversities that are not territorially grouped. It may be objected that the federal division of powers among territorial areas is in reality functional, since these areas differ from one another on questions that are functional in character. I agree. But the important point is that they are territorially organized. Such areas naturally differ in opinions, in interests, in composition, in functions; but this only brings us back to the point that they differ. If there were no functional differences, there might be no need for federalism. But the point to emphasize is that these functional differences are territorially grouped; and thus they provide a reason for and a demand for a federal system of government.

## *The Spectrum of Federal Societies*

The nature of a society is roughly reflected in the external forms of its political and constitutional arrangements; the extent to which it is federal can be roughly measured by the extent to which these external forms are federal. But the institutional arrangements and the constitutional structure by themselves are not an adequate test of the federal qualities of the society; dependence on them alone can lead to serious error in assessing the nature of the society beneath. Those who devise institutions can never be sure that the institutions so devised will be adequate to the needs they are designed to fulfil. Moreover, social patterns and social needs are constantly changing and, as the needs of a society change, its institutions tend to become obsolete. Finally, institutions mean different things to different peoples; the same set of institutions may produce widely different results when adopted and operated in different communities. Hence, for all these reasons, there can be no assurance that the institutional arrangements at a given time are well suited to the needs of the society below.

From this it follows that the real nature of the society cannot be divined merely by analysis of the institutions. Its nature can be examined only by observing how the institutions work in the context of that society. It is the operation, not the form, that is important; and it is the forces that determine the manner of operation that are more important still.

This is no less true of federalism than of other systems. Federalism is a function not of constitutions but of societies. A federal constitution, a federal government, and a federal society are all different things and each admits of infinite variations. A given community may well have a degree of one without the others. Federalism is thus not an absolute but a relative term; there is no identifiable point at which a society ceases to be unified and becomes diversified. The differences are rather of degree than of kind. All communities fall somewhere in a spectrum which runs from what we may call a theoretically wholly integrated society at one extreme to a theoretically wholly diversified society at the other. The differences between adjacent societies in this spectrum may be so slight or so incommensurable as to be incapable of assessment. But that there is a gradation is clear from observing societies that are widely separated in the spectrum.

As one moves across this hypothetical spectrum the societies encountered are more and more diversified. And the more diversified the society, the greater is the necessity of providing some means for articulating the diversities. But there is no point at which it can be said that all societies on one side are unitary and all those on the other are federal or diversified. If a society contains territorial groups sufficiently different from the rest of society that they require some instrumentality to protect and express their peculiar qualities, then the society is likely to provide some means for the creation of such an instrumentality. One such circumstance doubtless does not make a society or a constitution federal. But two or six or twenty may produce a result that may be properly so called.

It cannot be said that when a society is just so diversified, it requires a federal constitution. In the first place, we are unable to quantify social and political forces to the degree necessary to justify such a demarcation; and secondly the forces themselves are incommensurable. (Which is more diversified, a society rent by religious schisms or one in which the members are divided by differences of language?) Societies employ instrumentalities for the expression of diversities in accordance with what men in particular societies think is necessary; and this view of what is necessary and what is not will vary considerably from society to society. What is adopted by these particular men is an instrumentality to serve the needs of a particular diversity. If enough of these are employed, the result is a federal constitution or a federal government.

## *Diversities and Instrumentalities*

The social diversities that produce federalism may be of many kinds. Differences of economic interest, religion, race, nationality, language, variations in size, separation by great distances, differences in historical background, previous existence as separate colonies or states, dissimilarity of social and political institutions—all these may produce a situation in which the particular interests and qualities of the segments of the larger community must be given recognition.

In every community there is an indefinable complex of psychological and sociological attitudes and values that determines, in whatever fashion, the kinds of instrumentalities that are required in that community. In federal societies the territorial diversities within the community form the all-important elements in this complex.

The whole of this complex produces a demand for some kind of federal recognition of the diversities. This demand must in most instances meet a counter-demand (or inertia, which is equally a force) for increased unity or integration. The federal system is an institutionalization of the compromise between these two demands; and the federal constitution draws the lines of this compromise. The constitution will be more or less federal in accordance with the relative strength of the two demands. But what determines the federal quality of the government is not merely the constitution that draws the lines of the compromise but the whole system of instrumentalities employed as a result of these demands.

Now these instrumentalities are produced in order to express and protect the diversities in the federal society. Just as the diversities take many forms, so do the instrumentalities; the latter are designed to fit the needs of the former. But the relationship and correspondence between the diversities and the instrumentalities that express them will vary from society to society.

We are too prone to say that federal constitutions must contain a certain five or eight or ten characteristics and that all constitutions lacking any of these are not federal. Such a set of criteria ignores the fundamental fact that institutions are not the same things in different social and cultural environments. Two societies equally diversified in respect to a particular matter may require very different instrumentalities for the implementation of that diversity. By the same token, similar institutions or instrumentalities in different social contexts may serve to implement dissimilar diversities. No two societies are the same and each will require different instrumentalities in accordance with the complex of psychological and sociological determinants that is peculiar to it.

The word 'instrumentality' is a broad one and necessarily so; but we must be clear about what is meant. First of all, it does not mean merely a clause in the constitution, though such clauses may well represent such instrumentalities and the provisions of the constitution are a good rough guide to the pattern of instrumentalities. But the word includes not only the constitutional forms but also the manner in which the forms are employed; it includes the way the constitution and its institutions are operated. Beyond this it includes many things that are far from constitutional in importance in the ordinary sense of the word. It includes such things as habits, attitudes, acceptances, concepts, and theories. It includes perhaps the rules of the American Senate, the make-up of the Canadian Cabinet, the zeal of the Baptist Karens in Burma. All these may serve as instrumentalities for the expression of the diversities in a society, and whether a country is federal or not may best be determined by examining the nature and extent of these instrumentalities and not by checking its constitution against an *a priori* list of the characteristics of a federal constitution.

### *The Causal Relation Between Federalism and Its Instrumentalities*

The point has been made that the strength of the various forces within the society changes with the passing of time. *Pari passu*, the diversities within the society increase and decrease in intensity so that the need for their articulation becomes greater or less. Demands for new kinds of instrumentalities arise and are met by changing or abolishing old ones and substituting new ones in their place. But it can scarcely be hoped that the instrumentalities will keep pace with the changing pattern of social relations, and as a result the pattern of instrumentalities tends to lag behind the society itself.[1]

This is complicated further by the fact that the instrumentalities, once put into operation, become rigid and acquire a status of their own. (They become substantive instead of merely adjectival.) They become ends in themselves instead of merely means toward other ends. Their procedures become standardized; they may take on an honorific quality; they become matters of pride to the diverse elements that they serve; and ultimately the instrumentalities enter into and become part of that (psycho-sociological) complex which determines the nature of the instrumentalities.

[1] Though it may be observed that the functioning of the instrumentalities will not be so rigid in this respect as the constitutional forms.

This is by no means an unusual occurrence; it is manifested by almost every society in one form or another. The Scottish Committee in the British House of Commons is an example. This committee was at the outset a device, an instrumentality, to permit the expression of Scottish opinion on affairs that directly concerned Scotland; it is still that. But it is also much more, for it has become a thing of value in itself, a thing to be preserved because it is an essential part of the federal relation between England and Scotland.

Another example is to be found in many of the United States themselves. America adopted a federal constitution at the outset because the colonies were so diversified that they could be brought together in no other form. But since that time the federal constitution has continued in force and has collected around it all the aura of a highly revered institution. As other states have entered the union they have taken their places in the federal arrangement and have found that all the perquisites and particularities of the established states have accrued to them. Although at the time of their entry these later states may not have been sufficiently diversified to warrant such special treatment, they rapidly acquired such a consciousness of individuality that they would now be unwilling to part with the instrumentalities that permit the expression of that individuality. It is doubtful whether the two Dakotas warranted the dignity of separate statehood at the time of their entry into the union; but who can deny now that, having lived as states for a number of years, they would look with disfavour upon any proposal to deprive them of their individuality by merging them into one? The constitution, which endows the states with the characteristics of diversity, treats them indiscriminately, and thus tends to create diversity where none previously existed. The constitution with its federal plan, though designed as an instrumentality, has become a part of the complex of psychological and sociological values that is produced by the diversities in the American society. It is no longer merely an instrumentality serving to protect and articulate the diversities; it has itself become part of that complex of values that is the pattern of diversities and that determines the pattern of the instrumentalities.

Thus the problem of the student of federalism is greatly

increased, for he cannot clearly distinguish between society and the instrumentalities that it employs. Similarly with the problems of the statesman, for he cannot devise means to accomplish new ends without disturbing the old relationship, for the old means have themselves become ends; the old techniques have become values.

### *Types of Instrumentalities*

We must now look more closely at the kinds of instrumentalities that are employed to serve the needs of a federal society and which, taken all together, may produce a federal government.

Federal government is a form of political and constitutional organization that unites into a single polity a number of diversified groups or component polities so that the personality and individuality of the component parts are largely preserved while creating in the new totality a separate and distinct political and constitutional unit. But the instrumentalities of federal government, like the diversities they serve, vary tremendously. What is useful and produces a certain result in one society may be less useful and produce a different result in another. The problem of federalism is to make the instrumentalities fit the society beneath.

Various federal societies have attempted to solve this problem in various ways. But there is sufficient similarity in the various responses to it to suggest to observers that there may be certain things about federalism that are inevitable. Certain instrumentalities, certain institutions, have been so widely employed that it has been suggested that federalism requires such and such a kind of institution. Indeed a federal government is frequently held to be that kind of government that embodies a certain list of institutions. Perhaps this is valid; I do not suggest that it is useless. But it seems to place the cart before the horse. Federalism is a response to a certain need in the society. It is a form of government made necessary by certain diversities in the society that are distributed in a certain way. It must make use of certain instrumentalities to express and protect those diversities. The question whether certain particular instrumentalities are absolutely necessary in such a system is, or ought to be, yet an open one.

Some of those that have been found to be either universal or essential are the following:

*A written constitution* has been held by many to be necessary to a federal scheme. Since it appears in all sorts of systems, however, it can scarcely be considered a defining characteristic. The argument for its necessity in a federation rests on the fact that functions are distributed between the central government and the states and that this distribution must be precise in order to provide an adequate standard of action.

*A formal distribution of powers.* That the real key to the nature of a federation is in the distribution of powers seems to be agreed upon by nearly every writer who addresses himself to the question. Federalism implies the existence of two co-ordinate sets of government operating at two different levels in two different spheres. It seems clear that some precise method must be adopted for determining the contents of the two spheres. In all modern federations the line between the two spheres is drawn by the constitution, while the comparable line in a unitary state is drawn by the central government and is alterable by that government. There is no standard form for this distribution of powers, however, and several different schemes have been employed.

*Constitutional interpretation.* Since the terms of the distribution of functions can at best be very general, difficulties will be encountered in applying them to concrete situations. Hence some device or institution must be adopted by which these terms may be interpreted. Ordinarily this function is performed by the judiciary, as in Canada, Australia, and the United States. But in Switzerland the Supreme Court is subordinate in this process to the national legislature and in Imperial Germany it was performed by the Bundesrat, which was primarily a legislative and administrative body. It is the function, however, that is important and not the agency that performs it.

*Representation in the legislature.* Many federations have organized a second chamber in the national legislature in which the states are represented as states. The representation is not always equal but it is always the quality of statehood that is represented. Sometimes the state governments select, pay, and instruct their representatives, sometimes not. Some writers have considered state representation in the upper house of the central legislature to be the distinguishing mark of federalism, but this seems excessive. It is quite common and doubtless convenient, but scarcely essential.

*Dual citizenship*. To distinguish a federation from a confederation many students insist that the former has the ability to act directly upon its own citizens whereas the latter must act through the component states. Certainly the acceptance by the citizen of a federal society of allegiance to both governments is necessary to the healthy operation of the system; but whether duality of citizenship is absolutely necessary should still be an open question.

*The federal executive*. There is no standard type of executive in a federal system and wide differences are observable in modern federations. But nearly all admit some federal qualities. In the United States these include a state-based electoral college for choosing the president and the requirement of the Senate's consent to executive appointments. The Canadian Cabinet must be divided among religious and provincial interests in accordance with a precise ratio and a similar system prevails to a lesser extent in Switzerland and Australia.

These are by no means all the instrumentalities that are used in federations; the list could be very much extended. But these are the most common ones and, with one exception, include those that have most frequently been described as necessary to federal government. The exception is the process of constitutional amendment. Whether any one of them is in fact necessary to the operation of federalism or uniform throughout modern federations would require an intensive analysis based on extensive research. The present study is an attempt to make such an analysis of one of these instrumentalities.

## *The Process of Constitutional Change*

Every constitution is constantly undergoing changes of various kinds through the impact of new needs upon it. But the means by which these changes take place differ greatly. Necessity for alterations in the institutional structure of government arises under all systems, but in a federal government the problem is even more acute because the distribution of powers between states and nation, which is not present in unitary systems, gives rise to demands for shifts in the allocation of functions from one government to the other.

Federal constitutions change in the same way as other constitutions, though the procedures by which these changes are brought about may differ in form from those of more centralized systems. This study is devoted to those procedures or processes by which actual changes are effected in the wording of the formal constitutions of federations. But federations employ other means as well to alter their constitutional structures. If we attempt to list the elements, other than the written document, that compose the constitution in the larger sense of the word, it becomes apparent that each of these elements is subjected to changes in its own fashion. Constitutions, federal and otherwise, are composed of such things as the decisions of judicial tribunals, the acts of legislative bodies, the general pattern of customs and conventions, as well as the written instrument called the 'Constitution'. And each of these changes in a way peculiarly its own. Custom and convention change through slowly evolving modifications—sometimes accidental, sometimes deliberate—in the customary way of doing things. To the extent that legislative acts are part of the constitution, these can be changed by further acts of the same or higher legislatures. Judicial decisions are constantly modifying previous judicial decisions. Each kind of constitutional apparatus brings with it a distinctive mode of constitutional change.

Moreover, each of these methods may be employed to bring about modifications in the other elements. An act of the legislature may bring to an end a custom that has prevailed for years; a formal amendment may deprive an institution of a power that it has acquired by prescription over a long period of time; a decision of the high court may sharply alter the meaning of a legislative enactment. The pattern of change is a complex one; each element works on other elements, the whole producing a process of gradual evolution in the actual content of the constitution.

Federations have employed these various methods in different ways. Judicial interpretation has been a most significant force operating to modify the constitution in the United

States, in Australia, and in Canada; but it has had much less effect in Switzerland. In Canada perhaps the most significant changes have been brought about merely through evolving habits and customs, new conventions replacing old. Formal amendment has produced relatively few changes in Australia and the United States but has produced many changes in Switzerland. Of all these methods, judicial interpretation of the constitution has probably been the most important, producing far-reaching changes in the constitutions of the several states that have rendered them far different from what they would otherwise have been.

### *Formal Constitutional Amendment*

Formal amendment of the constitution is thus only one way in which it may be altered; but it is a most important way. It differs from all the others in that it is superior to them and may be employed to transcend or repudiate any change that may be brought about through these other means. Judicial interpretation may indeed produce many changes, but there are limits to what can be accomplished by interpretation alone. Courts may adapt constitutions to new needs, but they can do so only within certain limits; they cannot change the wording of the basic law; they cannot take a function from one agency and confer it upon another. Certain changes may be quite impossible without formal amendment of the provisions of the constitution.

Moreover, judicial interpretation is open to the objection that the means of popular control over the judges who exercise it are likely to be so attenuated by their indirect selection and length of tenure that the people can exercise almost no control over them, except indirectly and at long intervals. Those who believe in popular control can find little comfort in confiding to the judiciary the task of keeping the constitution up with the times.

The formal procedure of amendment is of greater importance than the informal processes because it constitutes a higher authority to which appeal lies on any question that may arise. While changing conventions, new legislative acts, and new interpretations may effect serious changes in the constitutional structure, the formal amendment is superior to them all; it may override any of the others and none of the others may override it.

It provides the ultimate authority and is the final arbiter of all disputes.[1] How it is to be exercised is therefore of the greatest importance.

Most students of federalism have agreed that a federation demands an amending procedure in which the states as separate entities play a part.[2] Just how the procedure should be devised has not been so completely agreed upon, since the several federations present differing evidence. Most are agreed that the unanimous concurrence of the states to the proposed change is not necessary and is indeed a matter of peril in federal government; unanimity is usually held to be a feature not of federations but of confederacies. On the other hand, it is generally agreed that the central legislature cannot be permitted to amend the constitution by itself, since this would endanger the states. Where between these extremes a 'proper' amending procedure would fall is the important question and one to which we shall give attention in the pages to follow.

The problem to which we address ourselves therefore is that of the formal amendment of the constitutions of federal states. The most important question to which we shall be seeking an answer is this: given the assumptions in regard to federal societies and federal governments that have heretofore been described, what significance can be attributed to the procedure by which the constitution is amended? Does the fact that a government is federal make necessary a certain kind of amending process? These questions are broad and doubtless the available data furnish a basis for only a tentative answer. But it is hoped that a method of approaching an answer may at least be suggested.

In the course of the investigation several other questions,

[1] 'The chief distinction between constitutions . . . is in the amending process. Who has the power to alter the constitution is master of the State, and the amending clause gives this power.' Herman Finer, *The Theory and Practice of Modern Government*, London, 1932, vol. i, p. 204.

[2] See, for example, James Bryce, *Studies in History and Jurisprudence*, Oxford, 1901, p. 173; Sidgwick, *Development of European Polity*, London, 1903, p. 435; Finer, op. cit., vol. i, p. 204; Friedrich, *Constitutional Government and Democracy*, Boston, 1937, p. 209; N. McL. Rogers, 'The Constitutional Impasse', in *Queen's Quarterly*, vol. 41, 1934, p. 479; W. Harrison Moore, *The Constitution of the Commonwealth of Australia*, London, 1902, p. 316.

subsidiary to the above, will demand attention. What is the role of the component unit in the processes of amendment as presently employed in modern federal governments? What of the suggestion that any kind of amending power at all is incompatible with the preservation of that state integrity that is considered to be the heart of federalism? Should it be (is it?) possible for the constitution to be changed with the consent of less than the whole number of component units? to be changed, by whatever formula, so as to imperil the position of the states, or of one or a few states in the system? Is a specific kind of amendment procedure an accurate test of whether a government or constitution is federal? What is the relation between the amendment procedure and the doctrine and practice of majority rule? If democracy be equated with the rule of majorities, can it be said that federalism is inconsistent with democracy? How are minority rights protected in federal states, especially with respect to the amendment process?

It is by no means suggested that the present study will provide answers to all these questions. But if a little light is shed upon them and others are stimulated to continue the examination, then something will have been accomplished.

# 2

# THE AMENDMENT OF THE CANADIAN CONSTITUTION

## *Means of Altering the Canadian Constitution*

WHETHER Canada is truly a federal country has been much disputed. It is true that, from a legalistic point of view, some doubt may be thrown on the federal qualities of the Canadian constitution, and it may be shown that there are elements in it that ill comport with the widely entertained conception of what ought to be included in a federal constitution. The central government may, for example, appoint provincial judges, name the provincial lieutenant-governors, and disallow provincial legislation. But these powers have by no means reduced the provinces to impotence, nor does the manner in which they have been exercised, especially in recent years, indicate that the country is becoming unitary because of them. Indeed the reverse if anything is true.

Lord Haldane argued that Canada was not federal, not only because the central government held the residuary powers, but because the original constitutions of the provinces had been completely replaced by new ones.[1] Others have urged similar views. Sir John Marriott felt constrained to speak of the 'distinctly unitarian bias of the Canadian constitution'[2] and some Australians have felt that although their country is truly federal, Canada's is not by reason of the institutional differences just mentioned.[3] Such arguments, I suggest, are largely irrelevant to the true question whether Canada is federal. It is scarcely to be denied that the Canadian society is very highly diversified and that these diversities are distributed on a territorial basis. Moreover, there are a great number of instrumen-

[1] See his opinion in *Atty. Gen. for the Commonwealth of Australia v. Colonial Sugar Refining Co. Ltd.* (1914), A.C. 237.

[2] Marriott, *Mechanism of the Modern State*, Oxford, 1927, vol. ii, p. 415.

[3] See, for example, Mr. Ashworth's minority report in the Royal Commission on the Constitution (Australia), 1929, *Report*, p. 278.

talities of various kinds that serve to implement these diversities. Whatever the constitutional forms, it is manifestly true that Canada operates her institutions as though they were federal.

Even as far as constitutional provisions are concerned, it is difficult to call Canada anything except federal. She does enjoy a written constitution; that constitution is subject to judicial interpretation; political competence in the country is divided between the central government and a number of regional governments; each unit is protected in the exercise of its functions from encroachment by the other; its citizens are directly subject to governmental action at both levels; its amending process is different from that employed for ordinary legislation; and its member units are at least roughly represented in the upper house of the central legislature. But the conclusion that Canada is federal rests not so much on these instrumentalities as on the diversities in the society for whose benefit the instrumentalities exist. These diversities are of two kinds and are so obvious that they need be no more than mentioned here: there is first the deep cleavage between the English-speaking and the French-speaking communities, a cleavage that embraces differences not only of language but of national origin, civil law, social customs, and above all of religion. Equally important is the division of the country into five distinct economic areas, the interests of which on some points are in sharp conflict; these areas are the Maritimes together with Newfoundland; Quebec; Ontario; the prairie provinces; and British Columbia. The diversities among these regions are very nearly as acute as those between the two language groups[1] and it may be argued that the continuation of federal government in Canada is made necessary no less by the former than by the latter.

The constitution of Canada was intended, according to the British North America Act, 1867, to be 'similar in principle to that of the United Kingdom'. It is ordinarily assumed that this meant that the Canadian system should be based on the principles of responsible cabinet government. But there are

[1] See, for example, the statements of the several provincial premiers before the Dominion-Provincial Conference of 1935. *Record of Proceedings*, 1936, King's Printer, Ottawa, pp. 10–21.

important differences between the two systems; whereas one gives great weight to conventions and embraces the principle of parliamentary sovereignty, the other employs a written fundamental law and has come nearer and nearer to the principle of judicial supremacy; the Canadian constitution, moreover, contains many federal elements that are lacking in the British. Though she inherited much of the spirit of British government, it cannot be said that Canada adopted all the principles of government that had developed in the mother country. At the same time, however, one must be wary of concluding that Canada's possession of a written constitution in the British North America Acts endows it with a constitutional system comparable to that of the United States. The truth is that she falls somewhere between British and American practice and resembles each in certain particulars. Much of the Canadian constitutional system rests, as does the British, not on law in the formal sense, but on convention. The operation of the cabinet system is not described at all by the British North America Acts and a perusal of those documents only leaves the impression that Canada is an absolute monarchy, ruled by an appointed and irresponsible figure called the Governor-General.

In view of all this, it will be apparent that constitutional change in Canada does not depend solely on the formal amendment of the written document. Indeed the most significant changes in constitutional practice have come about by other means. Among these may be mentioned such things as the gradual alteration of usages and conventions, acts of the Dominion and provincial legislatures, and, most important of all, new decisions and interpretations by the courts. It is not necessary here to show the tremendous impact of judicial interpretation upon the Canadian constitutional system, but it may be remarked that it has, among other things, almost directly reversed the intention of the framers of the constitution by according to the provinces numerous powers and functions that were expected to be exercised by the Dominion Government. Yet despite the very great significance of these informal means of constitutional change they must still operate within the framework of the written constitution, and the amendment of this fundamental law is in the last analysis the most certain, the most precise, and the most powerful method of changing the relationships of Canadian public life. It is this constitution that is, after all, the guiding principle and, regardless of the significance of the changes that take place within its perimeter, it is this perimeter itself that marks the limits of the informal methods of change. The perimeter is the boundary within which everything else moves; to alter it is to redefine the rules of the game and he who can do so controls the game itself. To the extent that Canada possesses such a written constitution, that constitution consists of the British North America Act of 1867 and the amendments that have been subsequently made to it.

### *The Absence of an Amending Clause*

But the problem of formal constitutional amendment is more complex and difficult in Canada than in any other federation, and perhaps more so than in any other country whatever. This is due to the fact that, although it was written, the Canadian constitution contained no provision for its own amendment.[1] There was no clause in the constitution setting out a procedure whereby the provisions of the constitution itself might be legally modified. Hence amendments to it still had to be made by the Parliament at Westminster which created the original statute. Just why such a provision was omitted cannot be told with certainty, though much speculation has been expended upon the question.

An examination of the debates and negotiations that preceded the act of federation discloses no discussion of this problem, though it is apparent that the Canadian fathers were quite familiar with the provisions of the Swiss and American constitutions in this regard, and were aware that the amendment procedure had been the subject of some controversy in

[1] This limitation does not apply to the provinces, which may amend their constitutions 'notwithstanding anything in this Act', except with regard to the office of Lieutenant-Governor. Section 92 (1). It was also anticipated that some of the provisions of the Act as regards the national government might be changed without recourse to another Act of Parliament. Many sections (e.g. 40) contain the clause 'until the Parliament of Canada otherwise provides' and several more the clause 'until the Queen otherwise directs'. About twenty sections anticipate their own modification by these means and several of them have been changed in accordance with them.

the American convention of 1787.[1] But they displayed no awareness of the significance of the problem. The most widely accepted explanation of the omission is that everyone recognized that the new constitutional Act could be brought into effect only by an Act of the Parliament at Westminster. No Act of the British Parliament provides for its own amendment; the normal and accepted method is merely to pass another Act. It was supposed that this new constitution, being an Act of Parliament, would naturally be subject to amendment by that Parliament. If a need for a change arose, Parliament would always be there to enact it. This emphasis on the character of the constitution as an Act of Parliament tended to obscure the necessity of securing agreement on a procedure for requesting such an amendment.[2]

The makers of the new dominion had no need to fear that Britain might take advantage of this power to amend the constitution; she had enjoyed that power for a long time. Moreover, under the legislative union the convention had grown up that no changes would be made by specific legislation except by the request or consent of the colonial legislature.[3] The Act of Union of 1840 had several times been amended in this fashion and it would naturally be expected that the same procedure would prevail in the Dominion.[4] Professor Rogers has suggested that no agreement would have been possible on an adequate amendment procedure,[5] which is very likely true; or it may be that the subject was deliberately avoided. One faction, led by Sir John Macdonald, wanted not a federal arrangement but a unitary legislative union or, failing that, at least a federal union in which great powers should be lodged in the central government. 'It may be that

[1] See Norman McL. Rogers, 'The Constitutional Impasse', *Queen's Quarterly*, vol. 41, 1934, p. 482.

[2] See Rogers, loc. cit. Also the testimony of Dr. O. D. Skelton before the 1935 Select Committee. Canada, House of Commons, Special Committee on the British North America Act, 1935, *Proceedings and Evidence and Report*, p. 29.

[3] On the other hand, general legislation for all colonies (i.e. not specifically for Canada) could and did make changes in Canadian law; this continued to be the case after 1867. See below, pp. 24 ff.

[4] See the testimony of Professor F. R. Scott before the Special Committee cited above at n. 2. *Proceedings and Evidence and Report*, p. 84. Also R. MacG. Dawson, *The Government of Canada*, Toronto, 1947, p. 142.

[5] *Proceedings and Evidence and Report*, pp. 107–8.

Macdonald used his influence to exclude the delicate question of an amendment procedure from the Quebec and London Conferences in the hope that in due course he could induce the provinces to accept a position of subordination which would leave the real power of initiating amendments in the hands of the Dominion Parliament.'[1] At least one of the fathers made explicit his awareness that the British Parliament would serve as the amending authority. The Hon. D'Arcy McGee observed to the Canadian legislature

> We go to the Imperial Government, the common arbiter of us all, in our true Federal Metropolis—we go there to ask for our fundamental Charter. We hope, that by having that Charter that can only be amended by the authority that made it, that we will lay the basis of permanency for our future government.[2]

So far as I have been able to find, this is the only time the subject was mentioned during the negotiations and debates that led up to the Act of 1867. A generation later, when Australia and South Africa were given constitutions, the pattern of imperial relations had considerably changed. It was no longer possible to think that Britain would provide the controlling force and neither of these countries was willing to leave to the British Parliament the amendment of its constitution; both documents therefore contained provisions for amendment.

Whatever the reason for the omission of an amendment provision in the original Act, the reason for its continued absence is clear. The peoples and provinces of Canada have simply been unable to agree on what method they would like to have inserted, and nothing can be done about it until some agreement is reached. In 1949, it is true, an important step was taken toward the solution of this problem. In that year an amendment to the constitution was adopted (by enactment of the British Parliament) which empowered the Canadian Parliament to alter those portions of the Canadian constitution that relate to the national government only.[3] But this act does not affect the rest of the constitution, and in particular it does not empower any authority in Canada to alter those portions

[1] Rogers, op. cit., pp. 482 f.

[2] Canada, Public Archives, *Confederation Debates*, 1865, p. 146.

[3] The British North America (No. 2) Act, 1949. See the discussion below at pp. 64–65, 92 ff.

of the constitution that deal with relations between the Dominion and the provinces. The federal element, therefore, which is of course the heart of the constitution, is still immune from local alteration and can still be amended only by the Imperial Parliament. This amendment is decidedly important and will be examined; but we must look first at the traditional processes by which the written constitution is amended, and in order to do this we must first turn attention to the nature of that written constitution and determine what it comprises.

### *Statutory Components of the Canadian Constitution*

It is generally considered that the constitution of Canada consists of the British North America Act of 1867 and the amendments that have subsequently been made to it. This is, of course, a no more adequate description of the operative constitution in Canada than that which describes the American constitution as the original document of 1787 together with the twenty-two amendments that have been added to it; indeed it is even less adequate, for the Act of 1867 was not intended to do all that the Constitution of 1787 did. The truth is that both definitions refer only to the formal documents around which and within the framework of which the constitutional law of each country has grown. All countries possess a constitution of much broader scope than what is contained in any written document and we must recognize that in Canada even more than in other countries this constitution contains such things as conventional usages, legislative enactments, judicial decisions, and orders-in-council.

But beyond the mere need of recognizing that not all the constitution lies in the written document, there is the additional problem that no one can say exactly what the formal written constitution itself comprises. In Australia and the United States, for example, this problem does not exist, for there the constitutions define themselves. But in Canada, while the most important element is undoubtedly the British North America Act and its amendments, there are other elements too that are equally part of the written constitution and the student of constitutional amendment processes must first address himself to the preliminary, but no less complex, question of just what composes this constitution.

To say that the formal Canadian constitution consists of the British North America Act of 1867 and its amendments is to beg the question, for there is no general agreement about what these amendments are; scholars differ on how many times the Act has been amended. The difficulty arises from the nature of the British statutes themselves; it would be a great convenience to Canadian constitutional lawyers if the Imperial Parliament had always plainly labelled any enactments that were intended to alter Canadian constitutional law and indicated that they were to be so construed. But such a practice has never been followed. There is no difference between such amendments and any other British statutes, except in the content of the Acts. In other words, so far as form, title, &c. are concerned there is no difference (except in very recent years) between British statutes that apply to Canada and any other British statutes. This is quite consistent with ordinary British practice. The Parliament at Westminster never distinguishes between statutes that are constitutional and those that are mere legislation; such a distinction would be meaningless in terms of the British constitution. Every British statute has the same status in law as any other British statute; if there is a conflict or inconsistency between two Acts, then the later enactment prevails over the earlier. It is true that some statutes specifically amend or repeal earlier laws, but it is not necessary that the earlier laws be so mentioned. Each statute affects earlier statutes so far as its content and necessary intendment require. The earlier statute need not be mentioned to be repealed or amended.

Now before 1931 at least this British Parliament was the supreme lawmaking agency for Canada,[1] and its enactments affecting Canada were patterned after the same principles that were employed in its own domestic legislation. Since these British enactments were supreme in Canada, they constituted a sort of constitution which the local legislatures in that country could not alter. And the fact that British legislation took such form led to a considerable haziness about what the

[1] Before 1865 any colonial Act in conflict with British law applying to the colonies, whether statute or common, was invalid. The Colonial Laws Validity Act, 1865 (28 & 29 Vict., chap. 63), removed this restriction so far as common law was concerned; but colonial laws in conflict with British *statutes* applying to the colonies continued to be invalid.

constitution of Canada really did consist of. The British North America Act was only a rough guide, for any British legislation subsequent to that statute prevailed against it and many enactments did so. Thus a British statute concerning immigration in the colonies would take precedence over Canadian legislation on the subject even though the Canadian legislature had been empowered to make laws on that subject by Section 95 of the British North America Act itself.

### *British Legislation in the Canadian Constitution*

It will be seen that there were two kinds of enactments that could affect Canada, those that applied generally to all colonies and did not exclude Canada by specific reference, and those that directly applied to Canada by name. Each of these must be considered in some detail.

1. Before 1867 there were forty-one Imperial Acts for the colonies in general that affected Canada along with the others.[1] Chief among these were the Renunciation Act, 1778, the Judicial Committee Acts, 1833 and 1844, and the Colonial Laws Validity Act, 1865. After 1867 there were over fifty more up to 1913.[2] These included such enactments as the Colonial Courts of Admiralty Act, 1890, the Merchant Shipping Act, 1894, and the Geneva Convention Act, 1911. In addition to the Acts themselves, many authorized the issuance of orders-in-council and many such (British) orders have been issued that have applied with the same force to Canada; these have been concerned chiefly with regulating judicial appeals or carrying out treaty obligations.[3] But further general legislation of this sort was precluded by the Statute of Westminster,[4] Section 4 of which provided that 'No Act of Parliament of the United Kingdom passed after the commencement of this Act shall extend . . . to a Dominion as part of the law of that Dominion, unless it is expressly declared in that Act that the Dominion has requested, and consented to, the enact-

[1] C. J. Tarring, *Chapters on the Law Relating to the Colonies*, 4th edn., 1913, pp. 168 ff.

[2] Ibid.

[3] H. McD. Clokie, 'Basic Problems of the Canadian Constitution', *Canadian Journal of Economics and Political Science*, vol. 8, 1942, p. 4. I have drawn heavily on Professor Clokie's excellent article throughout this section.

[4] 22 Geo. V, chap. 4. See text below in Appendix C.

ment thereof.' Thus general legislation for the colonies would be inoperative in a Dominion unless the Dominion requested that it apply; in this case it would be applied specifically and not as falling within the generality of the Act as applying to colonies. The Statute also relieved the Dominions of the repugnancy clause of the Colonial Laws Validity Act[1] and enabled them to repeal any British legislation then in force in the Dominion. Thus Canada was empowered to repeal or amend any law that had affected her in the past as a result of these general enactments applying to colonies as a whole.

2. More important for Canadian constitutional law were those British statutes that applied directly to Canada by name.[2] There was still no formal means of distinguishing even these Acts from other British statutes; again the only difference is in content. But they are much easier to find since they apply specifically to Canada and this fact is stated in the Acts themselves. Before 1867 there were twenty-five of these Acts that applied to the several colonies that now compose Canada[3] and an equal number since that date.[4] The British North America Act, 1867, is one of these and it might appear that the total list would comprise a record of the amendments to the Canadian constitution to date. But some are only temporary and trivial and some cannot be said to modify anything contained in the original Act of 1867. Even more important, some of them are not protected by the Statute of Westminster against amendment by the Canadian Parliament. For example, there were twelve statutes from 1867 to 1924 that dealt with loans and other financial questions, several of them confirming economic agreements between Canada and Great Britain or other countries. Another group of statutes and orders, more important

[1] Section 2.

[2] Mr. J. E. Read (now a judge of the International Court of Justice) has prepared a list of 'enactments of the parliament of Great Britain which by their express terms or by necessary implication apply to the Dominion of Canada'. In this list are found 53 such enactments before 1867 and 76 after that date down to 1943; it includes both general and specific Acts. Reproduced in Maurice Ollivier, *Problems of Canadian Sovereignty*, Toronto, 1945, Appendix iii, pp. 465–9.

[3] Tarring, op. cit., pp. 183–4.

[4] Clokie, op. cit., p. 5. It should be noted that these Acts too authorize orders-in-council and that several such orders have been issued by the British Government. Dawson states that 'the acts and orders-in-council of the British Parliament, which have been passed since 1867 and which apply *specifically* to Canada, number thirty-two'. R. MacG. Dawson, *The Government of Canada*, 1947, p. 139.

than the first, dealt with boundary questions and matters of extra-territoriality. Finally, and most important of all, is a third group that includes the real structural or jurisdictional changes in Canadian constitutional law. In this group are found all the statutes entitled 'British North America Acts' but it includes other statutes not so titled as well. The significance of this rough classification[1] is not that one group constitutes the amendments to the constitution and the others are excluded from this category, but only that some of the British statutes applying to Canada directly are of such a nature that they can hardly be called constitutional at all.

It is the third group with which we are primarily concerned, for it is these Acts that actually alter and clarify the British North America Act, 1867. Included in this category are the following statutes:

*a. Acts that merely remove doubts of interpretation and provide certain transient formalities*

1. Canada Copyright Act, 1875. This merely provided copyright legislation which was beyond the powers of the Canadian Parliament.
2. Canadian Speaker (Appointment of Deputy) Act, 1895. This authorized the appointment of a deputy speaker for the Canadian Senate, an office that had not been provided for in the Act of 1867.
3. British North America Act, 1916. This simply extended the life of Parliament for one year as a war-time expedient.
4. British North America Act, 1943. This postponed the redistribution of seats in the House of Commons until after the war.

*b. Substantive changes in the Act of 1867*

5. British North America Act, 1871. This removed any doubt of the Dominion's power to create new provinces and provide for their representation in Parliament; it

[1] The scheme of classification is that of Clokie who gives the statutes and orders in detail at op. cit., pp. 6–9; it is adopted by Dawson, op. cit., pp. 139 f. A slightly different approach to the problem of determining which Acts are constitutional amendments may be found in Paul Gérin-Lajoie, *Constitutional Amendment in Canada*, Toronto, 1950, chap. 1.

forbade Parliament to amend or repeal an Act establishing a province, except that boundaries could be changed with the consent of the provinces concerned.

6. Parliament of Canada Act, 1875. (Note that this is not even called a 'British North America Act'.) It confirmed the power of Parliament to authorize Senate and House committees to examine witnesses on oath by substituting a new provision in place of Section 18 in the Act of 1867.
7. British North America Act, 1886. This empowered Parliament to make provision for the representation in both Houses of Parliament of territories that were not a part of any province.
8. British North America Act, 1907. This provided a new basis for Dominion grants to provinces by inserting a new Section 118 in the Act of 1867.
9. British North America Act, 1915. This is the first Act to be called 'an act to amend the British North America Act, 1867'. It made several specific changes in that Act including the establishment of a new western senatorial division and a provision that no province should have fewer members of the House of Commons than it had senators.
10. British North America Act, 1930. This returned certain natural resources to the western provinces.
11. British North America Act, 1940. This added unemployment insurance to the list of Dominion powers in Section 91 of the Act of 1867.
12. British North America Act, 1946. This provided for a redistribution of seats in the House of Commons and a new basis of apportionment. It substitutes a new Section 51 in the Act of 1867.
13. British North America Act, 1949. This provided for the union of Newfoundland and Canada.
14. British North America (No. 2) Act, 1949. This provided an amendment procedure for certain parts of the constitution. Its effect is discussed below.
15. British North America Act, 1951. This added a new Section 94A to the Act of 1867 empowering the Dominion to legislate concerning old age pensions.

This list is quite arbitrary. Who can say that the statutes contained in the first two groups are not of sufficient 'importance' to be called constitutional? Other students of the subject have devised different lists.[1] In the foregoing list it should be noted that not all the statutes bear the title 'British North America Act' and none of them contain the term '(amendment)' in their short titles. But this has no legal significance, for their content, not their legal form, determines whether they amend previous acts.

It is apparent from the confusion attendant upon any effort to state precisely how many times the constitution has been amended that, at least before 1931, it was impossible to speak with any great accuracy about constitutional amendment at all. Even disregarding those elements of constitutional law that rest on judicial decisions, conventions, &c., one cannot talk meaningfully about the written constitution, as Americans do, and mean by it a certain document as amended. One must talk about fundamental law that cannot be touched by the Dominion Parliament. Or to put it another way, since Canada's documentary constitution consists largely of British Acts, we must try to ascertain which of those acts may be changed by

[1] R. MacG. Dawson in his *Constitutional Issues in Canada* (1933) held that the Act of 1867 had been amended eleven times. 'Four of these were temporary. . . three were largely declaratory and were passed "to remove certain doubts" in the Act; and only four were genuine amendments, viz. those of 1886, 1907, 1915, and 1930', pp. 3–4. On the other hand there was published in 1928 an official government list of the amendments which included the Rupert's Land Act, 1868, the Alberta Act, 1905, and the Saskatchewan Act, 1905. *British North America Act and Amendments, 1867–1927*, Ottawa, 1928. Two witnesses before the Special Committee of the House of Commons in 1935 gave different opinions as to what constituted the amendments to the Act. Mr. O. D. Skelton, Under-secretary of State for External Affairs, listed seven amendments (Canada, House of Commons, Special Committee on the British North America Act, 1935, *Proceedings and Evidence and Report*, pp. 31–35) but later in his discussion he included the Act of 1895 (ibid., p. 36) although this was not one of the seven he had listed. Dr. Maurice Ollivier, Law Clerk of the House of Commons, listed only six, omitting even the British North America Act of 1930 (ibid., pp. 56–57). Indeed, Dawson himself gives a different list in his *Government of Canada*, p. 141. *Constitutions of All Countries*, vol. 1, published by the British Foreign Office in 1938 lists as amendments only the Acts of 1875, 1907, 1915, and 1930. The most elaborate study of the subject is by Dr. Paul Gérin-Lajoie (*Constitutional Amendment in Canada*, 1950, chap. 3) who includes in his list of amendments fifteen different Acts, including the Canada (Ontario Boundary) Act, 1889, and the Statute of Westminster, 1931. For his criterion of what constitutes an amendment see op. cit., pp. 47–49.

the Canadian legislature and which are beyond its competence. This can best be done by a process of exclusion. If we can determine what statutes cannot be unilaterally amended by the Dominion Parliament, then everything else is within its competence.

### *The Statute of Westminster*

Before 1931 Canada, along with other colonies and dominions, was limited by the Colonial Laws Validity Act, which made invalid any colonial legislation in conflict with British statutes extending to the colony. Canada could not amend British legislation at all and all British laws that had affected the British North America Act in any way were part of the Canadian constitution, untouchable by Canadian legislation. By the Statute of Westminster in 1931, however, Canada gained the right to alter any British statutes that were operative in the Dominion. This Statute repealed the restrictive provisions of the Colonial Laws Validity Act (Sec. 2), gave to Dominions the right to enact extra-territorial legislation (Sec. 3), and surrendered the right of the British Parliament to legislate for the Dominions without their consent (Sec. 4). If this new competence of the Dominion Parliament had not been qualified, it would have bestowed upon that body the power to alter the British North America Act, 1867, at will, including the federal distribution of powers in Sections 91 and 92. The provincial governments, perceiving this, insisted that a clause be inserted in the Statute protecting them from this threat, and this was done. Section 7(1) of the Statute provides that 'Nothing in this Act shall be deemed to apply to the repeal, amendment or alteration of the British North America Acts, 1867 to 1930, or to any order, rule or regulation made thereunder.'[1] Moreover, it extended the powers granted in Section 2 to the provinces as well as to the Dominion and restricted the legislative powers thus granted to the already existing competences of the Dominion and the provinces.

The result of this section was to prevent the Dominion or any Canadian authority from altering the British North America Acts, 1867 to 1930; it was intended to retain at

[1] A similar provision protected the constitutions of Australia and New Zealand (Section 8).

Westminster the power to amend the constitution of Canada. But the section does not say 'the constitution of Canada'; it says 'the British North America Acts, 1867 to 1930'. If there is a difference between the two terms, it is the latter and not the former that was protected against alteration by the Dominion. And it is very clear that there is a considerable difference between them. It is therefore necessary to determine precisely what was included in the phrase 'British North America Acts, 1867–1930'.

### *Content of the Phrase 'British North America Acts, 1867–1930'*

First of all, any Act not bearing the title 'British North America Act' is excluded. This phrase is not by any means a general term covering any statute having to do with the British colonies on the North American continent, but is a precise legal denomination of a certain class of Acts. Those not so titled do not belong to this class and were not included within the scope of the phrase. This seems fairly obvious, but on reflection it appears to be of considerable importance. For among those Acts that must be excluded for this reason are the Canadian Speaker (Appointment of Deputy) Act, 1895, and the Canada Copyright Act, 1875, both of which were certainly constitutional amendments. Even more important, it excludes the Parliament of Canada Act, 1875, which specifically repealed Section 18 of the Act of 1867 and provided a new section in its place.

Secondly, it excludes any Act passed prior to 1867. The Short Titles Act, 1896,[1] had conferred the title 'British North America Act' retroactively on five Acts that had been passed before 1867. These dealt with Quebec, 1774 (14 Geo. III, chap. 83), fur trade and courts, 1821 (1 & 2 Geo. IV, chap. 66), trade and lands, 1822 (3 & 4 Geo. IV, chap. 119), seigniorial rights, 1825 (6 Geo. IV, chap. 59), and the union of the Canadas, 1840 (3 & 4 Vict., chap. 35). But since they preceded the early limit prescribed by the Statute they were obviously not intended to be protected.

The third consideration is of the Acts entitled 'British North

[1] 59 & 60 Vict., chap. 14.

America Acts' that were enacted between 1867 and 1930. There were seven of these, the Acts of 1867, 1871, 1886, 1907, 1915, 1916, and 1930. But even this is not a proper answer to the question of what is meant by the phrase in the Statute. For the expression 'British North America Acts, 1867 to 1930' is not merely a description of a group of laws, but a precise legal term referring to a collective statutory entity, the contents of which must be ascertained by precise legislative definition. It is unfortunate that the term, though it carries with it a precise denotation, has been carelessly employed. This will be apparent from an examination of the short titles of the several Acts in question. The appropriate sections of these Acts are as follows:

1867 Sec. 1: 'This Act may be cited as the British North America Act, 1867.'

1871 Sec. 1: 'This Act may be cited for all purposes as The British North America Act, 1871.'

1886 Sec. 3: 'This Act may be cited as the British North America Act, 1886.'

This Act and the British North America Act, 1867, and the British North America Act, 1871, shall be construed together, and may be cited together as the British North America Acts, 1867 to 1886.'

1907 Sec. 2: 'This Act may be cited as the British North America Act, 1907, and shall take effect as from the first day of July, nineteen hundred and seven.'

1915 Sec. 3: 'This Act may be cited as the British North America Act, 1915, and the British North America Acts, 1867 to 1886, and this Act may be cited together as the British North America Acts, 1867 to 1915.'

1916 Sec. 2: 'This Act may be cited as the British North America Act, 1916, and the British North America Acts, 1867 to 1915, and this Act may be cited together as the British North America Acts, 1867 to 1916.'

1930 Sec. 3: 'This Act may be cited as the British North America Act, 1930, and the British North America Acts, 1867 to 1916, and this Act may be cited together as the British North America Acts, 1867 to 1930.'

Thus the first definition of 'British North America Acts' appears in the Act of 1886 which brings together the Acts of 1867, 1871, and 1886 as the 'British North America Acts,

1867 to 1886'. It might have been expected that a similar clause would be included in the next Act, that of 1907, but such was not the case. The next definition occurs in 1915, when the Act of that year is added to the group included in the definition of 1886. At that time then, the phrase 'British North America Acts, 1867 to 1915' included all previous Acts *except* that of 1907 which had not been included in any of the definitions. The Acts of 1916 and 1930 added themselves to the foregoing so that the final phrase 'British North America Acts, 1867 to 1930' would seem to include the following: 1867, 1871, 1886, 1915, 1916, and 1930. But a further confusion is introduced by the fact that the Act of 1916, as well as a small part of that of 1915, had been repealed by the Statute Law Revision Act, 1927.[1] This repeal took place, it should be noted, not only before the Statute of Westminster, but also before the Act of 1930; the short title section of the latter added itself to the Acts, 1867 to 1916, even though the Act of 1916 had already been repealed, which can only be attributed to oversight. In any case the Act of 1916 cannot be included in the final list.[2]

Nor was the Act of 1907 included in the list of protected statutes; it had not added itself to the definitions of its predecessors and was ignored by its successors, apparently inadvertently. In any case, it was not included in the list of Acts

[1] 17 & 18 Geo. V, chap. 42.

[2] Professor Clokie excludes 1916, but for other reasons which do not appear to be borne out by the statutes themselves. He says, 'a third definition was unhappily made in the temporary Act of 1916, but this was subsequently dropped from the fourth definition made in the Act of 1930, which added itself to the 1885 [*sic*] and 1915 lists. The result is that the British North America Acts, 1867 to 1930, as protected by the Statute of Westminster, are the five following: those of 1867, 1871, 1886, 1915 and 1930.' Op. cit., pp. 10–11. I think this a valid conclusion, but not for the reasons stated. There seems to be no difference between the definition of 1916 and those of other years; it adds itself to that of 1915 and produces an entity entitled 'British North America Acts, 1867 to 1916'. The Act of 1930 does not add itself to the definitions of 1886 and 1915, as Mr. Clokie suggests, but to that of 1916.

The Act of 1916 was merely a transitory enactment providing for the postponement of an election. Whether it is protected or not is unimportant; but it seems clear that, whatever its content, it could not be protected in view of its repeal in 1927.

K. C. Wheare lists 1916 as one of the protected statutes; he makes no mention of the difference to which Mr. Clokie refers, but at the same time does not allude to the fact of its repeal. *The Statute of Westminster and Dominion Status*, 5th edn., 1953, p. 188. Regarding the Statute Law Revision Acts see below, p. 36, n. 2.

comprised in the phrase 'British North America Acts, 1867 to 1930' as employed in the Statute of Westminster.[1] In the British North America Act, 1940, an attempt was made to rectify this error by redefining the phrase to include it. Section 2 of that Act reads: 'This Act may be cited as the British North America Act, 1940, and the British North America Acts, 1867 to 1930, the British North America Act, 1907, and this Act may be cited as the British North America Acts, 1867 to 1940.' Whether this new definition has any effect, however, is open to serious doubt, as is indicated below.

Finally, we must exclude all British North America Acts after 1930, by the same argument that excludes those enacted before 1867. They could be included only by amending the appropriate clause of the Statute of Westminster and this has never been done. Simply to give them short titles and include them in such an entity as 'the British North America Acts, 1867 to 1940 (or 1951)' is not sufficient, for the Statute limits the protection to 'British North America Acts, 1867 to 1930'.

There have been six British North America Acts enacted by the British Parliament since 1930, the contents of which have already been noted.[2] The short title section of the Act of 1940 has been cited above; those of 1943, 1946, 1949, and 1951 conform to the model established in 1886 and 1915. Each adds itself to the preceding definitions for purposes of citation and interpretation. Professor Clokie, writing in 1942, argued that the Act of 1940 was protected by the fact that it added itself to the preceding definition and produced an entity called the 'British North America Acts, 1867 to 1940', which was beyond the competence of the Dominion. But he does not include 1907.[3] It seems to me that any argument that would include the Act of 1940 would also include the Act of 1907, for they

[1] The omission went unnoticed during the discussions at the time of the Statute of Westminster and was not mentioned before the Special Committee of 1935 or the Royal Commission on Dominion-Provincial Relations in 1938–9. Attention was apparently first called to it by Wheare in op. cit., 1st edn., p. 188, although Gérin-Lajoie points out that it was acknowledged indirectly in an amendment proposed by the House but refused by the Senate in 1936; that amendment was to have effect 'notwithstanding anything contained in the British North America Acts, 1867–1930, the British North America Act, 1907, the Parliament of Canada Act, 1875 . . . etc.' Canada, *House of Commons Journals*, 1936, pp. 333–4; 337–8; cited by Gérin-Lajoie, op. cit., p. 10.

[2] *Supra*, pp. 26–27.

[3] Op. cit., p. 11.

were both treated in the same fashion by the same authority at the same time. The only difference between the two Acts could be that the Act of 1907 had already been excluded by the Statute of Westminster, but this is not a good argument and Professor Clokie does not use it.[1] I think it a fair conclusion, on the basis of the statutes as they stood in mid-1949, to say that no Acts after that of 1930 could be included as protected by the Statute against amendment by the Dominion. This excludes 1940, 1943, 1946, and the first Act of 1949 and is to say that any of these might be altered unilaterally by the Dominion Parliament. The effect of the second Act of 1949 will be examined below. By the same argument, the Act of 1907 must be excluded; and by the argument already mentioned (i.e. the fact that it had been repealed) the Act of 1916 must also be excluded. Also conspicuously absent are the Canadian Speaker (Appointment of Deputy) Act, 1895, and the Parliament of Canada Act, 1875, neither of which possessed the necessary titles. Thus we may conclude that the following statutes were protected by the Statute of Westminster against alteration by the Dominion Parliament: the British North America Acts of 1867, 1871, 1886, 1915, and 1930. In addition there should be included the orders-in-council that have been issued pursuant to authority granted in the protected statutes; these have had to do primarily with the addition and organization of new territories.

With the exception of these five statutes and the orders-in-council issued pursuant to them, all other British legislation,

[1] It is not quite clear whether Professor Clokie thinks the Act of 1907 should be included or not. At one point on p. 11 he says so, but in his final list on that page he does not include it. On p. 12 he says it is doubtful. In his argument, however, it is clear that he thinks the Act of 1940 did accomplish this and if it does include 1940 then it must include 1907, for the same reasons. He is of the strong opinion that it should not have been done: 'The procedure of tacking an earlier Act to the short title section of a post-Statute amendment is undoubtedly a reprehensible method of producing a retrospective change in the provisions of the Statute of Westminster . . . it involves the propriety of withdrawing surreptitiously from the Canadian Parliament part of the freedom to repeal British statutes when this freedom had been secured by a solemn public agreement embodied in the Statute of Westminster' (p. 11). It is not quite fair thus to accuse the British Parliament of withdrawing this Act from the competence of the Dominion Parliament, for the deed was done at the latter's request. Like all such statutes it was enacted at the request and with the consent of the Dominion Parliament, and the address of the latter body is identical with the statute as enacted. See Canada, *House of Commons Journals*, vol. lxxx (1940), pp. 149–50.

in so far as it stood as part of the law of Canada, was left by Section 2 (2) of the Statute of Westminster subject to unilateral alteration by the Parliament of Canada. There are two qualifications, however, that should be added to this generalization. First, although the Dominion Parliament now had the power to alter any British legislation other than the British North America Acts, 1867–1930, it could not alter any such Act in such a way as to conflict with any provision of these protected statutes. Thus the continued protection afforded to these statutes acted as a limitation on the manner in which any other statute could be amended. A second limitation arose from Section 7 (3) of the Statute of Westminster. It will be recalled that Section 7 (1) had continued the protection of the Colonial Laws Validity Act with respect to the British North America Acts, 1867–1930; Section 7 (2) extended the effect of the repeal of the Colonial Laws Validity Act to the provinces as well as to the Dominion. As a result of this it was feared that the provisions of Section 2 (2), supplemented by those of Section 7 (2), might enable either the provinces or the Dominion to enact laws that would encroach upon the sphere of the other with respect to Acts other than the British North America Acts, 1867–1930. It was not intended that the area of legislative competence of either the Dominion or the provinces should be extended but only that within their respective areas of competence the disabilities of the Colonial Laws Validity Act should be removed.[1] There was therefore included in the Statute a further Section 7 (3) which provided that:

> The powers conferred by this Act upon the Parliament of Canada or upon the legislatures of the Provinces shall be restricted to the enactment of laws in relation to matters within the competence of the Parliament of Canada or of any of the legislatures of the Provinces respectively.

The result of this subsection was to preserve the distribution of powers with respect to acts other than those protected in subsection 7 (1) from alteration either by the Dominion or the provinces in view of the greater powers granted by Sections 2 (2) and 7 (2) of the Statute. For our present purpose

[1] Cf. Wheare, *Statute of Westminster and Dominion Status*, 5th edn., 1953, p. 193.

its effect was to restrict the amending power of the Dominion Parliament by guaranteeing that no alteration of a non-protected statute by the Dominion Parliament could operate to deprive a province of a power granted to it by such a statute. Examples of such powers are few in number, but the principle is clear.[1]

In summary then it may be said that after 1931 the power of the Dominion Parliament to alter the constitution of Canada extended to all parts of that constitution except the five protected statutes mentioned above and the orders-in-council issued pursuant to them, subject only to these two restrictions, viz., that no alteration of any Act could effect an amendment of the protected statutes and that no alteration of any Act could extend the area of Dominion activity into the fields of competence of the provinces.

Henceforward, when the terms 'constitution' or 'constitutional amendment' are used, they will refer to these fundamental elements that were protected by the Statute of Westminster.

### *Requesting the Amendment*

Having described the composition of the Canadian constitution, we face next the task of examining the methods by which it may be amended. We have seen that until 1949 no part of this constitution might be altered save by the British Parliament,[2] but to say this merely scratches the surface, for it is

[1] Dr. Gérin-Lajoie interprets subsection 7 (3) so broadly that he is led to argue that nearly every Act that has affected the Act of 1867 in any way was protected against Dominion alteration since many of them contained provisions that were beyond Dominion competence before 1931. See *Constitutional Amendment in Canada*, pp. 12 ff. I think this conclusion goes somewhat beyond the actual meaning of subsection 7 (3) since it is concerned only with the actual distribution of powers between Dominion and provinces. The difference between his view and mine is, however, one of approach rather than of substance. The point is of little practical significance in view of the slight importance of the substantive issues involved and, with the passage of the British North America (No. 2) Act, 1949, its interest has become largely antiquarian.

[2] Technically there are certain amendments to the Canadian constitution that have been made by the British Parliament without any consultation with Canadian authorities. Periodically the Statute Law Committee re-examines the statutes in force and recommends that certain spent or obsolete sections be repealed. The Parliament then passes a Statute Law Revision Act which repeals these sections as a group. The British North America Acts have been affected principally by the Acts of 1893 and 1927; no important provision of constitutional

a settled convention of that Parliament that it will not enact such amendments unless they are requested by the Dominion.[1] The problem is thus projected back a step to the Dominion itself. What agency in the Dominion has the power to request or consent to Acts of the British Parliament amending the British North America Acts, 1867 to 1930? The answer to this question is not found in any law, but it now seems clear that settled custom requires the Dominion Parliament to exercise this power by means of a joint address by the two Houses. But this was not always the case; in the early years of the Dominion's history there was some disagreement about whether this function should be reserved to the Parliament or whether it could on occasion be exercised by the executive government acting alone.

The question arose in connexion with the first effort to amend the Act of 1867. Section 146 empowered the Queen, subject to advice from the Privy Council and from the appropriate legislatures, to admit certain areas into the union as new provinces. But in 1870 the Canadian Parliament, acting on its own initiative, passed the Manitoba Act, the object of which was to prepare the way for the admission of parts of Rupert's Land and the North-West Territory into the union as the Province of Manitoba. There being some question whether this action was *ultra vires* the provisions of Section

law has been involved, although the 1927 Act repealed the British North America Act, 1916. For the precise sections that have been affected see the footnotes in *British North America Act and Amendments*, ed. Ollivier, Ottawa, 1943, *passim*. See also F. R. Scott, 'Forgotten Amendments to the Canadian Constitution', *Canadian Bar Review*, vol. 20, 1942, p. 339. Gérin-Lajoie has an interesting discussion of the effect of these Acts on the law and on the Canadian constitution in which he argues that so far as the constitution is concerned the Statute Law Revision Acts should be regarded as having no effect. See *Constitutional Amendment in Canada*, pp. 129 ff.

[1] It may be pointed out that this is by convention only and not by law. Although Section 4 of the Statute of Westminster states that no Act of the British Parliament will have effect in a Dominion unless requested and consented to by that Dominion, nevertheless this section does not apply to constitutional amendments, for Section 7 (1) states that 'Nothing in this Act shall be deemed to apply to the . . . alteration of the British North America Acts, 1867 to 1930 . . . etc.' The principal purpose of Section 7 (1) was to limit the powers of the Dominion Parliament to amend British legislation under Section 2 (2), but it applies to Section 4 as well. So far as the law is concerned, the British Parliament may still amend the protected British North America Acts without the request or consent of the Dominion.

146, the Canadian Government (not the Parliament) in 1871 petitioned the Imperial Government to present to the Imperial Parliament a bill to remove these doubts about the Dominion's power to admit new territories and to organize them as provinces. The Imperial Government then transmitted to the Dominion a bill which it proposed to introduce. At this point the Dominion Government was subjected to severe criticism in the House of Commons for proceeding in the matter without the authorization of the Parliament and an extensive debate followed.[1] The Government did not insist on a right to seek such amendment on its own authority and Sir George Cartier, in its behalf, admitted the error and accepted a resolution (which was carried unanimously) to the effect that 'No changes in the provisions of the British North America Act should be sought for by the Executive Government without the previous assent of the Parliament of this Dominion.'[2]

The principle thus pronounced received a supporting precedent when in the following year a Canadian Copyright Bill was reserved for royal consideration on the ground that it conflicted with British legislation. Fearing that the bill would lapse under the two-year rule of Section 57 of the Act of 1867, the Canadian Parliament in 1874 presented an address[3] requesting Her Majesty's assent to the bill. As a result of this address, the British Parliament passed the Canadian Copyright Act, 1875,[4] authorizing Her Majesty's assent to the Canadian bill. So far so good.

But in the next year the principle was again violated. In 1873 the Canadian Parliament adopted a measure entitled the Oaths of Allegiance Act, which permitted parliamentary committees to exact oaths from witnesses appearing before them; this bill was disallowed on the ground that it exceeded the powers of the Dominion Parliament under Section 18. Acting on its own authority and without any authorization from the Parliament, the Dominion Government petitioned the Imperial Government to secure the passage of British legislation validating this Canadian Act. The British Parliament then

[1] See Maurice Ollivier, *Problems of Canadian Sovereignty*, 1945, pp. 363–5.

[2] Canada, *House of Commons Debates*, 1871, vol. ii, pp. 649–50.

[3] Canada, *House of Commons Journals*, 1874, vol. viii, p. 232.

[4] 38 & 39 Vict., chap. 53.

passed the Parliament of Canada Act, 1875,[1] authorizing the assent to the Canadian legislation and substituting a new Section 18 in the Act of 1867. There is no record of any immediate objection in the Canadian Parliament, but in the following year the proceeding was challenged in the House of Commons and the Government was again severely criticized for its action. A defence was offered on the ground that the Government had merely sought the validation of an Act already passed by the Dominion Parliament, since in passing the Oaths Act the Parliament had previously approved the principles of the Parliament of Canada Act.[2] But this argument was weakened by the fact that two years before, when a corresponding validation had been sought for the Copyright Act, the Government had resorted not to its own authority but to a parliamentary address; the House was not satisfied with the explanations.

In 1895 a third instance of executive request occurred when the Canadian Speaker (Appointment of Deputy) Act[3] was passed by the British Parliament at the request of the Government of Canada without any address having been made by the Dominion Parliament. Here too a previous statute had been in doubt. An Act of 1894 authorizing the appointment of a deputy speaker in the Senate had been questioned because such an office was not provided for in the Act of 1867. At the Government's request, the Imperial Parliament enacted legislation to authorize such an office. Strangely enough, although the circumstances were very nearly the same as those of twenty years before, no comment or criticism was voiced in the Parliament this time. This might have been construed as an acceptance of the method of request by the executive government, but it was apparently not so interpreted,[4] for every amendment since that time has been made only upon the presentation of an address by the two Houses of Parliament.

This then may be considered the settled practice in the matter. Not for more than half a century has the Government undertaken to secure an amendment to the British North

[1] 38 & 39 Vict., chap. 38.
[2] Canada, *House of Commons Debates*, 1876, pp. 1140 ff.
[3] 58 Vict., sess. 2, chap. 3.
[4] See the explanation in Gérin-Lajoie, op. cit., p. 74.

America Act, except by a joint address. And in the only instances in which the executive acted without the Parliament, the latter body had already approved the substance of the legislation by antecedent acts of its own. The normal procedure has been for the Government to take the initiative by presenting the resolution for the approval of the two houses. The address when passed is presented to the Governor-General for transmission to London. It takes the form of a request to the Imperial Government to advise Her Majesty to lay before the Imperial Parliament a bill to accomplish a specified action. In recent times a draft bill has been drawn up by the Canadian authorities and included in the address in a form suitable for passage by the British Parliament. In most cases, too, the British statute has included the address as a schedule to the Act. But whether or not the address is scheduled to the Act, it has been customary for the Act to mention in its preamble the fact that it has been enacted upon receipt of such an address. On two occasions, however, this was not done. The Acts of 1915 and 1916 contained no mention of Canadian initiative in the matter.[1]

It is unfortunate that the Statute of Westminster is not clearer on the issue of the source of the request. Section 4 indicates that British legislation for Canada will be enacted only at the 'request and consent' of the latter, but it does not indicate who is to furnish this necessary element. In regard to Australia, the Statute is quite explicit; Section 9 (3) states that 'the request and consent referred to in section four shall mean the request and consent of the Parliament and Government of the Commonwealth'. But despite the absence of a comparable statement in regard to Canada (an omission that seems intentional in view of the third clause of Section 9), the precedents clearly indicate that the principle is the same.

Thus, except for the Statute Law Revision Acts and the three instances mentioned above, no British statute has been enacted specifically for Canada without a Parliamentary Address requesting the same for over half a century.[2] There have

[1] But the addresses were made all the same. See Canada, *House of Commons Journals*, vol. li, 1915, pp. 190–1, 248, 322, and vol. lii, 1916, p. 75.

[2] Perhaps another exception may be found in an ancient practice known as 'conditional legislation' by which the British Parliament provided loans for certain purposes subject to the enactment by the Canadian Parliament of speci-

been only two instances in which the executive government has actually secured an amendment without action by Parliament (1875 and 1895); both of these were in the nineteenth century and both were for the purpose of affirming the validity of an Act already passed by the Parliament. It would be difficult to dispute the contention that the practice of seeking amendments by Parliamentary Address is by now an established convention of the constitution.

### *Consultation with the Provinces*

But a more important question remains unanswered. Under what circumstances will the Dominion Parliament make such a request? The issue at the heart of this problem is the federal one. What has been and what ought to be the role of the provinces in the formulation of requests for constitutional amendment? Is their consent necessary? If the provinces do have a role in the process, then how should that role be performed? Must all the provinces consent to the proposed amendment, or may it be requested with something less than their unanimous approval? This problem has plagued Canadians for half a century or more and remains today one of the most important obstacles to the smooth operation of Canadian federalism.

There are two principal schools of thought on the matter; one holds that the constitution can be amended only with the unanimous consent of all the provinces, the other that no such unanimity is necessary. The suggestions of the latter group vary considerably; some argue that the power to amend (i.e. to request amendments) lies in the discretion of the Dominion Parliament; others hold that the Parliament need not but ought to consult the provinces; still others hold that some system of provincial consultation should be worked out but that it is not necessary that the consent of all be secured. Some propose a majority of the provinces, some say other fractions; some urge legislative approval, some urge referenda. Canada is widely split on the question and, thus far at least, it has been impossible to reconcile the differences of opinion.

These diversities of opinion strike directly at the heart of

fied guarantees. The practice was abandoned before the turn of the century. See Clokie, op. cit., pp. 17 f.

Canadian federalism. The essential aspect of the dispute is not merely the disagreement on procedure, for this is but the outward manifestation of the deeper schisms in the society itself. The question is that of the degree of protection that must be guaranteed to the diverse interests that are grouped generally within the provincial boundaries. We have argued above that the federal pattern of the society is reflected in the system of instrumentalities employed by that society to give expression and protection to the diverse groups. Every such instrumentality represents a social decision. But 'society' in the abstract never makes decisions; decisions are made by men. Hence every decision of 'society' is merely the common denominator of the diverse opinions in the society; it represents a compromise among these various opinions. The instrumentalities of federalism then, being the product of such social decisions, actually represent such a compromise.

Now in any federal society, one of the most important of the instrumentalities of federalism is the method of amending the constitution. In Canada no such instrumentality has been adopted; no social decision has been made; no compromise has been reached. I do not mean to imply that such decisions are not sometimes made (or that they should not be made) by default. It is by no means true that the compromise represented by a decision of society always leaves the diverse elements satisfied with the result; it is also true that the lack of a compromise is in effect a decision. But the point is that in Canada not only has a compromise not been reached on the instrumentality but no decision has been made even by default. Every time the instrumentality has been called upon its nature has been different. There have been nearly as many methods of constitutional amendment in Canada as there have been amendments to the constitution. No one can say what the instrumentality is, for no decision, no compromise, has ever been made in the matter.

### *The Compact Theory of Confederation*

The difference between those who urge the necessity of unanimous provincial consent and those who deny it turns in large part on their divergent interpretations of the early history of the Dominion and on their views regarding the nature of the British North America Act of 1867. The former group adheres for the most part to what is called the compact theory of confederation; the latter group denies the validity of this theory. Much of the controversial literature on the problem of constitutional amendment in Canada has taken the form of attacks on or defences of the compact theory.

The purpose of this theory is to show that the union of the North American colonies in 1867 was the result of a pact or treaty among them, by which they agreed to surrender certain powers, rights, and revenues to a central government, retaining certain others for themselves. Its proponents ordinarily rest their contentions on historical grounds, arguing that each colony represented at the Quebec Conference in 1864 agreed through its representatives to seventy-two resolutions which formed the basis of confederation. The agreement to these resolutions was then ratified by the colonial legislatures and the Act of 1867 which followed was merely the enactment into law of the treaty relationship. Since the Act provides nothing to the contrary, the future amendment of the Act must follow the same procedure as that employed for arriving at the original agreement, namely the unanimous concurrence of the participating groups. To buttress this interpretation, there are cited various remarks of the fathers of confederation in which the words 'treaty' or 'pact' appear, thus indicating the binding force of the agreement and emphasizing the separate identity of the contracting provinces as constituent bodies.

This interpretation of the events leading up to the Act of 1867 has received the very nearly unanimous denunciation of scholars who have treated of the subject.[1] Professor Dawson argues that 'the theory, while plausible, is constructed on sheer invention which has been subsequently propped up by an occasional precedent. It has no legal foundation.'[2] And W. P. M. Kennedy, perhaps Canada's most eminent constitutional lawyer, adds, '. . . it is true neither in history nor in law. The British North America Act is a statute, and has

[1] For example, in 1935 a Special Committee of the House of Commons called as witnesses seven eminent men, including both scholars and men in public life. Each was asked what he thought of the compact theory; of the seven only one failed to repudiate it unequivocally and even he denied that it implied a necessity of unanimous consent.

[2] Robert MacG. Dawson, *The Government of Canada*, p. 143.

always been interpreted as a statute.'[1] The latter comment strikes at the heart of the matter, for if the Act is not a treaty but a statute and is interpreted as a statute in accordance with British principles of interpretation, then there is no foundation for an argument for unanimous provincial consent. Since nothing can be read out of the statute that is not explicit in it, and since the Act mentions nothing at all about amendment, let alone unanimous consent, the provinces have no legal claim to any consultation at all. This leaves the legal question right where it was before 1867. All that can be said of the law on the matter is that the Act of 1867 is a statute of the British Parliament and (barring the exceptions provided in the 1949 Act) can be amended only by that body.

### *Historical Validity of the Compact Theory*

But the historical validity of the theory has also been subjected to severe criticism and has been found to rest on no more solid a foundation than the legal validity. Probably the most exhaustive examination of the historical basis has been that of Professor Rogers, who concluded that it was unsound.[2] The historical argument rests on the assertion that delegates of the provinces, meeting at Quebec in 1864 and again later in London, were empowered to conclude such a treaty on behalf of their governments, and that the treaty so concluded was then ratified by the legislatures of the several provinces and became the foundation of the British North America Act. This argument can be refuted at almost every point.

First of all, it is impossible to say who were the parties to the so-called pact. Though Quebec and Ontario were accorded separate representation at the two conferences, they were not separate colonies at the time, being united under the Act of 1840 in a legislative union. The Dominion was not a party, for it did not exist. Prince Edward Island and British Columbia made no agreement with the other colonies but with the Dominion only. Manitoba, Alberta, and Saskatchewan did not exist at all but were later created by Act of the Dominion

[1] Special Committee on the British North America Act, 1935, *Proceedings and Evidence and Report*, p. 69.

[2] Norman McL. Rogers, 'The Compact Theory of Confederation', in Canadian Political Science Association, *Proceedings*, 1931, vol. iii, pp. 205–30. The following paragraphs are drawn principally from this article.

Parliament. The conferences included only the representatives of New Brunswick, Nova Scotia, and the Province of Canada, the latter being represented by two separate delegations. This diversity of status among the provinces casts serious doubt upon the assertion that the conferences produced a treaty in which all participated and which can be changed only by the concurrence of all.

A consideration of the several steps in the argument reveals other important weaknesses. In the first place, it seems clear that the provinces possessed no power to conclude such a treaty. It has been suggested that such a power was granted by a letter of instructions sent in 1862 by the Imperial Government to the Governor of Nova Scotia. But an examination of this letter reveals only an authorization to hold a conference.[1] It speaks not of making agreements but of holding discussions. Professor Rogers argued, moreover, that the Imperial Government could not have authorized the provinces to conclude such a treaty, for at least one of them possessed a constitution that had been granted by an Act of Parliament.[2] The criticism is thus twofold: the Imperial Government did not intend to grant a treaty-making power, and it could not have done so even if it had so intended.

In the second place, the delegates were not empowered to conclude such a treaty, for no legislature authorized anything but a discussion.[3] In Nova Scotia there was not even this, for the legislature authorized a discussion only among the maritime provinces; the conference with Canada was undertaken on executive authority only;[4] and the same thing seems to have been true in the New Brunswick legislature.[5]

Finally, the compact theorists argue that the approval of the Quebec resolutions by the colonial legislatures constituted a ratification of the treaty. This would seem to have been expected by the conference itself, for the seventieth resolution read as follows: 'The sanction of the Imperial and Local

[1] The letter is given in Sir Joseph Pope, *Confederation Documents*, Toronto, 1895, Appendix v. See also the comments on this point in *Confederation Debates*, Quebec, 1865, pp. 110, 134, 136.

[2] Rogers, op. cit., p. 211.

[3] Ibid., p. 212.

[4] See *Debates of the Legislative Assembly of Nova Scotia*, 1865, p. 1, where the Speech from the Throne summarizes what was done.

[5] See *Debates of the Legislative Council of New Brunswick*, 1865, p. 117.

Parliaments shall be sought for the Union of the Provinces, on the principles adopted by this Conference.'[1] But the record shows that this sanction was not forthcoming. Only in the Province of Canada did the proposals receive legislative approval. They were never in fact submitted to the legislatures of Nova Scotia and New Brunswick. In these two provinces there was approval of the proposed discussions with the Imperial Government but none of the resolutions adopted at Quebec; the maritimes in general were dissatisfied with the Quebec scheme and hoped to secure new arrangements at the London Conference. In Nova Scotia the motion was for the purpose of avoiding the Quebec plan.[2] In New Brunswick the question was not posed because the Government had been decisively defeated in a general election,[3] and in Prince Edward Island the resolutions were defeated.[4] In the words of Stephen Leacock,

> . . . the maritime provinces, resisting and protesting, were dragged into the union, New Brunswick by a popular election on a momentary wave of indignation over the Fenian raids; Nova Scotia by a vote of the Legislature against the people's will. Prince Edward Island a little later in 1873 was bribed in by the purchase of its bankrupt railway. Newfoundland stayed out.[5]

Moreover, at the London Conference in 1866–7 substantial changes were made in the Quebec resolutions, but this changed basis for the confederation was in no instance referred back to the colonies for approval before being enacted into law by the British Parliament.[6] New Brunswick and Nova Scotia had in fact explicitly rejected earlier proposals that this be done.[7]

Neither the Quebec Conference nor the London Conference provides, then, an adequate basis upon which the historical validity of the compact theory can be defended. On the contrary a point-by-point refutation can be made. It can be

[1] Pope, *Confederation Documents*, p. 52.

[2] *Debates of the Legislative Assembly of Nova Scotia*, 1866, pp. 66–70. See also the speech of Mr. Miller, ibid., p. 189.

[3] W. P. M. Kennedy, *The Constitution of Canada*, Oxford, 1922, pp. 308 f.

[4] Rogers, op. cit., p. 211.

[5] Leacock, 'Is Canada Breaking Up?', in *Ottawa Journal*, 15 Dec. 1934. Quoted in Ollivier, *Problems of Canadian Sovereignty*, p. 350, note k.

[6] Rogers, op. cit., p. 217.

[7] Ibid., p. 216.

shown that the Imperial Government in London did not and could not authorize the provinces to make such a treaty; that not all provincial legislatures authorized such a treaty; and that the final arrangements were ratified by none of the provinces. Moreover, not all the provinces took part in the discussions that led up to the adoption of the Act. The British North America Act can therefore only be regarded as a statute of the British Parliament and nothing more.[1]

### *Views of the Fathers of Confederation on the Compact Interpretation*

It is unlikely that much credence would have been given to the compact theory at all were it not for the fact that several of the leaders of the confederation movement, both before and after the Act of 1867, employed the terms 'treaty' and 'pact' in their references to what had taken place in 1864–7.[2] Compact theorists have made much of these remarks, quoting Galt, Macdonald, Cartier, and others to show that what they really had in mind was a binding compact that would be changeable only by the unanimous consent of the contracting parties.[3]

We have shown above the difficulty of discovering just who were the contracting parties, but an examination of the remarks themselves casts even further doubt upon the compact interpretation, for it is fairly clear that this conclusion cannot

[1] But even conceding the falsity of the compact theory as described above, it has been argued in some quarters that there is a compact relation with the other provinces that entered the Confederation after 1867 and that these provinces have special rights, one of which is that no amendment is valid without their consent. This argument is examined and refuted by Gilbert D. Kennedy, 'Amendment of the British North America Acts in Relation to British Columbia, Prince Edward Island, and Newfoundland', *University of Toronto Law Journal*, vol. 8, 1949–50, pp. 208–17.

[2] See, for example, the remarks of the Hon. D'Arcy McGee in *Confederation Debates*, Quebec, 1865, p. 136; also the discussion at p. 110. Sir John Macdonald, then Attorney-General West for the Province of Canada, said that 'the Government presented the scheme as a whole, and would exert all the influence they could bring to bear in the way of argument to induce the House to adopt the scheme without alteration, and for the simple reason that the scheme was not one framed by the Government of Canada, or by the Government of Nova Scotia, but was in the nature of a treaty settled between the different colonies'. Ibid., p. 15.

[3] See, for example, one of the tracts submitted in 1938 to the Royal Commission on Dominion-Provincial Relations. Société Saint-Jean-Baptiste de Montréal, *Le Canada, pays anglo-français*, Montreal, 1938.

be read out of the remarks as they stand. Macdonald was a strong government man and, failing in his hopes for a legislative union, he wanted a federation with as strong a central government as possible. He was afraid that if the legislatures started amending the Quebec proposals there might be no end to it, and he saw in this a threat to federation itself. Consequently he and his colleagues were anxious to have the legislature accept the plan *in toto* without any amendments. To call it a 'treaty' was good floor tactics, for this meant that the legislature would be forced either to accept or to reject it as a whole. This was undoubtedly one of the reasons for the frequent reappearance of the terms during the debates. That this was not a hidden purpose is evidenced by the remarks of Macdonald cited above.

But the other governments did not resort to the same stratagems. It is significant that the words 'pact', &c., appear only in the debates in the Province of Canada. In neither New Brunswick nor Nova Scotia were the resolutions presented in the form of a treaty.[1] And in Canada the tactic did not pass without strong objection.[2]

But regardless of these terms and tactics, almost no one meant by them that the constitution should be amended only by the unanimous consent of the provinces. Several of the fathers of confederation are, indeed, on record as being directly opposed to that view. In 1869 a proposal was made to extend better financial terms to Nova Scotia. The objection was raised that this was a substantive change in the terms of confederation and should be effected by amending the constitution. A motion was offered to the effect that

> . . . any disturbance of the financial arrangements respecting the several provinces provided for in the British North America Act, unless assented to by all the Provinces, would be subversive to the system of Government under which the Dominion was constituted.

This motion was defeated in the House, and included among those voting against it were Galt, Macdonald, Tilley, Tupper, and Cartier.[3] In 1871 a similar motion was opposed by the

[1] Rogers, op. cit., p. 220.

[2] See the fascinating interchange between Mr. Christopher Dunkin and Sir George Cartier, Attorney-General East, in *Confederation Debates*, p. 540.

[3] Canada, *House of Commons Journals*, vol. ii, 1869, p. 260.

Government and defeated by the House.[1] Also in 1871 during the debates over the right of the executive to request amendments it was proposed that the principle of representation in the House of Commons should not be changed without the consent of the provinces that were signatory to the pact. This resolution was rejected without even being debated.[2] The compact theory, if it existed at all, at least did not have much strength in those days. It is very doubtful that it had yet been conceived in its present form.

### *Growth of the Compact Theory*

The compact theory with its implications of unanimous consultation and consent seems to have come into being only around the turn of the century. Certainly in these early days the use of the terms 'pact' and 'treaty' to characterize what had happened in the years leading up to 1867 conveyed no such meaning; the additional meaning was read into them in later years as a convenient means of bolstering a position otherwise difficult to defend on legal or historical grounds. Thus in 1889 Bourinot could write that

> . . . in entering into the federal compact the provinces never intended to renounce their distinct and separate existence as provinces when they became part of the confederation[3]

without saying anything about provincial consent to constitutional changes.

In 1890 Albert Bushnell Hart published his study of federal government and included in it a few pages devoted to the theories that underlie various forms of federations. He described two principal explanations—the 'constitution theory' and the 'treaty theory'. As examples of the latter he shows that it has given rise to the compact theory of the constitution of the United States (e.g. Hartford Convention, Virginia and Kentucky Resolutions, Civil War) and was also the justification of secession in Switzerland in 1847. Significantly he does not mention Canada at all in this regard, even though he was

[1] Ibid., 1871, p. 254.

[2] Ollivier, *Problems of Canadian Sovereignty*, pp. 364 f.

[3] J. G. Bourinot, *Federal Government in Canada*, Johns Hopkins Studies in Historical and Political Science, 7th ser., Baltimore, 1889, p. 124.

using exactly the same terminology later employed by the Canadian compact theorists.[1] Unless we are to conclude that Professor Hart simply had not heard about Canada's federal problems, the inference is clear that the compact theory in Canada had not yet been formulated—or at least that it had little currency.

But by 1907 it was clearly in evidence and was, indeed, given a boost by the discussions attendant upon the amendment of that year. These discussions gave rise to much speculation about the proper procedure for amendment, and the argument was often heard that such proposals required provincial consent. But even at this time the lines were not clearly drawn. During the debate on the 1907 address Sir Robert Borden remarked

> . . . I agree with what has been said . . . regarding the undesirability of lightly amending the terms of our constitution and am inclined to agree . . . on the necessity of some consultation with the provinces, although of course all the provinces are represented here.[2]

This was certainly the beginning of a concession to the compact theory, but the idea that representation in the Dominion Parliament was sufficient protection for the provinces would never have been accepted by the compact theorists.

After 1907 the theory was heard with increasing frequency until the 1920's, when it became a major constitutional issue. The twenties were in general a great era for the assertion of provincial rights.[3] The prairie provinces clamoured for the return of the natural resources that the Dominion had retained; the maritimes complained that the Dominion had never carried out the promises made at confederation and that these must now be redeemed; the Judicial Committee of the Privy Council virtually assigned the residual powers to the provinces through its broadening of the meaning of 'property

[1] Albert Bushnell Hart, *Introduction to the Study of Federal Government*, Boston, 1891, pp. 17 f.

[2] Canada, *House of Commons Debates*, 28 Jan. 1907, p. 2200. He continued: '. . . But inasmuch as this is a federal compact which we are to vary, it is only right that each province should be consulted and its decision given, in the right of its separate entity.' Loc. cit.

[3] See the discussion by D. G. Creighton, 'Federal Relations in Canada since 1914', in Chester Martin, ed. *Canada in Peace and War*, Oxford, 1941, pp. 47 ff.

and civil rights';[1] and Ontario joined Quebec in the affirmation of the compact theory of confederation.

By 1925 the leader of the Conservative Party, Mr. Arthur Meighen, was willing to say that 'undoubtedly, the pact of confederation is a compact and there are rights involved therein not represented by the Parliament of Canada'.[2] One of the best statements of the theory is that found in a memorandum sent to the Prime Minister of Canada by the Hon. G. H. Ferguson, Premier of Ontario, in connexion with that province's complaint about the repeal of the Colonial Laws Validity Act. The memorandum reviews the history of confederation, arguing that a treaty has been made, and concludes:

> . . . it is, therefore, earnestly represented that no restatement of the procedure for amending the constitution of Canada can be accepted by the Province of Ontario that does not fully and frankly acknowledge the right of all the Provinces to be consulted, and to become parties to the decision arrived at.[3]

Certainly the theory had enough vitality by this time to affect the Dominion's position on the Statute of Westminster, for it was at the insistence of Ontario and others that Section 7 was included in the Statute to prevent unilateral alteration of the constitution by the Dominion.

After a period of growth, then, through the twenties, the compact theory had by 1930 reached impressive proportions. All during the two decades from 1920 to 1940 the debates of

[1] Culminating, of course, in *Toronto Electric Commissioners* v. *Snider* (1925), A.C. 396.

[2] Canada, *House of Commons Debates*, 25 Feb., 1925, p. 335. That this opinion expressed more a personal than a party view seems evident from the fact that less than a decade later Mr. R. B. Bennett, Conservative Party leader and Prime Minister, proclaimed, 'I am not one of them who believe that unanimous consent on the part of all the provinces is necessary in order for the constitution to be amended'. *Canadian Problems As Seen by Twenty Outstanding Men of Canada*, 1933, p. 27. At party schools in 1934 both Conservative and Liberal Party speakers attacked the compact theory. Duncan McArthur, 'Revision of the Constitution', *Queen's Quarterly*, vol. 41, 1934, p. 127. After the war, however, the Conservatives again urged the necessity of consultation, while the Liberal Government has several times pushed through a joint address without it. See *House of Commons Debates*, 14 Feb., 1949, pp. 496 ff.; also 12 June, 1952, pp. 3156 ff.

[3] The memorandum was dated 10 Sept. 1930; it appeared in the *Toronto Globe*, 20 Sept. 1930, and is quoted at length by N. McL. Rogers, 'The Compact Theory of Confederation', in Canadian Political Science Association, *Proceedings*, vol. iii, 1931, pp. 206 f.

the Canadian Parliament abound in statements of the theory and arguments against it.[1] The principal proponents of the theory have presumed to speak on behalf of Quebec[2] and Ontario, though expositions of the doctrine have not been wanting in other provinces as well. The fact that these two largest provinces have been closely associated with the demand for unanimity indicates at least the weight of influence that has been thrown against any alternative proposals. Quebec's position on the question is readily understood; she has always considered herself unique among the provinces, as indeed she has been. Her differentiation from the rest of Canada in

[1] See especially the debate in the House on 19 Feb. 1925, pp. 328 ff. Statements in favour of unanimity of consent may be found in the *Debates* as follows: Mr. Cahan in the House, 11 May 1931, pp. 1485 f.; Senator Turgeon in the Senate, 28 Mar. 1935, pp. 229 f.; Mr. Cardin in the House, 5 July 1943, p. 4450; Mr. Hazen in the House on the same date, p. 4458. Statements opposed to that principle as follows: Mr. Garland in the House, 11 May 1931, p. 1481; Mr. Lapointe in the House, 1 Feb. 1937, p. 434; Mr. Woodsworth in the House on the same date, p. 444; Mr. St. Laurent in the House, 5 July 1943, p. 4459. Even in 1952 the Progressive-Conservatives were defending the compact theory; see 12 June 1952, p. 3170.

[2] Not all Québecois adhere to the theory of compact and unanimity; the late Minister of Justice, Mr. Ernest Lapointe, and the present Prime Minister, Mr. Louis St. Laurent, are notable exceptions. Moreover, the Liberal Party, which has more or less consistently opposed the theory, has drawn much of its support from Quebec. Others in that province, however, including regularly the government of the province, have felt most strongly about the matter. We may note here two submissions to the Sirois Commission by private French-speaking associations. Comité Permanent des Congrès de la Langue Française, *Mémoire à la Commission Royale*: 'A son (i.e. the Comité) avis, cet Acte n'a pas seulement le caractère d'une loi impériale; il comporte une entente préalable, un pacte arrêté entre les Provinces délibérantes, pacte que l'Acte impériale a fixé.' Also Société Saint-Jean-Baptiste de Montréal, *Le Canada, pays anglo-français* (*Mémoire à la Commission Royale*), p. 18: 'Pour réaliser une harmonie nationale, ces deux races ont librement consenti un contrat: le pacte de la Confédération qui a été sanctionné par l'Acte de l'Amérique Brittanique du Nord.' Note that in this version the parties to the pact are not the provinces but the two races. On the other hand, Dr. Ollivier (op. cit., p. 351) quotes a French cleric against any compact interpretation at all (the translation is Ollivier's): '. . . we believe it is not exact to speak of our constitution as a contract. It is without doubt a law of a particular nature but a law of indisputable authenticity. . . . In the defense of our most sacred interests and of our most incontestable rights we think that the dissemination of the truth renders much greater service than bad propositions, which, at first, appear to be able to support our legitimate claims and our sentiments of national pride.' *Revue de l'Université d'Ottawa*, vol. 5, 1935, p. 277. More recently there is a lengthy and enthusiastic defence of the compact interpretation by Father Richard Arès, S.J., 'La Confédération: Pacte ou Loi?' in *L'Action Nationale*, vol. 34, 1949 (2), pp. 194–230, 243–277. Cited in Gérin-Lajoie, op. cit., p. 205. The theory is by no means dead.

matters of 'race', language, and religion is protected by the Act of 1867 and she desires fervently to secure these guarantees against possible attack by the other provinces or the Dominion. Ontario came later to the support of the compact theory and her position seems to represent merely a desire to protect the prerogatives of her status as a large and powerful province. In the other provinces the compact theory had few supporters until the 1930's. At the Dominion-Provincial Conference of 1927 the other seven provinces indicated they would not be favourable to a rigorous application of the principle of unanimous consent,[1] but a decade later more support for it had been found.

In the testimony and submissions to the Royal Commission on Dominion-Provincial Relations in 1938–9[2] the issue was clearly drawn. Both Ontario and Quebec in their submissions to the Commission officially stated their adherence to the principle of unanimous provincial consent, while several other provinces officially refuted it.[3] Mr. Hepburn, Premier of Ontario, argued that 'if there is to be a change in confederation, it can be brought about only by renewed conferences between the representatives of the people and with unanimity of approval'.[4] Quebec enthusiastically supported this; the official submission by the provincial government read as follows:

> . . . It is the considered opinion of this Government that the British North America Act is the ratification of a compact. . . . The Government of this Province declares that it firmly adheres to this doctrine. . . . Neither the Federal Government, nor a majority of the Provinces, can change or alter its provisions.[5]

Saskatchewan and Nova Scotia unequivocally denied the principle of unanimous consent.[6] Most provinces, however, conceded that some measure for the protection of minority

[1] N. McL. Rogers, 'The Constitutional Impasse', *Queen's Quarterly*, vol. 41, 1934, pp. 484 f.

[2] Hereafter called and cited as the Sirois Commission. See below, pp. 85–87.

[3] The several positions are given briefly in British Columbia, *The Governments of Canada Before the Rowell Commission*, pp. 7 ff.

[4] Sirois Commission, *Evidence*, p. 7400.

[5] Quebec, *Statement of the Government of the Province of Quebec*, English text (submission to the Royal Commission), pp. 2–3. Also *Evidence*, pp. 8132–5.

[6] For Nova Scotia and Saskatchewan see British Columbia, *Governments of Canada Before the Rowell Commission*, respectively at pp. 11 and 7–8. Also see *Evidence* at pp. 3873 and 2277 respectively.

rights should be adopted, even though complete unanimity of consent should not be required on all questions.[1] Despite the quantity of testimony before it on the subject, however, the Commission did not make any recommendations concerning an amending procedure, since its terms of reference did not extend to this matter. It did, however, make several specific recommendations for changes in the constitution and urged Dominion and provinces to come to agreement on a general procedure.[2]

The compact theory and its corollaries of consultation and unanimity of consent pose one of the most serious constitutional problems that Canada has had to face. If the theory should be adopted, the constitution of Canada might well become very nearly inflexible; if it is repudiated and forcefully rejected by the anti-compact group, the unity of Canada will be imperilled. On the solution of this problem may hinge the future of the Canadian nation; and the prospects for such a solution must be measured by the experience of the provinces in the amending process thus far.

### *Consultation in Practice Before 1907*

It has been argued above that the theory that the unanimous consent of the provinces is necessary to alter the constitution is of fairly recent date. This may also be seen by examining the procedures employed in the early instances of amendment and inquiring to what extent the provinces have played a role in the process. We have seen that the House of Commons directly refused to subscribe to this conception on several occasions in the period immediately after the establishment of the Dominion. Indeed, there would seem to be no precedent for consultation with the provinces on such matters, let alone a necessity for their unanimous consent, before the enactment of the British North America Act, 1907. The Acts of 1871, 1875, 1886, and 1895 were all secured by the request of the Dominion Government or the Dominion Parliament, without

[1] See *Brief of Nova Scotia*, pp. 14–15; *Brief of Saskatchewan*, pp. 8, 330; *Brief of Manitoba*, pt. ii, p. 41; *Brief of British Columbia*, p. 351; *Brief of New Brunswick*, pt. ii; also *Supplementary Brief*.

[2] Sirois Commission, *Report*, bk. ii, p. 72.

any consultation with the provinces. This of course is not to say that no such suggestion was ever made, for we have already seen that it was made as early as 1871. But it was never adopted and the opinion of the provinces was never sought. Sir John Macdonald answered such a suggestion in 1875 by saying that 'there were occasions when this Legislature might fairly address Her Majesty in regard to Bills, the validity of which were questioned, without reference to the provinces, but with the greatest circumspection'.[1]

If much weight were to be given to the doctrine of consultation, it would appear most strikingly on occasions when the proposed amendment directly affected the position of the provinces. Yet even on the Acts of 1871 and 1886, which gave the Dominion the right to establish new provinces and provide for their representation in Parliament (thus actually changing the balance of sectional and provincial power), the provinces were not consulted and did not ask to be consulted.[2] There are only two occasions prior to 1907 when any provinces were consulted before seeking legislation from Westminster and no instance at all when all the provinces were consulted. The two instances mentioned were in 1889 and 1892; the Acts were not constitutional in nature and on neither occasion were any provinces consulted other than those that were directly concerned with the matter.[3]

## *The Precedents of 1907*

The Act of 1907, which provides the first precedent for consultation with the provinces, was different from its predecessors in that it so directly affected the provinces that their interest in its provisions could not be ignored. It inserted a new Section 118 in the Act of 1867, thus changing the amount of the subsidies paid by the Dominion to the

[1] Canada, *House of Commons Debates*, 1876, p. 1142.

[2] Special Committee on the British North America Act, 1935, *Proceedings and Evidence and Report*, p. 31.

[3] The first of these was the Ontario Boundary Act of 1889. 'When the Address was moved and the circumstances briefly outlined by Sir John Macdonald, Sir Wilfrid Laurier asked if it affected Quebec's boundary. On being informed that it did not, he offered no objection. Ontario's assent was reported as being secured by telegraph. Canada, *House of Commons Debates*, 1889, vol. ii, p. 1329.' Clokie, op. cit., p. 28, n. 43. The second was the British Columbia Loan Act of 1892.

provinces. The Act was in fact initiated by the provinces, for an increase in payments had been urged at the interprovincial conferences of 1887, 1902, and 1906. Despite the supposed rigidity of Section 118 of the British North America Act, the subsidies had been increased several times in the past by action of the Dominion Parliament without recourse to British legislation.[1] But on this occasion the Government insisted on resorting to an Imperial statute, probably hoping that this would put an end to the continuous clamour for increases.

Here for the first time all the provinces were consulted and only then was the address of the Parliament transmitted to the Imperial Government. It thus constitutes a valid precedent for the doctrine of consultation; but it seems clear that it was not intended to do so. Consultation was made necessary by the circumstances themselves and there was no intention on the part of the Government of indicating acceptance of the compact and consent principles. It was simply a matter of convenience; the Government wanted to settle once and for all the question of payments to the provinces and it had to ask the provinces how much they would accept. Sir Wilfrid Laurier remarked,

> We thought we could not do better than have a friendly conference with the provinces, and ascertain what was the most they deemed requisite in order to prevent their coming again to Ottawa and knocking at the door of this Parliament.[2]

That the 1907 Act constituted a precedent for provincial consultation can hardly be doubted; but it is also true that the precedent was not considered sufficient to bind future action, as will be shown below.

The Act of 1907 is of interest for another reason. All the provinces save one agreed to the terms proposed to the Imperial Government by the Dominion; but British Columbia felt that the new payments were still not high enough and refused to concur in the plan. Moreover, the suggested bill contained the words 'final and unalterable' in referring to

[1] Section 118 described the payments provided for as being 'in full settlement of all future demands on Canada', but it had always been interpreted as a minimum only. Despite the appearance of finality, this section has been changed more than any other, both before and after 1907.

[2] Canada, *House of Commons Debates*, 1907, vol. iii, p. 5304.

the payments, even though the fact that the payments were then being changed made meaningless similar expressions in earlier Acts. British Columbia, hoping for further increases, objected to this clause as well, and the provincial premier went to London to make the protest in person. As the matter turned out the finality clause was omitted from the Act, but the premier failed to secure an increased subsidy. The official reply of the Secretary of State for Colonies, indeed, casts doubt on British Columbia's claim that the omission of the finality clause was the result of her complaint. Since the schedule of payments was part of an Act of Parliament and could therefore be changed by any subsequent Act of the same Parliament, such words as 'final and unalterable' were clearly inappropriate, and it seems most likely that this was the reason for their exclusion.[1] The Act in its final form thus failed to meet British Columbia's objections and hence refutes the doctrine of unanimous consent.

The issue was further confused, however, by the words used by Mr. Winston Churchill to describe what had taken place. He said to the House that

> he would be very sorry if it were thought that the action which His Majesty's Government had decided to take meant that they had decided to establish as a precedent that whenever there was a difference on a constitutional question between the Federal Government and one of the provinces, the Imperial Government would always be prepared to accept the Federal point of view as against the provincial. In deference to the

[1] The letter to Premier McBride of British Columbia was in part as follows: 'I am directed by the Earl of Elgin to inform you that His Lordship has given the most careful consideration to the . . . views advanced against the proposed amendment to the British North America Act. . . .

'Lord Elgin fully appreciates the force of the opinion expressed that the British North America Act was the result of terms of union agreed upon by the contracting provinces and that its terms cannot be altered merely at the wish of the Dominion government.

'But . . . His Lordship feels that in view of the unanimity of the Dominion government and of all the provincial governments, save that of British Columbia, he would not in the interests of Canada be justified in any effort to override the decision of the Dominion parliament or to compel the reference of the question to arbitration.

'. . . no mention will be made in the Imperial Act of the settlement being "final and unalterable", such terms being obviously inappropriate in a legislative enactment.' Letter of 5 June 1907 to Premier McBride; signed by H. Bertram Cox. The letter is given in full in the testimony of Dr. O. D. Skelton before the Special Committee of 1935. See *Proceedings and Evidence and Report*, pp. 34–35.

representations of British Columbia the words 'final and unalterable' had been omitted from the Bill.[1]

This view can hardly be substantiated by the facts. The precedent had long since been established that the Imperial Government would accept the recommendations of the Dominion Government in such matters.[2]

Although some students of the problem concluded from the Act of 1907 that the doctrines of compact, provincial consultation, and provincial unanimity were henceforth to be the guides for constitutional practice,[3] such a conclusion would seem, even at that time, to have been premature. Certainly it did not demonstrate the necessity of unanimity, for the consent was not unanimous; nor did it conclusively indicate acceptance of the consultation principle since the subject, being directly concerned with the provinces, was different from that of former amendments. Finally, I have found no official recognition or mention of the compact theory at all and can only conclude that the supposed acceptance of this was inferred from the supposed acceptance of consultation and consent. Whatever precedents were established, they seem not to have been of great significance, since they were not followed.

[1] *British House of Commons Debates*, ser. 4, vol. 175, p. 1617.

[2] See Clokie, op. cit., p. 27, who adds: '(Churchill's) unfamiliarity with the details is shown by his reference later to the "Address of the Colonial Premiers which led up to this Bill".' *British House of Commons Debates*, ser. 4, vol. 179, p. 1456. Professor Rogers believed 'the reason for the omission of that phrase from the enacting portions of the Act was not to be construed as a deference to the objection raised by British Columbia, but rather as an expression of view always strongly held by constitutional lawyers in Great Britain that no Parliament can bind its successors'. Testimony before the Special Committee of 1935, *Proceedings and Evidence and Report*, p. 110. Professor Dawson says, however, that the 'objection raised by British Columbia was the probable cause of a slight change of wording when the British Parliament passed the statute'. R. MacG. Dawson, *The Government of Canada*, p. 144.

[3] See, for example, Sir George Ross, *The Senate of Canada*, Toronto, 1914, p. 115: 'It was not until 1907 that the Parliament of Canada formally admitted the doctrine of consent. The Subsidy Act of 1907 . . . was based upon the assent of all [*sic*] the Provinces by their Legislatures or representatives, and thus Parliament recognized for the first time that the Union Act was a treaty, to be amended only with the consent of the parties that were bound by it.' Also A. Berriedale Keith, *Responsible Government in the Dominions*, 2nd ed., Oxford, 1928, vol. i, pp. 586 f.: 'It was most expressly recognized in 1907 by the Imperial Government that the federal constitution is a compact which cannot be altered save with the assent both of the Dominion and of the provinces.' Keith held to this interpretation even in later years. See *Dominions as Sovereign States*, London, 1938, pp. 170 ff.

It must be conceded, however, that the events of 1907 left open the question of what the attitude of the British Parliament would have been if more than a single province had objected to the bill.

### *Consultation on Later Amendments*

That consultation with the provinces had not yet become a fast rule is demonstrated by the next amendment in 1915. This Act again made a substantial alteration in the position of the provinces by changing the scheme of representation in the House and in the Senate. But the only province that voiced a protest was Prince Edward Island, which made representations before a House of Commons committee. Its suggestions, however, were not accepted and no other provinces were consulted or asked to make representations. Suggestions were made in both the House and Senate that the provinces should be consulted, but neither was acted upon.[1] Similarly in the following year the provinces were not consulted in connexion with the British North America Act, 1916, which postponed the general elections for one year. No objections were raised against this procedure. In 1918 and 1920 there was no consultation with the provinces in connexion with the addresses requesting British action in respect to titles and extraterritoriality.

In 1930 another British North America Act returned to the western provinces certain natural resources that had been retained by the Dominion at the time of their admission to the union. In this instance the three provinces concerned were consulted, but no others, despite the fact that this was a specific amendment to the British North America Act.[2]

### *The Precedents of 1940 and 1943*

The best precedent for provincial consultation and unanimity of consent, because of both its recency and the clear-cut

[1] Special Committee on the British North America Act, 1935, *Proceedings and Evidence and Report*, p. 35. Also Gérin-Lajoie, op. cit., p. 88.

[2] It may be added that all the provinces were consulted in connexion with the enactment of the Statute of Westminster, but this Act, though full of significance for Canadian constitutional law, was not properly an amendment to the Canadian constitution. It was through the insistence of the provinces, however, that Section 7 was inserted in the statute. Gérin-Lajoie considers it to have been an amendment, however; see op. cit., pp. 93 ff.

way in which the issue was presented, was the British North America Act of 1940. This was the first instance in which a change was made in the provisions of Sections 91 or 92, and it is especially significant because of its effect upon the distribution of powers. The purpose of the Act was to assign to the Dominion the power to regulate unemployment insurance, a power that had been denied it in a recent decision of the Judicial Committee of the Privy Coucil.[1] In view of the nature of the amendment, the Government determined to seek the consent of the provinces and began such inquiries as early as 1937. All the provinces agreed to the transfer except Quebec, whose refusal held up the amendment for several years. There seems little doubt that the Dominion could have proceeded with the address to the Imperial Government without waiting for unanimous consent, but this was not done. The Government was faced with a considerable problem in making this decision, for as much as they wanted to secure the amendment they wanted even more to keep the support of Quebec for the Liberal Party. Finally, late in 1939, a political change occurred in Quebec's government and the consent of the new government was secured. The address was passed at once[2] and the Imperial Act was immediately forthcoming.

The Act of 1940 is thus a clear precedent not only for consultation but for unanimity of consent. The address was held up for several years while waiting for the consent of the ninth province. The Prime Minister, Mackenzie King, argued that this did not establish but rather avoided establishing a precedent:

> We have avoided anything in the nature of coercion of any of the provinces. Moreover, we have avoided the raising of a very critical question, namely whether or not in amending the British North America Act it is absolutely necessary to secure the consent of all the provinces, or whether the consent of a certain number of provinces would of itself be sufficient. . . . For the present at any rate we have escaped any pitfall in that direction.[3]

[1] *A.G. for Canada* v. *A.G. for Ontario* (1937), A.C. 355.

[2] Canada, *House of Commons Journals*, vol. lxxx, 1940, pp. 149 f.

[3] Canada, *House of Commons Debates*, 25 June 1940, pp. 1117 f. Dawson comments: 'This is a novel and seductively simple way of escaping a constitutional difficulty; . . . A few more avoidances and escaped pitfalls of this kind, and there is no doubt that the critical constitutional question would be most definitely settled.' Op. cit., p. 145.

It is not quite clear just how this procedure avoided the question, since it followed all the principles that the compact theorists could wish for.

But though the treatment of the 1940 Act came dangerously near acceptance of the principle of unanimous consent, the procedure followed in 1943 destroyed all hope that the question had been settled. The 1943 amendment was for the purpose of postponing the redistribution of seats in the House of Commons until after the war. The redistribution was prescribed by the constitution (Sec. 51) and it therefore required an Act of the British Parliament to postpone it. Quebec, whose population had increased more than that of other provinces, was to benefit considerably from the reassignment of seats and was loath to postpone it. But the inconvenience and injustice of reorganizing the basis of representation in wartime impelled the Government to push its proposal through the House. It was introduced and defended by Mr. St. Laurent, then Minister of Justice, and was supported by both Opposition parties;[1] the issue in the House was never in serious doubt. There was no effort on the part of the Dominion Government to consult the provinces, and this action evoked no protest except on the part of Quebec. This province, however, objected strongly to the Government's treatment of the matter and protests were voiced both at Quebec and at Ottawa. The provincial legislature passed a resolution of protest which the Government was requested to transmit to the British Government. Mackenzie King refused, however, replying that the matter concerned only the Dominion Parliament and not the provincial legislatures; that the compact theory was indefensible both in theory and in law; and that the British could not take cognizance of such a communication, since it was bound by the address of the Dominion Parliament.[2] In the House bitter complaints were heard that the Government was simply ignoring the official protest of the Quebec legislature and that such high-handedness abused the constitution and violated the rights of the provinces.[3] But the Government,

[1] Canada, *House of Commons Debates*, 5 July 1943, pp. 4429–40. Mr. St. Laurent, it may be noted, was the member for Quebec East.

[2] *Montreal Gazette*, 16 July 1943. Quoted by Dawson, op. cit., p. 146.

[3] Canada, *House of Commons Debates*, 5 July 1943, pp. 4447–57. The fervour of one of the members (Mr. Dorion) against the bill led him into a very interesting

secure in the support of the Opposition, pressed the matter to a vote without even replying to these protestations.[1]

The 1943 procedure is full of significance for the problem of constitutional amendment; it provides evidence against the compact theory fully as persuasive as that provided by 1940 in favour of it. The circumstances are particularly interesting since the protesting province was the one most closely associated with the doctrines of compact and unanimous consent. That the Liberal Government was willing to risk loss of the Quebec support is no less remarkable than the fact that it was seemingly repudiating the precedent that it had itself established in 1940. The important difference between the two amendments lies, of course, in the fact that that of 1940 clearly and significantly altered the distribution of powers, a part of the constitution which, it has been argued, is especially deserving of the protection afforded by the principle of unanimous consent.[2] But the facts themselves demonstrate that at least one of the provinces considered the alteration of 1943 sufficiently important to call for long and bitter protests at the disdainful attitude of the Dominion Government. If unanimity is for the protection of provinces, whether singly or collectively, it is reasonable to think that the provinces should be the ones to judge when it should be invoked. By the very operation of the principle, a province will not protest unless it considers the matter at hand worth protesting about.

### *Recent Amendments*

The British North America Act of 1946 which carried through the redistribution of seats in the House of Commons that had been postponed in 1943 was expected, desired, and

argument. He submitted that it was incongruous that a supposedly independent nation like Canada should have to appeal to the Parliament of a foreign country to amend its constitution. In fact he was so opposed to this humiliating procedure that he suggested it not be used and that the House should not pass the motion at all. Canada, *House of Commons Debates*, 5 July 1943, p. 4447.

[1] Ibid., p. 4461. The Prime Minister, however, in a letter to Premier Duplessis of Quebec, took the interesting position that to forward the latter's protest to the British Government would be to infringe on Canada's right to make such decisions by herself. 'Your attitude', he said, 'shows that you wished to have a matter of purely Canadian concern decided by the Parliament of Great Britain.' Quoted by Gérin-Lajoie, op. cit., p. 114.

[2] This distinction was urged by the Minister of Justice (Mr. St. Laurent) as justification for the different procedure employed. Ibid., p. 113.

required by the constitution. But the Act went farther than simply to reassign seats; it went on to provide a wholly new basis for such assignment, discarding the old rule of 'sixty-five seats for Quebec' and adopting in its place a new system of mathematical apportionment based on a total membership of 255.[1] The provinces were not consulted about the amendment by the Dominion; the address was passed without serious objection,[2] and the amendment was enacted by the Imperial Parliament.

In 1949 an amendment to the constitution provided for the union of Newfoundland with Canada. Section 146 of the British North America Act had provided that His Majesty in Council could admit Newfoundland to the confederation with the consent of the legislatures of the two countries. But for more than a decade Newfoundland had had no legislature, its government having been confided to a commission appointed by the Imperial Government. Hence legislative action by the British Parliament was necessary in order to effect the union.[3]

The movement for confederation came primarily from Newfoundland; Canada, throughout the discussions, carefully avoided exerting pressure on her eastern neighbour. After extended discussion in the press and in a convention elected for the purpose, the people of Newfoundland expressed through a referendum their desire to be admitted to the Dominion. Negotiations were undertaken between the two governments and the terms of union were agreed upon;[4] a motion for the approval of the terms was introduced in the House of Commons early in February 1949. All parties supported the proposal,[5] but when the motion for the joint address to the Imperial Government was introduced, the leader of the Opposition introduced a resolution requiring that

[1] The figure is now increased to 262 by the addition of seven members for Newfoundland. See the discussion that follows.

[2] Although a protest was made by the Government of Quebec and a motion to consult the provinces was offered and defeated in the House of Commons. See Gérin-Lajoie, op. cit., p. 118.

[3] See the explanation of Prime Minister St. Laurent in Canada, *House of Commons Debates*, 14 Feb. 1949, pp. 494 ff.

[4] The story of the discussions in Newfoundland and the negotiations between the two countries is recounted by the Prime Minister in ibid., 7 Feb. 1949, pp. 283 ff.

[5] Ibid., pp. 290 ff.

all provinces be consulted before passage of the address.[1] An intensive debate followed this proposal in which the government party (Liberal) opposed consultation on two grounds: (*a*) that the provinces were already represented in the Dominion Parliament,[2] and (*b*) that the Act to be requested was not an amendment to the constitution.[3] The C.C.F. supported the Government's position; the Social Credit Party supported the Conservative opposition. In the course of the debate, M. La Croix, a member from Quebec, introduced a second amendment requiring not only consultation but the consent of all the provinces.[4] Though the debates were long and bitter, neither amendment was adopted, the second receiving only twelve votes and the first being defeated by a vote of 137 to 66.

The debates present a good picture of contemporary opinion on the question of provincial consultation and consent and demonstrate fairly adequately that neither point of view is maintained by a majority of the country. The provinces were at no time consulted on the question, even though the admission of Newfoundland meant a decrease in the proportionate representation of the old provinces in the two Houses of the Dominion Parliament.[5] Moreover, none of the provinces made an official complaint, as was done in 1943, although it was reported to the House that the Premier of Quebec had expressed unofficially his dissatisfaction with the Government's refusal to consult with the provincial governments.[6] The address was passed by the Senate on 17 February 1949 and the British North America Act, 1949,[7] was enacted by the Imperial Parliament a short time later. The terms of union became effective on 31 March of the same year.

The second amendment of 1949 is perhaps the most interesting of all from the standpoint of the present study. The effect of this measure was to transfer to the Dominion Parliament itself the power to amend certain portions of the

[1] Canada, *House of Commons Debates*, 14 Feb. 1949, p. 501.

[2] Ibid., 15 Feb. 1949, p. 550.

[3] Ibid., 14 Feb. 1949, pp. 524 ff.

[4] Ibid., 15 Feb. 1949, p. 562.

[5] Newfoundland was to be represented by six senators and seven members of the House of Commons. See para. 4 of schedule to the British North America Act, 1949.

[6] Canada, *House of Commons Debates*, 8 Feb. 1949, p. 345.

[7] 12 & 13 Geo. VI, chap. 22.

constitution without resort to the Parliament at Westminster. It was closely tied to the announced intention of the reconstituted Liberal Government to abolish all remaining appeals from Canadian courts to the Judicial Committee of the Privy Council. In the Speech from the Throne in September the Government declared its intention to effect both these important changes as soon as possible. A resolution implementing the proposed partial transfer of constituent authority to Canada was introduced in the House by the Prime Minister on 17 October; it was slightly amended after debate and passed the House ten days later.[1] The address was quickly put through the Senate and the necessary bill was then passed by both Houses of the Imperial Parliament without significant change or even comment; it received the royal assent on 16 December.

The principal effect of this British North America (No. 2) Act, 1949,[2] was to empower the Dominion Parliament to amend those portions of the constitution of Canada that concerned the Dominion only. Safeguards were included to protect the provinces in the exercise of their rights and functions,[3] but even so several of the provincial officials were deeply concerned lest the new Dominion power should encroach upon the prerogatives of the provinces, and objections were voiced against this method of handling the problem. The Prime Minister intended this to be merely a first step in transferring to Canada the entire power of constitutional amendment; the second was to be a conference of Dominion and provincial officials, which would be held as soon as possible and would have as its task the effort to devise an amending procedure that would serve for the entire constitution.[4] The Premiers of both Quebec and Alberta protested against this unilateral action of the Dominion Government and urged that the legislation be postponed until after the conference could take place; other premiers, too, expressed varying amounts of dissatisfaction with the course being followed by the Dominion.[5] The Prime Minister, however, refused to

[1] Canada, *House of Commons Debates*, 27 Oct. 1949, p. 1218.

[2] 12, 13 & 14 Geo. VI, chap. 81. See the text below, in Appendix B.

[3] See below, pp. 92 ff., where the effects of the Act are discussed.

[4] See the letter from the Prime Minister to the provincial premiers reproduced in Canada, *House of Commons Debates*, 19 Sept. 1949, Appendix B.

[5] See Gérin-Lajoie, op. cit., pp. xvii ff.

postpone the proposed legislation and replied to the premiers by denying that the Dominion was under any obligation to consult the provinces on such a matter and asserting that with respect to the advisability—as opposed to the obligation—of such consultation the proposed amendment dealt only with matters of Dominion concern and that it 'would not be appropriate to consult the provincial authorities or to ask them to share our responsibilities'.[1] At no time during the entire process were the provinces consulted or asked to consent, although they were kept well informed of what was going on both by the press and by the Dominion officials. Moreover, none of the provinces took any official action in protest although the views of several of the premiers were made clear in the letters mentioned above.

Since the adoption of the altered amending procedure in the British North America (No. 2) Act, 1949, there have been two further amendments to the Canadian constitution, both of which provide significant precedents with respect to provincial consultation. The first of these, in 1951, made a distinct change in the federal distribution of powers by inserting a new paragraph in Section 94 empowering the Dominion to legislate with respect to old age pensions. Since this was clearly a matter of concern to both the Dominion and the provinces, it was outside the scope of the 1949 procedure and therefore required enactment by the Imperial Parliament. The other measure, in 1952, dealt with the reapportionment of seats in the House of Commons, and since this was considered a matter of concern to the Dominion alone the amendment was enacted by the Canadian Parliament, acting under the authority of the 1949 Act. For the first (and thus far the only) time the Canadian constitution was amended by the Canadian Parliament without recourse to the Parliament at Westminster.[2]

The British North America Act, 1951, came about as a result of a lengthy effort to provide a more extensive system of pensions for the aged. After an inquiry by a parliamentary committee and a discussion in a Dominion-Provincial Confer-

[1] Canada, *House of Commons Debates*, 17 Oct. 1949, p. 875. The quotation is from a letter from the Prime Minister to Premier Campbell of Manitoba.

[2] The citations for the two Acts are as follows: British North America Act, 1951, 14 & 15 Geo. VI, chap. 32; British North America Act, 1952, I Eliz. II, chap. 15.

ence, the Dominion Government undertook to provide pensions for persons over 70 while aid for persons from 65 to 70 was to be jointly financed by the Dominion and the provinces. Several of the provinces, however, felt unable to bear the increased burden without further authority to levy an indirect sales tax, and the Dominion Government expressed its willingness to secure two new constitutional amendments, one to confer on the Dominion the necessary power to provide old age pensions and the other to empower the provinces to levy such a tax; both would of course require enactment by the Imperial Parliament.[1] Only the first of these was ever carried forward, however, and the method of handling the two proposals constitutes a clear precedent in support of unanimous provincial consent.

No outright provincial objection was raised against the Dominion's assumption of responsibility for old age pensions, although there was considerable discussion of the details of the plan. What is important here is that the Dominion Government held up all action on the amendment until the agreement of each province was obtained to the exact wording of the address. A lengthy correspondence with the provincial premiers was carried on and several changes in the wording of the proposal were adopted as a result of their criticism.[2] The differences were over details and not the principle, but no action was taken until unanimous consent was reached.

To the indirect sales tax, however, there were numerous objections and the discussion was even more complex and heated. There is no need here to discuss the details of the controversy; the result of it was that, although eight provinces agreed to the proposal, two refused; and these two were Quebec and Ontario. In the face of this opposition the Dominion Government refused to sponsor the necessary amendment. Thus only one address was submitted to the

[1] Earlier, however, an effort had been made to determine whether the provinces might delegate power over old age pensions to the Dominion by a technique similar to that in the Australian constitution. A test case was brought by Nova Scotia to determine the constitutional question, but early in 1951 the Supreme Court held that such a reference or delegation was incompatible with the nature of the constitution. Neither the Dominion nor the province could refer or receive such powers. *A.G. Nova Scotia* v. *A.G. Canada* (1951) C.L.R. 31.

[2] The correspondence appears in full in Canada, *House of Commons Debates*, Appendix to 4 May 1951, pp. 2726–43.

Parliament[1] and only one amendment was enacted by the Parliament at Westminster. In the course of the debates the Prime Minister (Mr. St. Laurent) made it clear that he was unwilling to proceed in such a matter without the unanimous consent of the provinces, and, indeed, he was accused of saying that the Government would be bound by the decision of the unanimous provinces.[2] Clearly the handling of both these proposals constitutes an important precedent for the principle of unanimity. One was held up until unanimity was obtained; the other was abandoned for lack of it.

The amendment of 1952, however, tells a different story. The purpose of this Act was to amend Section 51 in order to reapportion the seats in the House of Commons in a manner different from that provided in the British North America Act, 1946. In the redistribution that was scheduled to follow the 1951 census Ontario, Quebec, and British Columbia stood to gain seats if the existing procedure were followed, while Nova Scotia, Manitoba, and Saskatchewan stood to lose. Strong protests arose as the time of reapportionment drew near, especially from Saskatchewan, whose representation was to be cut from twenty to fifteen seats. In response to this protest the Government proposed to amend the constitution to provide a different formula for the redistribution, assign new seats to Yukon and Mackenzie and, above all, to provide that no redistribution after a decennial census should reduce the representation of a province by more than 15 per cent. This reduced Saskatchewan's loss to three seats but did not help either of the others. It is a little surprising that no stronger objections were raised against this principle, but on the whole the provinces accepted the new formula, perhaps in recognition of the justice of the argument that the principle of strict mathematical representation of population had long since been abandoned to the benefit of several other provinces. The principal controversy was concerned with the kind of agency that should perform the redistribution and with the question of consulting the provinces before thus amending the constitution.

On the latter point the Progressive-Conservative Opposition

[1] Its passage is reported in Canada, *House of Commons Debates* for 7 May 1951, pp. 2749 f., where the address appears in full.

[2] Ibid., 22 May 1951, pp. 3273 ff.

raised vigorous protests against the Liberal Government's proposal to proceed unilaterally. They argued that this was obviously a matter in which the provinces were concerned and that the legislation, if not wholly beyond the powers of the Dominion Parliament under the 1949 Act, could at least be undertaken only after consultation with the provinces.[1] The Government denied both the necessity and the desirability of consulting the provinces and pressed the issue to a successful vote. Mr. St. Laurent declared that

> . . . if we consulted the provinces, that implies that we would not go ahead unless we got the consent of every one of them; and we are not prepared to take that risk.[2]

The Opposition, it should be noted, did not insist on the necessity of consent, but did strongly urge the necessity of consultation. At the 1950 constitutional conference (discussed below) eight of the provinces had insisted that Section 51 was a matter in which both Dominion and provinces were concerned and that it should not be subject to unilateral alteration by the Dominion. The Opposition made a great deal of these arguments but the Government refused to entertain them and denied the further argument, here again raised by the Opposition,[3] that the constitution was a compact that could be altered only by consultation among all parties. The proposal was carried to a vote and the amendment adopted. No province was ever asked to consent to its enactment.

### *Recapitulation of the History of Provincial Consultation*

A recapitulation of the practices employed in amending the constitution shows strong support for the unanimity principle (if not the compact theory) but only in a limited area. Although the constitution had been amended several times earlier, the first instance in which the provinces were consulted at all was in 1907. On that occasion one province registered a protest, but it seems doubtful that the change in the final statute was the result of that protest; in any case the Act was passed

[1] See the speech of Mr. Drew, leader of the Opposition, in Canada, *House of Commons Debates*, 12 June 1952, pp. 3170–2; also that of Mr. D. F. Fleming, ibid., pp. 3155–66.

[2] Ibid., p. 3158.

[3] Ibid., p. 3170.

despite the opposition of that province. Since 1907 there have been ten amendments to the constitution and in only two of these instances were the provinces consulted. These were the Acts of 1940 and 1951; on both occasions the address to the Imperial Parliament was postponed until the last province had consented. On other occasions, not only was there no consultation, but in 1943 the address was passed over the vehement protest of an important province. Thus only 1907, 1940, and 1951 can afford any comfort to the compact theorists, and the first of these can be explained away; the latter two therefore stand as the only real precedents for consultation and unanimous consent. It is of course highly significant that these are the only amendments that directly affect the formal distribution of powers between the provinces and the Dominion.

It is too early yet to see clearly what the effect of the 1949 procedure will be on the process of consultation, but the debates on the 1952 amendment certainly suggest that the Dominion will not feel it necessary to consult the provinces on any action taken under the 1949 provisions. Indeed the argument had long before been used that the Dominion need not consult the provinces on alterations in which only the Dominion was directly interested. On the other hand, the treatment accorded the two amendment proposals of 1951 provides powerful reinforcement for the 1940 precedent for consultation—and indeed unanimity—for any amendments that affect the federal distribution of powers. If a means is found by which the entire constitution may be amended in Canada, it is quite likely that the alteration of this distribution of powers will be subjected to the rule of unanimity or at least to a high extraordinary majority. But even if no such agreement is reached on a general procedure, it now seems established that an address to the Imperial Government and Parliament, having as its purpose the alteration of the federal distribution of powers, will be adopted by the Dominion Parliament only after each province has consented. For other matters the precedents are less convincing, but it seems equally well established that the Dominion will not feel obligated to consult the provinces on anything that it may alter under its 1949 powers. Finally, the older precedents suggest that the

Dominion need not consult the provinces on matters other than alteration of the distribution of powers, even though an address to Westminster is still necessary.

### *Relations Between the Provinces and the Imperial Government*

One other aspect of this complex series of relations remains to be explored, namely the relation between the provinces and the Imperial Government and Parliament. Since all subjects may petition the Crown and since the provinces derive their status from an Imperial Act, it has been argued that this gives the provinces the right to carry their complaints direct to Westminster, by-passing the Dominion Government. Compact theorists have on occasion pointed to certain efforts by the provincial governments to be heard in London,[1] but the difficulty with this evidence is that the efforts were seldom successful. In the early days of Confederation several provinces attempted by this means to secure alteration in the terms of union, including specific alterations in the British North America Act, but they were in no case successful. In 1868 a Nova Scotia delegation went to London seeking legislation that would permit that province to secede, but it was referred back to Ottawa by the Secretary of State. In 1874 British Columbia complained to London of the injustice of the terms of her entry into the union, but received the same reply. A similar circumstance in 1877 involved Prince Edward Island, and again in 1886 that province carried to London a protest that the Dominion had not performed its obligation of establishing steamboat communication between the island and the mainland. But the protest was ignored, the Secretary of State directly refusing to advise the Queen at all.[2]

A more important appeal came in 1887 at the first interprovincial conference, which was called by the Premier of Quebec and attended by representatives of five of the seven provinces. At the conference a number of possible amendments to the constitution were explored and the Dominion was thoroughly denounced for its negligence in meeting its

[1] The subject is explored by J. A. Maxwell, 'Petitions to London by Provincial Governments', *Canadian Bar Review*, vol. 14 (1936) pp. 738–49.

[2] Clokie, op. cit., p. 26.

obligations to the provinces.[1] The conference adopted twenty-four resolutions, all of them unanimous, of which eighteen proposed amendments to the British North America Act;[2] of the eighteen, twelve sought the increase of provincial powers at the expense of the Dominion. The eighteenth resolution had urged that the provinces should, through their legislatures,

> . . . take steps with a view to securing the enactment by the Imperial Parliament of amendments to the British North America Act in accordance with the foregoing resolutions.[3]

The proposals were therefore returned to the legislatures, all of which endorsed them,[4] and were then sent to the Governor-General for transmission to the Imperial Government. Thus the provinces were in effect claiming the right to initiate amendments to the constitution without even consulting the Dominion authorities. Had this been successful, and had a precedent thus been established, the constitution of Canada would quite possibly be very different from what it is today; certainly its amendment procedure would be even more confusing. The Dominion, however, hastened to make protest against the proposals in London. The Secretary of State acknowledged receipt of the resolutions but did nothing with them, perhaps accepting the Dominion's argument that they represented merely an effort by five provincial governments controlled by one political party to embarrass a Dominion Government controlled by the opposite party.[5] In any case the Imperial Government refused to act.

Other interprovincial conferences have been held on several occasions and the subject of constitutional amendment has

[1] The Dominion had also been invited to the Conference but Macdonald, then Prime Minister, declined, saying bluntly: 'In response to your letter, permit me to say . . . that it will be of no service to send representatives to this conference.' Quoted by Ollivier, op. cit., p. 369.

[2] The resolutions are given in full in the *Proceedings and Evidence and Report* of the 1935 Special Committee on the B. N. A. Act, pp. 98–104.

[3] Ibid., p. 104.

[4] The Upper Houses, however, in both Nova Scotia and New Brunswick refused to approve the resolutions. Indeed, the latter petitioned Her Majesty to ignore them. Gérin-Lajoie, op. cit., p. 143.

[5] See Professor Kennedy's testimony before the Special Committee of 1935, *Proceedings and Evidence and Report*, pp. 97–98. This interpretation is supported by the fact that the Governments of Prince Edward Island and British Columbia, which had refused to participate, were of the same party as that of the Dominion.

been several times discussed.[1] But never since 1887 have the provinces undertaken on their own initiative to send a request to London asking for amendments. In 1902, on the contrary, it was resolved 'that the Premiers of the various Provinces . . . (should form) a Committee to submit the foregoing Resolutions to the Government of the Dominion'.[2] It seems quite clear that the Imperial Government would not entertain such suggestions from the provinces, even from all the provinces, without the concurrence of the Dominion authorities. It is worth noting that while the effort of the provinces in 1887 was directed to expanding their own powers in twelve different areas at the expense of the Dominion, the latter has been guilty of such acquisitiveness on only two occasions, in 1940 and 1951, and then only with the unanimous consent of the provinces.[3]

### *The Relation Between the British Parliament and the Dominion*

But though the relation between the provinces and the Imperial Government is fairly well settled and affords no great problem, that between the Dominion and the British Parliament is more complex and complicated. The fact still remains that, apart from those portions that may since 1949 be altered by the Dominion Parliament, no one can amend the Canadian constitution except the Imperial Parliament. The relation between the two Parliaments is difficult to define, for there are two aspects or levels of this relation. At one level the British Parliament is bound by rigid conventions and by several of its own statutes; it is precluded from interfering in the affairs of Canada and can enact legislation for Canada only at the latter's request. At another level, however, the British Parliament is sovereign and unfettered; the limitations on it are conventional or are contained in its own statutes. No Parliament may bind its successors, and the present one could

[1] Canada, *Dominion-Provincial and Interprovincial Conferences from 1887 to 1926*, Ottawa, 1951.

[2] Ibid., p. 44.

[3] Actually only 1940 is in point. The Act of 1951 makes Dominion legislation on old age pensions subordinate to 'present or future' provincial laws on the subject. See F. R. Scott, 'Centralization and Decentralization in Canadian Federalism', *Canadian Bar Review*, vol. 29 (1951), pp. 1117–18.

modify, amend, or repeal any of these limiting statutes if it so chose. In the British system the legal and the constitutional are not always the same thing. Such an action would be quite within its legal powers.

It is not here suggested that the Imperial Parliament is likely to intervene in Canadian affairs on its own initiative or even that such action would be politically possible; indeed it would be unconstitutional in the extreme. But it is legally possible, for the sovereignty of that Parliament remains unimpaired. Even if Canada can settle its differences and decide upon an amending procedure, and a section embodying it is added to the constitution, an ultimate legal power will still reside in Westminster. This legal sovereignty is more important for Canada under present conditions than for any of the other Dominions; for Canada, lacking an amending clause in her constitution, must resort to the Imperial Parliament to secure alterations in her fundamental law. Thus, on occasion, the operation of this legal sovereignty is displayed quite vividly.

Now the important thing in any political process, in the amendment of the Canadian constitution as in other things, is not who has the legal power but how and by whom the decision is made. If the legal power wielder makes the decision, well and good; the problem is simplified. But if the decision is made elsewhere and the legal power is thus divorced from the political power, then the problem is more difficult. It is clear that the legal power of amending the Canadian constitution rests in the British Parliament, but there are few who would suggest that the political power, i.e., the real power to make the decision, rests there. But on the other hand, can we truthfully say that the two are wholly separated? Is there not some part of the decision on an amendment proposal that is made not by Canadians but by the British Parliament?

Long before 1931 it had been clearly established that the British Parliament would not legislate for Canada except at the request and with the consent of the latter. At no time after 1867 did any British legislation apply directly to Canada except at Canadian request. General legislation for the empire as a whole did at times affect Canada, and it was some time before the convention developed by which the imperial officials consulted with Canadian authorities on matters of a general imperial nature. But by the end of the nineteenth century even this was settled custom; after this time general legislation frequently exempted the self-governing colonies from its operation until the colonial legislature adopted it.[1] Thus by 1931 the Statute of Westminster could announce in its preamble:

> Whereas it is in accord with the established constitutional position that no law hereafter made by the Parliament of the United Kingdom shall extend to any of the said Dominions as part of the law of that Dominion otherwise than at the request and with the consent of that Dominion. . . .

The position is clear: no British Act affects Canada unless Canada so desires. But the problem has an obverse side. Is it equally true to say that British legislation will be immediately forthcoming upon the presentation of a request by the Dominion? This question is not so well settled.

### *Possible Discretion of the British Authorities*

Whether this request comes from the executive government in the form of a petition or from the Dominion Parliament in the form of a joint address seems to be a matter of indifference to the British Parliament. In the early controversy in Canada over the ability of the executive to request amendments to the British North America Act, the British authorities at no time indicated a preference for one procedure over the other. The amendments of 1871, 1875, and 1895 were all requested by the executive government and were granted without hesitation by the British Government and Parliament; the rest have been requested through a joint address of the Dominion Parliament. An even better example of this indifference is the matter of granting titles of honour to the King's subjects in Canada. In 1918 a parliamentary address requested that the practice of granting such titles be discontinued,[2] and this was done, although no legislation was necessary. In 1930 the Bennett

[1] Examples are the Reserve Forces Act, 1896; the Official Secrets Act, 1911; and the Copyright Act, 1911. An exception, however, is the Geneva Convention Act, 1911.

[2] Canada, *House of Commons Journals*, vol. liv (1918), pp. 312–13.

Government, without recourse to the Canadian Parliament, requested that such titles again be granted.[1] Again the British authorities complied, even though the request by the executive government countermanded an action by the legislature.

There seems to be no evidence that the Imperial Government will not act upon receipt of a request from the Government of the Dominion, whether that request proceeds from the executive or from the legislative branch. There is no reason for surprise at this indifference; Britain would not wish to place herself in the position of refusing a request from either source; the exercise of British judgement on such a matter would hardly comport with the principles of responsible colonial government, and even less with those of Dominionhood.

But a further question is whether a request, from whatever source, will always be followed by appropriate action of the British authorities. The overwhelming majority of precedents suggest that those authorities will always comply. But there are at least three instances in which some doubt has been thrown on the principle.

Section 146 of the British North America Act had provided that certain territories could subsequently be admitted to the union upon address to the Crown by the Parliament of Canada and by the appropriate colonial legislatures. In 1869 the Dominion passed an address[2] praying for the union of Newfoundland with Canada. But since the Newfoundland legislature passed no such address the conditions were not met and the British authorities necessarily took no action on the Canadian request.

In 1882 a Canadian address, though not disregarded, evoked no formal response for some eight years.[3] The address requested the establishment of a maritime court in Canada and the abolition of a vice-admiralty court in Nova Scotia that was appointed by the British, though paid by Canada. The form of the request was vague and delay in implementing it was inevitable. But the question involved general imperial policy

[1] See Clokie, 'Basic Problems of the Canadian Constitution', *Canadian Journal of Economics and Political Science*, vol. 8 (1942), pp. 20 f., from which these examples have been taken.

[2] Canada, *House of Commons Journals*, vol. ii (1869), p. 220.

[3] Ibid., vol. xvi (1882), p. 330. See Clokie, op. cit., pp. 21 f.

as well as policy toward Canada, and the British found it necessary to consult other opinions. Canadian wishes were finally complied with, however, by the enactment of the Colonial Courts of Admiralty Act, 1890.[1]

An even longer delay followed an address of 1920[2] in which a grant of extraterritorial jurisdiction was requested. This problem too involved general imperial policy, and by this time the Imperial Conference had grown up as a technique for handling such matters. This particular problem was part of the larger question of the status of the self-governing colonies, which was made the subject of the series of conferences that eventually produced the Statute of Westminster in 1931. The Statute included a special section (3) that granted to the Dominions the right to enact legislation having extraterritorial effect. Thus after eleven years the address of 1920 was implemented by imperial legislation.

Of these three instances, none offers valid evidence that the British Government is reluctant to respond to Canadian requests. Nothing could be done in 1869 without the concurrence of Newfoundland; the delays that followed the requests of 1882 and 1920 are easily explained and occasioned no dissatisfaction in Canada. None of the three casts serious doubt on the principle that the British Parliament will enact any legislation for Canada that is requested by the Dominion authorities.[3]

Some doubt still remains, however, about the role of the provinces in this matter. We have seen that the provinces are powerless to secure amendments from Westminster without the support of the Dominion, but can they hope to affect legislation requested by the Dominion, through direct appeal to London? Will the British Parliament comply exactly with a Dominion request in the face of serious opposition on the part of one or more of the provincial governments?

[1] 53 & 54 Vict., chap. 27.

[2] Canada, *House of Commons Journals*, vol. lvii (1920), p. 443.

[3] It should perhaps be noted that the amendments proposed and initially drafted in Canada are subject to British parliamentary scrutiny. In several instances (e.g. in 1940) minor changes in punctuation and other detail have been made without referring the question back to Canada; in 1943 and 1946 such changes were made after referring them to Ottawa. The Dominion Parliament has *not* been consulted in these instances. See Gérin-Lajoie, op. cit., p. 189.

The Act of 1907 poses this question but does not give a wholly satisfactory answer.[1] It is true that the Act in its final form differed slightly from the form in which it was requested, since the clause 'final and unalterable' in reference to the Dominion's subsidy payments to the provinces was omitted. But we have shown that the most likely reason for this omission was not that British Columbia objected to it but that the phrase was inappropriate to a legislative enactment and inconsistent with the principle that no parliament may bind its successors. Moreover, the efforts of British Columbia to persuade London to increase its subsidy payments were flatly refused. It must be conceded, however, that there were certain indications at the time from British officials that they were willing to look behind a request from the Dominion to ascertain the views of the provinces on the matter at hand. The letter from the Secretary of State for Colonies admits that there is 'force' to the argument that the constitution cannot be amended by the Dominion acting alone, although it does not concede the validity of this argument.[2] Moreover, the unfortunate words used by Mr. Churchill in the House of Commons give the impression that the Imperial Government will at least examine the opinions of both the provinces and the Dominion before making any decision about a controverted question.[3] But Mr. Churchill, as has been shown, manifests in the same statement a surprising misunderstanding of the nature of the mother country's relation to Canada at that time; his testimony would seem thus to be impeached. Whether good constitutional practice at that time permitted such discretion or not, it seems clear that that principle has not been followed and great doubt is cast upon its validity today, in view of the development of Dominion status since that time. The essence of that status is that decisions affecting the Dominion will be made in and by the Dominion, a principle that scarcely permits the British authorities to exercise their own judgement on such questions as these. Actually the problem is not that of the nature of the British response to Canadian requests for amendment but the political process in

[1] See above, pp. 55–59.

[2] See above, p. 57, n. 1.

[3] *British House of Commons Debates*, ser. 4, vol. 175 (1907), p. 1617.

Canada by which such a request is made. It is essentially a domestic problem for Canada, where no decision has even yet been reached about the nature of the province's role in the amending process. One can sympathize with the British officials who have been subjected to considerable embarrassment by Canada's inability to settle its own problems before taking them to Westminster.

The 1943 amendment also suggests that the British authorities feel bound to respond to addresses or requests for legislative action even in the face of provincial opposition. It will be recalled that this amendment was pushed through by the Dominion Government against the strong objections of the province of Quebec, objections expressed both in the Dominion Parliament and in the provincial legislature. The latter body formulated an official protest which the Prime Minister was asked to forward to London along with the address of the Dominion Parliament. Mr. Mackenzie King refused to comply, partly on the ground that the British Government could take no cognizance of it:

> Any such intervention by the Government or Parliament of Great Britain in the internal affairs of our country would be the negation of Canada's equality of status with the United Kingdom. . . . It is true that it is still legally necessary to ask the Parliament of Great Britain to amend the British North America Act. That situation, however, is acceptable only so long as such amendments are made automatically and without question on the request of the appropriate representatives of the Canadian people.[1]

The Prime Minister did not here make clear just what was meant by 'the appropriate representatives of the Canadian people', but that he meant the Parliament of the Dominion is clear from his insistence on pushing through the address. The point is that after the address was made and presented to the British authorities, the legislation followed immediately, and he was insisting that it had to follow. Quebec's protest was not forwarded to London and thus the British Parliament was not made officially aware of it, but that it was in truth unaware of it seems most unlikely.[2] The incident reinforces the principle that British responses are automatic.

[1] *Montreal Gazette*, 16 July 1943; quoted in Dawson, op. cit., p. 146.

[2] See Gérin-Lajoie, op. cit., pp. 115 f.

An interesting interchange, which is exactly in point, occurred in 1935 between W. P. M. Kennedy and the members of the Special Committee of the House of Commons on the British North America Act:

WITNESS (i.e. Professor Kennedy): I do not think there is the slightest necessity in law for the parliament of Canada to consult the provinces in the process. It may be very good politics, but politics is not the law.

MR. COWAN: Parliament could not do anything with the powers which come under section 92.

WITNESS: I think the Parliament of Canada can present any address to the Parliament of the United Kingdom.

MR. LAPOINTE: You would not advise this parliament to do so.

WITNESS: I do not think it would be a very wise thing.

THE CHAIRMAN: It would be a matter for the Imperial Parliament to say whether they would accept it or not.

WITNESS: I think they would accept it. I do not believe the parliament of the United Kingdom would refuse to pass an act implementing any address from any Dominion parliament. . . .

THE CHAIRMAN: The provinces hold their sovereign rights direct from the Imperial Parliament; why shouldn't they be able to go there?

MR. COWAN: The provinces would find some way of having representation. Your argument is, Professor Kennedy, that they would not be listened to.

WITNESS: I think they would be very courteously listened to.

MR. COWAN: But without effect being given to their representations.

WITNESS: I do not think they would be given effect to. I have known the law officers of the crown for many years, especially since the Statute of Westminster. I do not think any law officer of the crown would recommend his government to refuse legislation, it would put the Parliament of the United Kingdom in a very awkward position if it refused an Act implementing an Address from a Dominion parliament.[1]

Since the British Parliament has the legal power, it is pertinent to ask what the attitude of the British authorities has been. But it is difficult to find official statements of British opinion on constitutional law *before* the fact. The British habit is to solve such questions as these empirically, by the accretion of precedents, not by formal pronouncements of intention. But there exists at least one relevant statement by a British official on this point. When the Act of 1940 was presented to the British House of Commons the question was raised

[1] *Proceedings and Evidence and Report*, pp. 70 f.

whether the provinces had consented to the derogation from their powers that the Act effected. In reply to this the Solicitor-General, Sir William Jowett, made the following explanation:

> The true position is that we . . . (pass) these Acts only in the form that the Canadian Parliament require and at the request of the Canadian Parliament. . . . The sole justification for this enactment is that we are doing in this way what the Parliament of Canada desires to do. . . . *I do not know what the view of the Provincial Parliaments is.* I do know, however, that when the matter was before the Privy Council some of the Provincial Parliaments supported the Dominion Parliament. *It is a sufficient justification for the Bill that we are morally bound to act on the ground that we have here the request of the Dominion Parliament* and that we must operate the old machinery that has been left over at their request in accordance with their wishes.[1]

If this represents the true view of the British Government, as seems likely, then it appears that the provinces cannot hope to be separately heard on questions of amendment, but that the appropriate legislation will follow an address of the Dominion Parliament, regardless of provincial opposition.

The truth is, however, that the precedents are not yet conclusive for all cases. There has as yet been no instance where several provinces, or even both Quebec and Ontario, opposed such a measure. Nor has any proposal to alter Sections 91 or 92 been opposed by any province. We cannot be sure just what would happen in such a case. If, for example, the Dominion were to present an address to the British Government seeking to transfer from Section 92 to Section 91 the clause 'property and civil rights', and several provinces including the two largest ones[2] were to oppose the proposal, it is by no means certain what the attitude of the British Parliament would be. We can only hope that it will not be placed in a position where it has to decide such a question. Indeed, if the Canadian people ever do agree on an amendment procedure, the most relieved body of all will be the British Parliament. Under the present system it must undertake what is after all a thankless task in regard to matters about which it knows but little, and

[1] *British House of Commons Debates*, 5th ser., vol. 362, pp. 1179–80. Italics added.

[2] Of course, such a thing would be politically impossible; but this is only an example. Substitute a situation in which four or five or six smaller provinces oppose an important proposal—the problem is equally difficult.

which constantly expose it to criticism from dissatisfied Canadians on actions for which it has no responsibility. Britain can hope with Canada that the problem can somehow be solved.

### *Attempts to Devise an Amending Procedure*

The need for a standardized procedure for securing the amendment of the constitution has long been felt by many Canadians. But little effort was devoted to the problem until after the First World War. During the 1920's and 1930's it was discussed in many quarters and a number of proposals were put forward in an effort to solve the problem. The increasing interest in the matter seems to have been the result of several factors. The course of decisions in the Supreme Court of Canada and the Judicial Committee of the Privy Council tended more and more to increase the powers of the provinces at the expense of the Dominion, with an effect on the latter that bordered on disaster. This trend stimulated the feeling that the situation could only be remedied through recourse to the formal amendment of the constitution. Secondly, the decade of the twenties brought an active effort to define the position of the self-governing colonies, an effort that produced a definition of dominion status at the Imperial Conference of 1926 and led to the enactment in 1931 of the Statute of Westminster. The discussions during this period naturally led to an examination of Canada's inability to amend her own constitution and to the feeling that this left her somewhat short of complete independence. In the third place, the re-emergence of the compact theory and the embracing of it by Ontario led to a more widespread discussion of possible solutions to the problem. Finally, in the thirties the unsuccessful efforts of the Bennett Government to provide a Canadian New Deal made Canadians further aware of the nature of constituent power and of their own shortcomings in this regard.

From 1926 on a series of Dominion-Provincial Conferences has been held, at many of which the subject of an amending procedure has been discussed. But no agreement has ever been reached on what the procedure should be. There is almost universal agreement that Canada ought to have the power to amend its own constitution without the help of Westminster,[1] but there is wide disagreement on how this should be done.

Active official efforts to secure such a procedure began with the Dominion-Provincial Conference of 1927, at which the Dominion urged that the Dominion Parliament be assigned the power to amend the constitution, that the provinces be consulted in all cases, but that unanimous consent be required in only a few specified instances. The provinces refused to entertain the suggestion at all and the conference reached no conclusion other than failure.[2] A year later, when the impending Statute of Westminster was under discussion, the provinces were again called together to seek agreement on the question; but again no agreement was reached, and as a result Section 7 was included in the Act, excluding the amending process from its operation.

### *The Efforts of 1935*

Although public and even official discussion continued,[3] the next serious effort to solve the problem was made in 1935, when the House of Commons appointed a Special Committee on the British North America Act to investigate the matter and propose a method of amendment. This Committee interviewed seven expert witnesses and heard a great deal of argument, but it achieved only an airing of views. The provinces were requested to send representatives to discuss the question before the Committee but they unanimously refused, on the ground that it was beneath the dignity of a province to be called to

[1] Some, however, have preferred to leave the matter where it now stands, i.e., in the hands of the Imperial Parliament. See, for example, the remarks of Mr. Mackenzie King in *House of Commons Debates*, 24 Feb. 1920, p. 46. At the Conference of 1927 several provinces took this attitude; but most have since abandoned it. See the remarks of Mr. Taschereau, Premier of Quebec before the Conference of 1935. Canada, Dominion-Provincial Conference, 1935, *Record of Proceedings*, p. 51.

[2] See a brief summary of this and other conferences in Sirois Commission, *Report*, bk. ii, pp. 68–69; for the 1927 Conference see also *Report*, bk. i, p. 136. The most detailed history of the several conferences is Wilfrid Eggleston, *The Road to Nationhood*, Toronto, 1946.

[3] A more detailed survey of past efforts to secure agreement on an amending procedure may be found in Gérin-Lajoie, op. cit., chap. 8.

give its opinion to a committee of the Dominion House of Commons.[1] In their replies, however, most of the provinces expressed their willingness to discuss the matter at a new Dominion-Provincial Conference, and this the Committee decided to recommend. Although the seven witnesses submitted a variety of suggestions, the Committee came to no conclusion and refused to recommend any particular solution to the House.[2] At least one of the members conceded later on that the provinces were perfectly justified in their refusal to submit opinions.[3] But whether right or wrong, the Committee felt that in view of this provincial refusal there could be no point in making recommendations concerning an amendment procedure and that, indeed, such recommendations might prejudice the work of any later conference with the provinces.[4]

In consequence of the Committee's suggestion, a Dominion-Provincial Conference was called in December 1935, at which all the provinces were represented. A subconference was appointed to deal with the question of constitutional amendment and something of an advance was made. The report of the subconference offered a resolution, representing the opinions of the Dominion and eight of the provinces,[5] to the effect that Canada should have the power to amend its own constitution provided a method could be worked out satisfactory to all parties. This does not sound like much advance, but throughout the rest of the Conference the delegates exchanged congratulations on the progress that had been made. The point is that theretofore several of the provinces, notably Quebec, had been unwilling to abandon the arrangement whereby the British Parliament enacted the amend-

[1] The reply of Premier Taschereau of Quebec was highly indignant: 'Surely the Committee cannot expect that the views of the Province of Quebec will be discussed by an exchange of telegrams or letters. In a matter of such importance I suggest that a conference of the Dominion and the Provinces should be held.' All the provincial replies are given in the Committee's *Proceedings and Evidence and Report*, pp. 139–41.

[2] The Senate a little later authorized a separate investigation of the matter but this too produced no solution. See the *Report on the British North America Act by Parliamentary Counsel of the Senate*, Ottawa, 1939.

[3] Mr. Lapointe in *House of Commons Debates*, 1 Feb. 1937, p. 434.

[4] *Proceedings and Evidence and Report*, p. xiii.

[5] The dissenter was New Brunswick, whose representative, Mr. McNair, 'was unable to agree to the resolution in its entirety'. *Record of Proceedings*, pp. 37 f. The discussions of the subconference were never published.

ments. Here all save one were in agreement that it ought to be a domestic process. The Conference went on to recommend that the Minister of Justice convene a committee of experts from the Dominion and the provinces to work out a scheme, which would later on be laid before another conference.[1] Such a committee was appointed and began its work, but the project was never finished. The chairman, Mr. Lapointe, reported to the House in 1937 that the committee had been at work for some time and that although 'agreement was reached on many important matters . . . there are still some matters upon which agreement has not been reached'.[2] In this same year there was an attempt in the House of Commons to appoint another select committee to study the British North America Act and to make recommendations for specific amendments to the Act. But the House refused to repeat the failure of 1935. The Government pointed out that what was needed was not recommendations for amendments but a procedure for accomplishing them, and that the provinces had already shown themselves to be unwilling to discuss that with a House committee.[3] Meanwhile the committee of experts under the Minister of Justice had got lost in the shuffle that attended the appointment later in the year of the Royal Commission on Dominion-Provincial Relations.[4]

## *The Sirois Commission*

The Royal Commission was intended to investigate and make recommendations about the whole field of intergovernmental relations and its work was of the greatest importance, but its terms of reference did not extend to recommendations for an amendment procedure. It therefore made no such

[1] Ibid., p. 50.

[2] Canada, *House of Commons Debates*, 1 Feb. 1937, p. 433.

[3] Ibid., pp. 425–63.

[4] No report of the committee of experts was ever published. A discussion of its work was included in a report submitted in March 1936 by the Attorney-General to the Legislative Assembly of Saskatchewan. This seems to be the only available source on the work of the committee, which is unfortunate, for its work was of interest. The provincial Attorney-General's report was published as a pamphlet entitled *The Canadian Constitution and Its Amendment* (Regina, 1936). My reference to it is taken from Gérin-Lajoie, op. cit., pp. 246 ff., where there is a discussion of its content.

recommendations, though it did venture the opinion that such a procedure was needed.[1]

It was suggested to the Commission, however, that increased flexibility could be given to the constitutional structure if a provision were adopted similar to that in the Australian constitution (Sections 51 and 105A) by which functions could be transferred by reference from one government to the other. The suggestion has the advantage that it would enable a needed reform to be accomplished over the objection of a single province merely by leaving that province out of it; desirable changes could be effected in respect to one province without waiting for the accumulation of public opinion necessary to carry through a nation-wide constitutional amendment. Nova Scotia, Saskatchewan, and British Columbia[2] all urged that the Commission recommend the adoption of this delegation procedure and the Commission did so.[3] In particular the Commission suggested that the delegation technique could be applied very readily to the management of old age pensions, marketing, and fisheries.[4] The Report argued that by this method an arrangement could be made whereby the Dominion could shoulder some of the burdens of the smaller provinces which the larger ones would be unwilling to give up. Thus uniformity would not have to be preserved if the best interests of all could be served by sacrificing it. But the incorporation of such a provision into the Canadian constitution would require a constitutional amendment and this has not been tried.[5]

Though the Sirois Commission's report caused a great stir in Canada, the Government was unable to secure a general

[1] Royal Commission on Dominion-Provincial Relations (herein cited as Sirois Commission), 1940, *Report*, bk. ii, p. 72.

[2] Sirois Commission, *Evidence*; for Nova Scotia, p. 3878; for Saskatchewan, p. 2299; for British Columbia, p. 5557.

[3] *Report*, bk. ii, pp. 72–73.

[4] Ibid.; for pensions, p. 32; for marketing, p. 56; for fisheries, p. 59.

[5] Ibid., p. 73. Some time later the effort was made to use this device with respect to old age pensions, but the effort was thwarted by the Supreme Court in *A.G. Nova Scotia* v. *A.G. Canada* (1951), C.L.R. 31. It would thus require an amendment to authorize such a technique of avoiding the necessity of amendments. So far as old age pensions were concerned, the problem was solved by the British North America Act, 1951. It may be added that the procedure provided for in the Australian constitution has never been successfully employed. See below, pp. 164 f.

agreement on its proposals, particularly on those concerning finance. A new Dominion-Provincial Conference in 1941 broke up after two days because of the refusal of Ontario, Alberta, and British Columbia to use the Sirois Report as a basis for discussion.[1] It had been hoped that this Conference would endorse a series of amendments arising out of the Sirois recommendations, but the collapse of the Conference prevented any such agreement. There was no opportunity to raise the question of any amending procedure; any further discussion was then postponed by the war.

### *The Extreme Views and a Possible Compromise Between Them*

There have been many different procedures suggested for amending the constitution. Ordinarily they have fallen somewhere between what may be called the two extreme positions; one of these is the argument that the Dominion Parliament should be enabled to amend the constitution on its own initiative and without consulting either the provinces or the British authorities. Given the assumption that the British Parliament will enact any amendment requested by the Dominion Parliament, this seems to be essentially the legal position as it stands today. On the other extreme are those who urge that the consent of every province should be necessary before any amendment can be put into effect. These two positions were brought into sharp focus in 1925 when the Privy Council declared the Industrial Disputes Investigation Act to be *ultra vires* the Dominion.[2] Mr. W. F. Maclean proposed an address to the Crown praying that thereafter the British North America Act might be amended by a majority vote of the two Houses of Parliament. The House was unwilling to pass such an address and, during the course of the debate, Mr. Woodsworth proposed an amendment to the effect that any amendment to the constitution had first to be approved by all of the provinces. The House was no more pleased with the amendment than it had been with the motion itself, and at the end of the debate both were withdrawn.[3] The

[1] Canada, *Dominion-Provincial Conference, 1941*, Ottawa, 1941, *passim.*
[2] *Toronto Electric Commissioners* v. *Snider* (1925), A.C. 396.
[3] Canada, *House of Commons Debates*, 18 Feb. 1925, pp. 283–341.

incident not only points up the two opposing views but indicates that neither has enough support behind it to have a very great chance of being adopted. The general attitude towards these two proposals today seems to be very much the same as it was in 1925. It is not likely that either will ever be incorporated into the constitution.

The essence of the problem is that there is here an attempt to accomplish two seemingly contradictory ends. It is desirable that the constitution be kept rigid so that the guarantees it affords to minorities may not be impaired against the will of the minorities: hence a desire for unanimous consent. But it is also desirable that the constitution be kept flexible so that it may be adapted when necessary to the needs of changing circumstances: hence a desire for a procedure requiring less than unanimous consent.[1] To state the problem in these terms is very nearly to suggest a solution of it, for the parts of the constitution that afford protection to the minority groups are for the most part not those that would need to be changed to fit altered needs. A proper solution would seem therefore to require the unanimous consent of the provinces for the first parts and to require something less than unanimity for the rest. This idea of dividing the constitution into segments and adopting different kinds of procedures for the various segments according to their different natures has suggested itself to many people. The solution of the problem, in the words of Professor Rogers, involves the need

> to seek for an amendment procedure which will avoid, on the one hand, the extreme of unilateral action by the Dominion Parliament and on the other hand the doctrine of unanimous consent of the provincial legislatures. A reasonable view of the problem in its historical setting leads inevitably to the conclusion that an amendment procedure for the British North America Act should represent a compromise between these extreme positions.[2]

The first significant advocacy of such a compromise seems to have come from Mr. Ernest Lapointe at the Dominion-Provincial Conference of 1927. He introduced a proposal for dividing amendments into two classes, those requiring the

[1] Dawson, op. cit., pp. 147 f.

[2] N. McL. Rogers before the Special Committee in 1935; *Proceedings and Evidence and Report*, p. 108.

consent of a majority of the provinces, and those requiring unanimous consent. In the latter class were to be placed Sections 93 and 133 (education and languages) as well as certain subsections of Section 92.[1] Most of the compromise suggestions since then have followed this general pattern.

It is not necessary here to examine every such proposal. They do not agree in details, although in general the principle is the same as that urged by Mr. Lapointe. Several of the witnesses before the Special Committee of 1935 made detailed proposals of this nature. Professor Scott, Professor Kennedy, and Dr. Ollivier all offered such proposals[2] in which, although they agreed as to the desirability of compartmentalizing the constitution, they disagreed on the particular clauses to be assigned to the several compartments. This has been a recurring difficulty and one that is not yet overcome.

The suggestion is frequently made that the best thing to do would be to rewrite the whole constitution, using the present one as a basis. Dr. Maurice Ollivier, in his testimony before this same committee, argued that the constitution should be divided into compartments, that each compartment should include certain classes of subjects, and that each should have its own amending procedure. This was quite in line with the others' recommendations; but he added an interesting and important statement about how this new constitution should be brought into force. In his opinion it should be enacted as a Canadian statute, and after this is done the Imperial Parliament should then repeal all the British North America Acts. This was necessary because

> . . . even if we succeed in obtaining from the Imperial Parliament the insertion of a clause in the British North America Act allowing us the power to amend the constitution, the Act will still remain an Imperial Act, and as the British Parliament is sovereign they would still retain the right to amend it theoretically. It is true that a clause could be inserted similar to the one in the Statute of Westminster stating that no amendment shall be made by the United Kingdom to the British North America Act unless requested by the Dominion of Canada, or even that, having given the power to amend the Act, they would not interfere with

[1] Précis of discussions, Dominion-Provincial Conference, 3–10 Nov. 1927 (Canada, *Sessional Papers*, 1928, no. 69, pp. 11–12). See Clokie, op. cit., p. 30.

[2] *Proceedings and Evidence and Report*, respectively at pp. 85, 73, and 61.

it in any way, but this clause would not be legally binding on the Parliament of Great Britain as a statute cannot bind future parliaments and can always be repealed in a subsequent session.[1]

This is a clever and intricate device, but the objection may be raised that such a constitution adopted as a Canadian statute would violate the present constitution at dozens of points and, since the present constitution would at that time still be in force, the Canadian Act would be invalid. Moreover, on this strictly legal argument, the repeal by the Imperial Parliament of the British North America Acts would not affect the supremacy of that Parliament over the Dominion; the Imperial Parliament could re-enact any legislation for Canada that it desired and neither the Statute of Westminster nor any proposed Canadian constitution would bar its effect. It is doubtful that such a complicated plan is either necessary, desirable, or legal.

### *Opposition to the Compromise Plan*

This compromise plan, though it is the most popular reform proposal, still meets considerable opposition. The leading defenders of the doctrine of unanimity have only recently been willing to make even this concession. Quebec has always been desperately afraid that constitutional changes might pose a threat to its cherished privileges, and until 1950 was consistently unwilling to agree to such a proposal; in this opposition it was frequently joined by Ontario and, on occasion, by others. In 1932 Quebec's premier stated:

> . . . As leader of the government I am not prepared to permit the British North America Act to be changed by the will of a majority of the provinces. We have built certain things here in this old province; we have created institutions that are dear to us, and we don't want them done away with to suit the caprice of even a majority of the provinces.[2]

Similarly, in 1938, in its submission to the Royal Commission the Government of Quebec voiced its opposition to a scheme for compartmentalizing the constitution in the manner described above. The difficulty lay in the classification:

[1] *Proceedings and Evidence and Report*, p. 61.

[2] Quoted by Senator Turgeon in *Senate Debates*, 28 Mar. 1935, p. 230.

. . . Who will decide whether a given matter is or is not of interest to the Provinces and where will we stop, once the principle is conceded? In a constitution there are no secondary clauses.[1]

Other objections, too, have been raised against the plan. One of these turns on the difficulty of classifying amendments that might in the future be made. It would be possible to divide the present constitutional documents into sections and assign to each section a different amending procedure. But an amendment might easily be proposed that would have a serious effect on two or more parts of the constitution to which different procedures are assigned. If a wholly new clause were to be added, it might be very difficult indeed to decide which of the constitutional provisions were most affected. Argument and disagreement would inevitably follow. More serious still, constitutional provisions and amendments have far-reaching effects, involving indirectly things that they may not seem to affect directly. It is quite possible for a clause to lose its importance and strength indirectly by changes that seem to be directed to other clauses entirely. One need only cite the tremendous effect upon the division of powers in a federal state of the changing fiscal relations of the states to one another and to the central government. Even though Section 92 might be protected by the most rigid amending procedures, it is not impossible that some of its provisions could be vitiated by the gradual and indirect tranfer of fiscal power to the Dominion, a transfer that might be effected indirectly through the employment of easier procedures to change other clauses or indeed through some wholly extraconstitutional process; Section 92 might remain untouched in form while losing important parts of its substance. And, of course, the same is true of other clauses. The plan to compartmentalize the constitution is deserving of serious study, but there are very great difficulties involved which may not be ignored.

But these objections, although they are very real and quite valid, do not seem impossible to overcome. It seems clear that if Canada is ever to settle upon a solution to this problem without making the constitution so rigid as to be impossible of amendment, the solution will most likely come in some

[1] Quebec, *Statement of the Government of the Province of Quebec*, English text (submission to the Royal Commission), 1938, pp. 3–4.

such form as this. And it was in this form that the very significant proposals of 1949 and 1950 were cast.

### *The British North America (No. 2) Act, 1949*

The most significant amendment thus far to the constitution of Canada is that embodied in the British North America (No. 2) Act, 1949.[1] It represents the most important as well as the latest result of the long series of efforts already described to secure in Canada some means of amending the Canadian constitution without resort to the British Parliament. It places in the hands of the Dominion Parliament the power to alter certain portions of the constitution and in so doing it helps to establish the desired constituent authority in Canada.

But the change is far from complete, for the grant is limited in scope; there are a number of extremely important areas to which it does not apply, principally those in which the provinces are most interested. The important section of the Act is as follows:

> 1. Section ninety-one of the British North America Act, 1867 is hereby amended by renumbering Class 1 thereof as Class 1A and by inserting therein immediately before that Class the following as Class 1:—
>
> 1. The amendment from time to time of the Constitution of Canada, except as regards matters coming within the classes of subjects by this Act assigned exclusively to the Legislatures of the provinces, or as regards rights or privileges by this or any other Constitutional Act granted or secured to the Legislatures or the Government of a province, or to any class of persons with respect to schools or as regards the use of the English or the French language or as regards the requirement that there shall be a session of the Parliament of Canada at least once each year, and that no House of Commons shall continue for more than five years from the day of the return of the Writs for choosing the House; provided, however, that a House of Commons may in time of real or apprehended war, invasion or insurrection be continued by the Parliament of Canada if such continuation is not opposed by the votes of more than one-third of the members of such House.

It will be seen, however, that despite the restrictions with

[1] 12, 13 & 14 Geo. VI, chap. 81. The Act is so titled because another British North America Act had already been enacted in the same year, namely that which united Newfoundland with Canada.

which it is hedged, the authority granted to the Dominion is considerable. Indeed, many of the provincial officers have concluded that it is much too extensive for comfort. The amendment was conceived by the federal government as a first step in a general transfer of constituent authority to Canada, and was explained by the Prime Minister as merely extending to the Dominion the same power to amend the constitution with respect to national matters as that which the provinces had already long enjoyed with respect to provincial matters by virtue of the first clause of Section 92.[1] This explanation did not satisfy some of the provincial representatives, who pointed out that rights or privileges guaranteed the 'legislature or government' of a province might not be the same as those claimed and thought heretofore to have been secured to the province itself or to its people;[2] they pointed out further that in any case, in view of the vagueness of the new statute, the Dominion had become the judge of its own amending power.[3] All agreed that the authority thus conferred was considerable and that it was difficult to determine just what its limits might be.

The analysis of the Act's significance must begin with a reminder of the situation prevailing before its enactment. We have seen that the original Act of 1867 contains no amending procedure and that until 1949 every amendment had to be made by the British Parliament since the Colonial Laws Validity Act did not permit the Canadian Parliament to alter any British statute. Then in 1931 the Statute of Westminster empowered the Dominion to alter British statutes with the exception (according to the present analysis) of the British North America Acts of 1867, 1871, 1886, 1915, and 1930. These Acts and these Acts only were outside the amending power of the Canadian Parliament. Now comes the British North America (No. 2) Act, 1949, which is a clear amendment of that of 1867 and which grants to the Dominion Parliament the power to amend substantial portions of the constitution of Canada.

[1] *Proceedings of the Constitutional Conference of Federal and Provincial Governments, January 10–12, 1950*, Ottawa, 1950, p. 7.

[2] Ibid., pp. 23 ff.

[3] Ibid., pp. 23, 35, 42. The Premier of Quebec referred to the Act as 'most inappropriate and certainly a definite encroachment on provincial rights' (p. 68).

One might conclude from the logic of the foregoing argument that 1949 (No. 2) is not protected by the Statute of Westminster against alteration by the Dominion since it was enacted after 1930 and would thus be excluded for the same reasons as those that excluded the Acts of 1940, 1946, &c. Thus Parliament could alter it at will under the general powers of Section 2 (2) of the Statute of Westminster. But this argument does not hold up under close scrutiny in the light shed by the Act of 1949 itself. For this Act destroys the distinction drawn by the argument between those parts of the constitution that were alterable in Canada and those that, being protected by Section 7 (1) of the Statute of Westminster, were not so alterable.

The Act of 1949 (No. 2) is the latest enactment of the British Parliament on the subject of the amendment of the Canadian constitution and it prevails over any earlier Act with which it may be in conflict. It clearly states that the Canadian Parliament may amend any part of the Canadian constitution except with respect to certain specified matters. The Statute of Westminster provided differently. Hence, so far as Canada is concerned, the Act of 1949 (No. 2) constitutes by necessary intendment an amendment to the Statute of Westminster as well as to the British North America Act, 1867. Before its passage the Canadian Parliament could amend anything except the five Acts named above. The Act amends the Act of 1867 to allow Parliament to amend anything in the *constitution of Canada*—except with respect to the following items, the protection of which is continued:

*a.* Powers assigned exclusively to the provinces (principally Section 92).
*b.* Rights or privileges granted (by whatever constitutional act)[1] to the legislatures or governments of the provinces.
*c.* Rights or privileges granted to any class of persons with respect to schools or the use of languages.
*d.* The requirement of annual Parliaments and the five-year limit on the life of a House of Commons (with the proviso that this may be extended in times of real or apprehended emergencies).

[1] The use of the term 'constitutional act' raises the interesting question whether some (i.e. non-constitutional) acts were meant to be excluded here. This is doubtful, however, since no such distinction exists in British law.

The parts of the constitution that are thus protected are difficult to determine. They are described in terms of subject-matter rather than in terms of statutes and sections of statutes. This is unfortunate, because it increases the difficulty of interpretation; for the situation before 1949 could be set out in terms of statutes and not in terms of subject-matter.

What does the 1949 Act do to the distinction drawn in 1931? First and most obviously it divides the Act of 1867 into two parts, the first of which may be amended by the Canadian Parliament and the second of which may not. It is impossible at this time to draw up a precise list of those sections that are protected,[1] but certainly among them would be Section 92 which contains the exclusive powers of the provinces, Sections 58 to 90 which deal with the provincial constitutions and other provincial matters, Section 93 which concerns education, Section 133 which concerns the use of the English and French languages, and probably as well several others of lesser importance.

But before 1949 four other Acts in addition to that of 1867 were protected against amendment by the Dominion Parliament, namely those of 1871, 1886, 1915, and 1930. The new Act divides these into two parts in the same way; we may therefore inquire to what extent they continue to be protected under the new statute. Two of these Acts clearly confer rights or privileges upon the governments or legislatures of the provinces. Hence they are, in part at least, protected by the new guarantees. The Act of 1871 confirms the power of the Dominion to establish new provinces subject to certain limitations and requires the provincial legislatures' consent to any subsequent changes in the provincial boundaries. The Act of 1930 returned certain natural resources to the western provinces and assigned the control of them to the provinces concerned.

Whether anything in the Acts of 1886 and 1915 is still protected against Dominion alteration is doubtful. Such protection is extended only to rights or privileges granted to the *government* or *legislature* of a province and not to those granted merely to the province itself or to the people of a province.

[1] See the *Proceedings of the Constitutional Conference of Federal and Provincial Governments, January 10–12, 1950, passim.*, where several tentative attempts were made to formulate a list of such sections.

Both these Acts are concerned (in part) with the representation of the provinces in the Dominion Parliament; this would seem to be a right or privilege granted to the province but not necessarily to the government or legislature of the province. If this is a proper interpretation, as seems likely, then these privileges are not protected by the 1949 Act.[1] The Dominion Government, in pressing through the British North America Act, 1952, certainly considered that its power under the 1949 Act extended to the regulation of provincial representation in the Dominion Parliament.

Thus an examination of the subject-matter of the Acts protected before 1949 reveals that although substantial portions of them continue to be protected under the new formula, there are also important clauses that are no longer protected.

A further question arises from the comparison of the Statute of Westminster with the Act of 1949. Under the former only certain named statutes were unalterable by the Dominion. The latter deals not with a series of specific statutes but with something called the 'constitution of Canada'; it grants to the Dominion the power to alter that constitution except with respect to certain named subjects, mainly those in which the provinces are most concerned. Now the 'constitution of Canada' is a much broader term than the 'British North America Acts, 1867–1930', and it includes elements that the latter does not, such as, for example, all the British North America Acts since 1930. In view of this greater breadth of meaning it would seem that some features of this constitution may be protected against alteration by the Dominion by virtue of the exceptions in the Act of 1949 that were not so protected in the Statute of Westminster. This is certainly true of any provision of any Act not protected before 1949 that conferred rights or privileges upon the government or legislature of any province. With respect to such instances the Dominion has *lost* rather than gained power as a result of the passage of the 1949 Act. One example of this curious circumstance seems to be the first British North America Act, 1949, which conferred upon the legislature of Newfoundland certain

[1] See, for example, the remarks of the Premier of Nova Scotia, who argued that such privileges are protected. Ibid., p. 73. Prime Minister St. Laurent denied this contention at p. 70. See also Gérin-Lajoie, op. cit., p. xxx.

rights and privileges which would be protected under the new scheme but could not have been protected under the Statute of Westminster since the Act was passed after 1930. Another example may be found in the Statute of Westminster itself, Section 7 (2) of which removes from the legislatures of the provinces the disabilities that still existed under the Colonial Laws Validity Act and grants them the right to make laws in conflict with British statutes. Finally, the British North America Act, 1907, may be cited as a doubtful example of the same thing. That Act requires that certain minimum grants shall be made by the Dominion to each province 'for its local purposes and the support of its Government and Legislature'. The provisions of this Act still constitute a statutory minimum for Dominion grants to the provinces, but whether this provision may be construed as a 'right or privilege granted to the Legislature or Government of a province' within the meaning of the 1949 Act is uncertain. It seems clear at any rate that there are certain elements of the law of the constitution that were subject to Dominion alteration under the former plan but which are now protected by the exceptions in the Act of 1949. One may be permitted to wonder whether anything of this kind was intended by the Dominion Government when it was pressing for the joint address that led to the passage of the Act. At the very least the provisions of the new Act cast doubt upon the ability of the Dominion Parliament acting alone to enact laws that might be construed as affecting provincial privileges, and it is quite possible, as Dr. Gérin-Lajoie has pointed out,[1] that the validity of such an Act may be questioned in the courts, a device that was not available before 1949, when all Acts of amendment were enacted by the British Parliament.

All the same, the change in the amendment procedure introduced by the Act of 1949 is important. It will no longer be necessary to go to the British Parliament for alterations respecting a great number of subjects. Many of the British statutes enacted in behalf of the Dominion of Canada since 1867 could have been effected in Canada itself had the new procedure been in operation. No one will be more relieved than the British officials themselves that much of this scurrying back and forth will no longer be necessary.

[1] Op. cit., p. xxxv.

## *The Constitutional Conferences of 1950*

But the problems of the amending process in Canada have by no means been solved. The area that remains outside the Dominion's power to amend is still very large. Nearly half of the operative sections of the Act of 1867 contain provisions that would still be protected, and the whole problem of Dominion-Provincial relations remains untouched. Any changes in these provisions must still come, as before, through an Act of the Imperial Parliament, and the procedure by which this machinery may be set in motion is no clearer than before 1949.

The Act of 1949 was conceived as a first step towards the achievement of an amending procedure that Canada could operate wholly by herself. But this first step was the easiest; the really difficult task was still ahead, namely that of securing agreement between the Dominion and the provinces on a procedure by which the provisions affecting provincial rights and functions might be altered. The attempt to secure this agreement was initiated promptly. In January 1950 a conference of the Dominion and provincial prime ministers was called to examine the problem again. A greater measure of agreement was reached than by any other similar group in the past and the discussions were marked by a striking degree of amity and co-operation. A unanimous agreement was concluded by which the constitution would be divided into six different compartments and an amending procedure suited to its own peculiar nature would be assigned to each compartment.[1] The divisions were to be as follows:

1. Those provisions affecting the Dominion only could be amended by the Dominion Parliament.
2. Those provisions affecting only the provinces could be changed by the provinces alone.
3. Those in which the Dominion and some, but not all, provinces were concerned could be changed by the Dominion jointly with the legislature of each of the provinces concerned.
4. Those in which the Dominion and all the provinces were concerned (and this would comprise the most important parts of the constitu-

[1] *Proceedings of the Constitutional Conference of Federal and Provincial Governments, January 10–12, 1950*, pp. 93 f.

tion) could be amended by the Dominion Parliament with the concurrence of such majority of the provincial legislatures as might later be decided upon.

5. Those provisions concerning the fundamental rights of education, language, justice, the solemnization of marriage, and the amending procedure itself could be amended only by the unanimous consent of the Dominion and all the provinces.

6. Finally, certain spent or obsolete provisions would be repealed entirely.

It was the fifth category that was to be the most troublesome. The agreement was careful to state that the list of items suggested for inclusion in it was 'for instance but without restriction';[1] and the inclusion of more and more items in this category at the insistence of the less trustful provinces would pose a very serious problem.[2] But if problems like these could be solved there was much reason for hope in this proposal; it offered the very great advantage of providing a workable (though extremely complex) procedure while at the same time giving due weight to the federal composition of the country and to the intensity of feeling concerning the privileges of provinces and minorities.

But although agreement was reached on this formula, the formula was not the solution; it was only the framework of a solution. It remained yet to assign the clauses and provisions of the constitution to these various categories and procedures, and this task was to prove long and difficult, if not impossible. The bulk of informed opinion has been favourable to some such arrangement but the controversies over detail have been endless and, indeed, in many instances have resolved themselves into conflicts of principle.[3]

The premiers were unable to settle these questions at the January Conference and, after a lengthy and discursive discussion, they decided to establish a continuing committee of Dominion and provincial Attorneys-General to continue the

[1] Ibid., p. 117.

[2] The Premier of Ontario, Mr. L. M. Frost, immediately indicated that he considered the provisions on property and civil rights to be among the fundamental rights to be protected by the unanimity procedure. Ibid., pp. 77 f.

[3] A helpful summary of the controversies is that of Paul Gérin-Lajoie, 'Du pouvoir d'amendement constitutionnel au Canada', *Canadian Bar Review*, vol. 29 (1951), pp. 1168–79.

effort.[1] The committee thus organized received statements from each of the provinces and in August 1950 its members assembled again to try to reconcile the differences among the various statements. It secured agreement on the classification of about a hundred sections of the British North America Act but had to report failure on the rest. Needless to say, the most critical questions went unsolved. In September the full Constitutional Conference was reassembled at Quebec to consider the report of the continuing committee and to complete its work. It was anticipated that this session would then submit an over-all plan to the several legislatures as a preliminary to a final request to the Imperial Parliament for an amendment that would create a complete amending power in Canada itself. But this hope was dashed by the inability of the September conference to reach complete agreement.

In three days of discussion, both in public and *in camera*, the prime ministers could add but a few clauses to the classifications of the Attorneys-General and in the end could only refer the problem again to the continuing committee.[2] A Dominion-Provincial Conference on fiscal matters had by this time been scheduled to meet in Ottawa in December, and the Constitutional Conference decided to reconvene immediately after that meeting to hear a further report of the committee.

The continuing committee did its best but it had to deal with issues that were beyond its powers and abilities. It assembled again in November, but was unable to accomplish anything.[3] It could report only stalemate, especially on the vital problem of the fifth category. But in fact no formal report was ever made to the Constitutional Conference, for that body has never again been convened. The December meeting of the Dominion and provincial premiers was largely devoted to the problems of taxation and old age security and, indeed, it provided the basis for the 1951 constitutional amendment on the latter subject;[4] but the effort to secure a general amending

[1] *Proceedings of the Constitutional Conference of Federal and Provincial Governments, January 10–12, 1950*, pp. 91, 118.

[2] *Proceedings of the Constitutional Conference of Federal and Provincial Governments (Second Session), Quebec, September 25–28, 1950*, p. 131. The provincial briefs submitted to the committee are included as an appendix to these proceedings, pp. 86–130.

[3] *Montreal Standard*, 25 Nov. 1950.

[4] See above, pp. 66 ff.

procedure was abandoned. Both the continuing committee and the Constitutional Conference itself were discontinued. The press release agreed on at the December conference spoke confidently of renewing both these bodies after the amendments then under discussion had been disposed of,[1] but until then both were to be suspended. And suspended they remain.

The reports of the proceedings of the three sessions of the Constitutional Conference are a rich source of information on the diversity of views on the whole problem of constitutional amendment. The discussions are sometimes sweet and amicable, sometimes harsh and bitter, but throughout runs the constant theme of provincial jealousy and apprehension. At the September session there was a surprising amount of support for a proposal to create a wholly new constitution, but nothing was done about this and one may doubt whether it could have been successful. In both sessions the greatest obstacle, as would be expected, was Section 92, the exclusive powers of the provinces. Nobody challenged Quebec's insistence on unanimous consent for the alteration of the fundamental guarantees regarding education, language, and the like, but few would agree to the inclusion of all of Section 92 in this category. Interestingly, it was Ontario rather than Quebec that argued most forcefully for the protection of unanimity for this broad field of provincial action. There was no hope and the effort was abandoned. At the time of this writing it has not been revived.

### *The Form of Provincial Consent*

Even if agreement on some such procedure can be secured, however, there would still remain the problem of how to secure the consent of the provinces when such consent is required. The two alternatives that have most frequently been proposed are (1) resolution in the legislature and (2) referendum to the people of the provinces. The evidence seems to point to a preference for the former, but it is by no means conclusive. The techniques of direct legislation (i.e. initiative and referendum) are not often found in countries that employ

[1] *Proceedings of the Conference of Federal and Provincial Governments, Ottawa, December 4–7, 1950*, p. 137.

a responsible parliamentary system and the arguments against this combination are strong, although Australian experience has shown that the combination is not unworkable.

During the discussions of 1929 the problem was raised in several places and a strong advocacy of the referendum appeared. An editorial in a Winnipeg newspaper presented an argument that deserves reproduction:

> . . . the right to pass upon proposed amendments should in no case be exercised by the provincial legislatures. Nearly all the amendments will in some way or another touch upon some right claimed by a province; and if approval is sought from a body which, from its very nature is bound to think provincially, it will never be obtained. Ratification should be sought . . . from the people of the provinces who are citizens both of the Dominion and the provinces, and therefore competent to judge between conflicting interests. . . . But if the ratification of the provincial legislatures is required we shall never get anywhere, because there will always be some pin-headed provincialists who will see in every proposition some diabolical conspiracy against provincial rights.[1]

But in 1935 most of the witnesses before the Special Committee who commented on the point were opposed to a referendum for deciding the question of provincial consent. Dr. Ollivier left it out of his proposal deliberately, as he said, because it is 'too cumbersome, too complicated, and too expensive'.[2] Others, too, commented on the referendum scheme, but it was Professor Kennedy who made the most interesting observation and the most unhesitating criticism:

> . . . I do not believe it is possible to drive in double harness referendum and cabinet government. I believe that referendum is something that politicians have invented for 'passing the buck'. I throw the responsibility where it belongs, on the legislature. A referendum has an extraordinarily bad effect. Take a proposition like this: 'do you believe in the St. Lawrence waterways?' or something like that. You ask the people to vote 'yes' or 'no'. It is like asking them if they believe in eternity. You cannot isolate important questions and answer them with 'yes' or 'no'. The ramifications of a question are too profound, and I should like to have the question argued out in each provincial house. I am very strongly opposed—I cannot say it too emphatically—to referenda.[3]

[1] *Manitoba Free Press*, 1 Aug. 1929; quoted by Ollivier, *Problems of Canadian Sovereignty*, pp. 386 f.

[2] *Proceedings and Evidence and Report*, p. 59.

[3] Ibid., p. 76.

The Committee discussed the question at some length and several members recorded their objections to the referendum[1] but, as in many of its discussions, it came to no conclusion.[2]

Another interesting device for measuring the consent, not of the provinces but of the nation, to parliamentary proposals for amendment has been suggested (though not with much enthusiasm) by Dr. Gérin-Lajoie. He suggests that since the interests of the several population groups are more accurately grouped in areas than in the provinces themselves, these areas or regions might be used as the basic groups from which such consent might be sought.[3] The areas that have traditionally served as the basis of representation in the Senate would seem to be suitable for this purpose as well. Thus before any amendment would take effect it would have to be agreed to by each of the four areas—the maritimes, Quebec, Ontario, and the western provinces. In the multi-province areas a majority of the provinces would represent that area's consent. To the objection that this scheme would make necessary the consent of both Ontario and Quebec but that any other province could be overridden he replies that such a special position is justified by the fact that each of these provinces contains about a third of the total population of the country.

Another suggestion that is sometimes heard is to combine the requirement that a certain portion of the provinces must consent, with the further requirement that these provinces must represent a certain portion of the total population. In its simplest form this is the system employed in Australia, though in that country the system takes the form of a popular referendum. At the Dominion-Provincial Conference of 1935 Ontario submitted a proposal that divided the constitution into compartments in the manner already described and then required for the amendment of certain parts of the constitution the consent of the Dominion Parliament and of the legislatures of two-thirds of the provinces representing at least

[1] e.g. Lapointe at p. 63, Skelton and Scott at p. 83.

[2] It is of interest that objections to ratification by referendum on the same score were raised against the proposed procedure for the commonwealth constitution during the convention in Sydney in 1891. See Sir John Quick and Sir Robert Garran, *The Annotated Constitution of the Australian Commonwealth*, Sydney, 1901, p. 987.

[3] *Constitutional Amendment in Canada*, pp. 265 ff.

55 per cent. of the total population.[1] Such a proposal would naturally give weight to the large populations of certain provinces while at the same time taking account of the individual nature of provincial participation. Other schemes of a similar nature have simply varied the proportions involved. Dr. Gérin-Lajoie has proposed (with greater enthusiasm) such a scheme. He suggests that any amendments affecting certain classes of subjects should 'require the concurrence of two-thirds (or possibly three-fourths) of the provinces representing at least seventy-five per cent. of the population of Canada'.[2] This procedure he conceives as having very nearly the same effect as his suggestion about regional consent mentioned above. It would moreover have the advantage of being flexible enough to meet the needs of future shifts in population, whereas the regional plan might easily result in unintended inequities in a few years. He suggests too that this plan might be employed in conjunction with a popular referendum on some kinds of amendments and that the choice between referendum and legislative consent might best be left to the Dominion Parliament.[3]

## *Conclusion*

From the foregoing examination of the principles of constitutional amendment in Canada certain conclusions may be drawn. Certain parts of the previously protected fundamental law may since 1949 be amended unilaterally by the Dominion Parliament; the rest may still be altered only by the Imperial Parliament at Westminster. For the latter portions the request for amendment must come from the Dominion Parliament and not merely from the executive government alone. The Dominion Parliament has full legal power to request any kind

[1] *Constitutional Amendment in Canada*, p. 245.

[2] Ibid., pp. 268 ff.

[3] There are problems involved in the use of the referendum with the above procedure that ought to be more fully explored. For example, how is the necessary 75 per cent. of the population to be determined? If legislative consent is employed, presumably the vote of the legislature will stand for the total population of the province; if, however, a referendum is held, does its result count for the total population or merely for that part voting affirmatively in the referendum? These proposals, when all are considered, seem rather too complicated to have much chance of being adopted.

of amendment that it desires, and is not compelled to consult with the provinces before passing the address. It is most probable that the Imperial Parliament will respond automatically to any request from the Dominion Parliament without inquiring into the measure of provincial consent that has been secured. The provinces have no legal claim to be consulted in such matters and whether they are so consulted is within the power of the Dominion Parliament to decide. It seems probable, however, that the Dominion would not undertake to introduce changes in the formal distribution of powers or to modify the clauses that provide for the protection of minorities without the consent of all the provinces. It is also clear that an amendment providing for a general procedure of amendment will not be enacted without the consent of all the provinces. But there are political restraints and not legal or even constitutional limitations.

This is about all that can be said. It should be emphasized that the essential problem is not legal but political and social. It is not so important that the Dominion has the legal power as it is that the Dominion is not likely to abuse that power. Federal government, in Canada as elsewhere, places a premium on the willingness of people and groups of people to listen to opposing views and to compromise with them. There is a tendency in Canada (as there is in most federations) to credit the central government with an abstract existence wholly apart from the people it represents; similarly the provinces are considered as being separate from and in opposition to this central government. What this conception of federalism ignores is the essential fact that both central and local governments are instruments of the same group of people. Disagreements between the central government and certain local governments or between two groups of local governments are nothing more than disagreements between two groups of people. It is logically impossible to talk in terms of a conflict between the central government and *all* of the component units; moreover, to the extent that representative government is actually representative, it is not only logically impossible but institutionally impossible as well. For two sets of institutions purporting to represent the same group of people cannot disagree if they truly represent those people. It may be objected that there are instances where the central government has disagreed with nearly all, or at least a majority, of the states or provinces. I agree that such examples can be found. But the answer to this objection is that representative institutions are far from perfect instruments for the reflection of public opinion and that the office holders, both at national and regional levels, are sometimes mistaken in their estimates of that opinion. Moreover, local officials tend to acquire a vested interest in the prerogatives of the local government, just as national officials do in the national government. Each tends to think that the best solution to a problem is to permit his level of government to handle it. If he continues to conceive his own function as a representative one, he concludes that the officials at the other level are wrong in their calculation of public opinion. No effort is made here to suggest a solution to this problem, although it is one that desperately needs solving; I shall be satisfied if the point is made that every official in a federal system, whether he is working at the national or the local level, must understand that he represents the same group of people as do the officials at the other level.

The lesson that should be drawn from this is that any situation that seems to set the central government over against the regional governments is a false situation and indicates that someone, somewhere, has drawn improper inferences from the materials on which an estimate of public opinion is based. Such a situation being false, steps should be taken at once to improve it; whether this means a change of policy, a reorganization of institutions, a dissolution of legislatures, or another Dominion-Provincial Conference is unimportant. What is important is that when the steps are taken, they should be taken with the realization that someone is wrong and that it may be anyone.

The most important principle upon which federalism rests is that of respect for opinions with which one disagrees. If policy making in a federal state is not guided by this idea, then there is little chance for the federation to endure. The moral basis of a federal state is much more important than its legal basis. In Canada this is reflected perhaps best of all in this problem of an amendment procedure. If those who believe that the provinces ought not to take part in the process succeed in pushing through an amendment procedure that embodies this belief, they can expect only the dissatisfactions and difficulties that their efforts are bound to produce. Not because such a procedure might not offer perfect protection to the minority interests, but because the minority interests do not believe it will offer such protection. If, on the other hand, Quebec or Ontario, or other provinces, insist on the adoption of the principle of unanimous consent, then they can expect similar discontents. It has become clear that neither of these extremes can satisfy Canada's needs and that the only hope is to settle on some compromise procedure such as has been described.

But the difficulty with such a compromise is that it is not a compromise at all, but a concession of the adherents of the compact theory to their opponents. Unanimity does not admit of degrees and Quebec has for the most part been able to see no protection for herself in any other procedure; until 1949 at least she insisted that it be recognized in law, if any law was to be adopted. This intransigence has been carried so far as to threaten the foundations of the confederation.[1] In 1917 the Quebec legislature went so far as to debate a resolution which visualized the secession of the province from the union.[2] It has been manifested at nearly every Dominion-Provincial Conference at which the question of an amending clause has been raised.

The stubborn insistence of Quebec and Ontario on unanimous consent has been matched by equally stubborn insistence on the part of others that the Act of 1867 is not a compact and that there is no foundation for the doctrine of unanimity. This is true, and it is certain that the legalization of the unanimity principle might be disastrous for Canada. But it is far too easy to say that the compact theory has no basis either in law or in history and to dismiss it at that. There is a sense in which every federation is based on a compact, not

[1] See Léopold Richer, *Notre problème politique*, Montreal, 1938, p. 12: 'Nous exprimons toute notre penseé en disant que les pires agents du séparatisme sont les centralisateurs. Si l'on avait respecté les engagements de 1867, on n'aurait jamais entendu parler du séparatisme québecois.' Also, 'Il n'est pas de notre pouvoir, il n'est de pouvoir de personne, de dire: "Nous resterons dans la Confédération", ou bien: "Nous en sortirons". Mais si l'on veut absolument du séparatisme, les centralisateurs n'ont qu'à mettre leurs projets à exécution' (p. 9).

[2] D. G. Creighton, 'Federal Relations in Canada since 1914', in Chester Martin, ed. *Canada in Peace and War*, p. 41.

in a legal or even in an historical sense, but in a moral or social sense. Federations are formed instead of unitary unions because the component elements are unwilling to give up their individuality to such a union. So long as the federation continues, the component units have a right to have that individuality respected; once it is submerged into what is sometimes called the 'will of the majority' or the 'common good', then the basis of federalism has been destroyed. There is a profound truth in MacKay's observation that although 'legally the British North America Act of 1867 is merely a statute of the British Parliament, morally it is a compact between the provinces of Canada'.[1] It is to be hoped that the compact theorists will abandon their insistence on the incorporation of that theory into a legal procedure; but if they are persuaded to do so, their opponents should recognize the validity of the moral basis of the compact.

Quebec and her supporters should have no great fears on this score; for there is no evidence that her interests and rights would be jeopardized by the adoption of a compromise measure dividing the constitution into compartments, each with its own amending procedure. The record of the Dominion Parliament has on the whole been very good in this respect; it has not abused its legal power or insisted on its own desires while ignoring provincial objections. Indeed, in recent years the Dominion Government has granted in practice much of what Quebec and Ontario have sought in law. In the two instances where new powers were given to the central government, no action was taken until the consent of Quebec (and all other provinces) was obtained; in 1940 action had been postponed several years in deference to Quebec's objections. The only real aberration has been that of 1943, when the address was passed over Quebec's formal protests. Both the Dominion leaders and the representatives of the English-speaking provinces have evinced every concern that the rights and guarantees that the present constitution affords to Quebec should be rigorously maintained. No proposal for an amending clause is now seriously urged that does not require the consent of Quebec or of all the provinces for any changes in the significant clauses of Sections 91, 92, 93, and 133. Quebec may well

[1] Robert A. MacKay, *The Unreformed Senate of Canada*, Oxford, 1926, p. 207.

find hope and faith as well as charity in the consideration that is being shown her by the rest of Canada. And indeed the discussions of 1949 and 1950 seem to suggest that she has begun to do just this.

But Quebec, like the other provinces, has a responsibility to Canada as a whole. If one of the purposes of federalism is to guarantee certain things to the component elements, another is to bring these elements together into a whole that is greater than, or at least different from, the sum of its parts. No doubt the states of a federation have a right to a guarantee of their existence and position, but these states, by joining in a federation, contribute to the formation of a wholly new political and legal entity. In doing so they undertake a certain risk of losing some of the individuality that would otherwise be theirs. If confederation in Canada was a pact there were responsibilities on both sides, whereas the compact theorists have been concerned to emphasize only one side of it. If Quebec and Ontario insist on unanimity they may well be insisting on the impossible and may by that insistence contribute to the break-up of an entity to whose protection the pact commits them. Canada is a federal society, but it is a common society too; the diverse elements within it have an obligation to subordinate some of their own diversities for the common advantage. To insist on the primacy of the diversities, to insist on unanimous consent, is 'the negation of the existence of a common state'.[1] The moral obligation works both ways.

Canada, like any federation, displays both centralizing and decentralizing forces, each with institutions and habits of thought that support it. The two forces must be bent to serve the needs of the whole; if either completely overcomes the other, then federalism cannot last. We may say with Professor Kennedy[2] that

> . . . in giving reasonable weight to the provinces, the provinces should not control the federation; and in giving reasonable weight to the federation, the federation should not control the provinces. The real problem is not the revision of legislative powers, it is the integration of Canadian interests.

[1] Stephen Leacock, 'Is Canada Breaking Up?', in the *Ottawa Journal*, 15 Dec. 1934. Quoted in Ollivier, op. cit., p. 347.

[2] Testimony before the Special Committee on the British North America Act, 1935, *Proceedings and Evidence and Report*, p. 75.

# 3

# THE AMENDMENT OF THE AUSTRALIAN CONSTITUTION

THE problems of constitutional amendment in Australia are considerably different from those in Canada. The most obvious difference lies in the fact that the Australian constitution, unlike the Canadian, provides for its own amendment without recourse to the British Parliament. In Canada the process of amendment had to be determined before the role of the provinces in that process could be defined; in Australia the procedure is given; it is left for us to examine how it has worked and what role the states play in it.

In Australia too, however, there is some problem in identifying the constitution. There as elsewhere there is a sense in which the fundamental framework of government consists of more than the formal or written document. It includes such things as judicial decisions, statutes, unwritten customs, and conventions. And these elements change in other ways than by the formal amendment procedure. Indeed this process has been employed successfully so few times that most of the changes in the Australian constitutional structure have come about through changes outside the formal documentary constitution. The changing course of judicial decisions has been of particular importance here. The relations between the states and the central government were sharply altered by this method in 1920,[1] and since then there has been a steady increase in the power of the central government. The difficulty of the formal amending procedure has more than ever thrown the burden of adapting the constitution to changing needs upon the shoulders of the High Court. But the judiciary can do only so much. It can adapt but it cannot amend; it can amplify but it cannot change the constitution. The ultimate power to do this lies in the forces that control the amendment procedure

[1] *Amalgamated Society of Engineers* v. *Adelaide Steamship Co.* (1920), 28 C.L.R. 129.

itself. Any decision of the judiciary, any change in the conventions of the constitution, any statute of any legislature, may be overridden by amending the constitution. It is this power that is the ultimate authority in the state.

### *Britain's Role in the Amending Process*

The constitution of Australia is contained in a statute of the British Parliament[1] and, strictly speaking, is still subject to alteration or repeal by that body. No one, of course, would argue that the British Parliament is likely to do anything of the sort or that such an alteration would be accepted as valid law in Australia. But legally the power is there, just as the power is there to repeal all of the British North America Acts. It is no answer to say that the Statute of Westminster would forbid such action (which it does), for that very Statute of Westminster is also an enactment of the British Parliament and like any others is legally subject to similar alteration. The point is that although on a political or even on a constitutional level Australia's independence is complete, there is still a legal (perhaps a better word would be formal) sense in which Britain still holds dominion over her. This formal power, then, constitutes a perfectly legal way in which the constitution of Australia could be amended.[2]

It would of course be quite unconstitutional for Britain to exercise this power except on request from the Commonwealth authorities, but if such a request were made after the fashion

[1] The Commonwealth of Australia Constitution Act, 1900. 63 & 64 Vict., chap. 12.

[2] See David Maughan, 'The Constitution of the Commonwealth—Strength and Weakness', in *Constitutional Revision in Australia*, Australian Institute of Political Science, Sydney, 1944, p. 15. The author quotes from the report of the joint committee of the Lords and Commons which dealt with Western Australia's 1934 petition for secession to the effect that such action by the Imperial Parliament is still quite legal. He adds: 'This is still the position, notwithstanding the adoption of the Statute of Westminster by Australia.' Such an amendment actually took place as late as March 1937, when by the Geneva Convention Act of that year the Imperial Parliament conferred upon the Commonwealth Parliament the power to pass laws to give effect to the convention. The amendment attracted no attention in Australia and was not even brought to the Cabinet's attention. Op. cit., p. 15. Another discussion of this question of British intervention which reaches a similar conclusion may be found in Henry John May, *The South African Constitution*, Capetown and Johannesburg, 1949, pp. 19–23. See also a discussion of its historical aspects in L. F. Crisp, *Parliamentary Government of the Australian Commonwealth*, New Haven, 1949, p. 141.

of such requests from Canada, then the British authorities would have to decide. The Canadian precedents suggest that the British officials would be unwilling to refuse such a request from a Dominion Government; but it is possible. There is an important difference, however; since Australia does possess her own amending procedure, prescribed by that same British Parliament in the Constitution Act itself, Britain might simply refer the Australian Government back to its own amending procedure; or she might comply with the request. No Australian precedents exist that suggest an answer. We may hope that they never will, for if the problem is ever posed, it can be posed only by a request for an amendment by the Commonwealth Government, and this request, since it would ignore the prescribed procedure, would be if not *ultra vires* at least highly unconstitutional; it would be a mark of the break-up of the Australian federal polity.

It may also be argued that there is a certain relation between British policy and the Australian amending process in the fact that the Crown must approve any action taken in Australia to amend the constitution. That consent is given by the Governor-General in the Queen's name. But this is no limitation upon Australian constituent authority, for the same reasons as those mentioned above which restrict the power of Britain to alter the constitution. The Governor-General, though the representative in Australia of the British Crown, acts on the advice of Australian, not British ministers. It is inconceivable that he would insist on an action, such as refusing to assent to a constitutional amendment, in the face of contrary advice from his Australian advisers.[1] Nor is it any more likely that

[1] The history of the Crown in Australia has not, however, been entirely free from the exercise of discretion on the part of its representatives. On three separate occasions (1904, 1905, and 1909) the Governor-General refused to grant a dissolution of the House of Representatives when requested by the Ministry. (See Herbert V. Evatt, *The King and His Dominion Governors*, Oxford, 1936, pp. 50–54.) Even more spectacular was the dismissal in 1932 of Premier Lang of New South Wales together with his Ministry for their refusal to pay interest on debts owed to the Commonwealth. The Governor in this case explained that the Crown could not be a party to any illegality. Ibid., chap. xix. In May 1950 the Governor of Victoria refused to comply with the advice of the Premier (Mr. Hollway) to dissolve the Legislative Assembly, apparently on the ground that an election had just been held and that majority support had been assured for a different government. See *Melbourne Age*, 26 June 1950. A similar incident occurred in Oct. 1952. It is none the less true that the refusal of the Governor-General to assent

he would be advised to refuse his assent in such an instance, since in a responsible system such as Australia's the advice would come from the very leaders who had secured the passage of the amendment proposal through the legislature. The Crown's role in the amending process is negligible and must be performed, in accordance with good constitutional practice, upon the advice of the leaders of the Australian Government.[1]

## *The Statute of Westminster*

Section 2 (2) of the Statute of Westminster granted to the Dominions the right to amend or repeal any British legislation in so far as that legislation had effect in the Dominion. In Australia, as in Canada, it was feared that such a blanket authorization might work ill to the states, since it could be interpreted as giving the Commonwealth Parliament the right to amend that Act of the British Parliament that comprised the constitution of the Commonwealth. Despite the fact that the Constitution Act provided a definite procedure for its amendment by Australian agencies, the Statute of Westminster, being a later enactment of the same Parliament, would take legal precedence over the earlier act. Therefore an unqualified authorization to amend any British legislation, orders, or regulations could easily be construed as an amendment by the British Parliament of the amending clause of the constitution, empowering the Commonwealth Parliament, without consultation with the states or the use of the referendum procedure, to alter the constitution in any way it desired.

In view of this possibility and upon the insistence of the Australian states, a further clause was inserted in the Act to protect the states from such an interpretation. The clause (Section 8) was similar to that inserted for the protection of the Canadian provinces and read as follows: 'Nothing in this Act shall be deemed to confer any power to repeal or alter the Constitution or the Constitution Act of the Commonwealth of Australia . . . otherwise than in accordance with the law

to an amendment upon proper advice would be unthinkable unless he were somehow convinced of the illegality of the amendment or of the manner in which it had been adopted.

[1] See the *Report of the Conference on the Operation of Dominion Legislation and Merchant Shipping Legislation*, 1929, Cmd. 3479 (1930).

existing before the commencement of this Act.' The amending procedure prescribed by the original constitution was thus preserved intact.

Another problem was raised, however, at the Imperial Conferences of 1926 and 1930. Even with the above limitation imposed on the operation of Section 2 of the Statute, it could still be construed to confer upon the Commonwealth the power to alter any British legislation that constituted a part of the law of the *states*,[1] and such a power could be used to restrict the functions of the states to the advantage of the Commonwealth. In consequence Section 9 (1) was incorporated into the Statute:

> Nothing in this Act shall be deemed to authorize the Parliament of the Commonwealth of Australia to make laws on any matter within the authority of the States of Australia, not being a matter within the authority of the Parliament or Government of the Commonwealth of Australia.

Still other problems arose. Section 4 stated that no Act of the United Kingdom Parliament would thereafter extend to a Dominion unless 'it is expressly declared in that Act that the Dominion has requested, and consented to, the enactment thereof'. In Australia a question was raised about the identity of the officials or agencies who would be empowered to make such a request or give such consent. It was feared that the clause might be construed as referring to the executive alone. If the government of the day did not control both Houses of the Parliament (as was true in 1931) then the constitution might be effectively amended without the concurrence of both Houses as the constitution prescribes. As a result of these arguments Section 9 (3) was added to the Statute providing that '. . . the request and consent referred to in section four shall mean the request and consent of the Parliament and Government of the Commonwealth'. No other Dominion desired such a definition and no others were included in its scope. The problem was discussed briefly in the British Parliament, but an amendment applying the definition to all Dominions was defeated.[2]

[1] Examples were the Australian States Constitution Act, 1907, and the Merchant Shipping Act, 1894.

[2] *British House of Commons Debates*, vol. 260, 5th ser., p. 279.

But if 'request and consent' were to be so defined, the consent of the Commonwealth Parliament might be construed as necessary to any request by a state for British legislation that would apply to that state alone. It was conceded that such legislation was unlikely to be needed,[1] but it might be, and in such a case it would be inconvenient to require the consent of the Commonwealth to such a request. Section 9 (2) was therefore included in the Statute denying the need for such Commonwealth consent except as it may have been necessary before the commencement of the Act.

No attempt is made here to estimate the effect of the Statute of Westminster on the constitution of the Commonwealth, but it may be said that it had little effect on the provisions in that document for constitutional amendment. Indeed, the various qualifying clauses described above were adopted largely to prevent the Statute from having any effect on the amending procedure. The procedure established in the constitution continues to operate exactly as it did before the Statute and no efforts have been made to interpret the Statute in such a way as to produce therefrom any new modes of constitutional alteration.

The Statute of Westminster did not become part of the law of the Commonwealth, however, for more than a decade. Shortly after its enactment in 1931 the Labour Party lost control of the Government and a coalition of the Country Party and the United Australia Party took over. Despite the urging of Labour, now in opposition, and the half-hearted and intermittent support of the Government, no proposal for the adoption of the Statute was carried through until 1942 after Labour had come back into power. In the meantime Australia's legal position *vis à vis* Britain remained unchanged. The relation between the two continued to be governed by the Colonial Laws Validity Act, 1865, and the several conventions concerning Dominion status that had grown up. British legislation still applied to Australia,[2] and during this period several

[1] Commonwealth of Australia, *Parliamentary Debates*, vol. 132, p. 1085.

[2] It is unnecessary to discuss here in detail the various ways in which British legislation has had effect in Australia. The discussion of Canada's position above in chapter 2 applies as well to Australia, subject to a few qualifications. By the turn of the century the convention had grown up that British legislation would not

Acts of the British Parliament had legal effect in Australia, though all were consented to by the latter. Among these were the Geneva Convention Act, 1937, the Emergency Powers (Defence) Act, 1939, and the Prize Act, 1939. After war broke out Australia suffered some confusion and delay because she had not yet adopted the necessary sections of the Statute of Westminster. She was unable to enact legislation having an extraterritorial effect and her power to control shipping was limited by the Merchant Shipping Act, 1894, to ships of her own registry or in her own coastal trade. Most Australian bills dealing with shipping had therefore to be reserved, and considerable delay was sometimes encountered in securing the royal assent to them,[1] a source of great inconvenience in a country engaged in war and threatened by invasion. It was because of these disabilities that the war government decided to press the adoption of sections two to six of the Statute. The bill was passed after considerable debate and received the royal assent on 9 October 1942.[2]

## *The Amending Procedure of Section 128*

With respect to the problems of amending the constitution in a federal state, Australia offers a much better field of investigation than does Canada. It provides a better laboratory for the student of the problem and more data from which

apply to the self-governing colonies except when requested by those colonies. Australia achieved her constitution a generation later than did Canada and thus avoided many of the problems involved in the evolution of Dominion status that Canada had to face in her early days. But British legislation of a general nature, i.e., that applied to all colonies in general and not to specified ones, still affected Australia as well as the other Dominions; it was not until the Statute of Westminster that this disability was removed. The Colonial Laws Validity Act still operated and subjected Australian legislation always to its test of validity. A more significant difference for present purposes was the fact that Australia possessed her own amendment procedure and therefore did not have to resort to Westminster for changes in the basic British legislation for Australia. Whereas Canada could not amend her basic Act at all, since to do so would violate the Colonial Laws Validity Act, Australia was not thus restricted, for there the Constitution Act provided for its own amendment.

[1] Dr. Evatt reported that delays of up to four months had been encountered. *Parliamentary Debates*, vol. 172, p. 1397.

[3] The Statute of Westminster Adoption Act, 1942. The text is given in the appendix to K. C. Wheare, *The Statute of Westminster and Dominion Status*, 5th edn., 1953. The above discussion of Australia and the Statute is based on Professor Wheare's treatise.

inferences may be drawn, since it has a precise method of amendment provided in the constitution itself. Canada has had to grope her way forward from precedent to precedent, and whatever amending procedure she possesses today has been the product of a slow evolution that is by no means yet complete. The social and political conflicts that have marked the stages of this evolution provide the better opportunity to view the interplay of the social forces that make up the federal state, but Australia provides the better opportunity for examining the nature and operation of the institutional devices.

The amending procedure is described in Section 128 of the Australian constitution.[1] Briefly its provisions are these: the proposed amendment must be agreed to by an absolute majority of both Houses of the Parliament, after which it is submitted to a referendum; in the referendum it must receive the approval not only of a majority of all those voting but also of a majority of those voting in a majority of the states. If one House refuses twice to concur in an amendment proposal the Governor-General may submit it to the electors anyway. The representation or the territory of a state cannot be diminished without its consent.

The Australian constitution, alone among those of modern federations, was adopted not as a result of war, threat of war, or an acute sense of the ills that would follow continued disunion, but developed from a deliberate calculation of the advantages of union by a people that had never been subjected to any serious disturbances of its peace. The constitution was formulated at a series of conventions extending over nearly a decade; its framers had ample time to study the operation of other constitutions and to make a careful selection of those features that seemed most suited to their own needs. The amending clause occasioned considerable debate at each of the conventions, and in these discussions the intensive study devoted to other constitutions shows up very clearly. The Swiss and American constitutions in particular were subjected to a very close scrutiny and served as models for the craftsmen who created the Commonwealth; the amending process of the former is clearly reflected in that adopted for Australia.[2]

[1] It is reproduced in full below, in Appendix A.

[2] A summary and analysis of the various proposals for an amending procedure,

### *Experience with the Amending Process*

Since 1901 twenty-four proposals have been referred to the voters, having been approved by the necessary absolute majorities in both Houses of Parliament.[1] These referenda have been held on twelve different occasions, usually at the same time as a general election. Out of the twenty-four proposals only four have succeeded in acquiring the necessary majorities both in the nation as a whole and in the four states that constitute a majority. The successful referenda took place in 1906, 1910, 1928, and 1946.

The first attempt to amend the constitution occurred in 1906. It merely provided for a change in the dates of Senate elections and of the beginning of senatorial terms. All parties supported the proposal and there was little opposition to it. It passed by a very large majority of the whole electorate (774,011 to 162,470)[2] and was approved in all six states. Thus the first attempt to amend the constitution was successful.

The second effort came in 1910, when two proposals were put before the electorate. The first of these was intended to substitute for the provisions of Sections 87, 93, and 94 a new system of grants to the states based on their population, together with a special grant to Western Australia. The second measure was designed to change the provisions of Section 105, which permitted the Commonwealth Parliament to assume only those state debts in existence at the establishment of the Commonwealth. It was proposed to make the section apply to all state debts whenever contracted.

In Parliament there was general agreement that the assumption of state debts was necessary to save the states from finan-

together with appropriate references to the convention debates, may be found in Sir John Quick and Sir Robert Garran, *The Annotated Constitution of the Australian Commonwealth*, Sydney, 1901, pp. 985–95.

[1] The Royal Commission on the Constitution in 1929 summarized the efforts to amend the constitution up to that time; see its *Report*, pp. 232–4. More extensive data on particular referenda are given in the *Official Year Book of the Commonwealth of Australia*, published annually by the Commonwealth Government; see the editions for the years in which referenda took place. In the edition (No. 18) of 1925 a summary is given of all referenda up to that date (pp. 86 ff.). No such recapitulation has been made since that time. The results of the referenda are also announced in the *Commonwealth of Australia Gazette* about a month or six weeks after the date of the referendum.

[2] Royal Commission on the Constitution, *Report*, 1929, p. 232.

cial disaster and the second of the two measures was passed in the House by a large majority[1] and in the Senate without even a roll call.[2] The first measure, however—concerning the grants to the states—had more difficulty; in the House it commanded a majority of only 39 to 27[3] and in the Senate its margin of safety was only two votes.[4] The difference in legislative enthusiasm was also reflected in the referendum results. The state debts amendment was adopted with the considerable majority of 715,053 to 586,271, being approved in every state save New South Wales.[5] The finance amendment, however, was defeated in three states (New South Wales, Victoria, and South Australia) and received only 645,514 votes in the nation as against 670,838 opposed.[6] Thus out of the first three efforts to amend the constitution two had succeeded and one had failed. There was as yet no indication that the referendum would prove to be the obstacle to constitutional amendments.

It is significant that Australia's party system was at this time just beginning to take form; party lines had not yet been clearly drawn and support of public measures was still largely determined by individual choice rather than by allegiance to party group. Moreover, whatever party organization did exist at the time was rallied to the support of the two measures that were successful. Significantly, party opposition did develop to the 1910 proposal on finance.

In 1911 there appeared the first of a long series of amendment proposals (continued to the present day) seeking to enlarge the powers of the Commonwealth Government. Two proposals were offered to the voters in that year, one dealing with the control of monopolies and the other empowering the Commonwealth Parliament to regulate all commerce, both interstate and intrastate. The proposals passed the two Houses without difficulty[7] but both were defeated in the referenda,

[1] *Parliamentary Debates*, 1909, p. 5745.

[2] Ibid., p. 6592.

[3] Ibid., p. 5801. The delegations from each state were split almost evenly.

[4] Ibid., p. 6592. The roll call result was 19 to 16.

[5] Royal Commission on the Constitution, *Report*, p. 232.

[6] Ibid.

[7] *Parliamentary Debates*, 1910; for the House votes see p. 5413 for the commerce powers proposal and p. 5614 for monopolies; the Senate votes on both proposals appear at p. 6184. The proposals may be found summarized by the Royal Commission on the Constitution, *Report*, pp. 232–3.

and by almost identical votes.[1] Only Western Australia voted in favour of the proposals, the other five states opposing both measures.

In 1913 these same proposals were again submitted to the electorate by the same Labour Government, though the terms were not quite identical with those of 1911. The complex proposal on commerce powers was split into several different measures and a new proposal was added regarding employees on State railways, under which jurisdiction over labour disputes might be conferred upon a Commonwealth tribunal. Altogether in 1913 six proposals were submitted to referendum, on which the voters were to vote separately. Support for the proposals was about the same in both Houses of the Parliament, the House dividing 41 to 26 on most votes and the Senate about 20 to 12.[2]

In the referendum, however, all six proposals were defeated, though not by large margins:

| | *For* | *Against* |
|---|---|---|
| Trade and commerce | 958,419 | 982,615 |
| Railway disputes | 956,358 | 990,046 |
| Trusts | 967,331 | 975,943 |
| Industrial matters | 961,601 | 987,611 |
| Corporations | 960,711 | 986,824 |
| Nationalization of monopolies | 917,165 | 941,947[3] |

None of the proposals received a popular majority, but the vote was very close. The states split the same way on all measures, Queensland, South Australia, and Western Australia voting in favour of them and New South Wales, Victoria, and Tasmania opposing them. Had any one of the three latter states cast a few thousand votes more for the proposals they

[1] On commerce powers: 483,356 in favour against 742,704 opposed; on monopolies: 488,688 in favour against 736,392 opposed. Ibid.

[2] *Parliamentary Debates*, 1912. The votes may be found in this volume as follows:

| | *House* | *Senate* |
|---|---|---|
| Trade and commerce | p. 6323 | p. 7325 |
| Railway disputes | p. 6584 | p. 7326 |
| Trusts | p. 6585 | p. 7341 |
| Industrial matters | p. 6588 | p. 7341 |
| Corporations | pp. 6588–9 | p. 7348 |
| Nationalization of monopolies | p. 6722 | p. 7365 |

[3] Royal Commission on the Constitution, *Report*, 1929, p. 233.

would all have passed and the subsequent story of federal power in Australia would have been much different.

In 1919 another effort was made to secure two of these powers for the Commonwealth. The House initiated proposals to expand the powers of the central government over industrial disputes and to enable the Commonwealth to nationalize monopolies; the majorities in the lower chamber were tremendous, only two votes being cast against the resolutions;[1] in the Senate both measures were amended and passed by similar majorities without roll calls, only one negative vote being recorded.[2] The House agreed to the Senate amendments, though by less substantial majorities.[3] But the results of the referenda were very similar to those of 1913. Each proposal failed by a narrow margin to receive a popular majority[4] and three states voted against each one. However, although the states again split three to three, it was a different three states that opposed the new proposals. Of the three opposing states in 1913 only New South Wales and Tasmania again voted against the measures. Victoria now approved them while South Australia now opposed them.

The next effort came in 1926, when another omnibus proposal was offered to the people. The purpose of this bill was to amend paragraph xx of Section 51 to give the Commonwealth increased powers over corporations; it also empowered the Commonwealth Parliament to deal with industrial disputes of all kinds by removing the qualification 'extending beyond the limits of any one state' in paragraph xxxv; and finally it enabled the Commonwealth to control trusts and monopolies. In addition to this omnibus proposal there was submitted to vote another measure to confer upon the Commonwealth the power to make laws protecting the interests of the public in the event of an interruption of any essential services. Both measures passed the two Houses by considerable majorities; on the

[1] *Parliamentary Debates*, 2nd sess., 1917–18–19, pp. 12993, 13034.

[2] Ibid., p. 13217.

[3] Ibid., pp. 13300, 13303.

[4] The vote for the proposal on legislative powers over industrial disputes was 911,357 to 924,160; that on nationalization of monopolies was 813,880 to 859,451. Strangely enough over 160,000 people voted on the former issue who did not vote on the latter. Royal Commission on the Constitution, *Report*, 1929, p. 233.

omnibus bill there were only two dissenting votes in the House[1] and only one in the Senate;[2] on the essential services bill the majorities were smaller but still more than adequate. Curiously, this bill received much more support in the Senate,[3] which was supposed to protect the rights of the states, than it did in the House.[4] In the referenda the measures failed even more decisively than had their predecessors. Only New South Wales and Queensland supported them,[5] and they were defeated in the nation-wide poll by about 400,000 votes.[6]

The most significant amendment thus far adopted was approved in 1928. It was passed to ratify the Financial Agreement of 1927 concluded between representatives of the Commonwealth and state governments. In 1923 an experimental Australian Loan Council had been established to control the flotation of loans by the various governments. Experience with this experimental council had been satisfactory and it was consolidated by Commonwealth and state legislation in 1927. But in order to make binding the arrangements for its operation and to extend the scope of these operations, an amendment to Section 105 of the constitution was necessary. In 1927 state and national governments agreed on the form for this amendment, and after lengthy debates in the several legislatures it was formally proposed by the federal parliament. There was general agreement that the measure was necessary and, since its form had been agreed upon by the state governments as well as by the Commonwealth Government, there was almost no opposition to the proposal in either House. In the Senate only two members opposed the bill[7] and in the House it was passed without objection, no roll call being taken.[8]

The bill was probably not fully understood by the electorate, since it was a rather complicated financial measure; but for several years the experimental council had been in operation

[1] *Parliamentary Debates*, 1926, p. 2945. [2] Ibid., p. 3534.

[3] Loc. cit. The vote was 28 to 8.

[4] Ibid., p. 3111. The vote was 39 to 19 with 10 pairs.

[5] New South Wales had voted in favour of the proposals in both 1913 and 1919.

[6] 1,247,088 for the omnibus bill against 1,619,655; 1,195,502 for the essential services bill against 1,597,793. Royal Commission on the Constitution, *Report*, 1929, pp. 233–4.

[7] *Parliamentary Debates*, 1st sess., 1927–8, p. 6732.

[8] Ibid., p. 6721.

without apparent evil results. Moreover, since the proposal was supported by the state governments, by the Opposition party, and by most of the press, it succeeded in the referendum by large majorities in every state and in the Commonwealth as a whole.[1] Thus after eighteen years and four referenda on twelve proposals the people of Australia accepted another amendment to their constitution. But the importance of this one successful amendment overbalanced many of those that were defeated.

The new amendment became Section 105A of the constitution. It empowered the Commonwealth to enter into such agreements as that of 1927 'with respect to the public debts of the states'; it enabled the Commonwealth Parliament to make laws carrying out any such agreements and in effect empowered it to coerce any state failing in its obligations under the agreement; and it provided that these provisions should be valid notwithstanding anything else in the constitution. The amendment constituted the legal and constitutional ratification of the financial agreement and it validated the Loan Council, which was now made a permanent part of the Australian federal structure.[2] The Council has control over all state and federal borrowing and serves to prevent competition between the several governments in the flotation of loans. At the same time the Commonwealth took over all outstanding state debts and made provisions for their servicing and future management. On the Council each state has one vote while the Commonwealth has two votes and a casting vote, so that the latter's influence is great. If it can secure the support of two states it can control the Council's actions.[3]

But the 1928 amendment by no means satisfied those who desired greater economic controls in the hands of the Common-

[1] The total vote in the referendum was 2,237,391 to 773,852. The totals in each state may be found in the *Official Year Book of the Commonwealth of Australia*, No. 22, 1929, p. 68. This publication is hereafter cited as *Year Book*.

[2] Financial Agreement Validation Act (1929).

[3] Detailed discussion of the Council's origin and work may be found in Kenneth O. Warner, *Problems of Australian Federalism*, Seattle, 1933, chap. ix. See also the articles by R. C. Mills and Norman Cowper in Garnet V. Portus, ed. *Studies in the Australian Constitution*, Australian Institute of Political Science, Sydney, 1933, pp. 76–147. For a discussion of the Council as a solution to one of the problems of federalism see K. C. Wheare, *Federal Government*, 3rd edn., Oxford, 1953, pp. 103 f.

wealth Government. The question was raised again in 1937 when two more proposals were placed before the voters. One of these sought to confer upon the central government the power to control marketing; the other would have given it increased controls over aviation. Both were defeated in the referenda. The marketing proposal failed in every state and received only 1,259,808 votes compared with 2,214,388 votes against it.[1] The aviation proposal, however, received a majority of the total votes cast, 1,924,946 against 1,669,062, but received majorities in only two states, Victoria and Queensland.[2] This was the first instance in which a measure had received a majority of the total votes but failed of adoption because of the 'federal' requirement that four states approve it. Two other such instances have subsequently appeared, however, in 1946.

During the war the Labour Government again took steps to increase the powers of the Commonwealth, this time as a means of carrying out Australia's obligations as a partner in the United Nations, which had pledged themselves to internal reconstruction with a view to implementing the 'four freedoms' declaration of the Atlantic Charter. Late in 1942 Dr. H. V. Evatt introduced in the House of Representatives a proposal to amend the constitution by giving the central government full powers to make laws putting into effect the war aims and objects of Australia as one of the United Nations, 'including the attainment of economic security and social justice in the postwar world, and for the purpose of postwar reconstruction'.[3] The move caused instant difficulties among the states, not only because of its boldness but because it would require a referendum during a period when thousands of Australian soldiers were out of the country on war service. The Government invited discussion and criticism of the proposal and received it in full measure. A conference was called at Canberra at which were represented members of both Government and Opposition in each state as well as in the Commonwealth. The conference met in November and December of 1942 and agreed on a different method of providing

[1] *Year Book*, No. 30, 1937, p. 68. [2] Loc. cit.

[3] Quoted by K. H. Bailey in C. Hartley Grattan, ed. *Australia*, Berkeley, Calif., 1947, p. 102.

the federal government with power to carry out plans for postwar reconstruction.[1]

A compromise was reached whereby the Commonwealth Government gave up its plans for a war-time referendum in favour of a proposal to have the states refer to the Commonwealth, under the provisions of Section 51 (xxxvii), power to make laws on certain specified subjects. The reference was to be for a period of five years beginning with the cessation of hostilities; it was to provide the Commonwealth with powers during the reconstruction period roughly comparable to those that it had been exercising during the war. The plan gave the Commonwealth control over employment and unemployment, marketing, trusts and monopolies, prices, production, air transport, a health programme, and family allowances.[2] But although all parties agreed to the scheme and a draft bill for use in the states was drawn up, the plan came to nothing. Before the national government could assume the powers concerned, it was necessary that they be referred to the Commonwealth Parliament by the legislatures of the states. And despite the tentative agreement by the state delegates at the conference, the legislatures refused to sanction the arrangement. New South Wales and Queensland passed the bill in the desired form; Victoria passed it with the condition that the reference should be effective only if it were passed in similar form in all other states; South Australia passed it but with some omissions and with crippling amendments to the matters to be referred; Tasmania refused to pass it at all.

Faced with the refusal of the states to carry out the reference plan, the Labour Government had no alternative to dropping it completely but to submit the measure to a general constitutional referendum. The bill for the alteration was very similar to the draft bill that had been defeated. It granted fourteen specified powers to the Commonwealth Parliament for a period of five years after the war to enable it to carry out the tasks of reconstruction and the transition from war to peace.[3]

[1] Australia, *Convention of the Representatives of the Commonwealth and State Parliaments to Consider the Reference of Powers by the States to the Parliament of the Commonwealth*, Canberra, 1942.

[2] The text of the draft bill is given in *Year Book*, No. 35, 1942–3, pp. 62–64.

[3] Two excellent discussions of the problem may be found in the following

It was by far the most comprehensive grant of power to the central government that the people of Australia had ever been asked to ratify.

But it failed. Although it had carried the House by a large majority[1] it had scraped through the Senate with only two votes to spare.[2] This reluctance of the Senate foretold the attitude of the electorate, for the measure received only 1,963,400 votes while 2,305,418 were cast against it. Only South Australia and Western Australia approved it.[3] The Labour Government gave up in despair. There seems little doubt that the measure would have been most helpful in a difficult period, but the 1944 proposal was too comprehensive; it tried to secure everything at once. In effect it would have transferred so many items to the control of the Commonwealth that it would have radically changed the structure of Australian federalism, even though the transfer of powers was to be temporary. Given the history of previous amendments it is not surprising that the proposal failed to pass.

Another effort was made in 1946, when three more proposals were submitted to the people. These were designed to confer upon the Commonwealth the power to regulate the organized marketing of primary products, the terms and conditions of industrial employment (but not so as to authorize any form of industrial conscription) and to provide for such social services as maternity benefits, widows' pensions, medical and dental care, unemployment and hospital benefits, and family allowances. The three proposals passed the two Houses without difficulty, that on social services being practically unopposed, since the Opposition had lent its support to it.[4] In the referendum, however, the proposals did not fare so well. That on social services, supported by the Opposition, was accepted in all states, with a total popular vote of 2,297,934 to 1,927,148.[5]

articles: H. V. Evatt, 'Reconstruction and the Constitution', in D. A. S. Campbell, ed. *Post-War Reconstruction in Australia,* Australian Institute of Political Science, Sydney, 1944; and P. C. Spender, 'The Constitutional Alteration (Post-War Reconstruction and Democratic Rights) Bill, 1944', in *Constitutional Revision in Australia,* Australian Institute of Political Science, Sydney, 1944.

[1] The vote was 44 to 18. *Parliamentary Debates,* 1944, 1st sess., p. 1432.

[2] Ibid., p. 1904.

[3] *Year Book,* No. 36, 1944–5, p. 61.

[4] *Parliamentary Debates,* 1945–6, 3rd sess.; for the House see pp. 1217–18, 1230, 1231. For the Senate see pp. 1515, 1535–6, 1542.

[5] *Year Book,* No. 37, 1946–7, p. 65.

The proposals regarding the marketing of primary products and the control of industrial employment, though they received a majority of the total vote, were accepted in only three states, New South Wales, Victoria, and Western Australia.[1]

Another attempt to change the constitution occurred in May 1948. The Labour Government, commanding large majorities in both Houses, passed a bill conferring upon the Commonwealth the power to regulate rents and prices.[2] But in the referendum that followed the measure was decisively defeated by a vote of 2,618,183 to 1,793,712.[3] Not a single state returned a favourable majority.

The most recent attempt to change the constitution took place in 1951 as a result of apprehensions concerning the internal activities of the Communists. The Menzies Coalition Government sought in 1950 to enact legislation dissolving the Australian Communist Party and confiscating its property.[4] The Act was easily passed but was immediately challenged in the High Court, which in March 1951 declared it to be *ultra vires* the Commonwealth Parliament.[5] Parliament then submitted to referendum[6] a proposal to enlarge Commonwealth powers sufficiently to validate this and similar legislation. After a bitter and excited campaign during which Labour strongly opposed the measure, it was defeated at the polls in September 1951 by the close vote of 2,370,009 to 2,317,927. Only three states approved it.[7]

Thus out of twenty-four referenda only four have resulted in modifications of the constitution. Two of these, those of 1906 and 1910, have had relatively little effect. The 1928 amendment created a new financial arrangement that has enabled the Commonwealth to exercise an important influence

[1] Ibid. The total vote on the marketing proposal was 2,116,264 in favour and 2,068,171 opposed; on the industrial employment measure there were 2,060,275 votes in favour and 2,035,860 opposed.

[2] *Parliamentary Debates*, 1946–7, 1st sess., 3003 for the House and pp. 3170–1 for the Senate.

[3] *Year Book*, No. 37, 1946–7, p. 1247.

[4] Communist Party Dissolution Act, 1950.

[5] *Australian Communist Party* v. *Commonwealth* (1951), 83 C.L.R. 1.

[6] The votes may be found in *Parliamentary Debates*, 1951; for the House see p. 1437, for the Senate, p. 1515.

[7] Queensland, Tasmania, and Western Australia. *Year Book*, No. 39, 1953, p. 1342.

in state matters; the 1946 amendment on social services made a substantial enlargement of the area of Commonwealth functions and achieved a real shift in the distribution of powers.

### *Parliamentary Government and the Proposal of Amendments*

All amendments must be initiated in the Commonwealth Parliament; there is no provision for their initiation by the states as is found in the constitution of the United States, nor is it possible for amendments to originate in the mechanics of popular initiative, as is true in Switzerland. Most proposals have first been brought forward in the House of Representatives, though on a few occasions the Senate has taken the first step. Either, of course, satisfies the constitutional requirement.

The process achieves at the outset what Bryce and others have called 'rigidity' in the requirement that the two Houses must pass the proposal by absolute majorities. But this has not greatly hindered the amending process; most proposals that have failed of adoption in the Parliament have failed in both Houses, and even in those cases where one House has approved, the failure in the other House has not been the result of the requirement of an absolute majority.

A system of responsible parliamentary government like Australia's assures that the Ministry of the day will be able to control the policy decisions of at least the Lower House if not the Upper. To the extent that this holds true, the Government is able to control the House attitude towards questions of constitutional amendment. Most such proposals are therefore introduced by the Government and are supported by the Government party, so that very few fail to pass the first hurdle of parliamentary approval. But the Ministry is not always able to control the House and still less the Senate; moreover, private members' bills are not restricted in Australia as they are in Britain. So there are several ways for bills to get before one of the Houses without the support of the Government; but unless the Government adopts them as part of its own programme, they have little chance of final passage. Up to 1949 the total number of moves to amend the constitution in the two Houses had amounted to seventy-seven, of which only twenty-three had been submitted to referendum. Professor Parker's study has shown that all of these twenty-three were government bills and all but one had been initiated in the House of Representatives.[1] Of the entire 77 moves, 16 were motions that lapsed or were defeated; 38 reached the stage of bills, but then lapsed, were defeated, or for some other reason were not submitted to referendum;[2] 23 had been submitted to referendum and of these only four had been accepted by the necessary majorities in the states and in the nation. Of the 73 unsuccessful attempts (including abortive motions that were never introduced), 40 were initiated by private members and the remainder by governments. Although only one of the bills that were finally submitted to referendum originated in the Senate, 29 of the 50 attempts that did not reach the referendum stage were initiated in that chamber.[3] These figures offer a great contrast to those of the United States, where since 1789 there have been introduced in the Congress something in excess of four thousand measures that have had for their purpose the proposal of an amendment of the constitution. The difference may largely be attributed to the control exercised by the Government over legislative activity in Australia and the lack of such control in America.

### *The Senate as the Protector of the States*

When the constitution was adopted it was hoped and expected that the Senate would serve as the agency within the structure of the national government that would protect the rights of the states. But this has not been realized. The equality of state representation in the Upper House provides a mathematical overweighting for the smaller states, but this has not

[1] R. S. Parker, 'The People and the Constitution', in *Federalism in Australia*, Australian Institute of Political Science, Melbourne, 1949, p. 171. This article is the latest and most complete study of the constitutional referenda in Australia. Some exceptionally valuable tables are included in an appendix. These and the following figures are of 1949 and do not take account of the 1951 referendum.

[2] In 1915, for example, 'it was proposed to alter the constitution in regard to the legislative powers of the Commonwealth Parliament somewhat differently from the proposals submitted in 1911 and 1913, but the writs issued for the submission of these modified proposals were . . . revoked before any vote was taken', Royal Commission on the Constitution, *Report*, 1929, p. 233. The referenda were abandoned 'by an arrangement with the State Premiers'. Ibid., p. 231.

[3] Parker, op. cit., p. 171.

served the intended purpose. Senators, as well as Representatives, are elected as members of the national political parties and the success of their individual campaigns for election depends very largely on the support accorded them by those parties. It would be a very difficult task for a prospective senator, facing the difficulties of a state-wide candidacy and campaign, to win out alone against an opponent who had the support of a political party machine. Only loyal party men have any real chance of winning Senate elections.[1]

This dependence on party is reflected in the manner in which the members of the Senate cast their votes. Despite the fact that they represent their states, and despite the fact that all states are equally represented, these votes are cast not along state lines but along party lines. This is nowhere better shown than in the record of votes cast on the various proposals for constitutional amendments. Here, if anywhere, where the issue has been on so many occasions drawn clearly between the expanding powers of the national government and the dwindling powers of the states, the state foundation of the Senate should appear. But it does not. Even in this arena, where states' rights struggle against centralization, there is almost no tendency for the votes of senators to be determined on state lines. They vote for the party programme, including the party's announced stand on the particular issue of constitutional revision, almost never for the maintenance of the positions of their respective states.

A few figures will bear out this contention. In the voting in the Senate in 1948 on the proposal to grant to the Commonwealth power to control rents and prices the vote on the proposal was 28 to 3.[2] At this time the Labour Government had in the Senate a majority of exactly 33 to 3. The three votes against the proposal were all cast by the three members of the Opposition. Despite this huge majority in the Senate, the proposal failed in the subsequent referendum in every state. Queensland, from which the three opposing senators came, turned down the proposal by 422,000 to 187,000.[3]

On the industrial employment proposal in 1946 the votes

[1] See Alexander Brady, *Democracy in the Dominions*, 2nd edn., Toronto, 1952, pp. 183 ff.

[2] *Parliamentary Debates*, 1946–7, pp. 3170–1.

[3] *Commonwealth of Australia Gazette*, No. 104, 8 July 1948, p. 2590.

for and against the measure by the state representatives in the Senate were as follows:[1]

| | |
|---|---|
| New South Wales | 5 to 0 |
| Queensland | 3 to 2 |
| Tasmania | 2 to 3 |
| Victoria | 2 to 4 |
| South Australia | 3 to 3 |
| Western Australia | 4 to 2 |

Only rarely does a group of senators from one state return a unanimous vote; only rarely do a state's senators show any indication at all that they are voting together because they are from the same state. In 1913 six proposals were adopted by the two Houses all tending to increase the powers of the central government. On these proposals the delegations in the Senate voted as follows:[2]

| | |
|---|---|
| New South Wales | 3 to 3 |
| Queensland | 3 to 3 |
| Tasmania | 3 to 2 |
| Victoria | 3 to 2 (on one measure 3 to 0) |
| South Australia | 3 to 2 (on one measure 3 to 3) |
| Western Australia | 5 to 0 |

Only one state here showed any coherence, the rest being divided almost evenly between those in favour of and those opposed to the proposals. Other examples manifest the same lack of coherence. Only among the senators of Western Australia does there seem to be any regular tendency to stick together, and even here the influence of party in such votes cannot wholly be written off.

Yet if one views the groups of senators as representative delegations of the states, the record of the votes shows an interesting feature. Conceding that a state delegation's vote may be split, the votes of the Senate delegations as whole entities are more nearly in agreement with the results of the referenda in the several states than are the votes of the members of the House of Representatives considered in the same way. An examination of the table on page 132 shows that when the state representatives in the two Houses disagree the Senate delegations have concurred with the results of the respective state referenda on twenty-seven occasions as compared

[1] *Parliamentary Debates*, 1945–6, p. 1542.

[2] Ibid., 1912, pp. 7325, 7326, 7341, 7348, 7365.

*Table showing the correlation between votes of State Representatives in the two Houses of Parliament and those in the State Electorates in Constitutional Referenda*

| | *New South Wales* | | | *Victoria* | | | *Queensland* | | | *South Australia* | | | *Western Australia* | | | *Tasmania* | | |
|---|---|---|---|---|---|---|---|---|---|---|---|---|---|---|---|---|---|---|
| | *H* | *S* | *R* | *H* | *S* | *R* | *H* | *S* | *R* | *H* | *S* | *R* | *H* | *S* | *R* | *H* | *S* | *R* |
| 1951 . . . . . | yes | yes | no | yes | yes | no | yes | yes | yes | no | yes | no | yes | yes | yes | yes | yes | yes |
| 1948 . . . . . | yes | yes | no | no | yes | no | yes | yes | no | yes | yes | no | yes | yes | no | yes | yes | no |
| 1946 | | | | | | | | | | | | | | | | | | |
| Industrial Employment | yes | yes | yes | no | no | yes | yes | yes | no | yes | no | no | yes | yes | yes | yes | no | no |
| Social Services . | yes | yes | yes | yes | yes | yes | yes | yes | yes | yes | yes | yes | yes | yes | yes | yes | yes | yes |
| Organized Marketing | yes | yes | yes | yes | no | yes | yes | yes | no | yes | no | no | yes | yes | yes | yes | no | no |
| 1944 . . . . . | yes | yes | no | no | no | no | yes | yes | no | yes | no | yes | yes | yes | yes | yes | no | no |
| 1937 | | | | | | | | | | | | | | | | | | |
| Aviation . . | yes | yes | no | yes | yes | yes | yes | yes | yes | yes | yes | no | yes | yes | no | yes | yes | no |
| Marketing . . | yes | yes | no | yes | yes | no | yes | yes | no | yes | yes | no | yes | yes | no | no | no | no |
| 1928 . . . . . | yes | yes | yes | yes | yes | yes | yes | yes | yes | yes | yes | yes | yes | yes | yes | yes | yes | yes |
| 1926 | | | | | | | | | | | | | | | | | | |
| Essential Services . | yes | yes | yes | yes | yes | no | yes | yes | yes | yes | yes | no | no | yes | no | yes | yes | no |
| Industrial Disputes . | yes | yes | yes | yes | yes | no | yes | yes | yes | yes | yes | no | yes | yes | no | yes | yes | no |
| 1919 | | | | | | | | | | | | | | | | | | |
| Monopolies . . | yes | yes | no | yes | yes | yes | yes | yes | yes | yes | yes | no | yes | yes | yes | yes | yes | no |
| Industrial Disputes . | yes | yes | no | yes | yes | yes | yes | yes | yes | yes | yes | no | yes | yes | yes | yes | yes | no |
| 1913 | | | | | | | | | | | | | | | | | | |
| Commerce . . | yes | no | no | yes | yes | no | yes | no | yes | no | no | yes | no | yes | yes | yes | yes | no |
| Railway Disputes . | yes | no | no | yes | yes | no | yes | no | yes | no | no | yes | yes | yes | yes | yes | yes | no |
| Trusts . . . | yes | no | no | yes | yes | no | yes | no | yes | no | yes | yes | yes | yes | yes | yes | yes | no |
| Industry. . . | yes | no | no | yes | yes | no | yes | no | yes | no | yes | yes | no | yes | yes | yes | yes | no |
| Corporations . . | yes | no | no | yes | yes | no | yes | no | yes | no | yes | yes | no | yes | yes | yes | yes | no |
| Monopolies . . | yes | no | no | yes | yes | no | yes | no | yes | no | yes | yes | no | yes | yes | yes | yes | no |
| 1911 | | | | | | | | | | | | | | | | | | |
| Commerce . . | yes | no | no | yes | yes | no | yes | no | no | yes | yes | no | no | yes | yes | yes | no | no |
| Monopolies . . | yes | no | no | yes | yes | no | yes | no | no | yes | yes | no | no | yes | yes | yes | yes | no |
| 1910 | | | | | | | | | | | | | | | | | | |
| Finance . . . | no | yes | yes | yes | yes | yes | yes | no | yes | no | no | yes | yes | no | yes | yes | yes | yes |
| State Debts . . | yes | yes | no | yes | yes | yes | yes | yes | yes | yes | yes | yes | yes | yes | yes | yes | yes | yes |
| 1906 . . . . . | yes | no | yes | yes | yes | yes | yes | yes | yes | yes | yes | yes | yes | yes | yes | yes | yes | yes |

H = The total vote of the representatives of a state in the House of Representatives. S = The total vote of the Senators from a state. R = The state's vote in the popular referendum. Tie votes within a state's delegation are counted as negative. Source: *Parliamentary Debates*.

with only fourteen times in the House. Party allegiance may split the delegation and cause the group vote to be close, but it is difficult to account for the fact that there is a greater correlation between Senate and referenda than there is between House and referenda, unless one attributes it to some kind of kinship of the former body with state jealousies and desires. The worth of this comparison is suspect, of course, because neither House shows a very great correlation; the closer one is the Senate, but that body concurred with the referendum results only 75 times out of a possible 144. But it must be remembered that these figures take into account only those measures passed by the Parliament, and since we begin with the knowledge that most referenda have failed, no very close correlation can be expected in either House. The difference therefore does seem to possess some significance.

It is unusual to find all three elements—the Senate group, the House group, and the people of the state—voting the same way on a question. The table shows that this occurs most frequently in Western Australia, the state that has been the most willing of all to amend the constitution; but even here this three-way concurrence has occurred only twelve times out of twenty-four. In South Australia there have been only four such instances. The discrepancy among these three agencies, all of which are supposed to represent the same body of opinion at approximately the same time, suggests at the very least that the devices of representative government have not yet been perfected. Both the House and the Senate have been inadequate in representing the wishes of the electorate on issues of constitutional change.

### *Disagreements Between the Two Houses*

Although the Senate is controlled by political parties and although it is directly elected by the same suffrage as the House of Representatives, it is elected for longer terms and at different times. There is therefore no assurance that the two bodies will reflect the same opinions or that the same party will possess a majority in both Houses at the same time. There have been several occasions when the two Houses have been controlled by opposing political parties. The result is that the two sometimes fail to agree on legislative proposals, a predicament that may ultimately be resolved by recourse to the complicated procedure of double dissolution and a joint session, as provided in Section 57 of the constitution. This procedure has been utilized but twice.

The same kind of disagreement may arise on amendment proposals. In 1914 the Senate initiated an amendment which failed to obtain the support of the House,[1] and on at least three occasions the Senate has refused to concur in a House proposal. In general, however, the two Houses have not differed much. Most of the time they are controlled by the same party and there is always a tendency in the Upper House of a parliamentary legislature to give way to the Lower. The requirement that both Houses must agree to proposed amendments has not been an important deterrent to their adoption.[2]

In the event of serious disagreement between the two bodies, however, the constitution provides a way out. This is not the same procedure as that provided in Section 57 for ordinary legislation. The amending clause itself (Section 128) provides that the Governor-General may submit a proposal to referendum, despite its lack of support in both Houses, if one House passes it twice.[3] He is not required to submit it, but he *may* submit it. The Royal Commission on the Constitution pointed out that in exercising this apparent discretion the Governor-General must act on advice.[4] This suggests the further observation that the clause might mean more in practice than the words seem to indicate. For the advice upon which he would depend would be that of the Cabinet, which is responsible only to the House of Representatives, not the Senate. In the event of a disagreement between the two Houses in which this section were called into play, the Governor-General would almost necessarily follow the course of action taken by the body to which the Ministry is responsible. Thus the House could propose an amendment and, without the concurrence of the

[1] Royal Commission on the Constitution, *Report*, 1929, p. 231.

[2] There is at least one instance in Canada where the Senate's refusal has blocked action on an amendment. See Gérin-Lajoie, *Constitutional Amendment in Canada*, p. 149 and note 2. For the corresponding problem in the United States see chapter 5 below.

[3] The complete provision may be found in Appendix A, below.

[4] *Report*, p. 228.

Senate, succeed in getting it put to a referendum, but the Senate could not do so, for if the House refused to concur the Ministry would not advise the Governor-General to submit the question to the people. It would seem possible therefore for the House to push an amendment through without the consent of the Senate, but not possible for the Senate to do so without the consent of the House. The House's consent is always necessary; not so the Senate's. The question is largely academic, though not without importance; the two Houses have seldom disagreed in this fashion. The procedure has never been employed.

## *Referenda*[1]

> . . . Not less than two nor more than six months after its passage through both Houses the proposed law shall be submitted in each State to the electors qualified to vote for the election of members of the House of Representatives. . . . And if in a majority of the States a majority of the electors voting approve the proposed law, and if a majority of all the electors voting also approve the proposed law, it shall be presented to the Governor-General for the Queen's assent.[2]

In the half-century since federation a total of twenty-four proposals have been submitted to referendum on twelve different occasions. Of these only four have received the necessary majorities in the nation as a whole and in four states. It is in the referendum, not in the Parliament, that the rigidity of the Australian amending process is found.

The framers of the Australian constitution made extensive studies of the provisions of other constitutions on the procedure of amendment, especially those in other federal constitutions. They hoped to avoid the apparent difficulties of the American procedure and were determined to devise a system that would

[1] Despite a strong adherence to democratic doctrines, the Australians have never employed the device of the popular initiative and have used the referendum but very little, except in voting on constitutional amendments. In 1916 and 1917 there were national referenda on the question of drafting troops for overseas service, but aside from these instances the major use of the referendum has been in determining the popular attitude towards the sale of liquor. There is no provision in the national constitution for either device, except in Section 128. The present discussion pertains only to the use of the referenda in connexion with the amendment of the constitution.

[2] Constitution, Section 128.

be simpler and more flexible.[1] This they believed they had accomplished. In 1901 Quick and Garran observed that

> . . . the facilities for altering the Constitution of the Commonwealth are much greater than those for altering the American Constitution. In regard to origination, an amendment may be proposed by an absolute majority of one House of the Federal Parliament, whilst a two-thirds majority in each branch of the American Congress is required. In regard to ratification, whilst in the Commonwealth a majority of the people voting and a majority of States is sufficient to carry an amendment, in America it must be passed by the legislatures or by the conventions in three-fourths of the several States.[2]

Harrison Moore in his great constitutional study made a similar error:

> The great facility with which the Australian Constitution may be altered, makes it probable, that its development will be guided, less by judicial interpretation, and more by formal amendment, than the development of the Constitution of the United States.[3]

It is strange that these hopes and expectations have gone wrong, that a device that was expected to permit easy modification of the constitution has produced very nearly the opposite result.

Many explanations have been offered for the apparent rigidity of this procedure and for the continued failure of amendments in the popular referenda.[4] The explanation is necessarily complicated. In the first place the questions sub-

[1] See Brady, *Democracy in the Dominions*, 2nd edn., 1952, pp. 172 ff. In 1900 the U.S. constitution, though containing fifteen amendments, exacted from every observer a comment about its extreme rigidity. The first ten amendments had been adopted immediately after the initial ratification; the next two followed shortly thereafter; but in the ensuing century only three more were added and these were the result of a civil war. There had been no more amendments. For an especially bitter contemporary American complaint see J. Allen Smith, *The Spirit of American Government*, New York, 1907, pp. 46, 57.

[2] Quick and Garran, op. cit., p. 995.

[3] W. Harrison Moore, *The Constitution of the Commonwealth of Australia*, 1901, p. 332.

[4] On this point see especially the article by R. S. Parker in *Federalism in Australia*, cited above; also Gordon Greenwood, 'The Case for Extended Commonwealth Powers', in the same volume; Alexander Brady, *Democracy in the Dominions*, 2nd edn., pp. 173 ff.; K. H. Bailey, 'The Constitution and Its Problems', in C. Hartley Grattan, ed. *Australia*, Berkeley, Calif., 1947, pp. 100 ff.; P. H. Partridge, 'The Politics of Federalism', in G. Sawer, ed. *Federalism; An Australian Jubilee Study*, Melbourne, 1952, pp. 184 ff.

mitted to the electorate are not very simple. Many consist of several paragraphs of complicated legal terminology that the ordinary voter finds difficult to understand. All he really knows is that the Government down in Canberra is trying again to increase the power of the central government at the expense of the states. The complex questions of constitutional law do not readily lend themselves to a yes-or-no decision. The voter, being in considerable doubt of the result of the change, is inclined to vote no. When one is doubtful of the worth of a change it is very easy to decide against it. That ignorance of the issues involved is one of the reasons for the reluctance of the electorate to approve constitutional changes seems clear. It has been maintained by some[1] that adequate steps are not taken by the Government to educate the public on the complex issues involved. 'Adequacy' is, of course, a term relative in meaning to what one thinks is necessary, but it is true that a conscious effort is made to present the issues to the public. Each proposal is debated at length in the Parliament and the newspapers carry accounts of these discussions as well as other expressions of opinion on the questions. Before the referendum the Government publishes the arguments both for and against the proposals, distributes them during the campaign, and posts them at the polling places. Even so it can hardly be doubted that a better understanding on the part of the voters would be highly desirable.

Secondly, the people have been reluctant to approve changes in the constitution because they are slow to understand the embarrassments that arise from its outmoded parts. Men in the national government trying to devise legislation and conduct administration come up hard against the disabilities of the central government, particularly in the sphere of the division of powers between the centre and the parts. Seeing the difficulty clearly, they move to solve it by the only means immediately open to them, that of amending the constitution. But the voter has no such acute awareness of the problem and is likely to look with apprehension at any disturbance of the old allocations.

Thirdly, there is a very real antagonism to the increase of

[1] See the remarks of Mr. Menzies in *Parliamentary Debates*, 1938, pp. 1820 f.

federal power. Australia is a huge country and its states are very much larger that the states of America. To most people the Government at Canberra seems a very remote thing that is so far removed from the lives of the citizens that they dislike the idea of placing in its hands the control over their welfare. The preservation of the position of the states is frequently equated with the preservation of liberty. And as a result voters have frequently refused to transfer to that central government powers that have long been lodged in (though not necessarily exercised by) the states.

Even so, the evidence is not complete. It is very easy to conclude from the results of the referenda that the Australian people wish to preserve the states and do not wish to increase the powers of the central government. But one cannot be certain that the evidence supports so broad a conclusion. Many factors determine the way a man votes, in referenda as in elections; several are, indeed, suggested in this section. Certainly many voters have voted against increasing Commonwealth powers for reasons other than a general distrust of centralization or a desire to maintain the states. Results of some of the public opinion polls in Australia in recent years have, indeed, shown a considerable body of opinion in favour of abolishing the states altogether in favour of a unitary form of government. Complete unification seems to have more supporters than increased Commonwealth powers. In December 1943, for example, a poll reported by Professor Greenwood[1] produced these highly interesting results:

| | *Men* (%) | *Women* (%) |
|---|---|---|
| No change in federal system | 17 | 20 |
| Increase Federal powers | 16 | 14 |
| Complete unification | 61 | 41 |
| No opinion | 6 | 25 |

Similarly, polls in November 1942 and April 1944 displayed majorities respectively of 60 per cent. and 56 per cent. in favour of abolishing the states and creating a central unitary government for the entire Commonwealth.[2] The discrepancy between

[1] Greenwood, op. cit., p. 62.

[2] Parker op. cit., Appendix, p. 189. The 1944 poll is especially interesting in that it combined the question of abolishing the states with an indication of how the voter would vote in the 1944 reconstruction referendum: (*see opposite*)

the results of these polls and the results of the repeated constitutional referenda is not easy to explain. One might question the validity of the polls but for the fact that compulsory voting in Australia has enabled the Gallup organization there to establish a record of very nearly 100 per cent. accuracy. Perhaps Professor Greenwood comes close to the truth in his suggested explanation:

> It would seem that the electors believe that so long as a Federal system is in existence the States should be given a real function, but this does not necessarily imply a judgment in favour of retention of the States.[1]

But in the face of these discrepancies and the difficulties of interpreting them, the point is still worth making that a substantial group of Australian voters does oppose on principle the extension of Commonwealth powers; certainly this must be included as one of the important reasons for the repeated failure of efforts to increase those powers by constitutional alteration.

Finally, it is very nearly impossible for the voter to view these constitutional questions in the abstract. It is hard for him to weigh his decision in terms merely of a change in the constitutional structure without permitting his opinion to be coloured by considerations of persons and parties. Instead of

Question: 'Which of these three statements comes nearest to the form of government you would like Australia to have?' (April 1944)

| | *Choice of statement* | *Voting intentions at 1944 referendum* | | |
|---|---|---|---|---|
| | | *Yes* | *No* | *Undecided* |
| | % | % | % | % |
| 1. The Commonwealth the only government, with all powers, some of which would be delegated to regional or state councils | 56 | 37 | 13 | 6 = 56 |
| 2. The present Federal system, but with certain powers transferred from the States to Commonwealth | 17 | 8 | 6 | 3 = 17 |
| 3. The present Federal system, but the Commonwealth having no more power than before the war | 21 | 2 | 16 | 3 = 21 |
| 4. No opinion | 6 | 1 | 2 | 3 = 6 |

[1] Op. cit., p. 62.

asking himself, 'Is it good that the central government should have this power?' he asks himself, 'Do I want the *present* government to exercise this power?' The two are vastly different things. As Professor Bailey suggests,[1] an employer is unlikely to be willing to surrender the power to control prices to a Labour Government, while a working man may be equally reluctant to see such a power in the hands of a non-Labour government. Party considerations inevitably enter into the voters' deliberations on such questions. Abstract problems of constitutional power become confused with concrete questions of legislative policy, and a voter who might in some circumstances favour the adoption of a given measure will oppose it because of the framework in which it is proposed.

There is a tendency to vote in a referendum along lines dictated by one's party allegiance. Very few questions of constitutional change have been divorced from party considerations.[2] It is very difficult for any party, regardless of its general policy, to avoid trying to make capital out of such important public questions as constitutional amendments. The voters' attitudes are often coloured (though not wholly determined) by the stand taken by the party they support. Many of the constitutional referenda have been held on the same day as a general election.[3] The parties in their campaigns have discussed the questions involved and have urged the adoption or the rejection of the referendum proposals; the voter while he walks to the poll is presumably thinking not only about the referendum but also about the election. In many cases he is likely to vote a straight ticket—on the referendum as well as on the candidates.

Certain evidence from the referenda themselves points to this conclusion. In several instances a party in power has taken a referendum proposal to the people on the day of a general election and has found that not only has its amendment been defeated but that the party itself has been turned out of office. This happened to Labour in 1913 when the party submitted to the electorate a list of six different proposals for increases

[1] Op. cit., p. 101.

[2] Professor Parker concludes that 'all referendum compaigns except three (1906, 1928, and 1937) have been fought primarily on a party basis'. Op. cit., p. 147.

[3] On six out of twelve occasions.

in the Commonwealth's powers. All six proposals were repudiated and Labour lost its majority in the House of Representatives (though not in the Senate) to Cook and the Liberals.

An even more interesting case is that of the election of 1910. The embryonic Liberal Party led by Alfred Deakin went to the polls urging, among other things, the adoption of two amendments to the constitution, one altering the so-called 'Braddon clause' (Section 87) and one permitting the Commonwealth to take over state debts. At the election the Liberals were replaced by the Labour Party, but the amendment regarding state debts (which Labour had supported) was approved by a majority of the electorate and by majorities in five of the states. One of the Liberals' amendments, which the Opposition approved, was accepted but the Liberals themselves were defeated along with their other amendment.

But it is equally clear that party considerations are not the only influence. On several occasions a party has been retained in power at a general election at which the alteration proposals it has advocated have been repudiated by the electorate. In 1919, for example, Hughes and the Nationalists were retained in office, but the amendments they had proposed, empowering the Government to control industrial disputes and monopolies, were turned down by the very electorate that re-elected them. Similarly, in 1937 the Lyons Government (United Australia Party) proposed to increase the Commonwealth Parliament's powers over aviation and certain kinds of marketing processes. In the election of that year the two proposals were defeated, one by a very large majority in every state, but the Lyons Government was retained in power. It seems clear that although party considerations do contribute a great deal to the determination of questions in the referenda, they are by no means the only influence.

One other instance of the correlation between party programmes and the success of proposed amendments may be recorded. In 1946 the Labour Government took to the polls three amendment proposals, one concerned with industrial employment, another with the organized marketing of primary products, and the third empowering the Commonwealth to provide certain social services. The Opposition supported the proposal on social services, but opposed the other two.[1] In the election the Labour Party was retained in power, but of its three amendment proposals only the one on social services was accepted by the people—the one supported by the Opposition.[2] In this election Labour lost 4 seats in the House but gained 12 seats in the Senate, where the Liberal-Country alliance dropped from 15 seats to 3. Now a Senate election is more nearly akin to a referendum than is an election to the House, for the Senate election, like the referendum, is conducted in a state-wide constituency and is not broken down into smaller districts as with the House. In this election all the states voted pro-Labour in the Senate election, since Labour lost no seats and gained 12—from 21 to 33. But not all the states voted pro-Labour in the referendum, for two of the three proposals (all three of which were urged by Labour) were defeated—not because they lacked a popular majority but because they lacked majorities in four states. This suggests (but by no means proves) that the *electors* do *not* vote on party lines in referenda. Many of the Labour voters disapproved the Labour amendments. On the other hand, it has been shown that *members of parliament*, including Senators, *do* vote on party lines on questions of constitutional amendment.

The evidence is not conclusive. It is clear that considerations of party loyalty do have a certain effect on the voters' attitude towards constitutional amendments, but it is also clear that this is not the only influence, nor can its importance be estimated with accuracy. Moreover, the extent of such influence seems to vary from time to time; at times the electorate seems almost to ignore the desires of the party leaders. About the best that can be said is that there is a large segment of the electorate that does not vote on party lines as far as amending the constitution is concerned, and that there seems to be another segment that does. The consistent refusal of the Australian people to amend their constitution is probably best explained by the reasons suggested at the beginning of this section.

[1] *Parliamentary Debates*, 1945–6, pp. 1217 ff. (House) and 1515 ff. (Senate).

[2] The two 1937 proposals were also supported by the Opposition—then the Labour Party; but both failed.

### *Role of the States in the Referenda*

The purpose of the requirement that majorities in a majority of the states must approve a measure before it is presented for the royal assent was to protect the smaller states from being overwhelmed by the larger, since the latter would have a greater representation in the House of Representatives and might be able to propose measures favouring themselves. This requirement has, indeed, prevented the passage of some amendments and has presumably, therefore, served its purpose. An examination of the table on page 144 will show that in three instances proposals received popular majorities over the country as a whole but failed to be adopted because they lacked approval in the necessary four states. Two of the measures proposed in 1946 failed for this reason, three states having voted negatively. Similarly, the aviation referendum in 1937 produced a favourable total majority but lacked majorities in four states. It is worth noting that South Australia and Tasmania were found in the negative column in each of these three instances. In 1937 the total favourable majority was achieved despite the opposition of New South Wales, the largest state; this was due to the considerable majorities returned in favour of the proposal in Victoria (675,481 to 362,112) and Queensland (310,352 to 191,251).[1]

The table shows also that there is a tendency for all proposals voted on at one time to meet the same fate, though 1910 and 1946 constitute exceptions to the rule. The rule, in fact, as stated is of little value, for an equally good one, induced from the same evidence, is that all proposals tend to be defeated. It is true none the less that when several proposals are voted on at the same time, the voter tends to vote the same way on all measures. In 1911, 1913, 1919, and 1926 multiple proposals were voted on and the states voted the same way on each one.[2]

The table on page 144 also demonstrates another fact about the way the states have acted in the referenda. Some states

[1] *Year Book*, No. 30, 1937, p. 68.

[2] 'On only one occasion (aviation and marketing in 1937) has there been a discrimination of more than 10 per cent. of the formal votes in every state between the separate questions asked at a "powers" referendum.' Parker, op. cit., p. 145.

*Table showing the results of Constitutional Referenda in the States and in the Nation*

| Referendum | | Results | | National majority | | State majorities | |
|---|---|---|---|---|---|---|---|
| | | Pass | Fail | Yes | No | Yes | No |
| 1951 | Control of Communism | | x | | x | 3 | 3 |
| 1948 | Rents and Prices | | x | | x | 0 | 6 |
| 1946 | Industrial Employment | | x | x | | 3 | 3 |
| | Organized Marketing | | x | x | | 3 | 3 |
| | Social Services | x | | x | | 6 | 0 |
| 1944 | Reconstruction | | x | | x | 2 | 4 |
| 1937 | Aviation | | x | x | | 2 | 4 |
| | Marketing | | x | | x | 0 | 6 |
| 1928 | State Debts | x | | x | | 6 | 0 |
| 1926 | Essential Services | | x | | x | 2 | 4 |
| | Industrial Disputes | | x | | x | 2 | 4 |
| 1919 | Monopolies | | x | | x | 3 | 3 |
| | Industrial Disputes | | x | | x | 3 | 3 |
| 1913 | Trade and Commerce | | x | | x | 3 | 3 |
| | Railway Disputes | | x | | x | 3 | 3 |
| | Trusts | | x | | x | 3 | 3 |
| | Industrial Matters | | x | | x | 3 | 3 |
| | Corporations | | x | | x | 3 | 3 |
| | Monopolies | | x | | x | 3 | 3 |
| 1911 | Commerce | | x | | x | 1 | 5 |
| | Monopolies | | x | | x | 1 | 5 |
| 1910 | Finance | | x | | x | 3 | 3 |
| | State Debts | x | | x | | 5 | 1 |
| 1906 | Senate Elections | x | | x | | 6 | 0 |

have been much more willing to approve changes in the constitution than have others, and the spread between those at the extremes is large. As measured by the referenda the state most willing to accept changes has been Western Australia; the one least willing has been Tasmania. The others fall at regular intervals between these two, as is seen in the table on page 145.

Western Australia's place at the head of the list is not easy to understand. The largest state in the Commonwealth, she has next to the smallest population;[1] her financial problems have always been great. Her tax resources have not been adequate to her needs and she has had to depend largely on help from the Commonwealth. Moreover, she has always been

| *State* | *Number of favourable referenda* | *Number of unfavourable referenda* |
|---|---|---|
| Western Australia | 19 | 5 |
| Queensland | 17 | 7 |
| South Australia | 12 | 12 |
| Victoria | 10 | 14 |
| New South Wales | 8 | 16 |
| Tasmania | 6 | 18 |

dissatisfied with her position in the union and has chafed under the tariff policy, which she believes has done her increasing harm to the benefit of other states. This dissatisfaction led her in the early 1930's to make an earnest effort to secede from the Commonwealth, an effort that was carried so far as to petition London to grant power of secession. Since she has been the most dissatisfied with the present arrangement, it might be expected that she would be the most anxious to change it. But at the same time, since she has been so dissatisfied with the federal system, it is rather surprising to find her so regularly voting to increase the powers of the federal government. It may be that this consistent record is the result of a feeling of desperation, a feeling that nearly any change would be for the better. Western Australia has been dissatisfied with her place in the federal system; she has therefore voted to change that system. But this is only a suggestion, and it doubtless is an over-simplification; the matter is difficult to explain.

On the other hand, Tasmania's consistent refusal to approve alterations proclaims her desire to maintain the position of the states against the growing power of the federal government. Her small size, both in area and in population, her lack of industry, her different history, and above all her geographical separation from the rest of the country, all contribute to her

[1] Tasmania has fewer people but a much denser population. Western Australia's density is only ½ per sq. mile. One of her electoral districts (Kalgoorlie) has an area of 910,000 sq. miles, nearly one-third of the total area of the country.

insistence on the prerogatives of statehood. The people of Tasmania have voted 'yes' in only six referenda. These include all of the four successful amendments, for three of which the states voted unanimous approval, while five states approved the fourth. Her fifth affirmative vote was for the finance amendment of 1910, which was calculated to increase the grants to the states; and her sixth was for the Communist control proposal in 1951. From the evidence of the referenda it may be concluded that Tasmania has been willing to increase the powers of the Commonwealth only when the demand for the change has been so great that virtually all the states have been willing to make it. If the first three efforts to amend the constitution are not included in the tabulation (by reason of the fact that they are the only ones not designed to increase Commonwealth powers) then the total of Tasmania's affirmative votes is reduced to three—for the state debts proposal of 1928, for the social services amendment of 1946, and for the 1951 Communist bill.

Two devices were provided in the constitution for the protection of the states in the amending process. One was the requirement of the consent of a majority of the states in the referendum. The other was the requirement of an absolute majority in the Senate. The first of these devices has been effective, but the second, as we have seen, has been rendered largely useless by the intrusion of partisan politics. The states have therefore sought another guarantee of their interests in the process.

This was provided by an Act of the Commonwealth Parliament, first passed in 1906 and subsequently amended.[1] The Act gives to the states certain rights in connexion with the referendum that are designed to reassure them that the procedure is being properly carried out and that no action prejudicial to their interests is being taken. Specifically it provides that the state governments may appoint scrutineers at each polling place and may demand a recount of the votes when they deem it necessary; it provides that statements in election writs shall be forwarded to state governors and empowers the state governments to question the validity of any

[1] Referendum (Constitution Alteration) Act, 1906–28. It is consolidated in *Commonwealth Acts*, vol. 24, p. 237.

referendum return or statement by petition to the High Court of Australia; it empowers the High Court to entertain and make a determination in regard to such petitions.[1] No important controversy has ever arisen out of the provisions of the Act, or out of a state's dissatisfaction with the manner in which the referenda have been conducted.

### *Results of Formal Rigidity on the Power of the Courts*

The line of explanation suggested above for the apparent rigidity of the Australian constitution, as tested by the results of the efforts to amend it, is reinforced by the fact that quite different results have been produced by the informal methods of change. No one supposes that the constitution has been altered only by the four formal changes that have been incorporated into it by the procedure of Section 128; many other changes have taken place in the constitution if it is defined in the wider sense to include such things as statute law, conventions, and judicial interpretations. The point that should be made is that the constitution cannot be said to be inflexible merely because it has not often been formally amended. Flexibility is not a function of the amending procedure so much as it is a function of the willingness of the people to countenance changes in the basic structure of their institutions. The informal changes have been many: conventions have changed; statutory provisions of constitutional stature have been modified; and most of all the courts have produced changes in the constitutional structure by reinterpreting the meaning of the clauses of the constitutional document. The frequent failures of the referenda do not prove that the constitution is inflexible. They have failed because of reasons already suggested: the complication of party considerations; the desire, frequently unstated, to preserve the federal system; the reluctance to centralize power in Canberra; the ignorance of the voter in matters of constitutional law; the difficulty of overcoming the voter's natural tendency to oppose a new arrangement that he does not understand. But the voters have generally acquiesced in changes produced by other forces—the growth of new conventions and the changing nature of judicial

[1] See Kenneth O. Warner, *Problems of Australian Federalism*, Seattle, 1933, p. 8, note 24.

decisions. Indeed, their unwillingness to sanction formal constitutional amendments has influenced the shift to the judiciary of the task of keeping the constitution adequate to the needs of changing times; and the judiciary has not shirked this duty. The major increases in the powers of the Commonwealth since 1901 have come through judicial interpretation and not by formal amendment of the constitution.

The curious thing about this phenomenon is that the people have on the whole been willing to accept changes made in this fashion. There has been no great popular outcry against the decisions of the High Court. After the Engineers' case in 1920 the test of the validity of Commonwealth legislation was shifted from the doctrine of the immunity of instrumentalities to the repugnancy clause of Section 109. And this clause made most such legislation valid. From that time on the power of the central government has grown steadily although the people have continued, with rare exceptions, to refuse to increase the powers of that central government by means of formal amendments. All the while, however, the voters continued to return political parties that employed newly found Commonwealth powers to carry on activities of a sort that they had seemed to disapprove in the referenda. From 1928 to 1946 in every referendum the people denied new powers to the Commonwealth, yet all the while they sanctioned the use by the national parliament of similar powers found for it by the Courts. The growth of the power of the national government could have been stopped or at least slowed down by the use of political methods. It is no answer to say that no parties urged the return of power to the states; had there been any sort of widespread demand for such a policy, some party would have adopted it. But no such thing occurred. This seeming paradox can be explained only on the ground that the opposition of the people to the growth of the Commonwealth power has not been so great as is suggested by the referendum results, and that these negative results must be otherwise explained, as we have sought to do above. The constitution has proved to be much more flexible than the amending process and the people much less conservative than their referendum votes indicate.

There have been many devices by which the powers of the

Commonwealth have been expanded, but among them two seem to stand out. One is the control over the economic life of the country that has followed from Commonwealth regulation of labour disputes extending beyond the boundaries of a single state; second, and more important, is the fiscal subordination of the state governments that has resulted from their increasing reliance upon annual grants from the Commonwealth. Since the uniform tax scheme took effect during the Second World War the states have received no revenue from the all-important income tax but have been granted compensatory annual awards from the Commonwealth instead. The result has been the increasing predominance of the central government, which has led many observers to conclude that federalism in Australia is no longer an operative reality but has been replaced by a quasi-federal system in which the states have become little more than administrative subdivisions.[1]

### *Party Attitudes Towards Constitutional Amendment*

The most obvious fact about party views on amendments is that no party has had a monopoly on the desire to alter the constitution. Every party has proposed amendments and all parties have seen their proposals repudiated.[2]

The first amendment was introduced and carried through the polls by the combined forces of Deakin and Reid; it was not a party question and was adopted almost without opposition. The second effort in 1910, which saw the success of one measure and the failure of another, was made again by Deakin, who was by then the leader of what was becoming the Liberal Party. In the two proposals that had thus far achieved success the Labour Opposition had offered support; in the third measure, the finance amendment of 1910, the Labour Party had opposed the Government's plan, and its subsequent failure in the popular referendum emphasized the fact that interparty differences could save or defeat an amendment even with the

[1] See the remarks of Thomas Playford (Premier of South Australia) in *Federalism in Australia*, Melbourne, 1949, pp. 69 ff. Also the comment by K. C. Wheare, *Modern Constitutions*, Oxford, 1951, pp. 28 f.

[2] The whole question of the attitudes of the several parties may be traced in the many references to the problem of amending the constitution in Louise Overacker, *The Australian Party System*, New Haven, 1952, *passim*.

party system in the indeterminate state in which it then was. By 1911 Labour had again returned to power and it now began the long series of efforts to endow the Commonwealth with greater powers over economic and social policy that has continued to this day. In that year it proposed two amendments of this kind which were defeated at the polls; two years later it made a similar but more extensive effort to achieve the same end when it offered six more amendments to the people.

Then, after the defection of the Hughes faction during the latter part of the First World War, Labour lost power and did not return to office for more than a decade. But the effort to amend the constitution was continued by other groups. The 1919 proposals were submitted by Hughes and the Nationalists, but with no more success than their predecessors. Early in 1923 Hughes was driven out and the reins of government were taken over by a coalition of the Nationalists and the Country Party, led by Bruce and Page. This government proposed both the two unsuccessful amendments of 1926 and the successful state debts amendment of 1928 under which the Loan Council was established. Again, significantly, the successful amendment was supported by the Labour Opposition.

In the 1931 election Labour, which had suffered through two depression years in office, was replaced by the United Australia Party, which was to hold office, under Lyons and Menzies, for the next decade. It was this party that offered the two amendments of 1937, which failed despite the support of the Labour Opposition. Finally, in September 1941 Labour came again to office, where it remained until December 1949. It was Labour, therefore, that submitted the 1944 reconstruction amendment, the three 1946 amendments of which one was successful, and the rents and prices amendment of 1948.

Labour lost power in 1949, being replaced by Menzies and a Liberal-Country coalition. It was the coalition that submitted the Communist control proposal in 1951 which, with Labour strongly opposed, failed to pass. Thus, Labour has been responsible for submitting thirteen of the twenty-four amendment proposals thus far offered to the referendum; of this total only one has been successful (1946); the other twelve have failed. The other eleven measures have been divided among the various parties and splinter groups that have shifted about in opposition to Labour; in the latter group (non-Labour) three proposals have been successful, but two of these were adopted before the party system took on a definite form.[1]

The record shows that any party in power in the national government is likely to try to secure amendments to the constitution. Nearly all groups agree that the Commonwealth is in need of more powers—at least they agree to this when they are occupying office in the national government. The leaders of the party in power are the leaders of the national government. They come up against the limitations imposed upon that government by the constitutional distribution of powers, and they seek to make their administration more effective and to put through the policies they advocate by the only means open to them—that of altering the distribution of powers which they conceive to be an obstacle to their success. It is a wholly natural impulse and one to which all parties have succumbed. Moreover, in Australia there is no great reverence for the written constitution, such as is found in America, that might operate to make leaders reluctant to tinker with its provisions. The dominant note in Australian political attitudes has always been a self-conscious realization of power in the hands of a democratic people which may be used to satisfy the needs of that people. A constitution is not a thing to be worshipped from afar; it is an instrument to be used to accomplish desired purposes. No party need hesitate to alter it simply because it is the constitution; the only concern need be whether sufficient votes can be collected to effect the alteration. Since the leaders of the government have been so very conscious of a need for constitutional reform, the proposals have been many; but since the rest of the country has not been equally conscious of that need, the successes have been few. The Commonwealth Government has always been more willing to amend the constitution than have the people of the country, or the leaders of the state governments, even though the latter may be of the same party as the leaders of the national government. That party attitudes are not always consistent throughout both states and nation is shown by the difficulties that led to the rejection of the draft bills on references to the Commonwealth

[1] See the detailed account of the party origin of the abortive and defeated efforts to submit proposals in Parker, op. cit., pp. 171 f.

in 1942.[1] That the people take stands on these questions different from those taken by the national party leaders is shown by almost any referendum.

But though all parties have urged the adoption of amendments increasing national power, no party has been quite consistent in this advocacy. It is most difficult for a party in opposition to put away the temptation to oppose the Government on such questions as these; for to a populace normally disposed against constitutional amendments of the ordinary kind, there is a strong appeal in a posture that opposes change. As a result nearly every party has on one occasion or another opposed the adoption of amendments, even of the same sort that it may in previous years have urged as desperately necessary for the preservation of the Commonwealth. Thus in 1926 Labour opposed the Essential Services amendment although on earlier occasions it had advocated in different form the same kind of controls that were then being urged by the Government. In 1937 Labour opposed the grant of the marketing power which in 1946 it advocated. Better still are the examples of 1944 and 1946 when the United Australia opposition fought against the adoption of amendments giving the Commonwealth power to control various economic matters which they had previously advocated. This fact is made most clear by Mr. Menzies's speeches against the marketing proposal of 1946, for it was he who had led the debate for just this same control in 1937.[2]

Labour's record of consistency on this point has probably been better than that of the others. In 1919, 1928, and 1937 it lent its support to at least some of the Government's proposals for amendments, even though by doing so it sacrificed its opportunity to badger its opponents.

## *Policy of the Labour Party*

The Labour Party has been the principal advocate of changes in the constitution; on only a few occasions has it urged the rejection of amendments or failed to take active part in the campaign for their adoption. This attitude is a

[1] Labour at the time was in control of not only the national government but also of all the state governments except Victoria and South Australia.

[2] See the comment on this strange behaviour in the London *Times*, 28 Sept. 1946, p. 5.

natural one for Labourites to take. Their professed programme is one of socialization of property and industry by gradual degrees. In order to carry out their extensive plans for social welfare legislation, centralized planning, and collectivization they find it necessary to concentrate more powers in the hands of the Commonwealth Government. A reform movement such as Labour finds it far easier to press for central control; otherwise they must carry on their campaign on seven different fronts—in the national government and in six states. Moreover, the states' second chambers are quite conservative, three being elected on a restricted franchise[1] and one being chosen by an electoral college.[2]

The party has urged numerous amendments transferring specified controls to the Commonwealth, and in 1929 the Federal President of the Party argued before the Royal Commission on the Constitution that the Commonwealth Parliament should be given 'complete legislative powers, subject to such limitations only as will insure the control of Parliament by the people'.[3] Moreover, the party has on occasion urged that the amending procedure be changed so as to allow greater power to the central government in pushing through changes in the distribution of powers. The argument is the same as that against all rigid constitutions—that the people express their will in an election and that this will should not be thwarted by minority groups utilizing an amending procedure of extraordinary difficulty. President Kenneally in his testimony before the Commission declared that his party believed it necessary to grant to the Commonwealth Parliament 'power to alter the Commonwealth Constitution when and how desired by an absolute majority of the Commonwealth Parliament, in order to give effect to the will of the people declared at a general election'.[4]

As though to justify this statement of policy the Prime

[1] South Australia, Western Australia, and Tasmania.

[2] New South Wales. In Victoria the Upper House since 1950 has been elected by universal suffrage; the Queensland legislature is unicameral.

[3] Testimony of Mr. J. J. Kenneally before the Royal Commission on the Constitution. *Proceedings*, 1929, p. 1106. The limitations he suggested were that the Parliament should not be allowed to extend its own life, interfere with the initiative, referendum, and recall (which he proposed), interfere with the adult franchise, or impose conscription for military or naval service. Ibid., pp. 1106–7.

[4] Loc. cit.

Minister, Mr. Scullin, shortly afterwards introduced in the House a bill to alter the constitution to this effect. The bill added a new section (129) which altered the amendment procedure by providing that an amendment would become effective if the alteration bill '. . . be passed by an absolute majority in each House of the Parliament, and be assented to by the Governor-General'.[1] The bill was killed, however, by a non-Labour majority in the Upper House and was not pressed farther by the Government. There can be little doubt of the fate of such a proposal had it been submitted to referendum.

But Labour's policy has not been the same in all instances. We have seen that it has opposed several amendments in recent years. In earlier days the declared policy of the New South Wales Labour Party was one of opposition to centralization of power in the Commonwealth; and this attitude of the state party was a source of considerable irritation to the national leaders for years. The reason for it was that the state party feared that centralization in Canberra might give the rural and conservative interests a better opportunity to block social reform, since Labour at that time was not the powerful national party it later became.[2] Though these difficulties have disappeared, Labour now and then is still found in opposition to amendments which, according to the party's long-term policy, would seem to deserve its support. When in opposition, it has on occasion succumbed to the temptation to try to make political capital out of such questions; it is hard for the Opposition to resist an opportunity to oppose.[3]

Labour's socialist programme has never been militant or doctrinaire but has looked towards a gradual, step-by-step extension of trade unionism, social legislation, and industrial control. It has never attempted to achieve a socialist society by any decisive, all-embracing step; indeed, for it to do so would very likely be to sacrifice the middle-class support that

[1] The full proposal may be found in an article by A. C. Gain, 'Existing Provisions for Altering the Commonwealth Constitution', in G. V. Portus, ed. *Studies in the Australian Constitution*, Australian Institute of Political Science, Sydney, 1933, p. 223.

[2] See Brady, *Democracy in the Dominions*, 2nd edn., 1952, p. 174.

[3] On the attitudes of Labour and its opponents to the problem of constitutional change see Parker, op. cit., pp. 150-6; also L. F. Crisp, *Parliamentary Government of the Australian Commonwealth*, New Haven, 1949, pp. 80 ff.

has provided its margin of victory. Its amendment proposals have been designed to confer piecemeal upon the central government powers over limited sections of the economy. To make any large-scale alteration of the economic system would require more extensive modifications of the constitutional distribution of powers than it can hope to achieve. But it is significant that even in the states, where the necessary powers exist, the Labour Party, which has enjoyed many terms of office, has done nothing to implement any doctrinaire socialist plan. Socialism in Australasia, as Métin long ago pointed out, is 'without doctrines'.

### *Limitations on Section 128: the Covering Clauses*

The constitution of Australia, like that of Canada, is contained in a British statute; it consists of Section 9 of the Commonwealth of Australia Constitution Act, 1900.[1] The first eight sections of that Act, the so-called 'covering clauses', are not strictly speaking part of the constitution; they merely state the desire of the colonies to unite in the Commonwealth, define certain terms, and make certain transitory provisions. Section 9 begins by saying, 'The Constitution of the Commonwealth shall be as follows: . . .'; then appear the 128 sections of the constitution proper, which are actually sub-sections of the ninth section of the Constitution Act itself. In the final section of the constitution (128) a provision is made for an amending procedure whereby the provisions of 'this Constitution' may be altered by Australian authorities. Now there is no doubt that for purposes of the application of Section 128 the covering clauses cannot be considered as part of the constitution. The amending procedure specified in that section does not apply to the covering clauses 1 to 8, nor presumably does it apply to the introductory words of Section 9. These clauses could be amended only by the Imperial Parliament, though there is little doubt that the latter would amend them on request from the Australian authorities, and only on such a request. The question still remains, however, whether anything in the first eight sections limits the operation of the constitution itself.

[1] 63 & 64 Vict., chap. 12.

The question has arisen in connexion with the provision in the third covering clause, which says that the colonies 'shall be united in a Federal Commonwealth under the name of the Commonwealth of Australia'. In Australia there has been a considerable reform movement that has urged that the federal system should be given up in favour of a unitary state. To do this, whether otherwise possible or not, would seem to violate these words of covering clause three. The legal question is this: do the words of the covering clause bind the Australian people to a federal system or could that system be given up by appropriate use of the amending procedure in Australia? Does the third covering clause, in other words, constitute a limitation on the powers of amendment under Section 128?

Most students of the subject hold that it does not. It is usually argued that although the covering clauses could not be amended by use of the procedure of Section 128, this does not necessarily constitute a restriction on Australian constituent powers. One of the first treatises on the Australian constitution suggested that 'the description "Federal Commonwealth" is too vague to be available as a limitation of power',[1] and this view has been generally accepted. The Royal Commission of 1929 stated with approval in its report that 'it was suggested before the commission that "Federal" in covering clause 3 has not an exact meaning to which recourse might be had by the Courts for the purpose of restricting alterations of the Constitutions'.[2] Mr. Owen Dixon, later a member of the High Court of Australia, submitted to the Commission an opinion to this effect, which was incorporated by the Commission into its report without comment. The Dixon opinion has been widely accepted on the question and is frequently cited by those who discuss it.[3] It is certainly true that the words of the covering clause are vague enough to make it very nearly impossible for the courts to interpret them as a limitation. Whether such an attempt might be made or not, the amending procedure would permit changes so drastic that the reality if not the forms of

[1] W. Harrison Moore, *The Constitution of the Commonwealth of Australia*, 1901, p. 321.

[2] *Report*, pp. 365–6.

[3] A. C. Gain, op. cit., pp. 222–3; also K. C. Wheare, *The Statute of Westminster and Dominion Status*, 5th edn., 1953, p. 203.

federalism could be abandoned. Simply by increasing the scope of the powers of Section 51 the content could be taken out of the word 'federal' in the covering clauses.

It is arguable also that since the covering clauses establish the Commonwealth and provide for the inclusion within it of certain colonies, the Commonwealth could not be dissolved, nor could any of the states secede or be ceded by the Commonwealth without legislation by the Imperial Parliament changing the covering clauses. It can hardly be doubted, however, that that Parliament would conform to dominion wishes in such a matter. The question was posed in one form in 1934 when Western Australia sought by petition to Westminster to be separated from the rest of the Commonwealth.[1] The authorities in London replied that the matter was one for the Commonwealth to settle and refused to take any action. To accomplish such a thing the consent of the state, the Commonwealth, Westminster, and probably of the other states would be required.

### *Internal Limitations on Section 128*

A more important limitation on the power of amendment is contained in Section 128 itself. The final clause of the section reads as follows:

> No alteration diminishing the proportionate representation of any State in either House of the Parliament, or the minimum number of representatives of a State in the House of Representatives, or increasing, diminishing, or otherwise altering the limits of a State, or in any manner affecting the provisions of the Constitution in relation thereto, shall become law unless the majority of the electors voting in that State approve the proposed law.

Clearly the power of amendment extends to the whole constitution, including Section 128 itself. The amending procedure could properly be amended by use of that very amending procedure. But in this last paragraph certain things are protected by the requirement that any state affected by certain kinds of amendments must consent thereto. This means that

[1] See W. A. MacDonnell, 'Western Australia's Plea for Secession', *Dalhousie Review*, vol. 15, Oct. 1935, p. 315; also F. R. Beasley, 'The Secession Movement in Western Australia', *Australian Quarterly*, vol. 8, Mar. 1936, p. 31.

for certain amendments the consent of all states is necessary, since all might be so affected.

The kinds of amendments thus circumscribed are four:

1. Diminishing the proportionate representation in either House.
2. Decreasing the minimum number of representatives in the Lower House.
3. Increasing, diminishing, or otherwise altering the limits (i.e. boundaries) of a state.
4. Affecting the provisions of the constitution in relation thereto.

The question is whether this final paragraph may be amended by the ordinary procedure of Section 128 or whether the consent of all the states is necessary; for clearly it may be amended by the second method if not by the first. It is clear that under the constitution as it now stands those sections having to do with the matters named under heads 1, 2, and 3 could not be changed without the unanimous concurrence of the states. But could the final paragraph first be repealed by the ordinary procedure (i.e. without the unanimous consent of the states), and then those other sections changed by that procedure? The answer to this depends on the meaning of the phrase 'in any manner affecting the provisions of the Constitution in relation thereto'. Is the final paragraph a 'provision of the constitution in relation thereto' within the meaning of that final paragraph? On this point there is little agreement and no settled doctrine.[1] The crux of the question is the meaning of the word 'thereto', for the paragraph is not clear on what the word refers to. If the final clause is itself one of 'the provisions of the constitution in relation thereto', then it could be altered only with the unanimous consent of the states; if it is not, then

[1] W. Harrison Moore argued that the final paragraph was so protected. Op. cit., p. 322. So with F. A. Bland, *Government in Australia*, Sydney, rev. edn., 1944, p. 424. On the other side, arguing that the final paragraph is amendable by the ordinary procedure, are A. C. Gain, op. cit., pp. 219 ff., and K. O. Warner, *Problems of Australian Federalism*, p. 13. See also the joint legal opinion by A. P. Canaway and R. Windeyer in the appendix to the former's *The Failure of Federalism in Australia*. The most comprehensive treatment is accorded the problem in Canaway's two articles, 'The Safety Valve of the Commonwealth Constitution', in the *Australian Law Journal*, Aug. 1938 (vol. 12, p. 108), and 'The By-Pass of Constitutional Reform', in the Jan. 1940 issue of the same journal (vol. 13, p. 394).

the ordinary procedure of Section 128, involving only a majority of the states, could be used to alter the final protective clause; and then, with the protection gone, the formerly protected items (1, 2, and 3 above) could be altered against the objection of the affected state. The question is, what is the meaning of the 'there' in the 'thereto'? No attempt is made here to resolve this problem and no solution has found wide acceptance. It might be well to consult the intention of the framers, but the problem does not seem to have occurred to them. Quick and Garran discuss the final clause at some length, but the only alternative they suggest to unanimous consent of the states is a resort to the Imperial Parliament.[1]

But the double amendment, even if valid, is unlikely to be used. Federal government does not and cannot afford to operate in such a fashion. If unification is ever accomplished in Australia, it will be accomplished because the people in the states have decided to accomplish it and not because constitutional lawyers have succeeded in putting through two amendments in quick succession, one abolishing the protective clauses in the last section and the other abolishing federalism. When the diversities in Australian society have been reduced to the point where federalism no longer has meaning, the people will find a way to another form of government. The clauses of Section 128 are not as important as the lawyers think.

### *Reform of the Amending Procedure*

Since amendment of the constitution has been so difficult to achieve in Australia, there have been many complaints that the procedure itself is too cumbrous. Since amendments have customarily been for the purpose of increasing the powers of the central government, the complaints come from those who desire greater centralization or even the complete abandonment of federalism. There has arisen during the past two or three decades a growing movement in Australia demanding that a unitary system be installed in place of the present federal system, which, according to its critics, has served its purpose and is now merely holding up progress.[2] Having

[1] Quick and Garran, *Annotated Constitution*, p. 991.

[2] One of the clearest and most elaborate of the works setting forth these views is A. P. Canaway, *The Failure of Federalism in Australia*, London, 1930.

repeatedly failed to expand Commonwealth powers by amendment, these critics have turned to the reform of the amending procedure as a necessary condition to further progress. Thus most of the suggestions have been directed towards making amendments easier to secure, since opponents of centralization have few complaints here.

Since Australia has been so largely influenced by British precedents in her constitutional practices, the suggestion has naturally been made that the power to amend the constitution should be vested solely in the Parliament. This system would please the advocates of centralization, for the record of the Parliament has been excellent from their standpoint. We have already seen that the president of the Labour Party offered a suggestion of this kind to the Royal Commission and that a Labour Government sought the passage of an amendment in 1930 that would have conferred this power upon the Parliament.

Another advantage claimed for such a proposal is that it would permit the Commonwealth Parliament to absorb the functions of the states by degrees, thus easing the transition from a federal to a unitary system and avoiding the confusions of an immediate change from one to the other. Three members of the Royal Commission (Messrs. Ashworth, Duffy, and McNamara) declared themselves in favour of such a plan and submitted a minority report urging it.[1]

The proposal that the Parliament should have such a power has been heard in many quarters.[2] It is almost always predicated, however, upon a desire for a unitary system. Those who want to see federalism perpetuated naturally oppose the proposal. Such a procedure would not be without a certain merit if only one could be sure that the Commonwealth Parliament would exercise the power with the same degree of restraint and respect for established constitutional customs as has been manifested by the Parliament in London. In Australia, however, despite many similarities to Britain, politics is an entirely different matter. The country is still young and the game of

[1] *Report*, pp. 243–7.

[2] See also the suggestions made before the Commission by Mr. E. S. Pratt (*Proceedings*, pp. 1197 f.) and Mr. A. V. C. Melbourne (ibid., p. 1542); their proposals are summarized in the *Report* at p. 236 and p. 237 respectively.

politics is far more rough-and-tumble than in the mother country; it has by no means achieved the dignity that characterizes the corresponding processes in Britain. Moreover, the country possesses a written constitution, a fact that has importance not only for its institutions but for its practices as well. A written constitution tends to produce a respect for the written law, as distinguished from the conventional practice, that does not exist in Britain; but what is more important, it tends to produce a lack of respect for the latter, an attitude that countenances any action that is not prohibited by the written law, regardless of the custom in the matter. The same attitude is evident in the United States; a necessary emphasis on what is written tends to create a disregard of all that is not written. It is doubtful that the Australian Parliament could be depended upon to exercise this omnipotence with the prudence that would guarantee that the interests of the several states would be safeguarded.

The suggestion that the clauses of the constitution should be classified, some being amendable by Parliament and some by more difficult means, though often heard in Canada, has been less frequently made in Australia. Sir Frederic Eggleston, however, did urge such a suggestion upon the Royal Commission. He proposed that the referendum should be retained for altering some provisions of the constitution, e.g. the distribution of powers and the composition of the Senate, but that other provisions might be altered by an absolute majority in each House of the Parliament.[1] Such a proposal, though somewhat different in content, was also advocated by Messrs. Duffy and McNamara in their minority report;[2] but the Commission majority did not seriously consider it, commenting that 'it would be difficult to draw the line between the matters to which these two methods should be applied'.[3] Subsequent experience in Canada has certainly borne witness to the accuracy of this observation.

A further suggestion that is heard from various reform groups is to hold a new general constitutional convention at which the entire problem could be discussed by a body

[1] Royal Commission on the Constitution, *Proceedings*, pp. 727 ff.

[2] Ibid., *Report*, pp. 301 ff.

[3] Ibid., p. 237.

elected for that purpose. Some would employ such a convention merely as an advisory group to the Commonwealth Parliament; they would have its suggestions further considered by the two Houses of the Parliament and then submitted to the voters as ordinary alteration bills. Others have recommended that the proposals of the convention be considered as replacing the necessary submission by the Parliament and that the measures proposed be submitted directly to the people in a referendum. The latter kind of convention would clearly pose some obstacles in constitutional law, since it appears that the constitutional procedure prescribed in Section 128 would preclude any such direct proposal by a convention, unless a prior amendment authorizing it were adopted through the procedure now in operation. The first kind of convention would serve merely as an advisory group, and there seems to be no legal reason why this could not be done. Indeed, it has been done, if one accepts as a precedent the general conference of 1944 that devised the draft bills for the reconstruction amendment. That such a convention would have many proposals to consider seems plain from the fact that the Royal Commission had laid before it, in addition to various proposals for the reform of Section 128, suggestions for the amendment of the constitution in respect to more than forty different matters of a substantive nature.[1]

A proposal for holding a constitutional convention with a view towards general revision of the constitution was discussed in the Commonwealth Parliament in 1920,[2] and a bill for that purpose was introduced in 1921,[3] but the proposal could make no headway and was dropped. The proposal was heard again in unofficial circles from time to time and was raised again before the Royal Commission in 1929. Several witnesses urged that conventions of various kinds be held, but the Commission was unwilling to make any such recommendation. In its report it said:

> The value of a constitutional convention as a means of altering the

[1] A list of the matters thus proposed to be amended is included in the Commission's *Report* at p. 239.

[2] *Parliamentary Debates*, 1920, pp. 1233–47. A similar abortive motion had been brought forward in 1914. See Parker, op. cit., p. 182.

[3] Ibid., 1921, pp. 13019, 13472 ff., 14260.

Constitution was stressed by several witnesses. . . . It was suggested that the necessary provision (i.e., for periodic conventions) should be made in the Constitution. It was thought that a representative convention on the lines of the convention of 1897-98 could deal with matters which would be too numerous, as well as too disputable, to lend themselves to treatment at an ordinary referendum, and that such a convention would have the advantage of being composed of men who had experience of the working of the Constitution.[1]

But the Commission was not favourably impressed and, although there was a minority opinion on the matter,[2] the majority stated that they did not

recommend that provision should be made in the Constitution for the holding of a convention to consider and frame proposals for the alteration of the Constitution, whether the proposals are to be submitted as recommendations to Parliament or direct to the electors.[3]

The suggestion has not died, however, though the likelihood of its being accepted has not increased. During the discussions on the proposed amendments of 1946 it was again made.[4] Senator McLachlan argued that

. . . there should be no repetition of the fiddling attempts at reform made at the last two or three referendums. A long range view should be taken of this vital matter, and the whole subject should be thoroughly discussed by a competent body of men, charged with the task of making recommendations to the Government.

But still the old question of the constitutional status of such a body was raised and to this the honourable senator could only reply that 'the Constitution was framed by elected representatives of the people from each State. That was a very fair method, and I see no reason why it should not be adopted in regard to constitutional reform.'[5] The answer is, of course, that the constitution so framed now prevents such a device. If the convention were to be made a permanent feature of constitutional practice or if it were to be endowed with the power to

[1] *Report*, pp. 237 f. There is a list at this point in the *Report* of those who had urged the suggestion upon the Commission.

[2] Ibid., p. 269.

[3] Loc. cit.

[4] The Liberal and Country Parties supported the move for such a convention. See the *Round Table*, 1946, vol. 36, pp. 284 f. They have not again raised the question, however, since their return to power.

[5] *Parliamentary Debates*, 1946, 1st sess., p. 218.

submit proposals directly to referendum, some sort of constitutional sanction would have to be found for it; otherwise it would contravene the provisions of Section 128.

### *Reference of Powers from States to Commonwealth*

There already exists a method within the framework of the present constitution by which the terms of that document may be radically altered. This is the provision of Section 51, paragraph xxxvii, which authorizes the Commonwealth Parliament to make laws with respect to

> matters referred to the Parliament of the Commonwealth by the Parliament or Parliaments of any State or States, but so that the law shall extend only to States by whose Parliaments the matter is referred, or which afterwards adopt the law.

It seems clear that this provision was not intended to serve as a vehicle for any general reapportionment of the powers of government between the states and the central government, but that it could be used as such a vehicle seems equally clear. No limitations are placed on the matters that may be referred, though of course none could be referred that were not possessed by the state governments. The framers of the clause apparently intended that it might enable states to confer upon the Commonwealth the management of matters in which only two or three states were interested. Quick and Garran offer but one example of how the device might work:

> For instance, the Parliaments of New South Wales, Victoria, and South Australia might find it consistent with their interests to refer to the Federal Parliament such questions as the utilization of the Murray for irrigation purposes; the settlement of riparian rights . . . etc.[1]

This hardly envisages a general transfer by all states to the Commonwealth of some general governmental function not assigned to it by the constitution. But there seems to be no legal obstacle to its use for such a purpose.

The clause has the advantage that certain reforms could be made in the distribution of powers without the concurrence of all the states, but without, on the other hand, extending the effect of such transfers to those states that prefer not to take

[1] Quick and Garran, *Annotated Constitution*, p. 649.

part. It may be objected that this renders the clause of little use since to be effective the reference would have to be unanimous, else the power in the Commonwealth would be of only limited application. This objection is a valid one, but it poses the question, frequently forgotten in a federal system, whether it is desirable to take from a state a power which it has long enjoyed and which has been conferred upon it by the original constitution. Australians frequently forget, as do Americans, that theirs is, after all, a federal system, and that it is so for very good reasons. If the clause were to be utilized for these purposes, it is not likely that the states would refuse to refer any matter that could be conferred upon the Commonwealth by the normal processes of amendment. If unanimity of the states could be secured for the purpose of such a reference, then any procedure would serve the purpose.

There has been only one attempt to employ the clause for any purpose at all. This occurred in the 1942–4 effort to secure for the Commonwealth the extensive powers that would enable it to carry out its plans for post-war reconstruction. In this instance, though the reference was to be limited to a five-year period, the plan failed to carry in the states. It is well to recall, however, that the same plan failed in the later referendum by a considerable majority, succeeding in only two states.[1] Though there is little evidence upon which to base conclusions, there is at least no reason to think that the plan might not serve to make Australia's constitution more flexible than it now seems to be. It would avoid the part of the procedure of Section 128 that has defeated most amendments, i.e. the referendum, but there is no assurance that the state legislatures will be any more willing to see themselves deprived of their present powers than the voters have been. The plan as a whole poses several problems and, though it has been urged by many people, it is not likely to replace the normal amending process to any large extent. Thus far, it has never successfully been used.

## *Conclusion*

In summary it may be said that Australia's constitution may be changed by any one of four different methods: (1) by

[1] See above, pp. 124 ff.

Act of the Imperial Parliament; we have already seen how improbable this is under present conditions; (2) by Act of the Commonwealth Parliament. Many provisions of the constitution contain the phrase 'until the Parliament otherwise directs', and legislative Acts making such changes constitute real changes in the constitutional structure, though they are limited in scope and in no case of much significance; (3) by use of the reference procedure of Section 52, paragraph xxxvii, discussed in the preceding section; (4) by the formal amendment procedure provided in Section 128. This last is the only true method of amendment as the term is usually employed.

We have seen that Australia's utilization of the process of formal amendment has produced twenty-four constitutional referenda since 1900 and that of these proposals only four have been accepted by the appropriate majorities both in the states and in the nation as a whole. This fact has caused doubt in some quarters whether this amending procedure is effective, whether it is sufficiently flexible, whether it may not be stultifying the constitution by preventing changes that are necessary to adapt it to changing needs.

An adequate discussion of these questions would lead us into a lengthy examination of the nature of representative government and democracy which it is not our purpose here to make. But if one accepts the proposition that the structure and policy of a government should be determined by the wishes of the people over whom it governs and that these people are capable of deciding for themselves what these wishes are, then it is difficult to see how the Australian procedure is really open to such criticisms as these. Those who desire a unitary system in Australia are naturally dissatisfied with the results of the constitutional referenda, but their complaints should be lodged against their own inability to convince enough people that their views are correct and not against the devices by which these views are measured.

That the amendment procedure involves a recognition of the federal basis of the Australian polity none will deny. But it is not that federal element in the procedure that has held up constitutional reform in Australia. In the long series of constitutional referenda there have been only three instances in which an affirmative majority over the country at large has been thwarted in its approval of a measure by the lack of majorities in the necessary four states; and the first of these did not occur until 1937. The fact that in these three instances (one in 1937, two in 1946) the federal aspect of the procedure has been instrumental in defeating amendments that would otherwise have been adopted is testimony to the wisdom of the framers in providing a device by which the federal quality in their society, which they desired to preserve, could in fact be so preserved.

Nearly all the amendments that have been proposed have been directed towards the increase of the powers of the Commonwealth at the expense of those of the states. Hence, every time such a referendum has issued in the defeat of a measure, evidence has been offered that the Australian people desire to maintain the states with the powers conferred upon them by the original constitution. The federal nature of Australian society has been reflected by every constitutional referendum and not merely by those three where popular majorities were defeated by the lack of majorities in a few states.

It is not fair to say that the procedure itself is poor, or inflexible, or inadequate. The proposals have been made in the normal way, the people have voted, and the measures have been defeated. What the critics of the process forget is that perhaps it is they who are wrong, that perhaps the people of Australia are not yet ready to forsake their federal society. Certainly their record in the referenda has been clear on the point. It may be granted that the people have acquiesced in the increase in the powers of the national government when that increase came from another source, i.e. from the judicial modification of the constitution. It may be argued that there are other explanations for the negative results of the referenda. Public opinion polls may be cited to show that a majority of the people really prefer a unitary system. Yet when the question has been posed directly to the electorate, the people have said 'no' in almost every case.

There is a great deal of talk in Australia about the rigidity of the amendment procedure and not enough realization that the procedure is what it is because the society is what *it* is. A federal constitution with a 'rigid' amending procedure was adopted because the diversities within the society required that it be adopted. The purpose of the procedure was to enable the people of the states to protect their own particularities against subordination by the rest of the people in the society. It has been used in the manner and for the ends for which it was intended. How then can we criticize it on the ground that it has not served its purpose? What is rigidity, after all? When the people of Australia have been convinced that changes were necessary in the allocation of powers to the central government and the states, they have accepted these changes. The most difficult problem of Australian federalism has been a financial one. It is significant that out of the four successful attempts to amend the constitution, two dealt with financial questions. This suggests that the unwillingness to amend rests not on mere inertia but on the basis of a real refusal to transfer powers from the states to the Commonwealth; when the problems of greatest urgency were presented, the electorate rose to the occasion.

It is by no means suggested that this particular amending clause is essential to the preservation of federalism in Australia. Federalism is a function not of constitutional devices but of the diversities in society. If these diversities remain, as they clearly do in Australia, then the federal structure is likely to remain. No particular amending clause is needed to preserve it. Whatever institutional mechanics are employed, the political process is likely to produce very nearly the same public policy, unless decisions are reached by means of naked force, in which case a wholly different problem is posed and one with which neither federalism nor this essay is meant to deal.

Yet politics in Australia as elsewhere is an intensely dynamic thing. The pattern of diversities in a society is constantly changing. What was merely an instrumentality of federalism yesterday becomes part of the pattern of diversities itself today. The amending process was adopted because the states required some special means of protecting themselves against changes in the constitution that might be unfavourable to them. After living with this process for a long time and employing it for these purposes, the process, the procedure itself, has become more than a mere device; it has taken its place within the context of society; it has become part of the sociological pattern that is federalism. What in 1900 was a mere means has half a century later become an end in itself. Changing the amending procedure in Australia today would be a difficult thing to accomplish.

# 4

# THE AMENDMENT OF THE SWISS CONSTITUTION

WE enter next upon a brief consideration of the experience of Switzerland and the means provided in the constitution of that country for changing the fundamental law. Switzerland naturally follows Australia in our study, for the two amending processes are, as will be seen, quite similar in their essential features. But in both Switzerland and the United States there is found an attitude towards government and towards federalism that is lacking in the two countries already treated. In Australia and in Canada government operates in the shadow of the Crown; in Switzerland and America there is nothing comparable to that institution or to the concept it represents. The constitutions of the two Dominions are enactments of the British Parliament; they could, theoretically at least, be altered by that Parliament. The limits of government are not precise but shade off into the penumbra of uncertainty and security with which that undefined and undefinable entity, Crown power, surrounds them. In Switzerland and America the constitutions are the direct product of the peoples' exercise of constituent power; the functions of government are circumscribed by the written constitution in a way that is unknown in Britain and the Commonwealth. The methods of constitutional amendment are prescribed by those constitutions and one cannot even speculate about extra-constitutional ways in which formal change might be effected.

This is not to say that the constitutional structure of either country does not change informally in several ways, just as it does in the countries so far described. Conventions evolve, laws are amended, and statutes are reinterpreted in all countries; the framework of government is constantly shifting. The dynamics of the political process seldom wait for the slower procedures of formal amendment. Desires are awakened, demands are made, and the change is introduced. But not all changes are possible; when the constitution offers an obstacle to the evolutionary growth, its provisions must be modified. It is then necessary to stop and make the amendment that is needed; this crystallizes issues that may not theretofore have been clearly understood and provokes sufficient discussion to permit the change to be made in the light of public knowledge and public debate. The process of constitutional evolution must frequently be halted while the formal procedure of amendment is employed to effect the desired change; but this halt is healthy for the community, for it permits and requires that important changes be made self-consciously and with some understanding of what is going on. The need for formal amendment sometimes holds up the process of politics, but it is always the dynamics of that process that produces the amendment. If the procedure employed should prevent the adoption of the amendment, it proves only that the dynamic force was insufficient.

## *The Swiss Constitution*[1]

The Swiss constitution is the product of a long development that may be traced back nearly seven hundred years. In its present form it derives from the federal constitution of 1848 as thoroughly revised in 1874. The history of Switzerland through most of this period has displayed a conflict between the forces driving the country towards unification and those opposing this movement. By 1848 the constitution took a form that has satisfied most students of modern federalism that it was now truly federal and not merely a league of cantons.[2] The revision of 1874 made numerous changes in the original document and the constitution was readopted as a whole;

[1] The standard commentaries on the constitution are listed in the bibliography below. Two recent ones, both excellent, are William E. Rappard, *La Constitution fédérale de la Suisse 1848–1948*, Neuchâtel, 1948; and Christopher Hughes, *The Federal Constitution of Switzerland*, Oxford, 1954.

[2] See, for example, K. C. Wheare, *Federal Government*, 3rd edn., 1953, who argues that the constitutions before 1848 were not federal but that the constitution of that year was (pp. 22, 29). Wheare points out that even by 1848 there was no clearly accepted distinction between federal and confederate constitutions, and as an example of this he points to the title of the constitution of that year, which was styled '*Constitution fédérale pour la confédération Suisse*'.

but the essential elements remained the same.[1] The federal distribution of powers is similar to those of the constitutions of Australia and the United States in that the central government is granted a limited number of powers, all the rest remaining with the component units.[2] Actually, many more functions are assigned to the central government than in either of the other two countries, but the form of organization and the legal structure are nevertheless the same.

A significant difference between the constitutional structure of Switzerland and that of other modern federations lies in the function of the federal judiciary. Whereas in Canada, Australia, and the United States the supreme judicial tribunal has the power to review the acts of the federal legislative body and, if necessary, to declare them *ultra vires* and void, the judiciary in Switzerland does not have this power. The Federal Tribunal may review the acts of the cantonal bodies and of administrative officers of the federal government, but it must accept the decisions of the federal legislature as final. This does not mean, however, that the latter is to be regarded as possessing the unlimited legislative competence that characterizes the British Parliament. It must stay within the bounds of the constitution and can neither exceed the limits prescribed by that document nor amend it unilaterally. Moreover, even in the interpretation of its competences, the legislature is subject to the final decision of the people, as it may be expressed in the operation of the popular initiative or referendum.

The means by which the present constitution may be amended are described in the third chapter of that document. Provision is made both for total revision,[3] or the complete reorganization of the constitution, and for partial revision,[4]

[1] The texts of the 1848 and 1874 constitutions may be compared in French in K. Hilty, *Les Constitutions fédérales de la confédération Suisse*, Neuchâtel, 1891. The present constitution, as amended, may be found in English in Amos J. Peaslee, *Constitutions of Nations*, Concord, N.H., 1950, vol. iii, pp. 119–46.

[2] Article 3: 'The cantons are sovereign in so far as their sovereignty is not limited by the Federal Constitution, and as such they exercise all rights that are not delegated to the federal power'. But this distribution of powers is quite complex and displays important differences when compared with other federations. See Hughes, op. cit., pp. 5 f.

[3] Articles 119–20.

[4] Article 121.

or the alteration of limited parts. In both processes provision is made for the participation of the federal legislature, although, as will be seen, it is not always necessary for the legislature to concur in an amendment proposal. The most characteristic feature of the Swiss amendment procedure, and perhaps of Swiss government as a whole, is the extensive use made of popular participation in the process. The people take part both through the referendum, which is required on all constitutional amendments, and through the initiative, which may be used at any time.

## *Total Revision of the Constitution*

Total revision of the constitution may be accomplished in three ways:

1. It may be proposed by the two Houses of the Federal Assembly in the same manner as an ordinary law and then be submitted to the people for ratification by referendum. The proposal may be initiated by either Council and may be introduced by a member of one of the Councils or by a message from the government of one of the cantons, or by a message from the Federal Council (the executive body).[1] The new constitution must be agreed upon by the two councils in identical form, which would of course necessitate long and detailed discussions. After this is accomplished the revised constitution is submitted to referendum.

2. If the two Houses cannot agree on the form of the new constitution, or if one House desires a total revision and the other House does not agree, then the question whether there should be such a revision is put to the people in a preliminary referendum.[2] The voters do not, on such an occasion, give

[1] The lower house is called the National Council, the upper is the Council of States; together they constitute the Federal Assembly. The Federal Council is the plural executive.

[2] Deploige raises the interesting point that this preliminary referendum provided for in Article 120 is inconsistent with the statement in Article 119 that total revision takes place according to 'the forms required for passing federal laws'. When there is a disagreement between the Houses on an ordinary law, the project is simply dropped. Deploige explains Article 120 as being the result of 'the fear entertained by the authors of the constitution that the second chamber would systematically oppose the proposals for revision which might originate in the National Council'. Simon Deploige, *The Referendum in Switzerland*, tr. Trevelyan, London, 1894, p. 129. A strange fear to have been felt by the authors

any indication of what form they want the revision to take; nothing is offered to them to decide except the simple question: Do you want the constitution to be revised, yes or no? If the answer is 'no', the whole project is dropped. If the answer is 'yes', then the two Houses are dissolved, new elections take place, and the task of revising the constitution is undertaken by the new Federal Assembly.

The new Assembly is not bound by any instructions except those that it may read out of the general election programmes. The popular referendum provides no mandate other than one to revise the constitution. How it is to go about doing so is undetermined. What would happen if the two Houses were again unable to agree on the new constitution is unclear. The constitution makes no mention of such an eventuality, but it would not be unreasonable to expect such a disagreement to occur. Possibly another referendum and another dissolution would take place; the constitution offers no guide and there are no precedents, since the procedure has never been employed.

3. The third way in which total revision can take place is by use of the popular initiative. If 50,000 voters sign petitions calling for a total revision of the constitution, the same procedure is followed as has been described in the preceding case. A preliminary referendum is held in which the voters are asked whether they desire a total revision; if the answer is 'no', the project is dropped; if it is 'yes', the Federal Assembly is dissolved, re-elected, and then undertakes the revision. Just why the Assembly should be dissolved in this case is less clear than in the preceding one; if the two Houses cannot agree, their renewal is reasonable and is probably necessary before they undertake the revision. But when the proposal comes from a popular initiative the two Houses have not necessarily expressed any opinion on the matter and might therefore be given the opportunity of making a first effort at least. Presumably it was thought necessary even here because it was assumed that the normal method of revision would be through proposal by the two Houses and that the initiative would be resorted to only when it became evident that the Assembly was opposed to a revision.

of a federal constitution, in which a state-based second chamber is intended to provide a brake on constitutional changes inimical to state interests.

In any of the above instances the proposed revised constitution must be submitted for final ratification by the electors. This is called in Switzerland the 'compulsory referendum' since the constitution requires that it take place before any amendment of the constitution can be effected. It is to be distinguished from the optional or 'facultative' referendum which is used for ordinary legislation. In referenda on constitutional amendments the endorsement of a double majority is necessary, as in Australia. Not only must a majority of those voting approve the proposed amendment, but a majority of the voters in a majority of the cantons must approve.[1] The vote-counting is complicated by the fact that not all the voting constituencies are of the same rank. It is normally said that there are twenty-two cantons, but three of these are subdivided into half-cantons,[2] each of which has its own constitution and is separately represented in the federal legislature. For purposes of constitutional referenda the half-cantons are counted separately but are accounted as only half a voting unit; the vote in each is counted as a distinct unit and recorded as a half-canton in totalling the number of cantons that have approved the amendment. There are thus nineteen cantons and six half-cantons, making a total of twenty-two. Since the approval of a majority of cantons is required, all amendments must secure majorities of the popular votes in eleven and one-half cantons. This is true for both total and partial revisions of the constitution.

## *Partial Revision of the Constitution*

There are two general ways in which the constitution may be partially revised or amended:

1. The amendment may be proposed by the two chambers of the federal legislature and submitted for ratification by popular referendum. If the two chambers disagree on the proposed amendment, the question cannot be resolved by

[1] This is not true in the ordinary legislative ('facultative') referendum, in which a majority of the total number voting is sufficient.

[2] Unterwalden (Upper and Lower), Basle (Town and Country), and Appenzell (Interior Rhodes and Exterior Rhodes). For a brief account of the origin of these cantonal splits see William E. Rappard, *The Government of Switzerland*, New York, 1936, p. 33.

reference to the people, as is the case with a total revision. When one House desires an amendment and the other refuses to concur, the proposal is defeated or at least deferred until an agreement is reached. After the two Houses agree on the measure it is submitted to the people in a referendum in which it must be approved by a majority of all those voting and by a majority of those voting in a majority of the cantons.

2. The second way in which a partial revision may take place is through the use of the popular initiative. The initiative petition must be signed by 50,000 citizens and must be concerned with one subject only, that is to say, proposals amending more than one part of the constitution or adding more than one provision to it cannot be included in one petition. The proposal may be couched in general terms, indicating a desire to have the constitution amended or augmented in accord with a stated principle, or the petition may include a formal draft of the proposed amendment in the petition itself.

If the petition includes only a general statement of the desired change and not a formal draft suitable for incorporation into the constitution, then there are two courses open to the Assembly, between which it must decide by concurrence of the two Houses: (*a*) If it agrees with the general terms of the proposal, it formulates the amendment in precise terms for submission to the electorate in a compulsory referendum. (*b*) If it does not agree with the proposal, then a preliminary referendum is held to determine whether the electorate desires the amendment as described in the general terms of the petition. If the electorate votes 'no', then the proposal is dropped; if it votes 'yes', then the existing legislature must proceed to the formulation of the amendment in precise terms. This, of course, reduces the legislature to the status of a drafting committee under orders from a superior body. But the Councils are without very precise instructions in the matter and must interpret the popular decision as best they can. When the original petition is received by the Assembly, that body must decide within a year whether it will support the demand and formulate the amendment or whether it will disapprove and refer the question to the electorate.[1] If the preliminary refer-

[1] The electorate's original decision must, however, be made in a shorter time; all petition signatures older than six months are invalid.

endum results in an affirmative vote, however, there is no limit set on the time the legislature may take to draft the amendment and submit it to the final referendum. When the draft amendment is finally submitted to the voters, it must receive majorities both in the cantons and in the nation as a whole, as with other amendments. If it is successful, it becomes part of the constitution; just what happens if it is not successful is unclear. Whether the matter should be dropped or whether the legislature, still confronted with the mandate to devise an amendment, should make another effort to carry it out is not covered by the constitution. No such situation has ever arisen.

If the petition includes a draft proposal suitable for incorporation into the constitution, then the alternatives of the Federal Assembly are different. If it approves the proposal it merely submits it to referendum without comment; if it disapproves, two courses are open to it: it may submit along with the proposal a recommendation that it be refused by the people; or, if it agrees that some such amendment is desirable but dislikes the one in the petition, it may formulate a counter-proposal which is submitted to referendum along with the original. In no case, however, may the Assembly refuse to submit the proposal in the petition, nor may it alter any of its terms. If it disapproves it may offer an alternative to the people or it may recommend disapproval, but it must submit the original unchanged. The Assembly must make its decision within one year of the submission of the petition to it and, if it intends to formulate a counter-proposal, that also must be prepared within that period. If the Assembly fails to submit the question to referendum within the year, it is submitted by the Federal Council.[1] It may therefore be seen that 50,000 Swiss voters can compel a vote by national referendum on any proposal whatever, so long as they frame it in the form of an amendment to the constitution and assemble a sufficient number of signatures within a six-months' period. Nothing that either the Federal Council or the Federal Assembly may do can prevent the vote on the exact proposal so presented.

[1] These limits are prescribed in a law of 17 Jan. 1892. See Robert C. Brooks, *Government and Politics of Switzerland*, Yonkers, N.Y., 1920, p. 143, note 1; also Deploige, op. cit., pp. 131 f., 135.

## *Development of the Amending Procedure since 1848*

The constitutional referendum in its modern form seems to have originated in America in the 1770's. From there it passed to revolutionary France and thence to Switzerland in the early part of the nineteenth century. During the revolutionary disturbances of the 1830's and 1840's the use of the initiative and referendum became widespread in the Swiss cantons, and by 1848 there was little question that they were to be included in the newly framed constitution. Their use in the cantons was confirmed and required by Article 6 of the 1848 constitution, which guaranteed the cantonal constitutions only on condition that 'they have been accepted by the people, and that they may be amended by the people on the demand of the absolute majority of the citizens'. This clause was retained in the revised constitution of 1874 and still appears in the sixth article.

Amendment by means of the initiative and referendum was thought to render a constitution more flexible than the more rigid procedures of the American constitution, and Swiss experience would seem to have demonstrated the validity of this assumption. In regard to the amending procedure the drafting committee of the 1848 constitution said in its report:

> The committee proposes to render the constitution very easily amendable because a truly sovereign people must be able to change its fundamental law whenever it is so inclined. . . . In order to come into force, the Federal Constitution must be accepted by the majority of the Swiss citizens and by the majority of the cantons. Each element thus has its share in the supreme decision. The necessary concurrence of the majority of the confederate states constitutes a sufficient guarantee of cantonal sovereignty. We fully realize that all the cantons, the large as well as and perhaps more than the small, are attached to their sovereignty.[1]

The method adopted was thus to provide easy means of amending the constitution while at the same time guaranteeing to the cantons an integral part in the process.

The first concerted effort to change the provisions of the constitution took place in the middle 1860's. In 1866 the

[1] *Report of the Committee Which Drafted the Project of the Federal Constitution of 1848*, chap. iii; quoted in Rappard *et al.*, *Source Book on European Governments*, vol. i, p. 16.

Federal Assembly presented to the voters a series of nine amendments enlarging the powers of the federal government and guaranteeing certain civil and political rights. Of the nine proposals only one was accepted by the necessary majorities; this removed the disabilities imposed on Jews and made certain provisions regarding naturalized citizens. The agitation for modifications in the constitutional structure continued, however, and finally in 1872 resulted in an effort to revise the constitution completely. After long discussions[1] the Federal Assembly agreed upon a revised constitution which was submitted to the voters in May of that year. It was rejected by a vote of 260,000 to 256,000 with favourable majorities in only nine cantons.[2] The Assembly continued its efforts, however, and succeeded in effecting several compromises between the Radicals and their opponents as well as between the Catholics and the Protestants. A new draft was then drawn up and presented to the people in 1874. This time the revision was successful, receiving a majority of nearly 150,000 and the approval of 14½ cantons.[3]

The new constitution of 1874 had little effect on the amending procedure or the earlier scheme; it merely added two new paragraphs clarifying the manner in which the votes in the cantons should be counted in referenda.[4]

But a difficulty soon arose in the interpretation of the clauses that provided the amending procedure and this led to an important revision of the procedure itself. The constitution of 1848 had made no distinction between partial and total revision, though it spoke in general terms of *revision* of the constitution rather than of *amendment*. It was assumed that a partial revision might be undertaken in the same way as a total revision, either by a proposal of the two Houses of the legislature or by a popular initiative. Indeed the constituent assembly of 1848 adopted a resolution stating that in its

[1] The controversy evoked a number of pamphlets, which are summarized briefly in Deploige, op. cit., pp. 94 ff. The principal ones were Dubs, *Die schweizerische Demokratie in ihrer Fortentwicklung*, Berne, 1868; Gengel, *Aphorismen über demokratisches Staatsrecht*, Berne, 1864, and *Die Erweiterung der Volksrechte*, Berne, 1868; Bernet, *Nach zwanzig Jahren*, Berne, 1868; and Hilty, *Theoretiker und Idealisten der Demokratie*, Berne, 1868.

[2] *Statistisches Jahrbuch der Schweiz*, 1933, p. 395.

[3] Loc. cit.

[4] See below, Appendix A.

opinion the method prescribed in the constitution would be applicable to both kinds of change.[1] But this fact was not made clear in the document itself, with unfortunate results. The Federal Assembly initiated partial revisions in 1866 and this was not questioned even though the third chapter did not speak of anything other than 'revision'; there seemed to be general agreement that such an amendment was within the power of the Assembly to propose. But in 1879 an initiative petition was presented, bearing 56,526 signatures, requesting that Article 39 of the constitution be amended to establish a federal banknote monopoly. This was without precedent since 1848 and required an interpretation of the amending clause. The Federal Assembly, whose duty it would have been to submit the measure to the people, disregarded the express intention of the constituent assembly and, confining themselves to an interpretation of the clause itself, decided that it provided no right of popular initiative in partial revisions. According to this interpretation, the popular initiative could be used only to initiate total revisions of the constitution and this required a dissolution of the Assembly and new elections. Thus in order to secure a simple amendment to one article of the constitution it was necessary, unless the Assembly proposed the change, for the people to petition for a complete revision of the constitution and go through the unnecessary and complicated procedure of re-electing the two Houses of the legislature.

In accordance with this interpretation the Federal Assembly submitted to the referendum not the proposed amendment but merely the general question, 'Ought the present Federal Constitution to be revised?' This was in accordance with the provisions of the constitution for total revisions. The people, confronted with the need of using so difficult a means of getting such a small change, turned down the proposed total revision by a considerable majority, with 17½ cantons rejecting the measure.

An agitation for a constitutional amendment permitting the use of the initiative for partial revisions was immediately begun. Radical members of the Assembly joined in the movement and the Federal Council was directed to make a study

[1] Deploige, op. cit., p. 119, note 1.

of the problem and report to the Assembly. In June 1890 it reported that it favoured the amendment of the constitution to permit such a procedure[1] and the debate on the subject in the Assembly commenced in the following September. Two issues occupied most of the attention of the legislators: first, what should be the role of the Assembly in the process? and second, should the petition be drawn in the form of a legal amendment or should it be restricted to generalities? The solutions that were reached on these questions are reflected in the present form of the provisions, which have been described. Agreement was finally reached in April 1891 and the proposed amendment was submitted to referendum on 5 July. It was approved by 183,029 votes to 120,559; only four cantons returned negative majorities.[2]

The new provisions, as a glance at the Appendix below will show, made important modifications in the old amendment procedure. A few words were inserted into the old clause causing it to refer only to total revisions, and a whole new article was added prescribing in detail the manner in which the constitutional initiative should operate. An important element was the provision for the submission of petitions either in general terms or with the amendment set out in precise legal form.[3]

The only other major effort to alter the Swiss constitution occurred in 1934–5, when a heterogeneous aggregation of parties and interests tried to secure a total revision by use of the initiative. Agitation for the reform began in the early 1930's and soon collected about it at least three distinct supporting factions: (1) the Swiss fascist sympathizers, who desired a régime comparable to those that had appeared in Germany and Italy; (2) a group of Catholics, who desired a system based on corporativist principles; and (3) certain 'federalists',[4] who desired to return to the old scheme of

[1] See the *Message of the Federal Council to the Federal Assembly concerning the revision of the third chapter of the Federal Constitution*, 13 June 1890, p. 5; quoted in Deploige, op. cit., p. 120.

[2] *Statistisches Jahrbuch der Schweiz*, 1933, p. 397.

[3] The question of the banknote monopoly, which had originally raised the problem of partial amendment by initiative, had lain dormant during the intervening decade. It was now reintroduced and accepted by the people within three months of the adoption of the new procedure. But the new procedure was not used; the question was submitted to referendum by the Federal Assembly.

[4] The term 'federalist' has always meant in Switzerland just the opposite of

organization in which the cantons were much more nearly autonomous. All of these groups were considered to be well to the right and their demands were opposed by both Radicals and Socialists. They were essentially incompatible and were in agreement only on their desire for a change; on the nature of the change they did not and could not agree.

The petition requesting the general revision was signed by 78,050 voters[1] and was submitted on 5 September 1934. The debates in the Assembly were begun in December and continued into 1935. The referendum on the desirability of the revision was held on 8 September 1935 and the proposal was decisively defeated. 727,063 voters turned out to take part in the referendum, a figure not below the average but not high, in view of the grave consequences of the proposal. 511,578 voted 'no' and only 196,135 voted 'yes', a showing that was most disappointing to the revisionists. The latter were believed, both by themselves and by their opponents, to be able to command from 250,000 to 300,000 votes.[2] It was evident that the leaders of these groups were not able to discipline their followers. The ordinary voter was little interested in a general revision. Majorities were returned against the proposal in nineteen of the twenty-two cantons.[3] Significantly, the largest negative majorities came from those cantons that bordered on Italy and Germany.

The effort of 1935 is the only important instance of an attempt to secure a total revision of the constitution since 1874, and is the only one at all that has been submitted to a referendum. It may be noted that its supporters made no point of changing the amending clauses in chapter three, though there is every reason to suppose that some change would have been made had any of the three groups been able to impose its will on the new constitution.

The amending procedure today therefore is that of 1848

what it meant in the early days in America. Swiss federalists are decentralizers while the Federalists in the United States were those urging the establishment, and later the strengthening, of the central government.

[1] *Statistisches Jahrbuch der Schweiz*, 1946, pp. 522 f.

[2] Andrée Coste-Floret, *Les Votations populaires fédérales en Suisse de 1874 à 1935*, Montpellier, 1938, p. 270.

[3] In the canton of Schaffhausen the number of affirmative votes was less than the number of signatures secured there on the original initiative petition. Loc. cit.

with the additions incorporated into it in 1874 and 1891. The former merely clarified the method of counting the votes of the cantons and half-cantons. The latter made important alterations in regard to the popular initiative for partial revisions. The procedure as it now stands authorizes the initiation of both partial and total revisions either by the two Houses of the legislature or by means of the popular initiative. Any change, however, must be ratified by a majority of the whole population and of the cantons.

### *Experience with the Amending Process*

The Swiss constitution has probably been amended more times than that of any other modern national state.[1] Its authors claimed in 1848 that it was to be a very flexible thing, and experience seems to have borne out the wisdom of their estimate. From its inception up to the end of 1952 the Swiss voters had gone to the polls to approve or disapprove a total of 109 proposals to alter the constitution in one way or another, an average of about one per year. If one counts only from the revised constitution of 1874 the average is considerably greater than one per year: 98 referenda in 78 years. These figures mean little by themselves, but the frequent use to which the Swiss put their amending process will be seen from a more detailed examination of these efforts to amend the constitution.

In the period between 1848 and 1874 there were relatively few efforts to change the provisions of the constitution. The constitutional initiative was not operative at that time, as we have seen, and this naturally reduced the number of efforts. Apart from the unsuccessful effort in 1879 to secure a banknote monopoly through the use of the initiative, that device saw no service at all on a national level until after the passage of the amendment of 1891 permitting its use for partial revisions. Moreover, in the period before 1874 there was only one major effort to secure constitutional changes. This was in 1866, when the Federal Assembly submitted a series of nine amendments to the people, of which all but one were refused. This was the

[1] By far the most detailed study of Swiss constitutional amendment, and an invaluable source of information on the subject, is William E. Rappard, *La Constitution fédérale de la Suisse 1848–1948*, Neuchâtel, 1948.

only attempt in any form to secure amendments until the ill-fated total revision of 1872, which was finally completed successfully two years later. Thus to see the true nature of the Swiss amending process at work we will do well to base our estimate on the experience since the total revision of 1874.

Since this latter date there have been referenda on 48 amendment proposals emanating from the Federal Assembly and 50 that have been introduced by the process of popular initiative.[1] Of the 48 referendum proposals by the Assembly 38 have been accepted by the people and 10 have failed of adoption. Of the 50 initiatives only 14 have been successful and 36 have failed. The contrast between the two figures is significant.

There is little to explain about the referendum proposals. They are all of the same kind, so far as the mechanics of amendment are concerned, and the figures do not misconstrue the real activity. Each was proposed by the two houses of the Federal Assembly and was submitted to referendum according to the provisions of Articles 120 and 121. The outstanding feature of the referenda is the startling number that have been approved by the people.

The figures on the use of the constitutional initiative require some explanations. The table on page 187 displays the various forms it has taken. It will be recalled that several things can happen to an initiative petition, depending on the attitude of the two houses of the legislature. The Assembly may simply submit the proposal to referendum if it approves the content of it; or if it disapproves of the measure, it may submit it with a recommendation that it be refused by the voters; or it may submit along with it an alternative proposal. Of the 50 initiative votes, 41 have been straightforward referenda on questions proposed by petitions and submitted to the people by the Assembly. Of these 41 only 6 have been approved in the referenda: those concerning the slaughter of animals in 1893; the prohibition of absinthe in 1908; the provision for proportional representation in elections to the National Council in 1918; the requirement that certain treaties be

[1] This figure includes all the items in the right-hand column of the table on p. 187, i.e. it includes alternative or substitute proposals submitted by the Assembly as well as those submitted directly by petition. All data are reported as of 1 Jan. 1953.

# SWITZERLAND

*Constitutional Referenda on Proposals by Federal Assembly ('compulsory referenda')*

| Date | Subject | Popular vote | | Cantons | | Result |
|---|---|---|---|---|---|---|
| | | *Aff.* | *Neg.* | *Aff.* | *Neg.* | |
| 3 Sept. 1848 | Federal constitution of 1848 | 169,743 | 71,899 | 15½ | 6½ | yes |
| 14 Jan. 1866 | Regulation of weights and measures | 158,182 | 156,396 | 9½ | 12½ | no |
| 14 Jan. 1866 | Equality of Jews and naturalized citizens | 170,032 | 149,401 | 12½ | 9½ | yes |
| 14 Jan. 1866 | Communal affairs—right to vote | 137,321 | 181,441 | 8 | 14 | no |
| 14 Jan. 1866 | Civil rights and duties | 125,924 | 189,830 | 9 | 13 | no |
| 14 Jan. 1866 | Right to vote in cantonal matters | 153,469 | 165,679 | 10 | 12 | no |
| 14 Jan. 1866 | Liberty of conscience and religion | 157,629 | 162,992 | 11 | 11 | no |
| 14 Jan. 1866 | Abolition of certain punishments | 108,364 | 208,619 | 6½ | 15½ | no |
| 14 Jan. 1866 | Patents and copyrights | 137,476 | 177,386 | 9½ | 12½ | no |
| 14 Jan. 1866 | Lotteries and gambling prohibited | 139,062 | 176,788 | 9½ | 12½ | no |
| 12 May 1872 | Total revision of federal constitution | 255,606 | 260,859 | 9 | 13 | no |
| 19 Apr. 1874 | Total revision of federal constitution | 340,199 | 198,013 | 14½ | 7½ | yes |
| 18 May 1879 | Reintroduction of death penalty | 200,485 | 181,588 | 14 | 8 | yes |
| 30 July 1882 | Patents | 141,616 | 156,658 | 7½ | 14½ | no |
| 25 Oct. 1885 | Permitting creation of alcohol monopoly | 230,250 | 157,463 | 15 | 7 | yes |
| 10 July 1887 | Patents | 203,506 | 57,862 | 20½ | 1½ | yes |
| 26 Oct. 1890 | Insurance against sickness and accidents | 283,228 | 92,200 | 20½ | 1½ | yes |
| 5 July 1891 | Partial const'l revision by initiative | 183,029 | 120,559 | 18 | 4 | yes |
| 18 Oct. 1891 | Banknote monopoly | 231,578 | 158,651 | 14 | 8 | yes |
| 4 Mar. 1894 | Federal power over industry | 135,719 | 158,492 | 8½ | 13½ | no |
| 29 Sept. 1895 | Federal match monopoly | 140,174 | 184,109 | 7½ | 14½ | no |
| 3 Nov. 1895 | Centralizing army control | 195,178 | 269,751 | 4½ | 17½ | no |
| 11 July 1897 | Extending forest and water police | 156,102 | 89,561 | 16 | 6 | yes |
| 11 July 1897 | Pure food legislation | 162,250 | 89,955 | 18½ | 3½ | yes |
| 13 Nov. 1898 | Providing uniform civil code | 264,933 | 101,820 | 16½ | 5½ | yes |
| 13 Nov. 1898 | Providing uniform criminal code | 266,713 | 101,712 | 16½ | 5½ | yes |
| 23 Nov. 1902 | Federal grants to cantonal schools | 258,561 | 80,429 | 21½ | ½ | yes |
| 25 Oct. 1903 | Restricting sale of liquor | 156,777 | 228,094 | 4 | 18 | no |
| 19 Mar. 1905 | Patents | 199,187 | 83,935 | 21½ | ½ | yes |
| 5 July 1908 | Uniform industrial legislation | 232,457 | 92,561 | 21½ | ½ | yes |
| 4 May 1913 | Combating epidemics and epizootics | 169,012 | 111,163 | 16½ | 5½ | yes |
| 25 Oct. 1914 | Federal Administrative Court | 204,394 | 123,431 | 18 | 4 | yes |
| 6 June 1915 | Temporary war tax | 452,117 | 27,461 | 22 | 0 | yes |
| 13 May 1917 | Federal stamp tax | 190,288 | 167,689 | 14½ | 7½ | yes |
| 4 May 1919 | Navigation | 399,131 | 78,260 | 22 | 0 | yes |
| 4 May 1919 | War tax | 307,528 | 165,119 | 20 | 2 | yes |
| 10 Aug. 1919 | Election of National Council and Federal Council. | 200,008 | 79,369 | 21½ | ½ | yes |
| 16 May 1920 | Entry into League of Nations | 416,870 | 323,719 | 11½ | 10½ | yes |
| 22 May 1921 | Regulation of automobiles and bicycles | 206,297 | 138,876 | 15½ | 6½ | yes |
| 22 May 1921 | Regulation of aerial navigation | 210,447 | 127,943 | 20½ | 1½ | yes |
| 3 June 1923 | Alcohol monopoly | 262,688 | 360,397 | 10 | 12 | no |
| 25 Oct. 1925 | Regulation of aliens | 382,381 | 150,109 | 18½ | 3½ | yes |
| 6 Dec. 1925 | Old age, widows', disability insurance | 410,988 | 217,483 | 16½ | 5½ | yes |
| 5 Dec. 1926 | Grain monopoly | 366,507 | 372,049 | 8 | 14 | no |
| 15 May 1927 | Cantonal road payments | 334,206 | 199,305 | 21 | 1 | yes |
| 20 May 1928 | Naturalization | 316,250 | 131,215 | 19½ | 2½ | yes |
| 6 Apr. 1930 | Alcohol monopoly | 494,248 | 321,641 | 17 | 5 | yes |
| 15 Mar. 1931 | Election quotient for National Council | 296,053 | 253,382 | 13½ | 8½ | yes |
| 15 Mar. 1931 | Term of National Council | 297,938 | 256,919 | 16 | 6 | yes |
| 20 Feb. 1938 | Romansch a national language | 574,991 | 52,827 | 22 | 0 | yes |
| 27 Nov. 1938 | Federal financial arrangements | 509,387 | 195,538 | 21 | 1 | yes |
| 4 June 1939 | National defence | 445,622 | 246,082 | 19 | 3 | yes |
| 6 July 1947 | Economic controls | 556,803 | 494,414 | 13 | 9 | yes |
| 22 May 1949 | Swiss National Bank | 293,650 | 468,823 | 1½ | 20½ | no |
| 4 June 1950 | Federal financial management | 267,770 | 486,381 | 6 | 16 | no |
| 3 Dec. 1950 | Election of National Council | 450,395 | 218,541 | 20 | 2 | yes |
| 3 Dec. 1950 | Finance plan for 1951–4 | 516,704 | 227,131 | 20 | 2 | yes |
| 6 July 1952 | Armament financing | 256,195 | 353,522 | 3 | 19 | no |
| 23 Nov. 1952 | Price control extension | 489,461 | 289,837 | 16 | 6 | yes |
| 23 Nov. 1952 | Wheat supply | 583,546 | 188,044 | 21½ | ½ | yes |

Source: *Statistisches Jahrbuch der Schweiz*; the votes from 1848 to 1934 may be found in the volume for 1933, pp. 394–401; subsequent votes in subsequent volumes.

submitted to referendum in 1921; the subsidies for tourist spas in 1928; and the restriction of the plenary powers of the Federal Council in 1949. All the rest of the proposals were defeated, which indicates that the electorate is more receptive to advice from the legislature than from other citizens.

Moreover, the results have been considerably different in the nine instances in which the Federal Assembly has seen fit to offer a counter-proposal to the electorate along with the proposal initiated by the initiative petition. In five of these nine instances the submission of a counter-measure by the Assembly has resulted in the withdrawal of the original measure as proposed in the petition; in these five cases, therefore, the Assembly's proposal has gone before the voters by itself.[1] In four instances, however, the initiative proposal has not been withdrawn, with the result that both measures have been submitted to the referendum simultaneously.[2] It is significant that the measures proposed by the Assembly have been much more successful in these instances than have those proposed by petition. In the five instances in which the initiative has been withdrawn in favour of a legislative proposal, four of the latter have been approved; of the four instances in which the two proposals competed at the polls, the legislative proposal has been successful three times and the original initiative proposal once. These votes support the hypothesis suggested above, namely that the electorate is usually more sympathetic to the proposals of the legislature than to those of the petitioners. Of the fourteen successful measures listed in the table of initiatives on page 187 exactly one-half have

[1] Regulation of water power, 1908; Foreign decorations, 1931; Restriction on the urgency clause of Article 89, 1939; Family protection, 1945; and the Co-ordination of transport, 1946.

[2] Restrictions on gaming houses, 1920; Grain provisions, 1929; Private armament industry, 1938; Issue of banknotes, 1951.

---

* An initiative received 95,200 signatures but was withdrawn in favour of a counter-proposal by the Federal Assembly.

† An initiative received 75,234 signatures but was withdrawn in favour of a counter-proposal by the Federal Assembly.

‡ An initiative received 289,765 signatures but was withdrawn in favour of a counter-proposal by the Federal Assembly.

§ An initiative received 168,730 signatures but was withdrawn in favour of a counter-proposal by the Federal Assembly.

|| An initiative received 384,760 signatures but was withdrawn in favour of a counter-proposal by the Federal Assembly.

Source: *Statistisches Jahrbuch der Schweiz*; the votes from 1848 to 1934 may be found in the volume for 1933, pp. 394–401; subsequent votes in subsequent volumes.

# SWITZERLAND

*Table of Votes on Constitutional Referenda on Amendments proposed by Initiative*

| Date | Subject | Petition signatures | Popular vote | | Cantons | | Result |
|---|---|---|---|---|---|---|---|
| | | | Aff. | Neg. | Aff. | Neg. | |
| 31 Oct. 1880 | Total revision banknote monopoly | 52,588 | 121,099 | 260,126 | 4½ | 17½ | no |
| 20 Aug. 1893 | Slaughter of animals | 83,159 | 191,527 | 127,101 | 11½ | 10½ | yes |
| 3 June 1894 | Right to work | 52,387 | 75,880 | 232,409 | 0 | 22 | no |
| 4 Nov. 1894 | Split customs with cantons | 67,828 | 145,462 | 350,639 | 8½ | 13½ | no |
| 4 Nov. 1900 | P.R. in National Council elections | 64,675 | 169,008 | 244,666 | 10½ | 11½ | no |
| 4 Nov. 1900 | Direct election of Federal Council | 56,350 | 145,926 | 270,522 | 8 | 14 | no |
| 25 Oct. 1903 | Rep'n in Nat'l Council | 57,379 | 95,131 | 295,085 | 4 | 18 | no |
| 5 July 1908 | Prohibition of absinthe | 167,814 | 241,078 | 138,669 | 20 | 2 | yes |
| 25 Oct. 1908 | Regulation of water power* | .. | 304,923 | 56,237 | 21½ | ½ | yes |
| 23 Oct. 1910 | P.R. in National Council elections | 142,263 | 240,305 | 265,194 | 12 | 10 | no |
| 2 June 1918 | Federal direct tax | 116,864 | 276,735 | 325,814 | 7½ | 14½ | no |
| 13 Oct. 1918 | P.R. in National Council elections | 122,631 | 299,550 | 149,037 | 19½ | 2½ | yes |
| 21 Mar. 1920 | Gambling: | | | | | | |
| | (*a*) Initiative | 117,494 | 271,941 | 241,441 | 12 | 10 | yes |
| | (*b*) Counter-proposal | .. | 108,300 | 347,479 | ½ | 21½ | no |
| 30 Jan. 1921 | Referendum required on treaties | 64,391 | 398,538 | 160,004 | 20 | 2 | yes |
| 30 Jan. 1921 | Limiting military courts | 118,996 | 198,696 | 393,151 | 3 | 19 | no |
| 11 June 1922 | Naturalization of aliens | 59,812 | 65,828 | 347,988 | 0 | 22 | no |
| 11 June 1922 | Deportation for security reasons | 59,812 | 159,200 | 258,881 | 0 | 22 | no |
| 11 June 1922 | Federal officials in National Council | 57,139 | 160,181 | 257,469 | 5 | 17 | no |
| 3 Dec. 1922 | Capital levy | 87,535 | 109,702 | 736,952 | 0 | 22 | no |
| 18 Feb. 1923 | Preventive arrests | 62,323 | 55,145 | 445,606 | 0 | 22 | no |
| 15 Apr. 1923 | Tariff rights | 151,321 | 171,020 | 467,876 | ½ | 21½ | no |
| 24 May 1925 | Old Age, sickness, widows' insurance | 78,990 | 282,527 | 390,129 | 6 | 16 | no |
| 2 Dec. 1928 | Resort subsidies | 131,017 | 296,395 | 274,528 | 14½ | 7½ | yes |
| 3 Mar. 1929 | Grain provisions: | | | | | | |
| | (*a*) Initiative | 77,062 | 18,487 | 672,004 | 0 | 22 | no |
| | (*b*) Counter-proposal | .. | 461,176 | 228,357 | 21 | 1 | yes |
| 12 May 1929 | Highway regulation | 51,580 | 248,350 | 420,082 | 3 | 19 | no |
| 12 May 1929 | Communal liquor controls | 145,761 | 226,794 | 467,724 | ½ | 21½ | no |
| 8 Feb. 1931 | Foreign decorations† | .. | 293,845 | 124,804 | 17 | 5 | yes |
| 2 June 1935 | Economic crisis functions | 334,699 | 425,242 | 567,425 | 4 | 18 | no |
| 8 Sept. 1935 | Total constitutional revision | 78,050 | 196,135 | 511,578 | 3 | 19 | no |
| 20 Feb. 1938 | Modify legislative referendum | 53,416 | 87,638 | 488,195 | 0 | 22 | no |
| 20 Feb. 1938 | Private armament industry: | | | | | | |
| | (*a*) Initiative | 56,848 | 65,938 | 418,021 | 0 | 22 | no |
| | (*b*) Counter-proposal | .. | 394,052 | 149,025 | 22 | 0 | yes |
| 22 Jan. 1939 | Constitutional jurisdiction | 58,690 | 141,323 | 347,340 | 0 | 22 | no |
| 22 Jan. 1939 | Restrict urgency clause‡ | .. | 346,024 | 155,032 | 21 | 1 | yes |
| 9 Mar. 1941 | Alcohol regulation | 129,584 | 304,867 | 452,873 | 7½ | 14½ | no |
| 25 Jan. 1941 | Direct election of Federal Council | 157,081 | 251,605 | 524,127 | 0 | 22 | no |
| 3 May 1942 | Reorganize National Council | 75,740 | 219,629 | 408,821 | ½ | 21½ | no |
| 25 Nov. 1945 | Family Protection§ | .. | 548,601 | 170,278 | 21½ | ½ | yes |
| 10 Feb. 1946 | Co-ordination of transport‖ | .. | 289,935 | 571,566 | 1 | 21 | no |
| 8 Dec. 1946 | Right to work | 73,292 | 124,792 | 525,366 | 0 | 22 | no |
| 18 May 1947 | Economic reform; right to work | 161,477 | 244,415 | 539,244 | 0 | 22 | no |
| 11 Sept. 1949 | Abolish war powers of Federal Council | 55,796 | 280,755 | 272,599 | 12½ | 9½ | yes |
| 1 Oct. 1950 | Prevention of speculation | 54,698 | 158,794 | 429,091 | 0 | 22 | no |
| 15 Apr. 1951 | Banknote issue: | | | | | | |
| | (*a*) Initiative | 89,553 | 88,486 | 622,284 | 0 | 22 | no |
| | (*b*) Counter-proposal | .. | 490,326 | 209,636 | 22 | 0 | yes |
| 8 July 1951 | Taxation | 50,945 | 165,713 | 341,869 | 0 | 22 | no |
| 20 Apr. 1952 | Tax on corporate income | 88,025 | 129,243 | 552,122 | 0 | 22 | no |
| 18 May 1952 | Armament financing | 147,092 | 328,341 | 422,255 | 4 | 18 | no |

*(For notes * † ‡ § ‖ see opposite)*

actually been initiated not by petition but by the Federal Assembly as alternative proposals; thus while only seven[1] out of forty-one initiative proposals have been accepted (17 per cent.), seven out of nine legislative counter-proposals have succeeded (78 per cent.).

Finally, if one combines the two tables on pages 185 and 187 and determines the total number of proposals initiated by petition and by legislative action since 1874, one arrives inescapably at the conclusion that the legislative voice carries much greater weight with the electorate than does that of the popular initiative. Of the fifty-seven measures proposed by the Assembly forty-five, or 79 per cent., have passed; of the forty-one initiative measures submitted to referendum only seven, or 17 per cent., have been accepted.

The reasons for this phenomenon are fairly obvious. The legislative body rather accurately represents the diversities of public opinion. Hence it is unlikely that sufficient enthusiasm would be aroused for a measure in the Assembly if it were not supported by a substantial group of the electorate. Moreover, the legislature by organized debate, upon which public attention is focused, can discuss matters of this kind at length and can influence public opinion; many minds may be changed because of negative decisions in the legislative debates. The legislature is the obvious channel through which a movement towards constitutional amendment should flow. If the legislature can be brought to propose the amendment, the difficulties of amassing the necessary 50,000 signatures on initiative petitions are obviated. Hence the measures on which there is widespread agreement are likely to go first to the legislature; its proposals thus begin with the assumption of adequate support.

On the other hand, the reverse is true of initiative proposals. The purpose of the initiative is to provide a minority of the people a means of getting their proposals before the law-making body; it guarantees them a hearing that they might not otherwide obtain. Initiative measures are, for the most part,

[1] In 1920 the initiative proposal on gambling was accepted while the legislative counter-proposal was defeated. In 1946 an initiative proposal for the regulation of transport was withdrawn in favour of a counter-proposal; but the latter was defeated.

measures that the legislature has refused to entertain; the very fact that they are proposed by initiative suggests that they do not command a wide popular support. This is not always true, for legislators are sometimes wrong in their estimate of public opinion; and some measures are initiated by petition without a prior test in the Assembly. The successful initiatives are adequate evidence of this fact; but their rarity indicates that this is the exception rather than the rule.

Finally, the initiative in Switzerland has frequently been employed by minority groups as a propaganda device for calling their proposals to the attention of the electors. The Socialist Party in particular has pushed through several initiative petitions although it has apparently known in advance that they were doomed to failure even if they could be brought to referendum. The successive attempts to secure a 'right to work' amendment have been made for this purpose, despite the fact that none of them has ever achieved a majority in so much as half a canton.

### *The Federal Element in the Amending Process*

To become law an amendment must receive in the referendum a majority not only of all those voting but also of all those voting in a majority of the cantons. The requirement is the same as that found in the Australian constitution with the difference that in Australia a majority of the states actually constitutes two-thirds, whereas in Switzerland 11½ cantons out of 22 are all that are needed. We have seen in Australia that on three measures the will of the majority of the total electorate has been thwarted by the absence of a sufficient number of state majorities. This problem has arisen twice in Switzerland. In 1866 the Federal Assembly submitted a series of nine amendments to the voters, of which all but one were refused. Among these was a proposal authorizing federal control over weights and measures which was supported by a majority of the people, 159,182 votes against 156,396, but which failed of adoption because it obtained majorities in only 9½ cantons.[1]

An even more interesting example is that involving an

[1] *Statistisches Jahrbuch der Schweiz*, 1933, pp. 394 f.

initiative proposal in 1910 for the adoption of proportional representation in the National Council. This measure was defeated in the nation-wide balloting, receiving only 240,305 affirmative votes while 265,194 negative votes were cast against it; but it received local majorities in a majority (12) of the cantons. This situation has never occurred in Australia; all three of the Australian referenda mentioned above have resulted in favourable national majorities with insufficient state majorities.

Apart from these two instances all referenda in Switzerland have produced similar results in both cantons and nation. The majority of the cantons have always agreed with the result attained in the total vote.

### *The Frequency of Amendment Proposals*

The Swiss voters have been called to the polls to decide a question of constitutional amendment on an average of about once every nine months since 1874. This does not by any means represent the total number of efforts to secure a change in the constitution; these are merely the occasions on which an effort to amend was successful to the extent that a resolution proposing an amendment was *passed* by the legislature or on which 50,000 signatures were collected within a six-months' period on an initiative petition. There have been numerous instances in which motions failed or the required signatures could not be collected in time. Even so, the total number of referenda themselves is most impressive. No other federal state and perhaps no other country in the world can match the record of the Swiss in the past eighty years.

The explanation of this phenomenon is no easy thing. In search of it one most conveniently turns to the absence in Switzerland of any power in the judiciary to review and if necessary to invalidate the acts of the federal legislature. In most federations the constitutional structure is constantly being modified by means other than those of formal amendment, and one of the most important of these is the adaptation of constitutional law and doctrine by the judicial interpretation of the written constitution. In Switzerland the judiciary is called upon to interpret the federal constitution but it does not have the power to review the acts of the Federal Assembly. Such an avenue of constitutional change is therefore closed to the Swiss, and whatever might otherwise be accomplished in this fashion must be accomplished in others.[1] It is true that the judiciary does review the Acts of cantonal legislatures and of administrative officials at both local and national levels; but the important element of judicial review in the rest of the world is the review of national legislation; and the competence of the Swiss courts does not extend to this. The immediate result is to throw more responsibility upon the legislature which would thus seem to be endowed with the power to make such changes as would otherwise be accomplished by the judiciary, and to a certain extent this is true. But it is not wholly true. The legislature too is limited by the constitution; it cannot enact laws in violation of the fundamental law; and though it would seem to be the ultimate authority in the definition of its own powers, there still exists above it the power of the people to restrict or repudiate its acts through the initiative and referendum. Part of the constitution-changing function that might otherwise be performed by the courts passes to the legislature, but part of it also inevitably passes on farther to the amending process itself. And my argument here is that the absence of the power of judicial review tends to increase the use of the formal amending procedure.

Too much can, of course, be made of this point; its importance is difficult to assess. What the judiciary seems to do in America and in other countries where it has the power of judicial review is not to *amend* the constitution but to prevent its violation. It exercises a judicial veto over the acts of the other organs of government. It is the executive or the legislature

[1] Most commentators have followed Dicey's early insistence that federalism necessarily implies the right of the judiciary to appraise and invalidate the acts of all the legislatures, both national and local. See A. V. Dicey, *Introduction to the Study of the Law of the Constitution*, London, 1885, 9th edn. by E. C. S. Wade, 1939, pp. 157–80. This view has by no means been abandoned, despite Switzerland. Professor Wheare argues that '. . . federalism means that the last word upon whether a measure shall be law rests with the judicial branch of government and not with the legislature, subject to any decision taken by the body competent to amend the Constitution'. K. C. Wheare, 'The Impact of Federalism upon Parliamentary Government in the Commonwealth', *Parliamentary Affairs*, vol. 4, 1950, p. 166. See also P. A. Freund, 'A Supreme Court in a Federation: Some Lessons from Legal History', *Columbia Law Review*, vol. 53, 1953, pp. 597–619.

that proposes, while the judiciary disposes. It is too facile to say that the constitution is amended by judicial interpretation; in very many instances what the courts do is to permit or not permit someone else to amend it. And to the extent that this is the only role they perform we can scarcely argue that the absence of such a power in the Swiss courts transfers that function to the amending procedures; it would seem rather to transfer it merely to the legislature.

But changes in the constitutional structure do come about nevertheless through the medium of judicial interpretation. Judicial changes in the constitution may arise out of the initiative of other organs of government or of private groups, but the courts, though their function is in this sense restrictive, must now and then yield to these pressures and open up new avenues for action by appropriate reinterpretation of the constitution. In such an instance the court does play an important part in the process of constitutional change, even though the impetus towards the change may be said to come from some other source. And in many instances it is not at all clear that the impetus comes from outside the court. Certainly in such cases as *U.S.* v. *South-Eastern Underwriters Association*[1] and *Erie Railroad* v. *Tompkins*[2] there is a basis for arguing that the *court* changed the constitution. The difference in the Australian constitution as interpreted in *Deakin* v. *Webb* and as interpreted in the *Engineers' Case*[3] or the difference in the United States between *Hammer* v. *Dagenhart* and *U.S.* v. *Darby Lumber Company*[4] represents a highly significant change in the constitution and one that was produced by the judiciary. Admittedly the judiciary was subjected to considerable pressure to make the changes, but it was none the less the judiciary that made them. Moreover, this initiative or pressure may come from private groups as well, as has been true in the long series of civil rights cases in the United States. But the changing nature of the constitutional law on civil rights can scarcely be explained in any terms other than judicial decisions to change the content of the constitution. In the civil rights decisions, and

[1] 332 U.S. 533 (1944). [2] 304 U.S. 64 (1938).

[3] *Deakin* v. *Webb* (1904), 1 C.L.R. 585 and *Amalgamated Society of Engineers* v. *Adelaide Steamship Company* (1920), 28 C.L.R. 129.

[4] 247 U.S. 251 (1918) and 312 U.S. 100 (1941).

in the cases cited above as well, at least part of the initiative has come from the courts. To the extent that the courts do initiate changes, they serve as an active force in altering the constitution; and their ability to do this derives largely from the power of judicial review.

Perhaps of greater significance is the position that the courts hold in the popular mind. In a country employing judicial review the first test of the validity of legislative acts is in the courts; the courts are regarded as special guardians and interpreters of the constitution; they are much revered by the people. Opponents of questioned acts or proponents of new doctrines take them first to the judiciary; seldom is an appeal carried beyond its decision to the amendment procedure itself. In Switzerland the courts do not exercise this function; they do not serve as an intermediate testing-station between the legislature, the executive agencies, or the private groups, and the formal devices of amendment. Hence the appeals that would otherwise be carried to the courts can only be carried directly to the amendment procedure, or be abandoned. Instead of judicial review Switzerland has popular review. The courts do not receive the reverence that is accorded them in the United States and in other federations, where they are the final arbiters of the constitution. They do not possess the final veto on legislative action; they do not initiate changes in the constitution to the extent that they may elsewhere. The loss (by comparison) of the Swiss courts is greater than merely the loss of the power to review national legislation, for they lose too the esteem and exaggerated regard which that high position elsewhere confers upon them. I think we are justified in saying that the absence of judicial review is one of the important reasons for the greater use of the amending power in Switzerland.[1]

A second explanation lies in the absence of any right of initiative in the domain of ordinary legislation. The forms of direct democracy in Switzerland are more varied than those of most countries, but even there they are limited. They include both the initiative and referendum for constitutional amendments and they include an optional referendum for

[1] See the discussion of the problem as it appears in the United States in Fred V. Cahill, *Judicial Legislation*, New York, 1952, chap. 1.

legislative measures,[1] but they do not include the initiative for ordinary federal laws. But the Swiss live in an atmosphere of direct democracy; they are accustomed to employing the means of direct democracy in expressing their wills in law both at the national and cantonal levels. Since the national statute book is closed to the process of initiative, those groups advocating changes in the law, but which find no sympathy in the legislature, naturally turn to the constitutional initiative as the only means by which they can put their proposals to the voters. It seems quite apparent that if Switzerland permitted the initiative in ordinary legislation, the number of amendments to the constitution would be considerably less.

This disability also affects the nature of amendments that have been added to the constitution. Since the initiative must be used to amend the constitution and not merely to pass a law, measures that might be expected to become laws find their way into the constitution. The constitution thus contains provisions that in other countries would be assigned to the statutes and not to the fundamental law. A good example of this was afforded by the first amendment thus adopted, that of 1893, which prohibited the slaughtering of animals without previously rendering them unconscious.[2] The measure was pushed through with the support of the S.P.C.A. and certain anti-semitic interests and it was adopted by a comfortable majority. But one may doubt that a provision of this kind should have a place in a constitutional document; had the legislative initiative been provided, it most likely would not.

But the absence of a legislative initiative is not sufficient explanation either, for as many amendments have originated in the legislature as in the initiative; moreover, many of the amendments sponsored by the Assembly are also open to the criticism that they too deal with matters that might better be left to ordinary law. The explanation lies deeper in the Swiss

[1] The optional referendum takes place whenever 30,000 voters sign petitions calling for the reference of a legislative act to the electorate. It was first incorporated into the constitution in 1874 in the total revision of that year; it now appears in Article 89. For a discussion of its operation see Brooks, *Government and Politics of Switzerland*, pp. 152 ff. This referendum had been used sixty times from 1874 to mid-1953; twenty-one measures were confirmed and thirty-nine repudiated. *Statistisches Jahrbuch der Schweiz*, 1933, pp. 394–401; 1946, pp. 522–3; 1952, pp. 506–7.

[2] Now Article 25 *bis* in the constitution.

political mind. The extensive use of amendments for such purposes reflects a different attitude towards government from that commonly found in the English-speaking world. The Swiss have behind them a republican tradition of many centuries and they pride themselves on the fact that for hundreds of years they enjoyed the only republican system in Europe. Moreover, in many of the cantons this republicanism has meant democracy of the most direct kind for almost as long. The canton in the eyes of many Swiss is still more important than the federation and it is there that many issues of great importance are still fought out. In a few of the cantons even today the legislative body is the *Landsgemeinde* of the whole citizenry meeting together. The point is that the Swiss are used to living close to their government; they are accustomed to using it for their own purposes, and using it directly. The Australians, too, proclaim such an attitude towards government, but the Swiss make it operative in a way that the Australians (and perhaps every other nation) can never hope to achieve. If the constitution stands in the way of some particular need or desire, the Swiss does not merely bewail the fact; he changes the constitution. This results inevitably in a wholly different attitude towards constitutionality. It does not imply a lesser respect for law and order or even for the constitutional document itself; it merely means that the constitution and the law are called upon to respond to the purposes of the people they are designed to serve and that this response must be immediate and direct. The constitution becomes a tool to be used as needed rather than an idol to be worshipped from afar.

### *The Frequency of Successful Amendments*

This increased consciousness of the democratic process and this different attitude towards constitutionality help to explain not only the fact that many efforts have been made to amend the constitution but also the fact that a large share (about 55 per cent.) of these efforts have been successful. A long tradition of close participation in government breeds a self-consciousness in the citizen which is not found in large representative democratic states. When an amendment is proposed the Swiss voters can consider it a decision that they themselves must make. If the constitution is to be changed, it is they themselves who must change it. There is a personal responsibility involved; they are the ones who make such decisions; they do not feel that such an appeal is merely another effort to put something over on them. One reason for this is the fact that there has been no long series of efforts to increase the powers of the federal government at the expense of the cantons such as has been found in Australia. The amendments have been well divided among such subjects as economic matters, police regulations, financial measures, social legislation, and participation in international affairs.[1] When all amendments are of one kind, the citizen may easily develop a positive or negative attitude towards all amendments and may vote according to this preconception rather than according to his own careful appraisal of each proposal. The Swiss have been less troubled with this problem, since all sorts of changes have been proposed.

Furthermore, practice in this kind of situation perpetuates itself. An institution which may at the outset have been a mere mechanical device collects about itself with the passage of years an aura of sanctity all its own. Careful consideration and willingness to amend the basic law, once established, tend to continue. The Swiss voter today who feels the need of an amendment is not restrained by the fact that such an amendment would be a very unusual thing. Since his fathers and he himself have amended the constitution many times before, there is no presumption that he should disapprove of further amendment. The Swiss have always amended their constitution whenever necessary; therefore they continue to do so.

### *Amendment in Switzerland Compared with that in Australia*

A comparison with Australian experience is suggested by the fact that the procedures employed for constitutional amendment in the two countries are so very similar. Both employ the method of proposal by the national legislature,

[1] A brief classification of the amendments may be found in Brooks, op. cit., chap. vi; a more detailed and up-to-date discussion is that of Andrée Coste-Floret, *Les Votations populaires fédérales en Suisse de 1874 à 1935*; in the latter work the amendment referenda are classified topically and each is discussed in some detail. Still more valuable are the analyses in Rappard, *La Constitution fédérale de la Suisse, 1848–1948*, Neuchâtel, 1948.

both Houses ordinarily being required to consent; each then subjects the proposed amendment to the vote of the electors, who must approve it by majorities in the nation at large and in a majority of the component units.

There are, of course, differences in the two procedures. Australia makes no provision for the constitutional initiative; the Houses of the Australian Parliament must approve the measure by absolute majorities; whereas in Australia a measure to which the upper chamber objects may be submitted to referendum over its objection, this may be done in Switzerland only in the rare instance of a total revision. But the differences are less important than the similarities.

The outstanding fact that appears from a comparison of the records of the two countries is that the Swiss constitution has been changed literally dozens of times, while the Australian has been amended on only four occasions. The difference is one not only of absolute numbers but of percentages as well. We have seen that the constitutional referendum in Switzerland has resulted in the acceptance of approximately 55 per cent. of the proposals that have been submitted to it. In Australia the figure is about 17 per cent. If one discounts the proposals that have been introduced in Switzerland by the initiative procedure (because it does not exist in Australia) the discrepancy between the two countries becomes even greater.

In Australia the referendum has been a highly conservative device, since the people have generally been unwilling to alter their constitution; in Switzerland this has not been so, despite the fact that in essential features the two procedures are very nearly identical. The difference is difficult to explain satisfactorily. The institutions of government and a people's attitudes towards them are the product of social forces and historical evolution; and in these respects these two nations differ considerably. Those who conceive government as a mere set of institutional devices, a thing to be examined mechanically and constructed upon selected blue prints, would do well to examine the phenomenon here under consideration. If government be a mere matter of techniques and structures, then similar results should appear from a given institutional arrangement wherever employed. Clearly this is not the case. This method of constitutional amendment when used in

Switzerland has produced one kind of result; when used in Australia it has produced one that is wholly different. This is not merely a matter of one people being more democratic than the other or even of thinking that they are more so. Neither the Swiss nor the Australians would concede that any people has a higher regard for democratic government than they themselves. And probably they are both right.

The difference lies somewhere in the cultural background of the two peoples. Governmental institutions are inevitably coloured by the attitudes and acceptances of the peoples that employ them. To one nation they mean one thing and produce one result; to another they mean something quite different and produce results that are different. Switzerland and Australia, possessing widely different cultures, produce widely different results with the same institutional device. As a contrast it may be observed that Australia and the United States, possessing cultures that are more nearly similar, have produced results that are comparable to each other by using procedures that are very much different. The similarity here is not, however, so marked as is the difference between the first two countries.

The significant thing about constitutional amendment in Switzerland, however, is not merely the high percentage of successful amendments; it is the fact that amendments have been tried *and* adopted with such frequency. It is this willingness to amend the constitution that manifests its essential flexibility. By the most commonly accepted scheme of classification Switzerland's constitution would have to be called 'rigid'. But an examination of Swiss experience would seem to render this classification largely meaningless.

# 5

# THE AMENDMENT OF THE UNITED STATES CONSTITUTION

THE procedure by which the constitution of the United States may be amended is substantially different from those of the other countries that have been considered. It is unlike Canada's in that it is specifically provided for in the constitution itself; it is unlike Switzerland's in that it does not permit any popular initiative in its operation; and it is unlike both the Swiss and the Australian in that there is no popular referendum involved. Our consideration of America's experience with the problems of constitutional amendment will be somewhat different from that accorded to the other three countries because of these differences and also because a larger number of studies have already been devoted to the subject in the United States.[1] Our effort here will be devoted to exploring the connexion between the federal nature of the country's institutions and the procedure by which the constitution is changed.

[1] Although the literature on constitutional amendment in America is voluminous, it consists mostly of articles in various journals. A few monographs, however, have been devoted to it and these have been extensively employed in the preparation of the present work. The only monograph covering the field as a whole is that of Lester B. Orfield, *The Amending of the Federal Constitution*, Ann Arbor, Michigan, 1942. The pioneer work in the collection of data was by Herman V. Ames, *The Proposed Amendments to the Constitution of the United States During the First Century of its History* in the *Annual Report* of the American Historical Association for 1896. Ames's work was brought up to 1929 by Michael A. Musmanno, *Proposed Amendments to the Constitution*, published as House Doc. No. 551, 70th Cong., 2nd sess., and has been continued up to 1947 by other congressional documents at various times since then. The principal articles on the subject are noted in the bibliography at the end of this volume.

Orfield's work, within the limits of his method, very nearly exhausts the subject as it stood at the time of his writing, though the value of his monograph is limited in the present writer's view by the fact that it treats the subject almost exclusively as a problem of constitutional law. This chapter makes extensive use of the materials that Professor Orfield has collected; direct quotations are footnoted, but much of what is said here depends on his work even when the connexion is not so direct as to require citation.

The amending procedure of the United States constitution is found in Article V of that document. Its provisions were adopted only after considerable debate in the convention of 1787, but a compromise was reached that has endured to this day; the procedure has never been altered.

It consists of two principal steps—the proposal of the amendment and its ratification. Each of these may be accomplished in two different ways, although in practice nearly all amendments have followed the same course. A proposal may be initiated by the joint action of two-thirds of each House of the Congress, or it may be initiated by a convention called by the Congress on the petition of two-thirds of the states. The amendment may be ratified by the votes of three-fourths of the state legislatures or by conventions called for the purpose in three-fourths of the states.

Of the two methods of initiation, only the first has ever been successfully employed; all amendments have originated in the Congress and no convention for such a purpose has ever been assembled. Of the two methods of ratification, that by the state legislatures has been used in all but one instance; the twenty-first amendment was ratified by state conventions.

## *History of Amendments to the Constitution*

Since the constitution took effect in 1789 many efforts have been made to amend it in many different ways. Most of these efforts have begun in Congress, where more than 4,000 resolutions of amendment have been introduced.[1] The figure itself, however, is of little significance. Many of the proposals were identical, or at least were concerned with the same questions; many were trivial; many were ridiculous; and many were unnecessary. But the most significant explanation of the large number of proposals is the unlimited right of American Congressmen to introduce as many resolutions as they like

[1] The compilation begun by Ames and furthered by Musmanno has been continued by various students; most of the subsequent efforts to bring his listing up to date have been published as congressional documents. The latest was compiled by Carl A. Loeffler, *Proposed Amendments to the Constitution of the United States, Introduced in Congress from the 69th Congress, 2nd session, through the 79th Congress, December 6, 1926 to January 3, 1947*, Washington, 1947. The total given as of that date is 4,221, although it is admittedly inaccurate. Op. cit., p. 101.

on as many subjects as they like. A member of Congress is usually willing to satisfy a constituent by submitting a bill or resolution that he would not seriously support. As a result the Congressional hampers are full of resolutions of all kinds, including those for amendments to the constitution, that command no public support whatsoever. The number of amendments introduced annually in recent years has varied from thirty or forty to a hundred or more. Of these thousands of proposals the Congress has approved by the necessary majorities just twenty-seven; and of these the states have ratified twenty-two.

Even these figures, however, do not represent a true picture, for ten of these amendments were adopted immediately after the establishment of the constitution as a result of the apprehensions of the members of several state ratifying conventions concerning the omission from the new scheme of a bill of rights.[1] As a result of these complaints,[2] Mr. Madison introduced in the House of Representatives a long series of resolutions of amendment designed to mollify the objecting states; of these resolutions seventeen were passed by the House and twelve by the Senate. When put to the state legislatures for ratification, only ten of the twelve were adopted; these ten are the first amendments to the constitution.[3] Of the other two proposals submitted in 1789, one was concerned with the apportionment of seats in the House of Representatives and the other prohibited any change in the salaries of Congressmen until after the first election following the passage of the law. The amendments now comprising the bill of rights were ratified by eleven states and went into effect on 15 December 1791. Connecticut, Massachusetts, and Georgia took no

[1] The framers had considered the question of a bill of rights, but had decided against it on the ground that such protections were provided in the state bills of rights and that the powers of the national government were limited and did not extend to the subjects that would be thus protected. See Madison's Notes in *Documents Illustrative of the Formation of the Union of the American States*, 69th Cong., 1st sess., House Doc. 398, 1927, pp. 716, 726; also Hamilton in *The Federalist*, No. 84.

[2] The ratification resolutions of the various states mention many of the reservations that were made concerning the new constitution, although the ratifications themselves were necessarily unqualified. The resolutions are conveniently assembled in *Documents Illustrative*, &c., pp. 1009–59.

[3] See Ames, op. cit., p. 321, for the records of ratifications in the states.

action on them. The apportionment amendment was ratified by ten states, one short of the required three-fourths.[1] The compensation amendment was ratified by only six states.[2]

The next successful amendment proposed by the Congress was the eleventh. This arose from a decision of the Supreme Court in 1792 in which it was held that the jurisdiction of the Court extended to suits initiated by a citizen of one state against another state.[3] The outraged cries of the adherents to the principle of state sovereignty at this display of *lèse majesté* quickly called forth an amendment prohibiting such suits which was ratified by the necessary twelve states in less than a year.[4] The twelfth amendment followed in 1804 to prevent a recurrence of a tie in a presidential election such as had occurred between Jefferson and Burr in the election of 1800. The amendment was submitted by the Congress in December 1803 and was ratified by the necessary thirteen states within eight months, in time for it to take effect in the election of 1804.[5]

In 1810 Congress submitted to the states an amendment abrogating the citizenship of anyone who accepted foreign titles or honours. The amendment failed, but the decision was close and for a time it was thought that it had become part of the constitution. At the time of its submission there were seventeen states in the union, of which three-fourths would be thirteen (76·4 per cent.); after eleven ratifications had been made Louisiana was admitted to the union, bringing the number of states to eighteen, of which fourteen (77·7 per cent.) would constitute three-fourths. 'A record of twelve ratifica-cations, mistaken beliefs that South Carolina had taken favourable action[6] and that thirteen ratifications constituted the requirement contributed to the impression that the pro-

[1] The three states above named took no action and Delaware rejected the amendment outright. Ibid., p. 320.

[2] Delaware, Maryland, North Carolina, South Carolina, Vermont, and Virginia. Ibid., p. 317.

[3] *Chisholm* v. *Georgia* (1793), 2 Dall. 419.

[4] Ames, op. cit., p. 322.

[5] Ibid., p. 325.

[6] In South Carolina it was approved by the Senate and considered in the House, but consideration was postponed. A year later a committee reported unfavourably on it and the House did not reconsider the measure. See Ames, op. cit., p. 329.

posal was in force, though the Secretary of State did not certify it.'[1]

This occurrence raises the interesting question whether the three-fourths of the states required to ratify means three-fourths of those in the union when the proposal is submitted to the states or three-fourths of the total number of states in the union when the state bringing the total to three-fourths ratifies. The question has never been answered by any official authority, but it would seem that the latter is the only reasonable solution. Great difficulty would arise if it were considered that states admitted subsequent to the proposal but before the validation of an amendment were to have no part in the process. In the decade after the submission of the foreign titles amendment five states were admitted in addition to Louisiana. If two more of the original states had ratified the amendment during this period, it hardly seems proper that it should have gone into effect, since the fourteen ratifications would then have represented only 60 per cent. of the states.

In 1861 Congress submitted the so-called 'Corwin amendment' which provided that no amendment could be made to the constitution which should by its effect interfere with the institution of slavery in any state.[2] This amendment was an important part of the struggle over slavery in Congress and was actually an incident of the opening phases of the Civil War. It received no support among the states, being ratified by two legislatures only.

The most interesting of all the amendments, from the point of view of the procedure employed in adopting them, were the three 'Civil War' amendments adopted in the closing year of and just after the war between the states. Since one of the leading causes of the war had been the fundamental disagreement over the institution of slavery, many northern members of Congress were determined that success in defeating the South should be accompanied by success in defeating slavery. Accordingly an effort was made in April 1864 to submit to the states an amendment abolishing that evil, but it failed on this first attempt for lack of sufficient votes in the House. After

[1] Denys P. Myers, *The Process of Constitutional Amendment*, 76th Cong., 3rd sess., 1940, Sen. Doc. 314, p. 31.

[2] See Ames, op. cit., p. 196; Myers, op. cit., p. 32.

Lincoln's re-election in the fall it was again introduced and this time passed, though just barely.[1] At that time there had been admitted to the union a total of thirty-six states, of which eleven had seceded to form the Confederacy. Whether these southern states were competent to ratify amendments to the constitution was unclear. The view of the Congress was that they had forfeited their rights in the union and should not even be admitted to representation in the nation's legislature; in fact they were not at that time represented in Congress. But in his proclamation of the amendment on 18 December 1865, Secretary of State Seward stated that there were then thirty-six states 'in the United States' and that twenty-seven of them had ratified, a bare three-fourths of the total. Of these ratifying states, eight were former members of the Confederacy which were then under the ban of Congress.[2] According to this doctrine the southern states were competent to ratify amendments regardless of what their status might otherwise be. If, however, they had not been counted, the amendment would still have been adopted, for this would have left nineteen ratifications, constituting three-fourths of the twenty-five northern states whose position in the union was not questioned.

Similar difficulties were encountered with the fourteenth amendment, which was designed to make citizens of the former slaves and to guarantee them certain civil liberties. This amendment was proposed by Congress on 16 June 1866, at which time only the same twenty-five states were represented. In March 1867 the Congress declared the governments of several of the southern states (which had rejected the amendment) to be illegal and ordered their reorganization. With the aid of certain of these reorganized state governments, now dominated by Union forces, the necessary ratifications were secured. On 20 July 1868 Secretary Seward issued a proclamation stating that twenty-three states had ratified and that the amendment had also been approved by 'newly-constituted and newly-established bodies avowing themselves to be, and

[1] In the House the vote was 119 to 56; a difference of three votes would again have defeated the proposal. A. C. McLaughlin, *Constitutional History of the United States*, New York, 1935, p. 635.

[2] Alabama, Arkansas, Georgia, Louisiana, North Carolina, South Carolina, Tennessee, and Virginia.

acting as, the legislatures, respectively, of the States of Arkansas, Florida, North Carolina, Louisiana, South Carolina, and Alabama. . . .'[1] Counted among the twenty-three states were two (Ohio and New Jersey) that had subsequently withdrawn their ratifications, but the proclamation repudiated those withdrawals; the inclusion of these two states was necessary in order to make up the necessary three-fourths. On 21 July Congress adopted a concurrent resolution declaring that the amendment had been ratified and directing the Secretary of State to promulgate it as part of the constitution. On 28 July Seward issued a new proclamation in compliance with this directive, this time making no qualifications about any of the ratifications.[2]

The fifteenth amendment, forbidding the states to bar the Negro from the suffrage, was submitted by Congress in February of 1869. Three states, Virginia, Mississippi, and Texas, were required by Congress to ratify the amendment as a condition precedent to their readmission to the full status of statehood. In the Secretary of State's proclamation of 30 March 1870 these three were listed as among the ratifying states. The same constitutional difficulty still existed.

These three 'Civil War' amendments provide a perplexing problem to the student of American constitutional law; but they provide an even more interesting one to the student of federalism. What, after all, is the position of a state in a federation? The states that had carried their insistence upon their autonomy in regard to slavery to the point of an attempted secession from the union were compelled to return to the union and to assent to the abrogation of the rights they had sought to protect. Their ratification of the amendments implementing this abrogation was made a necessary condition to their re-establishment as states. That federalism is a device for protecting the states in the exercise of certain functions is clear, but what is not clear is what the functions so protected are to be. The Civil War is adequate testimony to the desirability of an understanding from the outset of the spheres of

[1] Horace E. Flack, *The Adoption of the Fourteenth Amendment*, Baltimore, 1908, p. 191, note 117.

[2] Myers, op. cit., p. 25. The inability of a state thus to withdraw a ratification is discussed below at pp. 229 ff.

authority that are to be possessed by the various units and levels of government in the federal system. But it is impossible to foresee all future developments and impossible so to allot powers and functions that no new problems will arise. In the middle of the last century one such problem arose, and America's experience in solving it is further proof that federalism demands of its users a sense of community that is sufficient to permit the peaceful settlement of such disputes. That the American federal experiment was not terminated abruptly in the 1860's is an indication not of the hardiness of the principle of federalism but of the fact that those who sought to preserve the federal union possessed greater military strength than those who would have destroyed it.[1]

No further amendment was made to the constitution until Congress, in 1909, proposed the sixteenth, designed to permit the federal government to levy a tax on incomes without apportioning the tax among the states. This amendment is an excellent example of the relation between the formal and informal methods of changing the United States constitution. The validity of an income tax had been sustained in 1880 by the Supreme Court,[2] which held that such taxes were not direct taxes within the meaning of the prohibition in Article I.[3] Fifteen years later, however, the Court reversed its earlier

[1] 'Federal government allows a strong and united nation to form by quieting all fear in the local unit that it is going to be unjustly treated in the matter of those peculiarities in which it differs from the rest of the nation, but to which it is deeply attached, or in which it represents a different civilization or important differences of local condition . . . the fifteenth amendment to the American constitution was a violation of the federal principle, and it is in this particular that the statement is true. It is an undoubted historical fact that the other states in the Union took advantage of the result of the Civil War to force upon the southern states a measure, negro suffrage, to which as a whole section of the country they were bitterly opposed, for which their local conditions were in no way prepared, and which could not be carried into practical operation without much local injustice. No better example than this could be devised of just the kind of action which it is the purpose of federalism to prevent, and the fact that the amendment was adopted by a majority of the nation from a righteous motive makes the example all the better. Federal government has for its object to prevent the righteous motives of the majority from unjustly oppressing the minority and thereby strengthening historical antagonisms.' George Burton Adams, *Federal Government, Its Function and Method*, New York, 1919, pp. 113 f.

[2] *Springer* v. *United States* (1880), 102 U.S. 586.

[3] Section 9, clause 4, requires that a 'capitation or other direct tax (be laid) in proportion to the census', an obvious impossibility with regard to an income tax.

decision, holding that such taxes were direct taxes and, in the absence of apportionment among the states according to population, were unconstitutional.[1] Agitation began immediately for a constitutional amendment authorizing Congress to levy such a tax. The first such attempt was made in December of 1895, and the next fourteen years witnessed forty-two different resolutions on the subject.[2] The proposal finally passed both Houses of Congress on 12 July 1909. It was ratified by the states without the haste that has marked many constitutional amendments, and was promulgated by the Secretary of State in February 1913, more than 3½ years later.

Before the sixteenth was adopted the Congress had also proposed a seventeenth amendment, providing for the popular election of senators in place of the election by state legislatures provided in the original constitution. This amendment had been the product of a slowly but steadily growing popular demand that had begun in the post-Civil War period.[3] Beginning in 1872, nearly every year had seen a proposal for this purpose; in all, 198 resolutions on the subject were introduced.[4] The principle obstacle to the reform was the Senate itself. On five occasions the House passed the proposal, the first time in 1894, but it was not until 1911 that it came to a vote in the Senate. After many months of conferences the two Houses agreed upon the form of the proposal and it was submitted to the states on 16 May 1912. The opposition in the Senate should doubtless be attributed not to any federal issue but to the unwillingness of the senators to endanger their seats by subjecting themselves to the perils of popular election. The amendment was rapidly approved by the states and the thirty-sixth ratification was given in April 1913, only two weeks after the promulgation of the sixteenth. It may be remarked that the state legislatures, by their ratification in

[1] *Pollock* v. *Farmers' Loan and Trust Co.* (1895), 157 U.S. 429 and 158 U.S. 601.

[2] Musmanno, *Proposed Amendments to the Constitution*, p. 212.

[3] James Wilson had proposed the popular election of senators in the Convention of 1787, but only Pennsylvania had voted for it. See Madison's Notes in *Documents Illustrative of the Formation of the Union of the American States*, pp. 168–73. An amendment to effect this principle was first introduced in Congress in 1826. Ames, op. cit., pp. 61, 340. Ames remarks that more amendments have been proposed on this point than on any other, p. 61.

[4] Musmanno, op. cit., p. 219.

less than a year, manifested no apparent desire to maintain their own function as electors of the Senate that was comparable to the latter's desire to maintain the old system. Indeed, by 1912 more than half the state legislatures were merely choosing between senatorial candidates named by the parties in the primary elections, though of course they were not legally obliged to do so.

The rapid adoption of the sixteenth and seventeenth amendments dispelled the long-held notion that it was nearly impossible to amend the constitution and encouraged the advocates of liquor prohibition to demand an amendment implementing their views. Support for such a measure was evinced by several regulatory statutes already enacted by Congress. By the latter part of the war period over half the states had adopted prohibition on a state scale. Proposals for a constitutional amendment on the matter were first introduced as early as 1876,[1] and by 1917 forty-six such proposals had been introduced.[2] Congress passed the resolution in December 1917 and in a speedy and rather bitter campaign it was adopted by the states in a little over a year.

This eighteenth amendment also introduced two new features into the process of amendment. One of these was the provision that it should not go into operation until 'after one year from the ratification of this article'. The other was that the amendment provided a time limit within which the ratification had to be consummated in order to be effective. That this was a reasonable exercise of Congress's power in the task of submitting amendments was upheld by the Supreme Court in 1921.[3]

The nineteenth amendment forbidding the exclusion of women from the suffrage came as a result of an agitation as lengthy and vigorous as that for prohibition. By 1919 forty-one of the forty-eight states had adopted woman suffrage in one form or another. When it was introduced again in Congress in that year there was little opposition to it[4] and the proposal

[1] Ames, op. cit., p. 272.

[2] Musmanno has provided a concise, useful summary of the growth of prohibition sentiment and legislation. Op. cit., pp. 225–37.

[3] *Dillon* v. *Gloss* (1921), 256 U.S. 368. See below, pp. 227 ff.

[4] The vote on the final resolution in the House was 304 to 90; in the Senate, where fears were expressed that the amendment would again raise the problem

was submitted to the states on 5 June. The forces supporting its adoption were well organized and effective campaigns were conducted in crucial states. In a little more than a year the necessary ratifications were secured, the thirty-sixth state (Tennessee) approving it on 18 August 1920.

The next effort made by the Congress to alter the constitution has thus far been unsuccessful. This was the so-called 'child-labour amendment' which was submitted to the states in 1924. This amendment was another of those attempts to change the constitution that have been stimulated by decisions of the Supreme Court. In the 1918 decision in *Hammer* v. *Dagenhart*[1] the Court invalidated an attempt by Congress to regulate the employment of children by banning the products of child labour from interstate commerce. Congress then turned to its taxing power and sought to impose a special tax on firms that knowingly employed child labour. In 1922 this effort too was repudiated by the Court in a decision that aroused much unfavourable comment.[2] Both these decisions were based on the principle of dual federalism. The Court acknowledged the power of Congress to tax and to control interstate commerce, but refused to permit such a use of these powers as would invade a sphere of action not delegated to Congress and therefore retained by the states. Thwarted in both these attempts, Congress resorted to a constitutional amendment as the only means of providing the control it considered necessary. In June 1924 an amendment was submitted to the states authorizing Congress 'to limit, regulate and prohibit the labor of persons under eighteen years of age'. The amendment was submitted to the state legislatures for ratification and contained no time limit on its effectiveness. Ratification was at first quite slow, only five states having approved the proposal by the close of 1930; another was added in 1931 and, after the Democratic victory in 1932 and an appeal for ratification by President Roosevelt, a number were added in the mid-thirties. 1933 produced fourteen ratifications and 1935 and 1937 each four more. No more ratifications have

of negro suffrage, there was more objection; the vote was 56 to 25. The Senate here, we may note, was serving a federal function. The figures here are taken from Musmanno, op. cit., pp. 251 ff.

[1] (1918), 247 U.S. 251.

[2] *Bailey* v. *Drexel Furniture Co.* (1922), 259 U.S. 20.

been added since then, so that the total now stands at twenty-eight, eight states short of the necessary three-fourths. Whether other ratifications could now be added is a difficult question.[1] Fourteen states have rejected the amendment in both Houses of the state legislature; in four states the two Houses have split on the question; and in two states no action has been taken.[2] Ratification has apparently come to a halt, partly because opinion is not wholly in favour of the amendment but also because recent shifts in the decisions of the Supreme Court have considerably diminished the need and demand for such an amendment.[3]

The next successful amendment was the twentieth, which was proposed by Congress on 2 March 1932; it changed the dates upon which the President and members of Congress begin their terms of office and eliminated the outmoded 'lame duck' or post-election session of Congress. Efforts to secure such a change had been made since very early in the history of the republic,[4] but no proposal had passed both Houses until the date mentioned. That public opinion was quite ready for the change was indicated by the prompt approval of thirty-six states in less than eleven months; the amendment received the necessary number of ratifications on 23 January 1933.[5] It repeated the practice first employed in the eighteenth, however, in specifying that it should not become operative until the 15th of October following ratification. It also continued the practice of specifying a seven-year time limit, which had first appeared in the eighteenth but had been omitted from the nineteenth.

The twenty-first amendment, also adopted in 1933, repealed

[1] See below, pp. 227 ff.

[2] These figures have been taken from the *World Almanac, 1943*, p. 339, and from the *Editorial Research Reports*, 1937, vol. 1, pp. 298 f. Three of the states rejecting have not notified the Secretary of State of their action; the official record therefore reads: 28 ratifications, 15 rejections, 5 states no action. Dept. of State Memorandum, *The Child Labor Amendment* (mimeo., no date).

[3] Of especial importance is *U.S.* v. *Darby Lumber Co.* (1941), 312 U.S. 100, which, in sustaining the Fair Labor Standards Act, 1938, permitted extensive regulation of child labour under the commerce power. This case rejected the whole principle of dual federalism and explicitly overruled *Hammer* v. *Dagenhart*, cited above. Even so, the amendment would confer on Congress more extensive powers than it now possesses.

[4] See Ames, op. cit., pp. 36 ff.

[5] All states ultimately ratified it.

the eighteenth. The question of liquor prohibition had by no means been settled in 1919 and agitation for the repeal of that ill-fated amendment began almost as soon as it was adopted.[1] Efforts to enforce it had been largely unsuccessful, and a substantial increase in crime in the 1920's was attributed to it. Numerous resolutions to repeal the prohibition were introduced in the ensuing decade and on 20 February 1933 Congress submitted an amendment to the states. This is the only instance in which the procedure of ratification by state conventions has been employed. During 1933 laws were passed in forty-three states providing for conventions in that or the following year.[2] During the same year conventions were held in thirty-eight states of which thirty-seven ratified the amendment and one (South Carolina) rejected it. The thirty-sixth ratification was received in the late afternoon of 5 December 1933 and the certificate was issued by the Secretary of State less than an hour later.[3] The next day the thirty-seventh ratification was received from Maine. Thus in less than eleven months after the submission of the amendment to the states it had been ratified by the necessary three-fourths and the sad experiment of prohibition on a nation-wide basis was ended.[4] The rapidity with which the amendment was ratified casts serious doubt upon the oft-heard contention that the convention method of ratifying amendments is too slow and cumbersome for practicability.

The most recent amendment to the constitution, the twenty-second, was submitted to the states by the Congress in 1947. It restricts the tenure of the president to two terms or to ten years if he has succeeded upon the death of his predecessor during the second half of a term. Both parties in the Congress

[1] One resolution for a repeal amendment was introduced in the House of Representatives on 19 May 1919, just four months after the adoption of the prohibition amendment. Musmanno, op. cit., p. 237.

[2] The exceptions were Georgia, Kansas, Louisiana, Mississippi, and North Dakota. Everett S. Brown, *Ratification of the Twenty-First Amendment of the Constitution of the United States*, Ann Arbor, 1938, p. 5. This is the standard monograph on the subject.

[3] Department of State, *Ratification of the Twenty-First Amendment* (no date), pp. 7–8.

[4] Or so we may hope. Since repeal there have been at least two resolutions introduced in the Senate proposing the repeal of the *twenty-first* amendment. Edwin A. Halsey, *Proposed Amendments to the Constitution of the United States, 1926–1941*, Washington, 1941.

professed a non-partisan attitude towards the question, but its principal support came from the Republicans, who had in that Congress (the Eightieth) gained control for the first time in sixteen years. The measure was severely criticized by its opponents not only for substantive reasons but also as being a partisan attack upon the memory of the late President Roosevelt. But these objections did not prevent the passage of the resolution. The question whether again to employ ratifying conventions was much debated but was finally resolved in the negative. The proposal was accordingly submitted to the state legislatures on 24 March 1947.

In the first few months following its submission the amendment seemed to find rapid approval among the states. Starting with Maine, five ratifications were received within the first month, and eighteen, or half the necessary three-fourths, within five months. But with the adjournment of the legislatures in the summer of 1947, the movement slackened somewhat. Few state legislatures meet in the even-numbered years, and by 1949 interest was lagging. By the beginning of 1951 only twenty-four states had ratified.[1] But upon the urging of anti-Truman forces early in 1951 more than a dozen states (controlled mainly by Republicans or southern Democrats) approved it, and the amendment became a part of the constitution when Nevada completed the thirty-sixth ratification on 26 February 1951. The total time elapsed from submission to consummation was three years, eleven months, and two days, the longest time thus far required for the ratification of an amendment.

## *The Initiation of Amendments*

Having briefly surveyed the history of amendments to the constitution, we turn now to a more careful analysis of the elements of the several procedures by which those amendments may be procured.

Since all amendments thus far submitted to ratification have originated in the Congress there are many questions about the convention method of initiating amendments that have not been answered by experience and cannot be answered from

[1] Two had rejected it and one had postponed consideration indefinitely.

the constitution itself, since the constitution's provisions are not detailed. It says merely that 'on the application of the legislatures of two-thirds of the several States, [Congress] shall call a convention for proposing amendments'.

One difficulty that arises immediately is that there is no principle to guide Congress in deciding when two-thirds of the states have submitted such petitions. Many have indeed been submitted, but they have varied widely in form and have in many cases included statements of purpose that vary just as widely.[1] If several states petition for a convention for the purpose of proposing amendments that are quite different, should they be counted together as a group, or should their different purposes preclude their being counted together as constituting the necessary two-thirds? Moreover, how close together must the various petitions come in order to be counted together? It would not seem reasonable for petitions received fifty or a hundred years apart to be considered together for the purpose of counting up the necessary two-thirds; but where should the line be drawn? Professor Orfield suggests, reasonably enough, that the seven-year time limitation imposed by Congress on the ratification of recent amendments would be a suitable limitation here as well.[2] But this, of course, is merely speculation. The reason why there is no clear law on most of such questions is, of course, that no such controversies have arisen; recent decisions of the Court[3] would seem to suggest that such problems would be left to Congress to resolve.

A further complication arises from the fact that among the many petitions now on record several were for the purpose of securing amendments that are no longer necessary; some of the changes have been achieved through ordinary amendments proposed by Congress and some by means other than formal amendment. Many that were concerned with the slavery question in the pre-civil war period would seem no longer valid at all, the question having been settled by other means.[4]

[1] Senator Millard F. Tydings compiled a record of such applications as had been received up to 1930; it was printed as Sen. Doc. No. 78, 71st Cong., 2nd sess., 1930.

[2] Op. cit., p. 42. See also W. B. Wheeler, 'Is a Constitutional Convention Impending?', *Illinois Law Review*, vol. 21, 1927, p. 782.

[3] Especially in *Coleman* v. *Miller* (1939), 307 U.S. 433.

[4] By 1909 twenty-six states had petitioned for a convention for the purpose

Finally, what should a state include in its petition: a mere statement of its desire for a convention or a detailed description of the amendment(s) it hopes the convention will initiate? Both techniques have been used, though most petitions have been for specific amendments.

Even if sufficient petitions were received and the convention were called, many questions would yet remain about the organization of such a body. Who would supervise it? Where would it meet? What basis for representation would be employed? How would votes be counted? Presumably the Congress in calling the convention would in some fashion give answers to many of these questions; but the constitution is wholly silent, not even confiding the power of giving answers to Congress.

A further and more serious problem is the uncertainty about what the powers of such a convention would be. Would it possess full power to propose amendments of any kind, or would its powers be restricted by the statements of purpose in the petitions of the state legislatures? Could Congress in calling the convention prescribe its functions and limitations? Could such a body present a wholly new constitution or could it offer only individual amendments to the old one? The ambiguities of the convention plan no doubt constitute one of the important reasons why it has never been used.

There were a few demands in 1937 to call such a convention on the sesquicentennial anniversary of the constitution. But the most concerted effort to use it in recent years was sponsored in the late 1940's by a tax-weary group calling itself the American Taxpayers Association, which urged a convention to propose an amendment setting a 25 per cent. limit on federal income taxes. In spite of its imprudence the movement received a surprising amount of support, and resolutions were passed in eighteen state legislatures requesting the convention. Leaders in organized labour and in the federal government opposed it strongly and the movement seems to have died.[1]

of amending the provisions for the election of senators. These petitions, limited in their scope, would seem now to be invalid. Orfield, op. cit., pp. 42 f.

[1] See a survey by the United Press reported in the *New York Times*, 15 Feb. 1953. In two states the resolution was vetoed by the Governor and in six states the legislature subsequently repealed its resolution of petition. Whether either action is legal is very doubtful.

Beyond these instances, no important demand for such a convention has been raised.

The method of initiation that has been used for every amendment, including those that have failed of ratification by the states, has been that of proposal by two-thirds vote of each House of the Congress. The powers of Congress in this regard are conferred upon it by Article V and are not among the legislative powers listed in Article I, Section 8. When it proposes an amendment, therefore, Congress is not legislating but is exercising a constituent function specially conferred upon it. This fact has furnished the foundation for the doctrine that the consent of the President is unnecessary to the proposal, a doctrine that was laid down by the Supreme Court early in the history of the republic.[1]

The provision that 'two-thirds' of the two Houses of Congress must consent has raised the question, two-thirds of what? The Congress early held that two-thirds of those voting was all that was required, and despite some claims that the phrase should be interpreted to mean two-thirds of the entire membership, the Supreme Court has upheld the former interpretation.[2] But the two-thirds applies only to the submission itself; amendments to the proposal may be made by majority vote. It would seem that the mode of ratification may also be selected by a mere majority, but the question has never been raised since the Congress has always included both questions in the same resolution.[3]

Whether Congress can withdraw a proposal after it has been submitted has not been settled. The only instance of this occurred in 1864, when Senator Anthony moved to repeal the

[1] *Hollingsworth* v. *Virginia* (1798), 3 Dall. 378. But though the Court early held that the president need not consent, several resolutions were subsequently signed by the president. Orfield reports (op. cit., p. 50, note 30) that in 1803 a motion in the Senate to submit the twelfth amendment to the president was defeated. In 1861 the President signed a proposed amendment without arousing comment. When the thirteenth amendment was proposed in 1864 Lincoln signed it, perhaps by accident; but Senator Trumbull immediately proposed and the Senate passed a resolution stating that the signature was unnecessary and should not be taken as a precedent. See A. C. McLaughlin, *Constitutional History of the United States*, p. 635. A corollary principle is that the state governor plays no part in the ratifying process and may not veto a ratification.

[2] *National Prohibition Cases* (1920), 253 U.S. 350.

[3] Orfield, op. cit., p. 49, note 28.

joint resolution submitting the Corwin amendment;[1] his motion failed, but it raises an interesting question. It might be argued that such repeal would be impossible on the analogy of the inability of the states to withdraw ratifications, but it should be remembered that this right is refused the states because the Congress has refused it. The question is unlikely to be an important one.

### *Relations between the Two Houses of Congress*

Since all amendments have been initiated by the Congress, it is pertinent to inquire whether this body has served as a proper agency for this function. The arithmetic of amendments suggests that the stumbling-block is the Congress rather than the states, since so few of the proposals introduced in that body have been submitted to the states. That this argument is without a solid foundation is, however, indicated by the fact that of all the proposals introduced in the Congress, only a small number are ever considered at all.

Almost every measure is introduced in the form of a joint resolution, although a few have taken the form of an ordinary bill. The measure is then referred to a committee, usually the committee on the judiciary unless there is a standing committee especially concerned with the subject-matter of the proposal. In a few instances, when there is a great deal of enthusiasm for the measure, its supporters may secure the appointment of a select committee to consider the matter.[2] The committee then considers the measure, or is supposed to, but few proposals are ever reported back to the floor of either House. Of the more than 1,800 proposals which Ames reported, 'over one-half received no further consideration beyond their reception and reference to a committee. The remainder have either been reported or received further discussion, but

[1] S.J.R. 25, *Congressional Globe*, 38th Cong., 1st sess., 1864, p. 522; cited in Orfield, op. cit., p. 52, note 33.

[2] Ames discovered two attempts to change the procedure in Congress, one by restricting the introduction of amendments to every tenth year and the other by establishing a standing committee on constitutional amendments. H. V. Ames, *Proposed Amendments to the Constitution of the United States During the First Century of Its History*, pp. 285 f.

only a very small percentage of these have been brought to a vote'.[1] To say, therefore, that several thousand measures have been proposed in Congress is totally misleading; Congress never has either an opportunity or a desire to consider more than a tiny fraction of such a number.

Even when a proposal does find its way to passage in one House, it must then go through the same procedure in the other and receive in that House, as in the first, a two-thirds majority of those voting. On most measures for which there is widespread support, similar resolutions are introduced in both Houses at approximately the same time; each House is then likely to adopt its own version of the amendment and the two measures are referred to a conference committee. Once a measure gets to conference it is likely to be passed, since both Houses have by that time indicated a desire for it, though in different forms. No proposal, so far as is known to the writer, has failed of passage because of failure of the two Houses to agree on the form it should take.[2]

Several proposals, however, have failed because of the unwillingness of one or the other of the two Houses to pass them at all. When Madison introduced his proposals for a Bill of Rights in 1789 the House passed 17 resolutions, of which the Senate would accept but 12; the other 5 failed of passage.[3] By 1924 16 House resolutions had failed in the Senate and 16 Senate resolutions had failed in the House;[4] several more such instances have occurred since then for which no accurate figures are available. Thus between 30 and 40 resolutions have failed of passage because of the opposition of one or the other of the Houses.[5] This is a very small part of the total

[1] Ibid., p. 285.

[2] Sharp disagreement between the two Houses on the proposed seventeenth amendment led to considerable difficulty in the conference. Ultimately, in order to save the principle of the amendment, the House gave in to the Senate's demands. See M. A. Musmanno, *Proposed Amendments to the Constitution*, 70th Cong., 2nd sess., House Doc. No. 551, Washington, 1929, pp. 222 ff., where citations from the *Congressional Record* are given.

[3] Madison's original proposals would have made the amendments restrictive of the states as well as of the national government; the Senate discarded this feature.

[4] Ames, 'The Amending Provision of the Federal Constitution in Practice', Amer. Philos. Soc., *Proceedings*, 1924, p. 69.

[5] As late as 1950 the Senate passed and the House defeated two proposals: (1) to alter the constitution so that each state's vote in the electoral college would

number of measures that have failed of passage after being introduced, but it is still true that the requirement that both Houses must agree has prevented the submission to the states of a considerable number of amendments. There is, of course, no assurance that very many of them would have been ratified.

The constitution of the United States provides no means by which disagreements between the two Houses may be resolved. The Australian constitution, as we have seen, does make such a provision, both for ordinary legislation and for constitutional amendments; but though the two Houses have differed on amendments in that country, the procedure has never been employed.

### *Total Revision and Partial Revision*

The Swiss constitution carefully distinguishes between the procedures for total revision of the constitution and those for partial revision or a single amendment. No such distinction is to be found in the United States constitution; that document speaks only of 'amendment'. Some have argued that the distinction should be read into the constitution; since the constitution was originally adopted by a convention, a new convention called at the instance of the states should have the right to draw up a wholly new constitution. This may well be true; but the converse assertion that Congress could not propose such a revision does not seem valid. The constitution makes no distinction between the powers of the Congress and the convention in the matter; both are empowered to propose 'amendments'. Whether this term encompasses total revisions is an open question, but there is no other way to bring one about. It seems clear that what one could do the other could do also. It is a very difficult task to draw an accurate line between amendment and revision, and the courts are unlikely to try it. The most reasonable suggestion is that either means of proposal could be used for either kind of constitutional change. And, of course, whatever form the change takes it would still have to be submitted to the ratification of the states.

be divided among the presidential candidates in proportion to their popular vote in the state; and (2) to guarantee women equal rights with men.

### *Ratification of Amendments*

After the amendment has been initiated it must then be approved by three-fourths of the states, acting either through their state legislatures or through special ratifying conventions, as one or the other procedure may be prescribed by Congress. Of the twenty-seven amendments thus far proposed by Congress twenty-six have employed ratification by legislatures; only one, the twenty-first, has been submitted to state conventions.

The use of the state legislatures instead of special conventions places a greater emphasis on the role of the state in the amending process. Members of conventions, though they are citizens of states, are not likely to be so concerned with state interests as the members of the legislatures, who are more self-conscious in their role of representatives of the state. The latter have something of a vested interest in the predominance of the state in public affairs; they have been elected largely on the basis of their views on state issues; they are likely to represent the interests of the state, even the selfish interests, more accurately than are the members of a convention. Whether this is desirable raises a different question. But the fact that the legislatures rather than conventions have been the customary method of ratification has placed a greater emphasis on the federal nature of the amending process than would otherwise have been the case.

The federal aspect of the process is thus brought out most clearly in the procedure of ratification. In the Congress the states are represented, it is true. But in the United States, as in most federations, the role of the Senate as the protector of the states has been exaggerated. This is not to say that it does not exist; certainly the Senate divides into regional blocs on occasion, blocs that function for the protection of the interests of particular regions and groups. But such groupings are the exception rather than the rule of ordinary Congressional activity, and even when they occur the alignment seems to be on regional rather than on strictly state lines. Party considerations are an equally important factor in the voting in Congress, and to the extent that party considerations are dominant, state and federal interests are suppressed. But party considerations are by no means the sole determinant, and one of the important influences on Congressional votes is the federal one, the desire to protect and perpetuate the state, to guard its interests in the legislative and constitutional processes. Federalism today does play a part in the Congress's role in the amending procedure; but the real area in which federalism functions is that of the ratifying process.

Ratification by state legislatures has raised a number of questions, many of which have been settled by court decisions, but many of which still remain unanswered. It has frequently been suggested that the legislature should not consider a question of amendment until an election has intervened, in order that the people may have an opportunity to elect representatives who will vote on the question in accord with the popular will. The difficulty in this theory is that no election turns solely on a question of amendment, and it is unlikely that a legislature elected after an amendment has been proposed will be any more representative of public opinion on that particular question than one that was already in office. The constitution itself says nothing at all about the matter; but at least one decision of the Supreme Court casts doubt upon the ability of a state to require such an election.[1]

Another question is whether Congress or the state legislature may regulate the manner in which the ratification is treated in the state. Article V gives no such power to Congress and the state is not required to consider a proposed amendment at all. If the legislature does not take any action, there would seem to be nothing that Congress can do to compel it. Several instances have occurred in which the states have taken no action on amendments.[2] Indeed, it was not until 1939 that Georgia, Massachusetts, and Connecticut ratified the bill of rights.[3]

[1] The Tennessee constitution (among others) required such an intervening election, but the legislature ratified the nineteenth amendment without waiting; the state Attorney-General held the ratification to be legal. In a test case the amendment was attacked on several grounds, among which was the contention that since the Tennessee ratification was in violation of the state law it was invalid. The Court rejected this argument: '. . . the function of a state legislature in ratifying a proposed amendment to the Federal Constitution, like the function of Congress in proposing the amendment, is a federal function derived from the Federal Constitution; and it transcends any limitations sought to be imposed by the people of a State.' *Leser* v. *Garnett* (1922), 258 U.S. 130, at pp. 136–7.

[2] See table below, pp. 236–7.

[3] See Julia M. Bland, *Georgia and the Federal Constitution*, Department of State Publication No. 1078, 1937; Denys P. Myers, *Massachusetts and the First*

The procedure for constitutional amendment has become standardized after many years, though the steps in the procedure could in many cases be altered by act of Congress since the constitution is silent on most of them. One student of the subject has outlined nine steps in the procedure which must be taken before the amendment becomes a part of the constitution:[1]

1. The two Houses of Congress, each by a two-thirds vote, adopt a joint resolution embodying the proposal of amendment;

2. The joint resolution bears the signature of the Speaker of the House of Representatives and of the President of the Senate, and is without the approval of the President;

3. The Secretary of State promptly transmits a certified copy of the resolution—formerly engrossed, now printed from the same type as the original—to the Governor of each state;

4. The respective governors transmit the resolution to the Legislatures in accordance with State legislation or practice respecting constitutional amendments;

5. The state legislatures (or conventions) reach a conclusion upon the proposal within the terms of their own laws and procedure;

6. Decisions of state legislatures to ratify, in the form of certified acts or resolutions, are notified to the Secretary of State by the governor or the secretary of the state; unless state law so provides, failure to ratify or rejection of the proposal may or may not be certified;

7. The amendment is 'valid to all Intents and Purposes, as a part of' the Constitution when its ratification is consummated by that state which brings the total up to three fourths of all the states;

8. The Secretary of State . . . is obliged to know what number of states constitutes three fourths of the total so as to determine when he has received 'official notice' that a proposed amendment 'has been adopted, according to the provisions of the Constitution';

9. When the requisite number of ratifications is received, 'the Secretary of State shall forthwith cause the amendment to be published, with his certificate, specifying the States by which the same may have been adopted, and that the same has become valid, to all intents and purposes, as a part of the Constitution.'[2]

*Ten Amendments to the Constitution*, Sen. Doc. No. 181, 74th Cong., 2nd sess., 1936; Thomas Le Duc, *Connecticut and the First Ten Amendments to the Federal Constitution*, Sen. Doc. No. 96, 75th Cong., 1st sess., 1937; Denys P. Myers, *The Process of Constitutional Amendment*, Sen. Doc. No. 314, 76th Cong., 3rd sess., 1940, pp. 10 ff.

[1] Myers (op. cit., pp. 4–9) gives detailed references for each step in the procedure, including certain exceptions to the rules he suggests.

[2] But the amendment goes into effect not on promulgation but when the thirty-sixth state ratifies. *Dillon* v. *Gloss* (1921), 256 U.S. 368.

This description is still an accurate summary with one exception. In 1950 the functions of the Secretary of State with respect to constitutional amendments were transferred to the Administrator of General Services and are now performed under his supervision by the Archivist of the United States.[1]

## *Ratification by Conventions*

The other method of ratification which Congress may select requires the approval of specially elected constitutional conventions in three-fourths of the states. It has been used only once. Efforts were made in Congress to use such conventions for the ratification of the thirteenth and fifteenth amendments, but without success. Ames makes the interesting observation that the debates in Congress on the point lead to the conclusion that those urging the convention method were doing so in an effort to defeat these amendments, believing that it would be more difficult to secure the approval of conventions than of state legislatures.[2] Of the fifteenth amendment it was argued that since this was the first change in the constitution that materially affected the rights of the people, the amendment should be submitted to conventions rather than legislatures, the convention being considered more directly representative of the public will. The suggestion was opposed in the Senate, however, on the ground that the convention system was 'dilatory, expensive, and unwise', and it was not used.[3]

A similar argument made more progress during debate on the eighteenth and nineteenth amendments; here it was argued that these amendments, because of their content, required ratification by conventions since they took powers away from the states and interfered with personal liberty.[4] The constitution offers no such distinction, however, and the courts have refused to recognize anything of the sort. In 1931 a lower federal court held the eighteenth amendment to be

[1] See *United States Code*, Title 5, Section 160. This transfer was accomplished by Reorganization Plan No. 20 of 1950 under provisions of the Reorganization Act of 1949.

[2] Ames, *Proposed Amendments to the Constitution*, pp. 286–7.

[3] *Congressional Globe*, 40th Cong., 3rd sess., pp. 828, 855, 1040. Cited in Ames, op. cit., p. 287.

[4] J. H. Smith, 'Is Prohibition Constitutional?', *Plain Talk*, vol. 4, 1929, p. 415.

invalid because it was of the nature of legislation and should not have been included in the constitution. The Supreme Court quickly reversed this decision, however, holding that no such distinction can be made, either between subjects that may be included in the constitution and those that may not, or between subjects that require ratification by conventions and those that do not.[1] The choice between the two types of procedure is entirely that of Congress, and there would seem to be no limitations at all upon this power to select.

Until the twenty-first amendment only one instance was on record of a ratification by a constitutional convention, and this was undoubtedly unlawful. In 1861 Congress, in proposing the Corwin amendment forbidding future anti-slavery amendments, prescribed that ratification should be by state legislatures. But in Illinois a convention happened to be in session which had been called for the purpose of altering the state constitution. It passed a resolution ratifying the amendment. Since only two other state legislatures ratified it, the amendment was lost and the validity of the Illinois ratification was never formally questioned. It seems clear, however, that it was quite invalid.

The only real experience with the convention method has been that connected with the twenty-first amendment which in 1933 effected the repeal of the eighteenth. Section 3 provided that:

> This article shall be inoperative unless it shall have been ratified as an amendment to the Constitution by conventions in the several States, as provided in the Constitution, within seven years from the date of the submission hereof to the States by the Congress.

Whether Congress should enact general regulations governing the time and manner of holding such conventions was much discussed,[2] but in view of the constitution's silence on the point no attempt was made by the Congress to regulate the

[1] *United States* v. *Sprague* (1931), 282 U.S. 716. It has also been argued that the tenth amendment places a limitation on the power of amendment. See Selden Bacon, 'How the Tenth Amendment Affected the Fifth Article of the Constitution', in *Virginia Law Review*, vol. 16, 1930, p. 771. This view embodies a misconception of the amending process and is clearly untenable. It was refuted also in *United States* v. *Sprague*, cited above.

[2] Orfield, op. cit., pp. 56 ff., gives the opposing arguments and cites numerous articles urging various views on the question.

states on the matter.[1] Many of the states, however, recognized the power of the Congress to call the conventions and to regulate them; twenty state laws calling the conventions provided that any subsequent effort by Congress to regulate the subject should take precedence over the state laws. Only one state, New Mexico, explicitly denied the power of Congress to regulate.[2]

Possibly the most important reason for the use of the convention procedure for the twenty-first amendment was the feeling that the question of liquor prohibition was one that so directly affected the people that they should be given as clear an opportunity as possible to express their will on the question. This was a lesson learnt from the bitter complaints and the great amount of litigation that had been aroused by the eighteenth amendment itself, which had been ratified by state legislatures.

The proposal passed both Houses of Congress in February 1933 and the movement for ratification spread rapidly through the states. Starting in Michigan and Wisconsin in April, state conventions approved the amendment with such rapidity that the thirty-sixth ratification was received—from Utah—by 5 December, at which time the new amendment became part of the constitution. It was ultimately ratified by thirty-eight states and rejected by two.[3]

The state conventions, each regulated by state legislation, varied greatly in their organization and method of operation. Over half were elected on a state-wide basis; some were selected from constituencies of various sizes; and some were based upon a combination of the two principles. They varied

[1] In 1937, however, Mr. Wadsworth of New York offered such a bill in the House, seeking to provide such regulation for the future. It was not accepted. See House Resolution 299, 75th Cong., 1st sess., 1937; cited and briefly discussed by Orfield, op. cit., p. 57.

[2] Everett S. Brown, 'The Ratification of the Twenty-First Amendent', *Amer. Pol. Sci. Rev.*, vol. 29, 1935, pp. 1008–9. A larger work by the same author entitled *Ratification of the Twenty-First Amendment of the Constitution of the United States*, Ann Arbor, 1938, assembles all the data on the states' treatment of the amendment.

[3] South Carolina rejected it outright. In North Carolina the voters selected convention delegates, but in a referendum that was held at the same time they voted against the amendment; therefore no convention was held. Of the states planning conventions for the following year, only Montana went ahead; its convention, too, ratified the amendment, bringing the total to thirty-eight.

in size from three members in New Mexico to 329 in Indiana.[1]

The most characteristic feature of ratifying conventions is that they more accurately reflect the popular will on the question than legislatures can hope to do. The convention is elected for one purpose only and its selection is not confused by other issues that inevitably creep into the election of a legislature. Moreover, in most ratifications by the legislatures the people have had no opportunity at all to pass on the question, even by voting for or against legislators, for most ratifications have taken place without waiting for intervening elections. In an effort to secure more faithful conformity to public opinion some states have adopted the practice of waiting until after an election before posing the question in the legislature, but it would seem that such a restriction on the legislature could not be made binding, inasmuch as the constitution does not prescribe it. Recent decisions, too, tend to suggest that such a restriction would not be accepted by the courts.[2] The convention, on the other hand, provides a ready-made mechanism for determining the public will on the question. Indeed, one of the criticisms that has been levelled at the twenty-first amendment is that the conventions did not deliberate at all, but served merely as a rubber stamp for the popular opinions expressed in the election.[3] Such a criticism does not seem entirely valid, however, for it is inevitable that a considerable amount of public discussion must have taken place in the Congress and in the general agitation that seems to be necessary before a proposal for amendment can be entertained in Congress. And, of course, the electoral campaign preceding the selection of the convention members would seem to afford ample opportunity for public debate.

Those democrats who are anxious to see the decision of public questions placed more and more in the hands of the people themselves welcome the convention method of ratification as a means of furthering this end. This consideration has led many people to believe that the convention system

[1] Everett S. Brown, *Ratification of the Twenty-First Amendment of the Constitution of the United States*, 1938, p. 516.

[2] *Hawke* v. *Smith* (1920), 253 U.S. 221; *Coleman* v. *Miller* (1939), 307 U.S. 433.

[3] Brown, op. cit., p. 5.

would be used rather more in the future than it has in the past, but with the twenty-second amendment proposed in 1947 the Congress again employed the technique of ratification by state legislatures.[1]

### *Ratification by Referendum*

A third method of ratification that has frequently been proposed is that of the popular referendum. This procedure, admittedly the most democratic of all, is provided in the constitutions of both Switzerland and Australia, but is not mentioned in the constitution of the United States. That a device so democratic in character was not included by the framers of the latter constitution is hardly surprising in view of the well-known bias of the majority of that group against direct democratic methods.[2] But agitation for some sort of referendum procedure has continued over a long period of time.[3]

The best-known effort to establish a popular referendum as a means of ratifying a constitutional amendment took place in Ohio after the submission to the states by Congress of the eighteenth (liquor prohibition) amendment. That state in 1918 amended its constitution to provide for a referendum on the state legislature's action in ratifying or refusing to ratify amendments to the federal constitution. In 1919 the legislature ratified the eighteenth amendment; but when the state officials prepared to submit the action to referendum a citizen of the state sought an injunction to prevent this

[1] The twenty-second amendment was initiated in the House of Representatives, which proposed to submit it to the state legislatures. In the Senate it was referred to the Committee on the Judiciary, which recommended that it be submitted to conventions instead. The Senate, however, refused to accept the recommendation and concurred in the House plan. The debates in the Senate are of considerable interest; several senators argued that the use of legislatures was actually more democratic in that conventions can so easily be 'rigged'. Of further interest was the widely held (though controverted) opinion that since the state legislature would prescribe the organization of the convention it could resolve *itself* into a convention for the purpose. See the *Congressional Record*, 80th Cong., 1st sess., 1947, pp. 1681, 1800–7, 1862.

[2] See Homer Cummings, 'The Nature of the Amending Process', *George Washington Law Rev.*, vol. 6, 1938, pp. 247 ff.

[3] Ames cites several instances from the *Congressional Globe* in the civil war period when members of Congress sought to secure some such procedure. Op. cit., pp. 293–4.

'unconstitutional' use of state funds. The Supreme Court of the United States upheld an appeal that the provision for referenda exceeded the state's powers, that the term 'legislature' in Article V referred not to the total legislative power of the state, which might be construed to include the whole electorate acting as a direct legislature, but to the representative legislative body to which the term was ordinarily applied.[1] The principle seems to be that the two modes of ratification provided in Article V are exclusive and that the state can do nothing of a formal nature to alter the method by which its own ratification is decided. Several states, however, have employed such referenda in an advisory fashion to furnish the legislature with an accurate indication of public opinion in the state.[2]

## *A Time Limit on Ratification*

Official action is taken on an amendment, however, only when it is ratified; when it is rejected by too many states or fails to be considered by a sufficient number, the proposal simply remains open. It was long supposed that these proposed amendments would still be pending indefinitely and that states could ratify them at any time without regard to the date of their submission by the Congress. In recent years, however, a change has occurred in the public and official attitudes towards these unratified amendments. Congress has in all proposed twenty-seven amendments to the constitution, of which only twenty-two have been ratified by the states; one of those that have not been ratified was submitted as late as 1924; two date from the period of the bill of rights. It is hardly reasonable to suppose that all of them are still equally available for ratification by the states, yet the constitution sets no limit on their effective life. Indeed, in 1873, after Congress had increased its own compensation retroactively in a measure widely criticized as a 'salary grab', the Ohio senate solemnly ratified an amendment proposed in 1789 which would have limited the power of Congress to make

[1] *Hawke* v. *Smith* (1920), 253 U.S. 221. It was on this decision that the subsequent decision in *Leser* v. *Garnett* depended. See above, p. 220, note 1.

[2] See W. A. Robinson, 'Advisory Referendum in Massachusetts on the Child Labor Amendment', *Amer. Pol. Sci. Rev.*, vol. 19, 1925, p. 69.

such a change.[1] This action caused considerable comment and stimulated demands that some sort of 'statute of limitations' be adopted.[2]

In the eighteenth amendment Congress included for the first time an express time limit on the ratification, stating that 'This article shall be inoperative unless it shall have been ratified . . . within seven years from the date of submission hereof to the States by Congress.'[3] When this limitation was challenged in the courts, the Supreme Court upheld it as a proper part of Congress's role in submitting amendments to the states. Proposal and ratification are parts of a single process, said the Court, and should not be considered as two wholly separate procedures; moreover, amendments are proposed when the Congress 'deems it necessary', and no one can suppose that the congressional estimate of necessity should last for fifty or a hundred years; finally, the ratification procedure presumes a general approval of the amendment at a given time and should not be construed as a mechanical device for eliciting just so many affirmative actions in states without regard to their comprising a general common opinion.[4]

The enactment of ordinary legislation by the Congress establishing such a time limit might be criticized, but there can be little doubt of the validity of the incorporation of such a limit in the amendment itself. Though no such limitation was included in the nineteenth amendment, it was again included in the twentieth, twenty-first, and twenty-second. In each instance the limit has been set at seven years. In the case cited above the Court held that it was a proper function of Congress to set a reasonable limit and that seven years was reasonable. The Court did not undertake to define what it meant by reasonable, and Congress could undoubtedly adopt a different limit if it so desired.

[1] Ohio Laws (1873) 409; cited by Orfield, op. cit., p. 75.

[2] See Ames, op. cit., pp. 291–2; also John A. Jameson, *Constitutional Conventions*, 4th edn., 1887, pp. 635–6.

[3] Amendment XVIII, section 3.

[4] *Dillon* v. *Gloss* (1921), 256 U.S. 510. But one distinguished scholar considered the seven-year limit 'an obviously futile proceeding. As part of an unratified amendment, the provision was inoperative, and if ratification had taken place after the prescribed date it would still have been inoperative unless the ratification was valid in spite of it'. Edward S. Corwin and M. L. Ramsey, 'The Constitutional Law of Constitutional Amendment', *Notre Dame Lawyer*, vol. 26, 1951, p. 200.

The Court, however, implied that an amendment was not to be considered as pending beyond a reasonable time, and the fact is that not all amendments thus far unratified have specified such a limit. The only one, however, about which there could be any serious question is the child-labour amendment proposed by Congress in 1924. This amendment contained no time limit and was presumably, therefore, still pending in 1937 when the legislatures of Kentucky and Kansas ratified it. It was argued that since thirteen years had elapsed the reasonable limit accepted in *Dillon* v. *Gloss* had been exceeded and that the ratifications were invalid. But the Court refused to invalidate them, holding that such a question was political in nature and was for Congress, not the Court, to decide.[1] Since the Congress has taken no action it may be assumed that the amendment is still pending, though it would probably be possible for Congress to reject any further ratifications. The 1939 decision, it will be observed, recognizes the power of Congress to apply such a time limit after the fact.

In all four instances in which Congress has specified a time limit, the limit prescribed has been seven years. This would seem to be a very generous limit, if experience be consulted, for no amendment thus far ratified has taken nearly that much time for its adoption. The amendment requiring the longest time for ratification was the twenty-second, which was approved in a little less than four years. The table on p. 230 sets out the times at which the several amendments have been submitted and ratified. It will show that seven of them required less than a year and that one, the twelfth, required only seven and a half months. Seven years would seem to be an eminently reasonable limit. The average time required has been about nineteen months.

### *The Finality of State Ratifications and Rejections*

Two questions of interest that have lately arisen are whether a state may ratify an amendment after once rejecting it, and whether it may reject it after once ratifying it. The answer to the first question seems to be in no doubt. Congress accepted the ratifications of several states that had previously rejected

[1] *Coleman* v. *Miller* (1939), 307 U.S. 433.

the fourteenth amendment,[1] and this action was sustained by the Supreme Court many years later.[2] Arkansas rejected the sixteenth amendment on 9 January 1911, but ratified it on 22 April in time to be counted in the certificate of the Secretary of State.[3] The twenty-second amendment was rejected by the legislatures of Texas and Idaho, both of which subsequently ratified in time to be included in the certificate.[4] These

*Times of Submission and Ratification of Amendments*

| *Amendment* | *Date proposed* | *Ratifications required* | *Date consummated* | *Time elapsed** | | | *Notice of validity* |
|---|---|---|---|---|---|---|---|
| | | | | *Yrs.* | *Mos.* | *Days* | |
| 1–10 | 25 Sept. 1789 | 11 | 15 Dec. 1791 | 2 | 2 | 20 | none |
| 11 | 4 Mar 1794 | 12 | 7 Feb. 1795 | 0 | 11 | 3 | 8 Jan. 1798 |
| 12 | 12 Dec. 1803 | 13 | 27 July 1804 | 0 | 7 | 15 | 25 Sept. 1804 |
| 13 | 1 Feb. 1865 | 27 | 6 Dec. 1865 | 0 | 10 | 5 | 18 Dec. 1865 |
| 14 | 16 June 1866 | 28 | 9 July 1868 | 2 | 0 | 23 | 20 July 1868 (Sec. of St.)<br>21 July 1868 (Congress)<br>28 July 1868 (Sec. of St.)† |
| 15 | 27 Feb. 1869 | 28 | 3 Feb. 1870 | 0 | 11 | 7 | 30 Mar. 1870 |
| 16 | 12 July 1909 | 36 | 3 Feb. 1913 | 3 | 6 | 22 | 25 Feb. 1913 |
| 17 | 16 May 1912 | 36 | 8 Apr. 1913 | 0 | 10 | 23 | 13 May 1913 |
| 18 | 17 Dec. 1917 | 36 | 16 Jan. 1919 | 1 | 1 | 0 | 29 Jan. 1919 |
| 19 | 5 June 1919 | 36 | 18 Aug. 1920 | 1 | 2 | 13 | 26 Aug. 1920 |
| 20 | 2 Mar. 1932 | 36 | 23 Jan. 1933 | 0 | 10 | 21 | 6 Feb. 1933 |
| 21 | 20 Feb. 1933 | 36 | 5 Dec. 1933 | 0 | 9 | 15 | 5 Dec. 1933 |
| 22 | 24 Mar. 1947 | 36 | 26 Feb. 1951 | 3 | 11 | 2 | 1 Mar. 1951 |

* Computed to the date of the ratification consummating the necessary three-fourths.
† See the explanation of these several notices at pp. 231 f.

Source: adapted from Denys P. Myers, *The Process of Constitutional Amendment*, Sen. Doc. 314, 76th Cong., 3rd sess., 1941, p. 29.

are the only instances in which a state ratification, following a previous rejection, has been counted in the three-fourths necessary for adoption. Many states, however, have ratified after the consummation of the necessary ratifications, but these add nothing to the validity of the amendment. The twentieth amendment was, indeed, eventually ratified by all forty-eight states and within a relatively short time. In 1937

[1] See above, pp. 205 f.; also below, pp. 231 f.

[2] *Coleman* v. *Miller* (1939), 307 U.S. 433. See also *Southern Calif. Law Rev.*, vol. 11, 1938, p. 472; Walter F. Dodd, 'Amending the Federal Constitution', *Yale Law Journ.*, vol. 30, 1921, p. 322.

[3] Myers, op. cit., p. 25.

*World Almanac, 1951*, p. 716.

a Kentucky court denied the right of the state legislature to ratify the child-labour amendment after it had once rejected it;[1] but this decision, when carried to the Supreme Court, was reversed, the higher body upholding the Supreme Court of Kansas in its contention[2] that the ratification of a state was valid, a previous rejection notwithstanding.[3] This is the accepted doctrine today. It is based on the principle that the act of ratification is an affirmative act and is the only act mentioned in the constitution. The fifth article does not mention rejections of an amendment or the possibility that a state may not act; nor do ordinary legislative principles preclude subsequent passage of an enactment on the ground of a previous failure of passage.

This principle that ratification is the only act of a state that may be officially recognized is seen elsewhere in the practice of the Administrator of General Services (and formerly of the Secretary of State) in taking no official notice that any state has rejected an amendment. It is unnecessary for a state to notify the Administrator of any action other than ratification, though in some instances this has been done. Indeed, in the two most recent instances the Secretary of State (whose function it then was) apparently suggested that whatever action is taken should be officially reported.[4]

A more difficult question, however, is whether a state, having once ratified an amendment, may withdraw that

[1] *Wise* v. *Chandler* (1937), 270 Ky. 1.

[2] *Coleman* v. *Miller* (1937), 146 Kan. 390.

[3] *Coleman* v. *Miller* (1939), 307 U.S. 433. See the discussion of the relation of this decision to the Kentucky and Kansas cases in Orfield, op. cit., pp. 70 ff.

[4] In 1933, in connexion with the twenty-first amendment, the letter of transmission sent by the Secretary to the state governors requested that the resolution 'be submitted to a convention in your State for *such action as may be had and that a certified copy of such action* be communicated to the Secretary of State'. Department of State, *Ratification of the Twenty-First Amendment to the Constitution of the United States*, Washington, 1934, p. 3. It may also be noted that South Carolina sent to the Secretary a certified copy of her *rejection* of the amendment. Ibid., p. 8. South Carolina's proceedings on the question are reported in Everett S. Brown, *Ratification of the Twenty-First Amendment*, pp. 375 ff. The letter of the Secretary of State of 27 Mar. 1947 submitting the twenty-second amendment to the states also requested a certified copy of 'such action' as the legislature might take. No rejections were reported, but the Governor of Oklahoma notified the Secretary on 5 June 1947 that the ratification had 'failed to pass' that legislature and the Secretary took notice of Oklahoma's adverse action. Letter to the author, 12 Apr. 1951, from Assistant Legal Adviser of the State Department.

ratification and reject the amendment. The question first arose in 1868 in connexion with the fourteenth amendment when the states of New Jersey and Ohio attempted to withdraw their ratifications before the amendment had achieved the necessary number of approvals. The Secretary of State in his proclamation of 20 July 1868[1] included both states in the required total, but stated that the amendment had been ratified only if these withdrawals were invalid. Congress immediately declared that that was the case and the Secretary issued an unqualified declaration of adoption a week later. Similarly with the fifteenth amendment, New York sought to withdraw its ratification, but was counted by the Secretary of State as among the twenty-nine ratifying states in his proclamation of 30 March 1870.[2] Oregon even passed a resolution withdrawing her ratification of the fourteenth amendment after it had become part of the constitution, but this, of course, had no effect.[3]

An attempt was made in the House of Representatives to include in the eighteenth amendment a clause providing that 'Any state may recall its rejection or ratification of this amendment at any time before three-fourths of the states have actually ratified the same'. But the resolution was rejected by the House.[4] A similar effort was made in 1928 to amend the constitution by providing such a clause in the amendment procedure of Article V, but this too failed. Other efforts of the same kind have been made from time to time.[5]

Congress has consistently refused to permit a state to withdraw a ratification once given, and the Supreme Court upheld this practice in *Coleman* v. *Miller*, holding that such a political decision was for the Congress to make. The present doctrine seems to be that a state may ratify after it has rejected an amendment, but it may not reject it after ratifying it. This seems wise in view of the confusion that would otherwise result.

## *The Role of the States*

In other federations we have been able to collect data from the actions of the component units that enable us to examine the ratifying process very closely. In Switzerland we can

[1] See above, p. 205. [2] Ames, op. cit., p. 388. [3] Ibid., p. 377.
[4] Musmanno, op. cit., pp. 236 f. [5] Orfield, op. cit., p. 191.

isolate the decision on an amendment at one point in time and say with assurance that so many cantons approved and so many rejected it; so also in Australia. But in the United States a similar profit cannot be derived from the arithmetic of ratification. There is no set time at which the states approve or reject the amendment; they may change their decisions before it is consummated, and they may add ratifications even after the amendment has become part of the constitution. Consulting the records of state ratifications is therefore less meaningful. It is impossible to get a clear estimate of the popular support for an amendment from the ratification records, even if we assume that the votes in the legislatures accurately mirror public opinion in the states. And after the amendment is adopted the interpretation of votes or lack of votes in other states is even more difficult.

With the thirty-sixth ratification the amendment takes effect; a later ratification may indicate only a desire to get on the bandwagon; some members of the state legislature who have vigorously opposed ratification may no longer care to hold out and the ratification is passed in a perfunctory way just for the record. On the other hand, certain states that might have ratified no longer take the trouble to do so, since further ratifications add nothing to the amendment's force or validity. This certainly occurred in connexion with the twenty-first amendment; within the year thirty-eight states held ratifying conventions and all but one of these approved the amendment. Half a dozen other states that had already made plans for conventions in the following year cancelled those plans, since the amendment had already been adopted; others too would undoubtedly have held conventions within a short time. There is no doubt that many of these states would have ratified the amendment.

In attempting to determine the number of states that should be counted as truly favouring an amendment on its merits, it may be assumed at least that those states that ratify within a very short time after consummation ought reasonably to be included. Ratifications, however, that take place several months or even years after the amendment has taken effect are suspect because the motives that affect such action are different. For four of the twelve amendments for which certificates have been issued,[1] more ratifications have been acknowledged by the Secretary of State than have been necessary to constitute the required three-fourths. For the fourteenth, 30 out of 36 states in the union were included; for the fifteenth, 29 out of 36; for the sixteenth, 38 out of 48; for the twentieth, 39 out of 48. When the twenty-first amendment was ratified, the Secretary made special arrangements to secure the decisions of the states whose conventions, being held on the same day, would constitute the last three necessary ratifications. As a result, the proclamation was issued on 5 December 1933 within an hour after the thirty-sixth ratification; on the next day the thirty-seventh was reported.[2] In other instances certificates were issued when the total number of ratifications reached three-fourths, although this has sometimes slightly exceeded an exact 75 per cent.

Perhaps the best way to discover whether the federal element in the procedure has been of any significance is to inquire whether the requirement that three-fourths of the states must ratify has prevented any amendments from being adopted. Five amendments submitted to the states have failed to secure the necessary ratifications. Two of these were submitted simultaneously with the original ten amendments. The first of these, concerning the apportionment of members in the House of Representatives, was approved by ten states, just one short of the necessary three-fourths. The bill of rights itself was ratified by only eleven states, and only the defection of Delaware from this group prevented the apportionment amendment from becoming part of the constitution. The ratifying states included all but Delaware, Massachusetts, Georgia, and Connecticut; they constituted 79·6 per cent. of the population of the United States.[3] Here at the outset an amendment was defeated because, though apparently favoured by a large majority of the people, it could not command the necessary number of states.[4]

[1] None were issued for the first ten.

[2] The details of these arrangements may be found in Department of State, *Ratification of the Twenty-First Amendment*, Washington, 1934, pp. 6 ff.

[3] According to the census of 1790. The percentages in this and the following paragraphs have been computed from the population reports in the *World Almanac, 1943*, p. 431.

[4] No great claim is made for this kind of analysis. It may be objected quite

The other unsuccessful amendment limited the right of Congress to change the compensation of its members. It was ratified by only six states whose population amounted to 49·8 per cent. of the population. This amendment commanded a majority neither of the states nor of the total population, but the vote was close and, had the United States a system comparable to that of Australia, the outcome would possibly have been different. At this time there were fourteen states in the union of which eleven were required for ratification.

The next unsuccessful amendment was that pertaining to titles of nobility, submitted in 1810. This proposal, like the first mentioned above, received the ratifications of a majority of the states, but failed because the majority was less than three-fourths. There were then eighteen states in the union and the three-fourths rule necessitated fourteen ratifications. The amendment received twelve, but these twelve constituted 56·9 per cent. of the total population.

In 1861 Congress proposed the Corwin amendment prohibiting any future amendment abolishing slavery. This amendment received only two ratifications and need not detain us here. Of greater interest is the child-labour amendment, proposed in 1924, which has been approved by twenty-eight states, three more than a majority, but eight less than the necessary three-fourths; these ratifying states comprised 55·6 per cent. of the population by the 1930 census.

These data suggest that the federal element in the amending procedure has indeed had an important effect on the operation of the process of constitutional amendment. Had ratifications of a mere majority of states been necessary instead of three-fourths, three more amendments would have found their way into the constitution: apportionment of the House, 1790; titles of nobility, 1810; and the child-labour amendment, 1924; and this would be true even if the requirement had also made it necessary that the majority of states ratifying constitute a majority of the population.

properly that the ratification of ten state legislatures representing states whose population amounted to a certain percentage of the national population does not necessarily indicate popular support of that extent. Certainly each of these states may have contained large minorities that opposed the amendment. But it is likely that others that did not ratify contained large minorities that did favour the amendment. These various minorities would roughly cancel one another.

## State Action on Amendments

| State | Date admitted to union | a 1789 | b 1789 | 1–10 1791 | 11 1795 | 12 1804 | c 1810 | d 1861 | 13 1865 | 14 1868 | 15 1870 | 16 1913 | 17 1913 | 18 1919 | 19 1920 | e 1924 | 20 1933 | 21 1933 | 22 1951 |
|---|---|---|---|---|---|---|---|---|---|---|---|---|---|---|---|---|---|---|---|
| | | Amendment and date | | | | | | | | | | | | | | | | | |
| No. of states | | 14 | 14 | 14 | 16 | 17 | 18 | ? | 36 | 37 | 37 | 48 | 48 | 48 | 48 | 48 | 48 | 48 | 48 |
| Ratifications required | | 11 | 11 | 11 | 12 | 13 | 14 | ? | 27 | 28 | 28 | 36 | 36 | 36 | 36 | 36 | 36 | 36 | 36 |
| Alabama . . . | 1819 | | | | | | | — | X | X | X | X | — | X | O | — | X | X | r |
| Arizona . . . | 1912 | | | | | | | | | | | X | X | X | X | X | X | X | — |
| Arkansas . . . | 1836 | | | | | | | — | X | X | X | X | X | X | X | X | X | X | X |
| California . . . | 1850 | | | | | | | — | r | — | O | X | X | X | X | X | X | X | X |
| Colorado . . . | 1876 | | | | | | | | | | | X | X | X | X | X | r | X | X |
| Connecticut . . . | 1788 | — | — | r | X | O | O | — | X | X | X | O | X | r | r | O | r | X | X |
| Delaware . . . | 1787 | O | X | X | X | O | X | — | r | r | r | X | — | X | — | O | X | X | X |
| Florida . . . | 1845 | | | | | | | — | r | X | X | — | — | X | — | O | r | X | — |
| Georgia . . . | 1788 | — | — | r | X | X | X | — | X | X | X | X | — | X | O | O | X | — | X |
| Idaho . . . | 1890 | | | | | | | | | | | X | X | X | X | X | X | X | X |
| Illinois . . . | 1818 | | | | | | | — | X | X | X | X | X | X | X | X | X | X | X |
| Indiana . . . | 1816 | | | | | | | — | X | X | X | X | X | X | X | X | X | X | X |
| Iowa . . . | 1846 | | | | | | | — | r | X | X | X | X | X | X | X | X | X | X |
| Kansas . . . | 1861 | | | | | | | — | X | X | X | X | X | X | X | X | X | — | X |
| Kentucky . . . | 1792 | | | | X | X | X | — | O | O | O | X | — | X | X | X | X | X | O |
| Louisiana . . . | 1812 | | | | | | | — | X | X | X | X | r | X | O | O | X | — | X |
| Maine . . . | 1820 | | | | | | | — | X | X | X | X | X | X | X | X | X | r | X |
| Maryland . . . | 1788 | X | X | X | X | X | X | X | X | O | O | X | — | X | O | O | r | X | r |
| Massachusetts . | 1788 | — | — | r | X | — | X | — | X | X | X | r | X | X | X | O | r | X | O |
| Michigan . . . | 1837 | | | | | | | — | X | X | X | X | X | X | X | X | X | X | X |
| Minnesota . . . | 1858 | | | | | | | — | X | X | X | X | X | r | X | X | X | X | r |
| Mississippi . . . | 1817 | | | | | | | — | O | r | X | X | — | X | O | O | X | — | X |
| Missouri . . . | 1821 | | | | | | | — | X | X | X | X | X | X | X | O | X | X | X |
| Montana . . . | 1889 | | | | | | | | | | | X | X | X | X | X | X | r | X |
| Nebraska . . . | 1867 | | | | | | | | | X | X | X | X | X | X | O | X | — | X |

| | | | | | | | | | | | | | | | | | | | |
|---|---|---|---|---|---|---|---|---|---|---|---|---|---|---|---|---|---|---|---|
| Nevada | 1864 | | | | | | | | X | X | X | X | X | r | X | X | r | X | X |
| New Hampshire | 1788 | X | O | X | X | r | X | — | X | X | X | r | X | X | X | X | r | X | X |
| New Jersey | 1787 | X | O | X | — | X | X | — | r | W | r | r | X | r | X | X | X | X | X |
| New Mexico | 1912 | | | | | | | | | | | r | X | r | X | X | X | X | X |
| New York | 1788 | X | O | X | X | X | O | — | X | X | W | X | X | r | X | O | X | X | X |
| North Carolina | 1789 | X | X | X | X | X | X | — | X | X | X | X | X | X | — | O | X | O | X |
| North Dakota | 1889 | | | | | | | | | | | X | X | X | X | X | X | — | X |
| Ohio | 1803 | | | | | X | X | X | X | W | X | X | X | X | X | X | X | X | X |
| Oklahoma | 1907 | | | | | | | | | | | X | X | X | X | X | X | — | O |
| Oregon | 1859 | | | | | | | — | r | W | O | X | X | X | X | X | X | X | X |
| Pennsylvania | 1787 | X | O | X | — | X | X | — | X | X | X | — | X | r | X | X | X | X | X |
| Rhode Island | 1790 | X | O | X | X | X | O | — | X | X | X | O | — | — | X | — | X | X | O |
| South Carolina | 1788 | X | X | X | r | X | O | — | X | X | X | X | — | X | O | O | X | O | r |
| South Dakota | 1889 | | | | | | | | | | | X | X | X | X | O | X | — | X |
| Tennessee | 1796 | | | | | X | X | — | X | X | O | X | X | X | X | O | X | X | X |
| Texas | 1845 | | | | | | | — | r | r | r | X | X | X | X | O | X | X | X |
| Utah | 1896 | | | | | | | | | | | O | O | X | X | X | X | X | X |
| Vermont | 1791 | X | X | X | X | X | X | — | X | X | X | r | X | r | r | O | r | X | X |
| Virginia | 1788 | X | X | X | X | X | — | — | X | r | X | — | — | X | O | O | X | X | X |
| Washington | 1889 | | | | | | | | | | | X | X | X | X | X | X | X | O |
| West Virginia | 1863 | | | | | | | | X | X | X | X | X | X | X | X | X | X | — |
| Wisconsin | 1848 | | | | | | | — | X | X | X | X | X | r | X | X | r | X | X |
| Wyoming | 1890 | | | | | | | | | | | X | X | X | X | X | X | X | X |

Dates are those of validation of successful amendments, of submission of unsuccessful ones.

Legend: Blank = not in union
X = ratified
r = subsequent ratification not counted in certificate
W = attempted to withdraw ratification
O = rejected
— = failure to act

Unsuccessful amendments:
a = apportionment of House
b = compensation of Congress
c = foreign titles
d = Corwin amendment
e = child labour

Source: adapted from Myers, *Process of Constitutional Amendment*, pp. 39–40.

## *Limitations on Amendments*

Article V of the constitution, after describing the procedures for the amendment of the constitution, goes on to provide that:

> . . . no Amendment which may be made prior to the Year one thousand eight hundred and eight shall in any Manner affect the first and fourth Clauses in the Ninth Section of the first Article; and that no State, without its Consent, shall be deprived of its equal Suffrage in the Senate.

The article thus imposes three restrictions on the power to amend the constitution, one of a permanent nature and two that expired in 1808. The two clauses protected by the temporary guarantee forbade the Congress to interfere with the importation of slaves before 1808 or to levy a direct tax without apportionment among the states according to population. The permanent limitation prevents any derogation from a state's equality in the Senate without the consent of the state so affected. The first two limitations have long since expired and, though they were both clearly federal instrumentalities, they are no longer of any but antiquarian interest. The third is still operative as a limitation on the power of amendment.

The limiting clause actually does not prevent interference with a state's equality, but only such interference without the state's consent. It is actually a restriction not of substance but of procedure; if the state consents, it could be deprived of its representation. Presumably also, if certain states had their representation increased, those whose representation was not increased would have to consent, since equality would be impaired.

Even so, this limitation is not absolute, for the prohibition in Article V could be amended by the ordinary procedure, thus abolishing the guarantee; after this the equality of a state could be infringed by that same procedure, since it would no longer be protected by the constitution.[1] Such a technique is not likely to be employed; if it were used for such a purpose

[1] Orfield seems to think this a poor statement of the position; he cites with approval Burgess and Mirabeau to the effect that 'we must not lose the *grande morale* in the *petite morale*', op. cit., pp. 84–85. But in a discussion like this we are speaking of morality only indirectly; the concern for the moment is with the legal provisions of the constitution. See William A. Platz, 'Article Five of the Federal Constitution', *George Washington Law Rev.*, vol. 3, 1934, p. 26; also W. F. Willoughby, *The Government of Modern States*, New York, 1924, p. 143.

it would be most likely to destroy the comity of the federal system. Many constitutions have included similar limitations on the amending power, but the present writer knows of no attempt to circumvent these limitations by two successive amendments.[1] Presumably, however, any such limitation could be abolished by the use of the amending power itself.[2]

Restrictions of this nature on the power to amend the constitution are in themselves instrumentalities of federalism wholly distinct from the procedural provisions of the amending clause itself. On occasion in the past certain states or certain classes of states have sought to increase the guarantees against amendments deleterious to their interests. In the Convention of 1787 Mr. Sherman sought to include a prohibition against amendments interfering with the states in their internal police.[3] Much later the Corwin amendment, proposed by the Congress in 1861, was another such attempt; it would have forbidden any future amendment abolishing slavery.

More recently several attempts have been made to read into the fifth article certain implied prohibitions that are not to be found set out in specific terms.[4] One of these is based on the idea that the amendment process cannot be employed to destroy the states or the federal system. That such a restriction was not implied by the framers of the constitution seems

[1] A relevant incident did occur, however, in New South Wales, where an Act of 1929 provided that the Legislative Council (Upper House) could not be abolished nor its powers altered without submitting the question to referendum; this protection was also extended to the 1929 Act itself. In 1930 two bills were introduced, one repealing the Act of 1929 and the other abolishing the Legislative Council. An injunction was sought to prevent their presentation to the Governor without a referendum. An appeal was carried to the Judicial Committee of the Privy Council, which held the 1929 Act binding and the new Acts invalid as violations of Section 5 of the Colonial Laws Validity Act, 1865 (28 & 29 Vict., chap. 63), which authorized colonies to alter their legislatures 'provided that such laws shall have been passed in such manner and form as may . . . be required by any Act of Parliament, Letters Patent, Order in Council, or *Colonial Law* . . . in force in the said colony'. See *Attorney-General for N.S.W.* v. *Trethowan* (1932), A.C. 526. Also the commentary by W. Friedmann in *Australian Law Journal*, vol. 24, 1950, pp. 103–8.

[2] There is some doubt about whether this is true in Australia. See above, pp. 157 ff.

[3] *Documents Illustrative of the Formation of the Union of the American States*, 69th Cong., 1st sess., House Doc. 398, p. 734.

[4] Orfield at op. cit., p. 87, note 12, cites a vast number of sources of suggestions of such implied limitation. See also Bacon, 'How the Tenth Amendment Affected the Fifth Article of the Constitution', *Virginia Law Rev.*, vol. 16, 1930, p. 771.

clear from the fact that they rejected Sherman's proposed restriction mentioned above. Others have argued that certain clauses in the constitution are so basic as to preclude their alteration by the ordinary processes. The bill of rights is held by some to place restrictions on the amending power.[1] The tenth amendment is also held to constitute such a limitation.[2] But there is nothing in any of these provisions that refers to the amending clause, nor can any such references reasonably be inferred. To assert that such limitations may be shown by inference is to misunderstand the legal nature of a constitution.

Certain amendments have been attacked in the courts on the ground that they violated implied restrictions of this sort. It was alleged that the eighteenth amendment was essentially statutory in character and belonged in legislation rather than in the constitution. This was doubtless true, but on a moral rather than a legal basis. Since the amendment was incorporated by regular means into the constitution, it possessed all the force of other elements of that instrument; and so the Supreme Court held when it was called upon to decide the issue. A second objection was that the amendment did not amend, that is change, anything in the constitution but added new matter to it. It is clear from the practice of every nation that this is a wholly false interpretation of the word 'amend' in its legal sense (whatever its etymological sense).[3] Still another attack on the eighteenth amendment was based upon the allegation that the adoption of it should have been as nearly as possible an act of the people and that it should therefore have been ratified by conventions. This contention was even upheld by a federal judge in a lower court, but was thrown out by the Supreme Court on the ground that Article V quite explicitly assigns to Congress the power to choose between the two methods of ratification.[4]

Although many such implied limitations have been suggested,[5] the Supreme Court has refused in every instance to

[1] George D. Skinner, 'Intrinsic Limitations on the Power of Constitutional Amendment', *Michigan Law Rev.*, vol. 18, 1920, p. 213. [2] Bacon, op. cit.

[3] These arguments were all contemptuously brushed aside without a reasoned opinion. *National Prohibition Cases* (1920), 253 U.S. 350.

[4] *United States* v. *Sprague* (1931), 282 U.S. 716.

[5] In addition to the sources mentioned see Wm. L. Marbury, 'The Limitations Upon the Amending Power', *Harvard Law Rev.*, vol. 33, 1919, p. 223; J. H.

accept this argument. The accepted legal doctrine now seems to be that there are no limitations whatever upon the amending power, with the single exception, explicitly stated in the clause itself, that no state shall be deprived of its equal suffrage without its consent. By following the prescribed procedures anything else can apparently be accomplished. The one restriction in regard to the Senate has not caused much discussion and has never been involved in litigation. Although it has not been of active importance, its presence serves as a significant guarantee to the federal entities and it is not impossible that it will one day serve as an important instrumentality of federalism.

### *The Question of Rigidity*

This survey of the experience of the United States with its amending procedure displays two phenomena of interest to the student of constitutional provisions and processes. After the adoption of the twelfth amendment there was a period of more than a century during which the only amendments to the constitution were the three that were produced by the stresses and strains of the Civil War. From 1810 to 1909 not a single amendment was submitted to the states that was not an outgrowth of the slavery controversy. Observing these facts, most commentators arrived reasonably enough at the conclusion that the United States constitution was rigid in the extreme and that only a revolution or a revolutionary change in opinion could effect a formal change in its provisions. But beginning in 1913 four amendments followed one after the other in quick succession and two more were added a decade later. In the twenty years from 1913 to 1933 six amendments were made to the constitution, and a seventh proposed by Congress but not accepted by the states. These developments led many students of the subject to reconsider the conclusions reached by their predecessors; the new amendments suggested that the constitution was not so rigid after all. This conclusion was equally valid, for the facts just as clearly demonstrated that the

Smith, 'Is Prohibition Constitutional?', *Plain Talk*, vol. 4, 1929, p. 415; D. O. McGovney, 'Is the Eighteenth Amendment Void Because of its Contents?', *Columbia Law Rev.*, vol. 20, 1920, p. 499; Orfield, op. cit., chap. 4, *passim*.

constitution was readily subject to alteration if only enough support for the amendments was aroused.

In the latter part of the nineteenth century attempts to amend the constitution increased considerably.[1] But people became more and more convinced that the constitution was very nearly impossible to amend. The writers on American constitutional subjects were almost unanimous in their complaints on this score. Woodrow Wilson, writing in 1885, stated: 'It would seem that no impulse short of the impulse of self-preservation, no force less than the force of revolution, can nowadays be expected to move the cumbrous machinery of Article V.'[2] Lord Bryce observed that 'If . . . comparatively little use has been made of the provisions for amendment, this has been due, not solely to the excellence of the original instrument, but also to the difficulties which surround the process of change.'[3] Even Chief Justice Marshall had once referred to the procedure as an 'unwieldy and cumbrous machinery'.[4] There is no need here to repeat similar arguments from other sources;[5] there were very few dissenters.

Moreover, the mathematical tricks that could be performed with the amending procedure were appalling to those who sought a more flexible process. As early as 1788 Patrick Henry had used this sort of argument against the adoption of the constitution: '. . . one-twentieth part of the American people may prevent the removal of the most grievous inconveniences and oppression, by refusing to accede to amendments'.[6] The

[1] Ames lists 765 proposals in the sixty-year period from 1789 to 1850 and 971 proposals in the forty-year period from 1850 to 1889. See op. cit., Appendix A, where the proposals are numbered.

[2] *Congressional Government*, Boston, 1885, pp. 242–3. By 1908 Wilson had not changed this opinion; see his *Constitutional Government in the United States*, published in that year, p. 193.

[3] *The American Commonwealth*, 3rd edn., vol. 1, pp. 368–9.

[4] *Barron* v. *Baltimore* (1833), 7 Pet. 242 at p. 250.

[5] Such compilations have been made, however; quotations and references on the subject may be found in the following: H. V. Ames, 'The Amending Provision of the Federal Constitution in Practice', in Amer. Phil. Soc., *Proceedings*, vol. lxiii, 1924, pp. 62–75; Charles E. Merriam, *American Political Ideas, 1865–1917*, New York, 1920, chap. vii; L. B. Orfield, *The Amending of the Federal Constitution*, chap. vi.

[6] Elliot's *Debates*, vol. iii, p. 48; cited by J. Allen Smith, *The Spirit of American Government*, 1907, pp. 45–46. Smith's book was one of the most bitter polemics against the undemocratic elements in American government, and the amending procedure was not spared: 'As a matter of fact, it is impossible to

argument is built on the fact that the one-fourth of the states that might block an amendment could theoretically be the smallest of all. Burgess used a similar argument. Using the 1880 census, he argued that 3,000,000 people could defeat an amendment desired by more than 45,000,000.[1] He could have done much better than this if he had really been determined to reduce the proposition to absurdity.

The trick can work in the other direction as well, by demonstrating that a relatively small number concentrated in the small states can put through an amendment opposed by the majority of the people concentrated in the large states.[2]

This kind of argument has not been dispelled by the easy adoption of amendments in the twentieth century. Former Attorney-General Homer Cummings in 1938 argued that the amending process was rigid because, according to the 1930 census, states comprising only 4·6 per cent. of the population could halt an amendment.[3] The difficulty with these arguments is not that they are not true; figures, as someone has said, do not lie. The argument could be carried even farther. To take the figures just cited, we may say accurately enough that it is mathematically possible for the opponents of an amendment to be so distributed as to constitute *bare majorities* in each of these thirteen smallest states. In that case 2·3 per cent. of the population would be thwarting the rest. Or, to make it worse, we might assume that the opponents represent bare majorities in the legislative districts of those states containing the smallest number of people. In that case the figure would probably be below 2 per cent.[4]

secure amendments to the Constitution, unless the sentiment in favor of change amounts almost to a revolution' (p. 46). Smith, too, used the mathematical parade of the horribles: 'In 1900 one forty-fourth of the population distributed, so as to constitute a majority in the ten smallest states could defeat any proposed amendment' (p. 46).

[1] John W. Burgess, *Political Science and Comparative Constitutional Law*, Boston, 1890, vol. 1, p. 151,

[2] Ames in *Proceedings* of Amer. Phil. Soc., 1924, p. 70, cites a study that had concluded that less than 32 per cent. of the total number of legislators in the forty-eight states could ratify an amendment.

[3] Homer Cummings, 'The Nature of the Amending Process', *George Washington Law Rev.*, vol. 6, 1938, pp. 247–58; reprinted by the Government Printing Office, 1938. The citation is from the latter, p. 10.

[4] See a discussion of these arguments and an interesting attempt to refute them by Carl J. Friedrich, *Constitutional Government and Democracy*, 1941 edn., pp. 200 ff.

These arguments are parlour tricks, not political science. There is not the slightest possibility of such an aggregation of voting strength either for or against an amendment. States vote in groups not because of their size but because of regional interests, economic and social considerations, and attitudes towards political parties.

The adoption of amendments sixteen to nineteen in the period of the First World War led to a reconsideration of the question of constitutional rigidity in America. It was still true that the amending procedure contained federal elements and it was still true that a small part of the population could theoretically thwart the will of a great part. But the rapid passage of these amendments made many re-examine their previous opinions on the possibility of amendment. In 1919 George Burton Adams recognized the new phenomenon:

> It was declared by high authority ten years ago that the Constitution of the United States would never again be formally amended. Since then two amendments have been easily and quickly adopted. . . . Two other amendments are now being pressed for adoption, and one of them is so rapidly being adopted by the states as to seem to show not merely that the constitution can be easily amended when there is sufficient popular demand, but that it may even be too easily amended without due consideration of the fitness of the amendment to belong in the constitution.[1]

Others too were forced to reconsider. Ames had written in 1896 that 'the real reason for the failure of those other amendments that have been called for repeatedly by the general public has been due to the insurmountable obstacles in their way'.[2] In 1924 he confessed that he had changed his mind: 'Although the speaker some years ago held the view that the amending process was too difficult . . . he believes (now) that a radical change in the method of amendment is neither necessary nor desirable.'[3] Professor W. F. Dodd reported in an article in 1921 that he repudiated his opinion on the subject expressed in 1910.[4] The simple truth of the matter seems to be

[1] G. B. Adams, *Federal Government, Its Function and Method*, New York, 1919, pp. 94–95.

[2] *Proposed Amendments to the Constitution*, p. 301.

[3] *Proceedings* of Amer. Phil. Soc., 1924, p. 74.

[4] Dodd, *The Revision and Amendment of State Constitutions*, Baltimore, 1910, p. 141 n.; cf. his article, 'Amending the Federal Constitution', in *Yale Law Journal*, vol. 30, 1921, pp. 348 ff.

that when sufficient public approbation is aroused for a measure, it is likely to be carried through without much difficulty. All of the amendments that have been adopted since the Civil War, except the twenty-second, have been rapidly carried through on a wave of popular approval.

The figures on the number of amendments proposed and ratified are not very significant with regard to the question of rigidity, but they cannot be ignored. We have seen that over 4,000 measures have been introduced in the Congress, out of which only 27 have been submitted to the states; the proportion is very low. On the other hand, out of the 27 measures submitted the states have ratified 22, which is a rather high proportion. But the difference between these proportions cannot be taken as an indication that all the rigidity lies in the Congress and none in the states. Measures are introduced in Congress for any reasons that please constituents. The figures do not disclose the measures that were duplicates of others, that were unsupported, unnecessary, ridiculous, or facetious.

Even so, it is true to say that an amendment has almost no chance of getting through Congress, but that when it does it has an excellent chance of being ratified by the states. The reason for this is not that Congress is unwilling to amend the constitution but that Congress is unwilling to amend it unless there is some assurance that public opinion largely favours the proposed change. The process by which Congressmen make this decision is difficult to analyse, but it is the same as that by which they ordinarily discover what the public wants. This again is the political process in action, the shifting of various kinds of opinion, the adjusting of differences, the compromising of conflicts, that leads to public policy. Since two-thirds of Congress must agree to an amendment, there must of course be a larger measure of public support than is necessary for an ordinary statute. But when this support has been present, the amendment has been forthcoming. Critics of the amending procedure tend to forget that not only have more amendments been *ratified* in recent years but Congress has *proposed* more amendments in recent years.

### *Other Criticisms of the Amending Procedure*

Opinions at the time of the original ratification of the constitution were sharply divided on the suitability of the amending procedure in the fifth article. We have seen that Henry and Marshall were both highly critical of it and considered the constitution far too rigid. Others took the view that it was too flexible. Hamilton devoted nearly the whole of the last *Federalist* paper to a demonstration that the procedure afforded a means of change both easy and convenient.[1] Madison thought that the procedure took a middle path, guarding equally 'against that extreme facility, which would render the Constitution too mutable; and that extreme difficulty, which might perpetuate its discovered faults'.[2]

In the preceding section we have observed that two of the major complaints raised against the amending procedure have been (*a*) that it is too difficult to permit the ready accommodation of the constitution to changing needs; and (*b*) that by requiring the consent of three-fourths of the states, it permits minorities concentrated in the smaller states to thwart the will of majorities concentrated in the larger. In addition to these criticisms, two other complaints have been raised against the amendment procedure: first, that, so far from being too difficult to achieve, amendments are in reality far too easy to achieve; and second, that the process of amendment is so far removed from direct popular control that it is undemocratic.

The first of these objections was seldom heard before the advent of the twentieth century. It was produced by the fact that in a short period of eight years (1913–20) four amendments were added to the constitution and that the single year of 1933 saw the addition of two more. In many cases the desire to make ratification more difficult seems to have been cloaked by an apparent desire to make it more democratic.[3] An amendment proposed in 1921 by Senator Wadsworth and Representative Garrett[4] would have *added* a referendum to the already

[1] *The Federalist*, No. 85, Modern Library edn., pp. 570–4.

[2] Ibid., No. 43, p. 286.

[3] See Orfield, op. cit., pp. 183 f., 193 f.; also Justin Miller, 'Amendment of the Federal Constitution: Should it be Made More Difficult?', *Minnesota Law Review*, vol. 10, 1926, p. 185.

[4] See a speech by the former in the *Congressional Record*, vol. 65, 1924, pp. 4491 ff.

existing process of legislative ratification, a change that would have required three steps in the process instead of two. Most of the complaints that the procedure is too easy apparently came from those who were dissatisfied with the content of certain amendments of the First World War period, and especially from the opponents of the eighteenth amendment. These dissentients were for the most part mollified when that amendment was repealed with an ease greater than that with which it was passed. Since 1933 there have been few complaints on the score that amendment is too easy.

Arguments that the amending process is undemocratic have continued, however, and it is this criticism that has in recent years led to most of the proposals for the reform of Article V. Several elements that are undemocratic can be found by the critics: the requirement that two-thirds of Congress must agree on the proposal; the requirement that three-fourths of the states must ratify; the fact that state legislatures have performed the function of ratifying in all but one instance; and the fact that there is under the present scheme no provision for a direct expression of public opinion on the questions of amendment.

The truth is that these criticisms are quite valid in so far as the assumptions on which they are based are not challenged. To criticize the amending procedure for being undemocratic is to assume that it was intended or expected or ought to be democratic. This involves a definition of democracy which it is no purpose of the present study to provide; but presumably one of the things that is meant by such criticisms is that the process does not guarantee that the constitution shall include just what the majority of the people in the country want it to include. Certainly this is true. But this criticism should be aimed not at the lack of popular control but at the federal system itself, for, as it is implemented in the United States, the federal principle refutes the principle of majority rule as applied to the problem of constitutional amendment. One of the instrumentalities of federalism in America is the requirement that three-fourths of the states must concur in changes in the constitution. If this should not be, we must explore the present attitude not only towards amendments but towards federalism itself.

The other aspect of the charge that the procedure is

undemocratic is the argument that the procedure does not permit direct popular participation in the amending process. This complaint is a valid one, though it does not involve any question of federalism. The ratifications of the states may be obtained either from state legislatures or from state conventions, as Congress may direct, but not from direct popular votes. The critics who urge that ratifications might better be obtained from popular referenda in each state do not necessarily suggest a disturbance of the federal arrangement; for each state could retain its own part in the process, and the requirement that three-fourths of the states must ratify need not be given up. We are concerned here not with the question whether it ought to be given up but only to distinguish between these two different aspects of the complaint that the procedure is undemocratic. One is actually a criticism of the federal basis of American government; the other is not.

## *The Reform of the Amending Procedure*

These dissatisfactions with the amending procedure have led to a vast number of proposals for the reform of the constitution's fifth article. But the surprising fact is that no such proposals were offered in Congress before the constitution had been in operation for three-quarters of a century,[1] although numerous efforts had been made to amend the constitution in other respects. The first such proposal recorded by Ames appeared in 1864, when a resolution was introduced for the purpose of reducing the majorities required both for the proposal and ratification of amendments. During the discussions attendant upon the submission of the 'Civil War' amendments, certain suggestions were made for changes in the procedure,[2] and such suggestions were heard with increasing frequency during the remainder of the nineteenth century; the twentieth has seen no diminution of such efforts.

Attempts to reform the procedure have taken many forms and have been aimed at the correction of all sorts of perceived faults. Most of them, however, have been directed towards

[1] Ames, 'The Amending Provision of the Federal Constitution in Practice', Amer. Phil. Soc., *Proceedings*, 1924, p. 66.

[2] Ibid., p. 67.

changing the process of ratification rather the process by which amendments are initiated, despite the fact that the data set out above tend to suggest that it is the procedure of submission rather than that of ratification that has been the greater obstacle. But the majorities required in the Congress for the submission of amendments have attracted considerable attention.[1] Various means of modifying the present system have been proposed, but the principal suggestion has been that ordinary majorities in each House should be sufficient.[2] Some have suggested ordinary majorities in two successive sessions.[3] Professor Burgess once suggested that the two Houses should sit in joint session after the French fashion and that a majority in such a session should be sufficient for the initiation of amendments.[4] Such a system, however, is open to the legal objection that it would affect the equal representation of the states in the Senate.

The requirement that both Houses must agree to a resolution of amendment has prevented the submission of more than thirty such resolutions,[5] which has led certain reformers to suggest that either House should be permitted to initiate amendments without the other's consent, when the first House passes the proposal two or more times.[6] Such a scheme, as we have seen, is provided for in the Australian constitution, though it has never been put to use. There has also been a certain amount of agitation for the establishment of a means whereby amendments may be proposed by popular initiative.[7]

[1] There have also been a few efforts to change the provision whereby Congress is required to call a convention at the instance of two-thirds of the states. See Ames, *Proposed Amendments to the Constitution*, pp. 281 ff.; also Wayne B. Wheeler, 'Is a Constitutional Convention Impending?', *Illinois Law Rev.*, vol. 21, 1927, p. 782.

[2] Orfield has collected an impressive array of resolutions introduced in Congress that propose such a plan. Op. cit., p. 173, n. 20.

[3] Munroe Smith, 'Shall We Make Our Constitution Flexible?', *North American Review*, vol. 194, 1911, p. 657.

[4] John W. Burgess, *Political Science and Comparative Constitutional Law*, 1890, vol. 1, p. 152.

[5] See above, pp. 217 f.

[6] J. David Thompson, 'The Amendment of the Federal Constitution', *Proceedings of the Academy of Political Science*, vol. 3, 1912, p. 65. Ernest C. Carman, 'Why and How the Present Method of Amending the Federal Constitution Should be Changed', *Oregon Law Rev.*, vol. 17, 1938, p. 102. Carman also suggests that a majority of the states be empowered to propose amendments.

[7] See Orfield, op. cit., pp. 177 ff.

But the procedure of ratification has attracted more attention from reformers than has that for the initiation of amendments. There have been many complaints that Congress should make use of the convention mode of ratification rather than that of ratification by the legislatures.[1] But the Congress has been most unwilling to employ the convention system, and the reversion to legislative ratification for the proposal of the twenty-second amendment in 1947 makes it clear that the twenty-first amendment established no presumption in favour of the greater use of conventions in the future. Moreover, if the purpose in insisting on conventions is to make the procedure more democratic, then the obvious goal to work for is the establishment of ratifying referenda. But the convention is certainly closer to public opinion than is the legislature, and it has the very important advantage of being available without requiring a constitutional amendment to put it into practice.

Ratification by the state legislatures has been subjected to even more serious criticism and the efforts to modify this scheme have been the most numerous of all. In the first place many attempts have been made to reduce the requirement that three-fourths of the legislatures must ratify the proposals.[2] The number has been set by various persons at two-thirds[3] and at a simple majority.[4] The experience of Switzerland and Australia has apparently had some influence as well, for there have been numerous proposals looking towards the establishment of a system comparable to the ones employed in those countries. Professor Orfield notes plans to make ratification follow on popular referenda in which adoption shall be depen-

[1] Charles W. Needham, 'Changing the Fundamental Law', *Univ. of Pennsylvania Law Rev.*, vol. 69, 1921, p. 223; George S. Brown, 'The People Should be Consulted as to Constitutional Changes', *Amer. Bar Assoc. Journ.*, vol. 16, 1930, p. 404.

[2] Rhode Island in 1790 ratified the federal constitution 'in full confidence' that certain amendments would immediately be incorporated; among these was one providing than an amendment to the constitution should require the consent of *eleven* of the original thirteen states. *Documents Illustrative of the Formation of the Union of the American States*, p. 1057. Orfield states that this is the only instance of a formal proposal to increase the number of states necessary for ratification. Op. cit., p. 185.

[3] See ibid., p. 185, n. 48, and p. 187, n. 56, for references to proposals of this sort in Congress.

[4] Notably by Senator LaFollette of Wisconsin, S.J.R. 131, 62nd Cong., 2nd sess., 1912. See Musmanno, *Proposed Amendments to the Constitution*, pp. 194 f.

dent upon approval by a majority of those voting,[1] by majorities in a majority of the states,[2] or by a combination of these methods. This last would be essentially the same method as that employed in Australia and Switzerland. It would combine the requirement of a majority of those voting with that of a majority of the states, preserving the federal nature of the process while making of it a more direct expression of the popular will; it would at the same time satisfy those critics who consider three-fourths of the states too large an obstacle to change.[3] An interesting variation on this principle was suggested by Mr. Juul of Illinois in 1919; his proposal included ratification by the legislatures, but assigned to the states a weight in the determination of the question equivalent to their votes in the electoral college.[4]

A change frequently sought and in a few states unofficially established has been the requirement that the state legislature shall not undertake to ratify an amendment until the Lower House has been re-elected. Efforts by the states to enforce this by law or constitutional provision have been declared invalid by the Supreme Court[5] as being inconsistent with Article V, but several states employ it as a customary practice without legal sanction. The value of the device seems to be slight, however, since it does not give a clear indication of public opinion. A better method, accomplishing the same thing, has been for the state to hold a popular referendum. This device also has been held unconstitutional as a formal device of ratification,[6] but it serves an excellent purpose as an advisory agency, indicating the will of the people of the state and providing the legislature with an unmistakable guide for its action.[7]

[1] Orfield, op. cit., p. 186, n. 53.

[2] Loc. cit., n. 54.

[3] In addition to Orfield, op. cit., p. 186, see K. C. Wheare, *Federal Government*, chap. xi; Munroe Smith, 'Shall We Make Our Constitution Flexible?', *North American Review*, vol. 194, 1911, p. 657; Frederic B. Johnstone, 'An Eighteenth Century Constitution', *Illinois Law Rev.*, vol. 7, 1912, p. 265.

[4] Musmanno, *Proposed Amendments to the Constitution*, p. 201.

[5] *Leser* v. *Garnett* (1922), 258 U.S. 130.

[6] *Hawke* v. *Smith* (1920), 253 U.S. 221.

[7] See W. A. Robinson, 'Advisory Referendum in Massachusetts on the Child Labor Amendment', *American Political Science Review*, vol. 19, 1925, p. 69. Also William Howard Taft, 'Can Ratification of an Amendment to the Constitution Be Made to Depend Upon a Referendum?', *Yale Law Journal*, vol. 29, 1920, p. 821.

There have been many proposals of amendments to Article V that would establish the popular referendum as the principal (or only) means of securing ratifications. As we have seen, these proposals have been associated with (or dissociated from) the federal principle in several ways, but a trend of opinion towards this device in, say, the past three decades seems very clear, whatever the details of the proposals. Such a scheme was included in the Progressive platform of 1912 and in the Democratic platform of 1924. The general widening of the suffrage and in particular the adoption of the fifteenth, seventeenth, and nineteenth amendments gave stimulus to the idea that amendment should be made to depend upon popular approval of a direct kind. Between 1917 and 1928 nineteen such proposals were introduced in Congress,[1] and such measures continue to be put forward. Two in particular have attracted widespread attention in recent years; one of these was the proposal of Senator Wadsworth and Representative Garrett[2] in 1921 which was investigated and discussed through most of the 1920's; the other was the proposal by Senator Norris in 1938.[3] The Wadsworth–Garrett proposal provided that any state could require that ratification by its legislature be subject to confirmation by referendum. It permitted referenda in the states, but did not require them.[4] Senator Walsh offered an amendment to this resolution abolishing legislative ratification and referring all questions directly to popular vote. Senator Jones proposed a method midway between these two that would employ advisory votes in the legislature but make the state's ratification dependent on the outcome of the referendum.[5] After many hearings and debates on the several proposals the resolution was recommitted without decision and no vote was ever taken on it.

Senator Norris's proposal in 1938 provided for popular referenda on amendments, with the approval of two-thirds of

[1] Musmanno, op. cit., p. 199.

[2] S.J.R. 40, 67th Cong., 1st sess., 1921, and H.J.R. 69, 67th Cong., 1st sess., 1921.

[3] S.J.R. 134, 75th Cong., 3rd sess., 1938.

[4] See Judson King, *American Principles and the Wadsworth Amendment*, Washington, 1925.

[5] The three forms of the proposal are discussed in Musmanno, op. cit., pp. 199–204; also Orfield, op. cit., pp. 193–6, 198–9.

the states being necessary; the states were to be deprived of their present right to initiate a constitutional convention. The hearings on this proposal are a source of much interesting material on the problem of amendment in the United States,[1] but they produced no effective result. The measure secured significant attention for some time, but no action was taken on it.

Those who advocate the popular referendum as the best means of ratifying constitutional amendments would do well to take warning from the experience of Australia, where such questions are almost always voted on at general elections and have become in most cases party questions. Whether this is desirable or not, it has not in general been true in the United States. Another consideration of the same type is that voters in the United States are already confronted with ballots containing an appalling number of offices and questions on which decisions must be made. It would be most unfortunate if the all-important questions of constitutional amendment should be smothered at general elections under the biennial avalanche of the long ballot.

## *Conclusion*

The long series of efforts to make formal changes in the procedures provided in Article V have thus far been unsuccessful—the article stands today with precisely the same wording it possessed in 1789. But it can hardly be said that the process of amendment has remained unchanged. The meaning of the various clauses of that article have been subjected to changing interpretations by the courts and the result of these interpretations has been a gradual modification of the content of the article. History has taught us, moreover, that the constitution can, after all, be amended when sufficient demand for amendment is aroused. The convention method of ratification was employed for the first time in 1933 after a century and a half of neglect. The question of the duration of the validity of pending amendments has apparently been settled by tagging each one with a seven-year time limit. Despite the lack of

[1] U.S. Congress, Senate, *Hearings Before a Sub-Committee of the Committee on the Judiciary, Ratification of Constitutional Amendments by Popular Vote,* S.J.R. 134, 75th Cong., 3rd sess., 1938.

formal changes in its provisions, the fifth article has undergone a few modifications. These do not by any means meet the demands of the critics of the amending procedure, but they do demonstrate that even in a federal system with a supposedly rigid constitution, change can be expected. Since the Second World War there has been relatively little agitation for reform of the amending procedure and, though it should not be inferred that there will be no more criticism or that the procedure is even quite satisfactory, it seems unlikely that any significant changes will be introduced in the near future.

A word of caution may be added. It is appropriate to suggest that the critics of the amendment process have been perhaps too eager to attribute evils to it that are inherent not merely in this procedure but in the American system of government itself. Since schemes of value differ, some things are evils to one man that seem good to another. Critics are always more articulate than defenders, and the student of the subject must be careful not to attribute more influence to the former than they deserve. This is not to suggest that the process is not deserving of criticism; the very fact that it has been gradually modified suggests that faults have been found. But it may also be suggested that the changes effected have not been great, and it may just be possible that no significant changes are needed; after all, the record does not provide much evidence that the system has been inadequate.

The reform of political and constitutional institutions is a very uncertain thing. Institutions in operation have a strong, though frequently concealed, effect on other institutions and on the people who operate them. To alter them without profound investigation of their precise place in the general scheme is to tempt fate. Political science has not yet advanced to the stage where all the complex interrelationships of sociology, psychology, politics, and constitutional law can be observed or analysed. A change in one of these can have a tremendous effect on the others; and this effect cannot always be predicted. Many critics would, for example, relieve the amending procedure of the burdens of its federal machinery by requiring only a nation-wide popular majority for ratification. Perhaps this would be a good thing. But the participation of the states in the amending process is an important instrumentality of federalism in America, in the sense in which that term has been here used. Modification of this instrumentality would carry with it implications for the rest of the political process that can scarcely be estimated. Severe changes in this one instrumentality would affect many others and would bear implications far more profound for the federal system than the mere tinkering with the amending procedure alone. Changes of this nature must be undertaken only with the utmost care and caution.

# 6

# CONSIDERATIONS ON OTHER COUNTRIES

WE have thus far examined the processes of constitutional change in the four countries that are generally acknowledged to be federal in their constitutional structures. Each of them employs procedures, however, that are peculiar to itself and differ from those of the others in important particulars. But despite these variations there is to be perceived among these four countries a principle common to them all, a principle that seems to be essential to federal government. This is that the constitution is not amended merely on the strength of a numerical majority in the country as a whole, but that such changes require consideration of the attitudes of the component units. In every case the question arises whether the states as states, and not as mere divisions of population distribution, approve the proposed change. The participation of the states in the process is institutionalized in various ways, and in one country it is hardly institutionalized at all; but in every country it is observable. This principle of state participation is present in every federation, whether constitutional provision is made for it or not, and we may suggest that it is the essential characteristic of the federal element in the amending process.

But the reader may recall the earlier suggestion that the essence of federalism is not to be found in constitutional provisions but in the psycho-sociological diversities within the nation and in the manner in which the institutions function. Bearing this in mind, we may inquire whether this common principle is restricted to those countries that political scientists have called federal. In this chapter we shall examine briefly the experience of certain other governments which are more often described as unitary but which seem to display a comparable or perhaps identical principle.

## A. THE UNION OF SOUTH AFRICA

The constitution of the Union of South Africa is contained[1] in a statute of the Imperial Parliament (9 Edw. VII, chap. 9) enacted in 1909 after lengthy deliberation by a constitutional convention in South Africa; the Act took effect in 1910. It united in a legislative union the four colonies of the Cape of Good Hope, Natal, the Transvaal, and the Orange River Colony. The first two of these colonies were peopled predominantly by Europeans of British origin and the latter two by the descendants of the early Dutch settlers. There was from the outset therefore a combination into one nation of two peoples who differed in language, religion, national origins, and even economic interest.

These differences were great and history has proved them important. But despite the precedents of Canada and Australia, whose diversities were no greater, a unitary constitution was adopted. The size of the country, the fact that the nationality groups were not perfectly distributed along provincial boundaries, the feeling that certain problems required central management (e.g. railways, racial questions)—all these things impelled the constitution-makers towards a unitary state.

### *Federal and Unitary Features of the Union*

Whether or not the union thus established was in fact federal or unitary has been a question much discussed by students of constitutional law and politics. The Union Government does display several features commonly associated with federalism and these have led a few scholars to argue that South Africa, despite its unitary qualities, is actually a federation.[2] The constitution establishes the four former colonies as provinces of the Union and empowers them to enact laws on a list of

[1] All of the constitution is, of course, not included in the Act of 1909; South Africa even more than the other Dominions finds her constitution in such features as statutory enactments and conventions. See W. P. M. Kennedy and H. J. Schlosberg, *The Law and Custom of the South African Constitution*, Oxford, 1935, pp. 71–75.

[2] See, for example, Herman Finer, *Theory and Practice of Modern Government*, London, 1932, vol. 1, p. 244. But see also E. M. Sait, *Political Institutions: A Preface*, New York, 1938, p. 380 n.

subjects[1] in much the same manner as Section 92 of the British North America Act. The provincial councils may exercise these powers as they like, being restrained by no limitations on the powers themselves, but only by the fact that the Union Parliament may override any provincial legislation. Another federal characteristic is the provision for equal representation of the four provinces in the Senate. Each province elects eight senators and sixteen others are chosen by other means. The senators from a province are elected not by popular vote but by the provincial council and by the members of the House of Assembly for the province. This equality of representation was provided by the Act of 1909, but there is no assurance that it is permanent, for Section 25 empowered the Parliament to change these provisions after ten years. Even so the equality has been maintained, and this fact is indicative of the vigour of federal feeling in the country. Another federal characteristic originally found was the perpetuation of provincial regulations concerning voters and elections.[2] But this was changed in 1918 with the passage of the Parliamentary Elections Act which replaced the provincial regulations with others applying to the whole Union.

The unitary characteristics of the constitution are more outstanding than the federal. While the provinces are empowered to pass laws on certain subjects, these laws are invalid if they conflict with any Union legislation and the Union Parliament may by simple act invalidate any provincial law. The powers of the Union are not listed but are contained in the single statement that 'Parliament shall have full power to make laws for the peace, order, and good government of the Union'.[3] This statement confers upon the Union Parliament plenary power over all matters and enables it to deal with the provinces in any fashion. It subordinates the provinces to the Union in a manner both unequivocal and absolute. The Union Parliament can add to or subtract from the powers of the provinces; it can override any Act of the provinces; it can legally abolish them altogether. Clearly the provinces of South Africa have no status comparable to that of the provinces of Canada or the states of Australia and the United States.

[1] Section 85.
[2] Sections 35–37.
[3] Section 59.

### *Federalism in Action*

But if we look beyond the constitutional clauses we find many elements in the governmental practices of South Africa that are federal in character. No country composed of groups so diverse can be entirely free of the qualities of federalism in its social organization. These diversities consist not only of the conflict between the Britisher and the Afrikaner but of the vast cultural differences of the black and the white and the brown. South Africa has a native population that is considerably larger than the white group and in addition there are several hundred thousand mixed breeds or 'coloureds' and several hundred thousand Indians who have never been assimilated. It is true that no one of these racial groups is concentrated exclusively in any one province and that no province can claim to represent any one of them by itself, but certain of the provinces nevertheless lend their support to the interests of one or another. Natal is peopled principally with British, though it has important elements of other groups; the Transvaal and the Orange Free State are predominantly Afrikaner. The fact that the nationality groups were not perfectly isolated in the several colonies was one of the chief reasons for the avoidance of a federal scheme of government; but neither are they perfectly distributed among all the provinces, with the result that the country functions in a large measure like a federation even though it formally is not one. The governmental system has displayed many of the features of federalism and has given rise to many of the peculiar problems that have troubled such federal governments as Australia and the United States. In 1934 a commission of inquiry declared itself to be

> . . . impressed by the battle for authority that appeared to wage continuously between Union and provincial officers on many subjects in which they were mutually concerned. The suggestion to decentralize Union powers to the provinces met with the most strenuous objection by Union representatives. On the other hand, proposals made to detach certain functions exercised by the provinces and to coordinate these with Union departments met with equally strenuous opposition on the part of provincial authorities.[1]

[1] *Report of the Provincial Finance Commission*, 1934, para. 21; cited by Alexander Brady, *Democracy in the Dominions*, 2nd edn., 1952, p. 353.

Once established, governments like those of the provinces, being constantly nourished by a steady growth of local patriotism and perpetuated by the vested interests of office-holders, are very difficult to reduce in stature. If anything, the South African provinces have increased rather than diminished in importance since union. Though the Union may have the legal power to solve a problem by legislative fiat, the political problem would be insuperable, since it would have to move in the face of animosities and jealousies that the provinces have acquired over a long period of years.[1]

We may mention a few of the problems that have troubled South Africa and made its status as a unitary state suspect. One is the great disparity between the sources of provincial income and the costs which the functions assigned to them cause them to bear. This in South Africa, as in other countries more properly called federal, has been managed by a system of grants by the Union to the provincial governments. The distribution of these subsidies has produced the same problems that are found in federal systems: each province is certain that its share should be increased at the expense of the others. Another such problem lies in the control of elementary education, which was assigned by the Union Act to the provinces for a five-year period only; but the subject has never been taken from them because of the fierce political opposition to such a transfer. Another such example is found in the relations between the two governments in the social welfare field. As the need for welfare legislation has increased, the responsibility of the Union in financing the various programmes has also increased because only the Union can bear the expenses involved, even though the subject was one of those allotted to the provinces.

Finally, one may cite the distinctive federal characteristics of the South African party system. It may be superfluous to point out that the parties rather sharply reflect the provincial and social diversities that divide the white population. The Nationalist Party, whose major themes are those derived from the Afrikaner tradition, is strongest in the old Dutch republics

[1] See Jan H. Hofmeyr, *South Africa*, 1930, 2nd edn. by J. C. Cope, New York, 1952, chap. 11, for a discussion of the compromise drawn by the constitution between federalism and unitarism.

of the Transvaal and the Free State; the United Party finds its greatest support in the British areas of the Cape and Natal. A striking illustration of the strength of this provincial attitude towards the party system was afforded by the formation in Natal after the 1953 election of a Federal Party whose aim was to bring about the adoption of a federal system. Some members of the British community in that province, dismayed by the electoral success of the Nationalists and their programme, sought by this means to protect its own very different views on racial policy and continued membership in the Commonwealth. It has even been suggested by some that this movement was coupled with an outright threat of secession.

Thus in many respects the government and especially the politics of South Africa take on the appearance of federalism even though she does not possess federalism's constitutional and institutional forms. The truth is that a country composed as South Africa is of four areas, each with its own political background, its distinctive nationality and religious characteristics, and each bearing the traditions derived from a separate existence, cannot avoid the difficulties that these characteristics bring with them.

### *The Amending Power and the Statute of Westminster*

The most interesting place to study the federal and unitary qualities of South Africa is in the operation of its amending process, all the more because the varying interpretations of that process have produced in recent years a bitter constitutional crisis.

For the most part the amending procedure is one of the marks of unitarism in the constitution. Section 152 of the South Africa Act empowers the Union Parliament to 'repeal or alter any of the provisions of this Act'. Thus the power of constitutional amendment is placed squarely in the Union Parliament; the provinces have no role in the process other than that effected by their representation in the Senate, and the Senate in South Africa, as in other Dominions, has never served as an agent of provincial interests.[1] The provision for

[1] See Henry John May, *The South African Constitution*, Capetown and Johannesburg, 1949, p. 132: 'The senate reveals the only real element of

constitutional amendment is, so far as the words of the constitution are concerned, an element not of federalism but of unitary government.

But the constitution placed certain restrictions on the use of the amending power.[1] In the first place, no provision for which a definite period of time was prescribed could be altered before the expiration of that period. With the expiration of all such periods, however, these temporary restrictions lapsed. Secondly, three sections could not be altered or repealed without resort to a special amending procedure that differed from the ordinary process of legislation. These three specially protected (or 'entrenched') sections were 35, which protected the franchise of non-Europeans in the Cape; 137, which assured the equality of the English and Dutch languages; and 152, the amending clause itself. In order to alter any of these entrenched clauses it was necessary for the two Houses to sit together in a joint session at which, on the third reading, the proposal had to be passed by two-thirds of the total membership of the two Houses. To this extent then the ability of the Parliament to amend the constitution was limited. All other sections could be altered by ordinary legislative processes.

The entrenchment of these clauses was actually what we have called an instrumentality of federalism. The Cape franchise was a step taken in that province towards the advancement of the non-European races. It was based on a policy of humanitarianism and assimilation that was repudiated in the Dutch colonies, and its protection in the constitution was a device to permit the continuation of a policy peculiar to one province. Of the desire to protect the constitutional provision for bilingualism little need be said. The inclusion of the protective clauses of Section 137 are as much federal instrumentalities as are those in the Canadian constitution which protect the education systems and languages of the two nationality groups in that country. These devices illustrate our earlier argument that federal instrumentalities are employed in many countries that cannot be classed as federal on the evidence of

federation in the constitution of the Union' but it is so negligible that it has 'had no effect on the politics of the Union . . . the election of senators and members of parliament has consistently been on party and not on provincial lines'.

[1] See the complete text of Section 152 in Appendix A, below.

the constitution alone. If the diversities exist and there is a demand for their protection, some sort of instrumentality will be adopted, whether the country be federal, unitary, or something else.

Before 1931 no one challenged the validity of these limitations. They were contained in the Imperial Act that constituted the South African constitution and there was little basis for such a challenge. But in that year was enacted the Statute of Westminster, which was widely believed to have abolished these limitations. The argument that led to this conclusion was, briefly put, the following. Before the Statute of Westminster South Africa, like other Dominions, was subject to the repugnancy provisions of the Colonial Laws Validity Act, 1865, and thus was unable to legislate in conflict with any British statute that was part of the law of South Africa. The British statute here in question was, of course, the South Africa Act, 1909. Under it the South African Parliament could alter any of the Act's provisions *except* those that were specially entrenched; these could be altered only by use of the special procedure provided in Section 152. But the Statute of Westminster repealed the repugnancy clause of the Colonial Laws Validity Act in so far as it operated against Dominion legislation and empowered the Dominions to enact laws in conflict with British statutes. Thus, it was argued, an Act of the South African Parliament was no longer restricted by anything in any British statute, and the restrictions on the amending power of the Union Parliament arising from the entrenched clauses and their special procedure were no longer valid. The entrenched clauses were no longer entrenched.

Special attention is given here to this interpretation because it made a great deal of difference in the amending process. It has now been rejected and is no longer a valid interpretation, but it was widely accepted both in Britain and in South Africa,[1] and was seemingly adopted by the Appellate Division of the Supreme Court of South Africa in 1937 in what was for years

[1] Scholarly opinion was almost unanimous; among those accepting this view were A. Berriedale Keith, *The Dominions as Sovereign States*, London, 1938, p. 177; K. C. Wheare, *The Statute of Westminster and Dominion Status* (in the first four editions), 1st edn., Oxford, 1938, p. 242. Henry John May, *The South African Constitution*, pp. 32 f.; Sir Ivor Jennings and C. M. Young, *Constitutional Laws of the Commonwealth*, 2nd edn., Oxford, 1952, pp. 346 f.

the leading case on the question.[1] Until 1951 it was virtually unchallenged.

### *Experience with the Amending Process*

One should bear in mind that this controversy over the entrenched clauses (to which we shall presently return) does not affect the rest of the constitution. In all other areas the Parliament is supreme and can alter any of the provisions of the constitution at will. Since there are no limits to this power, the Parliament may amend the constitution in any form. For an Act to constitute an amendment to the constitution, it need not specifically mention the affected provision or call itself an amendment. As in Britain an Act of the Parliament operates to amend an earlier Act or even the constitution itself if such amendment is required by the necessary intendment of the later Act. This principle has been endorsed by the Appellate Division of the Supreme Court.[2] Indeed, there have been several Acts of Parliament that have actually been amendments to the constitution that have not mentioned that instrument at all.[3]

But in the exercise of this sovereignty the Union Parliament has displayed a keen awareness of the existence of the federal qualities in the South African society. Though it may amend the constitution in any way it pleases (the entrenched clauses aside), the exigencies of politics require that the interests of the provinces be consulted whenever important changes are made. The consultation process is not standardized, but it is none the less an important factor in the determination of such questions.

A few examples of this federal element in the amending process may emphasize the point. In 1934 regional and provincial sentiment, especially in Natal, forced through the

[1] *Ndlwana* v. *Hofmeyr*, N.O. (1937), A.D. 229.

[2] *Krause* v. *Commissioner of Inland Revenue* (1929), A.D. 286.

[3] See Kennedy and Schlosberg, op. cit., pp. 108 ff., where the principal amendments are given, also their Appendix IV, where the text of the constitution includes all amendments to that date. 'In all sixty-six sections of the South Africa Act have been amended, while the enactments altering, interpreting, or amplifying the South Africa Act number one hundred and fifty six.' Ibid., p. 112. Note that this was written in 1935. In 1945 Henry John May reported that there had been 'nearly 200' amendments. 'The Union of South Africa, the Provinces and the Central Government', *State Government*, vol. 18, 1945, p. 117.

Parliament an Act guaranteeing that none of the functions of the provincial governments would be abolished or interfered with except with the consent of the local councils.[1] Though the legislation had no legal effect, it was an important indication of the strength of provincial feeling and its substance was directed towards the preservation of provincial autonomy.

Another illustration may be found in the hesitant and frequently equivocating attitude of the Nationalist Party with respect to the question of a republic. The Afrikaner community and its leaders have long desired to sever completely the ties with Crown and Commonwealth and establish a South African republic in the tradition of their forebears. This sentiment was never stronger than immediately after the 1953 election, but no steps have been taken towards the establishment of such a republic. That the republicans have hesitated is in part testimony to the existence, even among the Nationalists, of a strong federalist attitude. Fearing that the British will not accept such a republic, they have thus far been reluctant to push their plans to the point of an open break.[2]

When the Statute of Westminster was being discussed in the Union Parliament in April 1931 General Smuts, as leader of the Opposition, raised the question of the desirability of continuing the guarantees of the entrenched clauses, which the Statute was considered to abolish. The Government was unwilling to limit the powers of the Parliament in this respect but agreed to a motion by General Smuts asserting that the Statute was accepted 'on the understanding that the proposed legislation will in no way derogate from the entrenched provisions of the South Africa Act'.[3] The Government was quite willing to accept this principle and in its behalf Dr. Stals stated:

> I think no one in the House, or in the Union, doubts the moral obligation of the Parliament and the people to respect the basic principle in our constitution, and therefore, it appears to me to be unnecessary to include a provision for securing it.[4]

[1] Brady, op. cit., 2nd edn., pp. 357 f.

[2] This, of course, is not the sole explanation. Other practical deterrents are the economic and military advantages of membership in the Commonwealth, the desire to acquire the High Commission Territories, fear of Communism, &c.

[3] House of Assembly Debates, 22 Apr. 1931, vol. 17, col. 2739.

[4] Loc. cit. See Wheare, op. cit., 5th edn., p. 241.

This understanding between the leaders of the two parties constituted a sort of gentlemen's agreement under which no future alteration of the entrenched clauses would be undertaken except by use of the special procedure provided in Section 152. But it is clear that all considered the legal protection to have disappeared. In 1934, when the Status of the Union Act was being debated, the Speaker went much farther and announced that 'if it is desired to amend or repeal any of the entrenched clauses, then the procedure laid down in the South Africa Act must be followed'.[1] The limitation announced by parliamentary resolution in 1931 and the statement of the Speaker three years later clearly had no legal effect since they did not alter the power of Parliament, but they are of great significance to the student of federalism, for the entrenched clauses are, as we have observed, important instrumentalities of federalism in the South African community. That their entrenchment was continued by moral sanction after the legal sanction had apparently been withdrawn is further evidence of the toughness of the federal spirit that has prevailed. That the moral sanction was strong enough was indicated in 1936 when the Parliament, in legislating to abolish the Cape native franchise, which was secured by one of the entrenched clauses, employed the extraordinary procedure of Section 152 even though it was presumably no longer necessary in law.[2]

### *The Constitutional Crisis and the New View of the Entrenched Clauses*

In the spring of 1951 the Nationalist Government, in pursuit of its policy of *apartheid*, or racial segregation, introduced the Separate Representation of Voters Bill. Its circumstances and intent were much the same as those of the 1936 legislation except that it was now the coloured persons rather than the natives who were being taken from the regular voting lists. The Opposition again sought to invoke the special procedures of Section 152, but now without success. The Nationalist Government represented the first attainment to power by the extremists of the Afrikaner tradition, and it was much less

[1] Kennedy and Schlosberg, op. cit., p. 103.

[2] Wheare, op. cit., p. 242.

sympathetic to pleas for unity than its predecessors had been. The tradition of compromise represented by Smuts and Hofmeyr had given way to the 'purified' nationalism of Malan and Strydom; the gentlemen's agreement was cast aside. The Speaker, moreover, now had the judicial precedent of *Ndlwana* v. *Hofmeyr* to guide him and he now ruled that the joint session was not required by law and that the House might proceed with the bill. It did. But the employment of the bicameral procedure evoked a strong protest from many quarters and provoked a constitutional crisis that has still not been resolved. The Act thus passed was immediately challenged in the courts, and in *Harris* v. *Donges*[1] the Appellate Division held it to be in violation of the entrenched clauses and therefore void. To do this the Court had to re-examine the arguments of its own 1937 decision and recast its own interpretation of the effect of the Statute of Westminster on the South African constitution.

The new interpretation adopted by the Appellate Division was apparently first suggested in a monograph by Professor D. V. Cowen of the University of Cape Town, published in 1951.[2] Both the monograph and the later court decision are based on the assertion that the security of the entrenched clauses never depended upon the repugnancy clause of the Colonial Laws Validity Act and hence was not affected by the repeal of that provision by the Statute of Westminster. Briefly, the argument turns on the question, what is an Act of Parliament? The Union Parliament before the Statute of Westminster could repeal or alter anything in the South Africa Act by use of the proper procedure to produce an Act of Parliament. For most purposes such an 'Act of Parliament' would be produced by the agreement of the two Houses, acting bicamerally, and the Governor-General; but for the entrenched clauses such an Act could be produced only by the special procedure of Section 152, namely the concurrence of the Governor-General and the two Houses sitting unicamerally and approving by a two-thirds vote. Actions affecting the entrenched clauses were simply not Acts of Parliament unless

[1] *Harris et al.* v. *Minister of Interior*, 1952 (2), A.D. 428.

[2] *Parliamentary Sovereignty and the Entrenched Sections of the South Africa Act*, Cape Town and Johannesburg, 1951.

the special procedure was employed; hence there could be no question of repugnancy since no Act of Parliament was involved. This situation prevailed before the Statute of Westminster and that Act had no effect upon it. The entrenched clauses were specially protected not by the Colonial Laws Validity Act but by the South Africa Act itself, which must be viewed not as a mere statute but as a constitution for the Union. That constitution makes an Act of the Union Parliament supreme, but a measure passed bicamerally and affecting the entrenched clauses is no Act of Parliament and hence is void in that respect. Thus the Appellate Division disposed of and invalidated the Separate Representation of Voters Act. The entrenched clauses were still entrenched after all.[1]

Faced with this rebuff, the Malan Government passed a new Act creating a new High Court of Parliament, composed of all the members of the Parliament. This new High Court was given power to review any decision of the Appellate Division that challenged an Act of Parliament.[2] The High Court promptly met (the Opposition refusing to take part) and reversed the decision in *Harris* v. *Donges*. Shortly thereafter the Appellate Division declared invalid the High Court of Parliament Act on the ground that it sought to accomplish the same thing that had been declared illegal in the first case.[3] At this point the controversy was set aside temporarily to make way for the 1953 elections in which the Government won an impressive victory. After the election the reconstituted Malan Government accepted the Court's decision, though not very gracefully and perhaps only temporarily. Several efforts were made to secure enough support from members of the Opposition to provide a two-thirds majority in a joint session, but these efforts were unsuccessful. And there, at the present writing, the matter rests.

With respect to federal attitudes in the Union two differing

[1] Of primary interest, in addition to the decision itself and the Cowen monograph cited above, is the fifth edition of K. C. Wheare's *The Statute of Westminster and Dominion Status*, Oxford, 1953. Professor Wheare throughout the first four editions of this work had argued that the Statute of Westminster had freed the Union Parliament of the restraints of the entrenched clauses. In the fifth edition (Appendix VIII) he confesses himself to be convinced by Professor Cowen that these clauses remain entrenched.

[2] Act No. 35 of 1952.

[3] *Minister of the Interior* v. *Harris et al.*, 1952 (4), A.D. 769.

conclusions can be drawn from this controversy. It may be argued that the Government displayed less regard for federal sensibilities than had its 1936 counterpart, since it pushed through these strongly controverted measures without resort to the special procedures of Section 152.[1] Or one may point to the storm of protest aroused by the Government's action and use it to measure the continued vitality of federal sentiment. For there can be no doubt that it is a federal question that is involved. Doubtless, too, both arguments are valid. Moreover, the crisis also provoked a separatist movement in Natal after the 1953 election, which for a year or so excited speculation about both the adoption of a federal constitution and the possibility of outright secession.

The principle manifested by all these instances is this: although the constitution is unitary and although the legal forms of constitutional amendment contain no federal instrumentalities (the entrenched clauses apart), yet those forms have been employed in such a fashion that the amendment process displays many features found in federal systems. Though the institutions are doubtless not federal, they are frequently operated as though they were; and this may be more significant than the formal plan of the institutions themselves.

### B. THE UNITED KINGDOM

The experience of the United Kingdom provides an example similar to that of South Africa. The constitution is clearly unitary, the Parliament of the central government being both supreme in relation to other organs of government and sovereign in relation to the law. Even so, there are many elements of federalism in the British society, and the diversities that constitute this federal quality are reflected and articulated through various instrumentalities of a federal type. We have already called attention to the Scottish Committee in the House of Commons as an illustration of such instrumentalities; many others may be observed. Northern Ireland has a separate Parliament; Scotland has a separate Church; England, Scotland, and Ireland each has its own bench of judges, the members of which are not interchangeable; each has its own

[1] Doubtless the Government would have used that procedure had it been able to command a two-thirds majority in a joint session.

Attorney-General, in Scotland called the Lord Advocate. In the executive government certain ministers serve in relation to the whole of the United Kingdom, others are limited to England or to Great Britain. The Foreign Secretary, for example, serves the United Kingdom; the Home Secretary for the most part serves only England and Wales, Scotland and Northern Ireland being served in these functions by their own officials. In 1912 Mr. Herbert (later Viscount) Samuel concluded that of the fifteen members of the Cabinet who customarily dealt with the domestic affairs of the United Kingdom only four exercised their functions over the whole of that Kingdom; all of the others he found to be restricted to portions of it.[1] In Ireland, even before 1922, there was a separate executive and Privy Council under the Lord Lieutenant.

The Parliament itself is in the main unitary, yet in both composition and organization it displays certain features that may be termed federal. By the Act of Union of 1800 Ireland was guaranteed no fewer than one hundred members of the House of Commons, which resulted in an arithmetical over-representation of some 50 per cent. Similarly, in the House of Lords the special representation of the Scottish and Irish peers has constituted a federal instrumentality. In addition to the Scottish Committee in the House of Commons there is a further provision that private bills relating to persons or areas in Scotland are referred not to the ordinary Private Bills Committee but to a special committee of the same type composed of Scottish members and sitting in Scotland. In its activity more than in its composition the British Parliament manifests a consciousness of the federal nature of British society. The Parliament serves as the legislative body for several different areas: England, England and Wales, Great Britain, the United Kingdom, and the Empire; and its legislation may cover any one of these areas. In the article cited above, Lord Samuel mentioned that of the 458 public Acts passed between 1901 and 1910 only 252 extended uniformly to the three kingdoms of England, Scotland, and Ireland. The rest applied only to one or to two.[2]

[1] Herbert Samuel (Viscount Samuel), 'Federal Government', *Nineteenth Century*, vol. 72, 1912, p. 681.

[2] Ibid., p. 683.

The procedure for amending the constitution in Britain differs in no formal way from that of ordinary legislation. The Queen-in-Parliament, being sovereign or legally unrestricted, enacts statutes of constitutional stature with the same techniques as those employed for ordinary bills. But the political process varies according to the nature of the bill. The Parliament undertakes changes in the constitution only after long and careful deliberation, investigations by select committees or royal commissions, wide publicity and public debate, and in many instances only after receiving a popular mandate on the question through the medium of a general election in which the issue plays a prominent part. That this idealizes the process is readily conceded, but the point is clear that Parliament does not undertake constitutional changes of importance without the utmost caution and consideration of the various shades of opinion on the question. Legally the constitution must be classed as flexible, but this flexibility is none the less a function of public opinion and not solely of the legal powers of the Parliament.

It is in this practice of consultation that one finds federal elements in the process of constitutional amendment. Before bills of this nature are enacted, the interests and representatives of the component units are consulted and, if the interests of one of these areas are likely to suffer from the proposed action, then this is at least given full consideration. Particularly when measures are likely to affect the different units in a special way, or when directed at them in particular, the process is likely to take account of local opinion.[1] This process is not institutionalized; indeed, it may consist of little more than careful attention to the words of Irish or Scottish—or even Cornish—members of Parliament. But processes of this kind need not be institutionalized to be effective, particularly in a country like Britain where tradition binds so much of practice and where the spirit of representative government has for so long prevailed.[2]

[1] The subject of political limitations on parliamentary sovereignty is discussed at length by Harold J. Laski, *Studies in the Problem of Sovereignty*, New Haven, 1917, pp. 268 ff.

[2] We should refer also to the process employed in the past for changing the Imperial Constitution, which has been considered by many to possess federal qualities. Every major change in the imperial structure in the past hundred years

It may be objected that this consultative principle, as applied to the representatives of the areas affected by the proposed legislation, is nothing more than that which operates in every democratic country. This may be true. But it is especially worth noting in Britain, for that country has been held by all to be the archetype of unitary government and the one where the processes and forms of federalism are least likely to be found.

Too much should not be made of such an argument; it is not suggested that the United Kingdom is 'federal' by the criteria of any known scheme of classification. The constitution is not federal but unitary. The sovereignty of the Queen-in-Parliament is recognized in theory, in fact, and in law. But one may not ignore the presence of certain federal elements in the British society and in the processes of British government, including that process by which the constitution is amended.

If someone should say of these paragraphs that 'according to this argument, classifications become largely meaningless, since every country might contain elements that are federal', I should reply, 'exactly'.

## C. NORTHERN IRELAND

We may pursue a little farther our examination of the federal qualities of the British community by centring our attention briefly upon the system of government that has been provided in Northern Ireland.

That government was established by the relevant portions of the Government of Ireland Act of 1920[1] which had been intended to provide a dual system of government for the two Irelands, both being retained within the embrace of the British system. That the southern part of the island refused to accept the Act is well known; but the provisions for the north-eastern counties of the province of Ulster went into effect and serve today as the constitutional instrument of that area. Northern Ireland was separated from the rest of the island as a result

has been undertaken only after long discussions with the representatives of the colonial areas affected by the Acts. The constitution of each of the Dominions has been for the most part formulated by representatives of the Dominion, even down to the most minute details.

[1] 10 & 11 Geo. V, chap. 67.

of the very strong antipathy of the Presbyterians of the North to their inclusion with the rest of (Catholic) Ireland under any sort of Home Rule Parliament controlled by the South.

In Northern Ireland today the principle of devolution has been put into practice; though it has been applied in Scotland and, to a much lesser extent, in Wales, it is here that it has been carried the farthest. Northern Ireland possesses its own Cabinet, Parliament, and courts, and may legislate on all subjects not forbidden in the Act of 1920.

The creation of Northern Ireland is the story of the interplay of regional diversities and animosities. Ireland as a whole had long struggled to achieve some form of home rule, but as the movement neared success in the late nineteenth century the Orangemen of Ulster became more apprehensive about the possible evils of subordination to a Dublin Parliament. Yet within Ulster there was by no means a wholly homogeneous population; at least two counties were Catholic and nationalist; two more were split about evenly between the two groups. When the question of partition arose, Ulster decided to shear off three of the southern counties, leaving the Unionist Protestants clearly in control of the remaining area; the other six became Northern Ireland. The federal diversities of recent Irish political history have been highly complex. There is first of all the general relation between all of Ireland and Great Britain; secondly, at what may be called a lower level, there is the relation between Ulster and the rest of Ireland; thirdly, at a still lower level, there is the relation between the Catholic counties of Ulster and the rest of that province. All these complex relationships and the feelings and animosities they generate have served to colour the final picture of government in both the North and the South.

The Act of 1920 by no means created an independent government for the separated counties of Ulster. The British constitution continued to be unitary in respect to Northern Ireland and the British Parliament continued to be sovereign. But the Act did devolve upon the local legislature several functions of government, thus relieving Westminster of many duties and endowing the Northern Irish with the ability to control in large measure those affairs that were of the most direct concern to them. The Northern Parliament is empowered to make laws for the 'peace, order and good government' of Northern Ireland in matters relating exclusively to Northern Ireland. There are certain subjects, however, that are 'excepted' or 'reserved' upon which the Parliament cannot legislate. These include such things as the Crown, defence, foreign affairs, and certain reserved taxes.[1]

The point of interest, however, is not the limitations imposed upon the Northern Ireland Parliament, but the extensive powers of self-government that are conferred upon it. Here within the most unitary of unitary states is a local parliament elected by and responsible to a local area, which enjoys the right to legislate on an impressive list of subjects, and indeed on any subject at all not excluded by the limitations of the Act itself.[2]

A further federal element in this arrangement is the provision in the Act of 1920 (Sec. 19) for the continued representation of the separated counties in the Parliament at Westminster. The reason for this was that the Parliament of the United Kingdom reserved for itself under the Act a rather considerable share in the authority over the area, and it was felt that the area should still be permitted to share in its exercise. These representatives from Northern Ireland were reduced from thirty to thirteen, and at Westminster they occupy a rather peculiar position. Although they participate in general discussion in the Parliament, they do not take part in debates on subjects in respect to the United Kingdom which, in respect to Northern Ireland, have been devolved or transferred to the Parliament at Stormont. This exclusion derives not from law or even from written rules but from convention only; the Speaker at Westminster simply does not recognize the Irish members during such discussions.

In exercising its powers over Northern Ireland, however,

[1] Nicholas Mansergh, *The Government of Northern Ireland*, London, 1936, pp. 108 f. The present section is based very largely upon Professor Mansergh's excellent book. See also J. L. Montrose, 'Legal Aspects of Taxation and Grant Under Northern Ireland System of Devolution', in G. Sawer, ed. *Federalism; An Australian Jubilee Study*, Melbourne, 1952, pp. 1–33.

[2] In this federal-type situation the enumerated powers are retained by the originating authority, i.e., the Parliament at Westminster, while the residuary powers are exercised by the Parliament at Stormont. During the debates in the House of Commons it was objected that this was not in accord with good federal practice. See the discussion in Sir John A. R. Marriott, *The Mechanism of the Modern State*, vol. ii, 1927, pp. 412–13.

the British Parliament invariably pays careful heed to the views of the Irish representatives, though of course such matters occupy little time at Westminster. This, it may be said, is merely common decency; but it is more besides. It is an operative instrumentality of the federal relation between the people of Northern and the United Kingdom as a whole. In several instances, moreover, certain members of the Parliament at Stormont have also served as members of the Parliament at Westminster, which brings even closer together the two legislatures that exercise this joint control over Northern Ireland. Until 1929 the members of the two Parliaments were elected from the same constituencies by an identical set of electors.

Of the two Parliaments, however, it is the local one that seems to attract the greater attention from the people of Northern Ireland. Little interest is ordinarily aroused in the elections for the Parliament at Westminster and candidates in those elections stand less on national issues than on the issues of local Irish politics. Public interest in Northern Ireland is, in the words of Professor Mansergh, 'centred almost exclusively upon the operation of the local parliamentary institutions'.[1]

The powers of the local government over constitutional amendment, however, are strictly limited. The British Parliament remains the sovereign legislative body and the only agency that can change the 'constitution' of Northern Ireland. Section 75 reserved the power to amend the Act:

> Notwithstanding the establishment of the Parliament of Northern Ireland . . . or anything contained in this Act, the supreme authority of the Parliament of the United Kingdom shall remain unaffected and undiminished over all persons, matters and things in Northern Ireland. . . .

Nevertheless some provisions of the Act are subject to local change. As in most of the Dominion constitutions, certain provisions are made 'until the parliament may otherwise direct'. It is true that such provisions are not, strictly speaking, constitutional amendments; but they do enable the local government to make some changes in the content of its own basic law.[2]

[1] Mansergh, op. cit., p. 145.

[2] One such provision (Section 15) permitted local alteration of the electoral law. Thus in 1929 the Irish Parliament abolished the system of proportional representation and substituted one of single-member districts. Ibid., chap. vii.

More important, however, than these provisions (which are, after all, quite limited in scope) is the attitude that has been taken by the British Parliament towards real changes in the Act of 1920. On several occasions since that date it has been necessary to amend the basic Act,[1] and in each case the wishes of the subjects concerned have played the most important role in determining the nature of the amending legislation. This is not all altruism on the part of the Imperial Parliament; Britain has a very real interest in seeing that devolution in Northern Ireland is successful, since, if it fails, the old troublesome question of a united or a disunited Ireland will arise again. The Belfast Government is therefore in a position to apply judicious pressure when it is needed.[2] But the occasions for such pressure have been few. The British have no desire to impose upon Northern Ireland a system of government which the Irish do not want; changes that are desired are likely to be forthcoming. Experience with devolution is too limited to assert that the relation between the two Parliaments in respect to British legislation for the subordinate area is similar to that between Britain and the Dominions; indeed, it is not intended to be similar, since Northern Ireland is still an integral part of the United Kingdom. But so far as the amendment of the local constitution is concerned there is a very great similarity.

It would be improper to consider that the relation between Belfast and Westminster is a federal one on any acceptable definition of the term. Devolution is not federalism. Yet the two have many features in common. Devolution in practice demands from the parties concerned much of the attitude that is requisite for the proper functioning of federal government. So far as social psychology is concerned, there is a great deal of similarity between the two systems. Devolution in Northern Ireland is an instrumentality of federalism of the same sort as that found in the formal distribution of powers in a federal state. Though the constitutional forms are still those of a unitary government, and though the powers of the Parliament at Belfast are subordinated to the sovereignty of the British Parliament, yet the very existence of the Government of Northern Ireland and its successful operation over a period

[1] The Miscellaneous Provisions Acts of 1928 and 1932 are the most important.

[2] Mansergh, op. cit., p. 319.

of three decades stands witness to the vitality of the federal principle in this segment of British society.

### D. NEW ZEALAND 1852–76

In both Britain and South Africa we have observed countries whose constitutions are clearly unitary in the accepted sense of the word, but in which the processes of constitutional amendment display many features that are federal. In New Zealand there has been a wholly different kind of constitutional problem.

#### *Artificial Federalism and Unitary Government*

In New Zealand not only is the constitution unitary but it is difficult today to discern any real federal elements in the society itself. For a quarter of a century, however, from 1852 to 1876, that country possessed a constitution that resembled a federal scheme of government in several particulars, and this fact led some students to class it as federal or in most cases as 'quasi-federal'. The constitution laid down in the Imperial Act of 30 June 1852[1] divided the colony into six provinces (later increased to nine) which were provided with local councils and centrally appointed superintendents, and which were empowered to legislate on everything except certain restricted subjects set out in the Act. The powers of the provinces were quite extensive, and owing to the absence of subordinate local governments and to the difficulties of communication with the central government it was the provinces that occupied the larger place in the sphere of government for a number of years.

The constitution itself, however, was distinctly unitary. The Upper House of the central legislature did not consist of representatives from the component units; the latter had no share in the selection of the executive officers of the central government; the Governor could veto provincial legislation; and all legislation of the central government was superior to that of the provinces. The powers of the central government were not limited in respect of the provinces and any provincial law that

[1] The New Zealand Constitution Act, 1852, 15 & 16 Vict., chap. 72. The important sections may be found reproduced in A. P. Newton, *Federal and Unified Constitutions*, London, 1923, pp. 146 ff.

was in conflict with any law of the Assembly was to that extent invalid.

Whatever was federal in the system was created artificially by the Act itself and by considerations of the geography of the colony.[1] Communication among the several areas was extremely difficult; the two islands were separated by a considerable expanse of water, and each was divided by very high mountains which made extremely arduous any contact by inland routes. The six provinces centred around the six communities that had sprung up in various portions of the islands, and communication was almost wholly by sea. It was this factor that produced the provincial system, for experience had taught the difficulty of governing the whole colony from one central government.

The people themselves were culturally homogeneous; they had come from largely similar backgrounds in the same country; they were divided by no sharp differences of language, race, religion, or national origin. They were, moreover, nearly all in the same economic position, so that differences on this score could not easily have caused severe conflicts, at least in these early years. The only real reason for establishing the quasi-federal provincial system was the geographical structure of the islands; but this reason was so powerful that it made such a scheme of government a virtual necessity.

### *Conflicting Patterns of Thought*

Institutions once established, however, have a tremendous tenacity. They dig their roots deeper and deeper into the cultural soil until they take on values and characteristics that they do not at their planting possess. What begins merely as a device for the performance of certain functions may become worth more in the minds of the people who employ it than the functions themselves. What has begun as a mere means becomes an end in itself. So with the provinces in New Zealand. Imposed for reasons of terrain and lack of communication upon a people who otherwise had no need of them, the provinces tended to breed federalism where no federalism had before existed. They took on a value of their own apart from the needs they served, and when they became no longer neces-

[1] See Leslie Lipson, *The Politics of Equality*, Chicago, 1948, pp. 17–18.

sary it was found that their roots had spread until their eradication was a task of the greatest difficulty.

During this period, however, other developments took place. Communication among the provinces was greatly improved. Roads were built; huge loans were floated for the construction of railways; gold discoveries in the South Island brought a huge influx of immigrants; population increased tremendously. The several communities, formerly widely separated, were growing closer and closer together. The geographical considerations that had dictated the establishment of the provincial system were becoming less and less important. The need for the provincial division of the country was diminishing.

These two developments moved in opposite directions. The provinces after a few years were taking on values of their own and were collecting about themselves adherents who desired their perpetuation, not for the good they accomplished but for the particularities they stood for. At the same time the progress of colonization was making their existence unnecessary by bringing the country into a closer physical union.

### *Constitutional Amendment*

The constitution of 1852 made no formal provision for its amendment, but the powers it conferred upon the General Assembly were sufficient to permit it to alter many provisions without the benefits of a formal amending clause. In 1857 a second Act was passed[1] empowering the Assembly to amend the Constitution Act in all but a few particulars.[2] From this time onward, therefore, the power of constitutional amendment was lodged very largely in the hands of the New Zealand Parliament. But even under the constitution as it then stood the central government was not limited in its relation to the

[1] New Zealand Constitution Act Amendment Act, 1857, 20 & 21 Vict., chap. 53.

[2] Section 8 of the Statute of Westminster continued these exemptions, even after its adoption by New Zealand in 1947. After the adoption, however, the Imperial Parliament passed (at the request of the Dominion) the New Zealand Constitution (Amendment) Act, 1947, 11 Geo. VI, chap. 4, which repealed the Act of 1857 cited above, and expressly authorized the New Zealand Parliament to amend or repeal anything in the Act of 1852. See K. C. Wheare, *Statute of Westminster and Dominion Status*, 5th edn., 1953, pp. 328–33.

provinces; any of its enactments invalidated a conflicting law of a province, and by simply occupying a field with its own legislation the Assembly could effectively exclude the provinces from it. It possessed, moreover, under the Act of 1852 the authority to redistribute the functions of government between itself and the provinces and had as well the specific power to 'constitute new provinces', to which was added by Imperial Act in 1868[1] the power of 'abolishing any province heretofore or hereafter to be established in New Zealand'. The provinces were completely at the mercy of the central government.

As colonization and development advanced during the period 1852–76 provincial feeling was gradually overcome. The provinces were unable to provide for their own financial needs and came to depend more and more on the Assembly for assistance; it was this poverty that finally caused their abolition.[2] Provincial feeling through the latter part of the period gradually diminished, though in 1876 it was still strong enough to make the fight for abolition a long and bitter struggle. But though it was decreasing in importance, it was throughout the period a factor to be counted on, and the central government found it necessary to consult provincial opinion on all major policy questions. Indeed, it could not avoid doing so, for as a general practice the superintendents and other officers of the provinces were members of the Lower House of the central legislature. There they urged the case for the provinces, both individually and, as the question of abolition was raised, collectively. To the extent that provincial sentiment continued to exist, the policies of the country could be determined only after taking this sentiment into consideration. Decisions were frequently hard fought and bitterly resented. Provincial leaders resisted all efforts to narrow the scope of their functions or derogate from the powers of the units they represented.

### *Federalism in Practice*

New Zealand's constitution was never federal, but during this period there were many things that seemed federal in the

[1] 31 & 32 Vict., chap. 92.

[2] W. P. Morrell, *The Provincial System in New Zealand, 1852–1876*, London, 1932, p. 250.

way it worked. In practice the General Assembly, especially in the fifties and early sixties, left many functions to the provincial governments. 'So long as the people of New Zealand were . . . federally minded, the constitution could be worked as a federal constitution',[1] but the federalism of New Zealand was always a federalism of practice and never a federalism of legal forms. Its sanctions were those of opinion and convenience, never those of law.

During this period the country displays a picture of federalism quite different from any of those we have heretofore examined. Whatever was federal in its system was imposed artificially by reason of what may be called external considerations upon a people that was essentially unified. The principal instrumentality of this 'federal' system, apart from the existence of the provinces themselves, was the informal representation of the provinces in the Lower House of the legislature through the presence there of the chief provincial officers. Constitutional amendments, especially those having to do with the distribution of powers, could be made only after consulting the interest of the component units, but this consultation was never institutionalized as it is in other federations. Moreover, the federal spirit, as exemplified in the desire for preservation of the provinces, began to die almost as soon as it was born; when the time came for that constitutional amendment of the most profound significance for the federal system —that abolishing the component units themselves—there was not sufficient support for the provinces to prevent their complete extinction.

## E. GERMANY

The term federal has been applied, rightly or wrongly, to a number of states in the course of the past two centuries. Particular attention has been devoted in this study to those countries about which there has been general agreement concerning their federal quality. But it may be of value to note also the methods employed for effecting amendments in certain other states about whose federal nature there has been less than unanimous agreement. One of these is Germany,

[1] Morrell, op. cit., p. 56.

which has produced a whole series of 'federal' constitutions. To these we briefly turn.

### *Imperial Germany*

The Imperial German constitution proclaimed itself to be federal and was conceded to be so by many nineteenth-century students of federalism and constitutional law. But its classification as federal had always to be qualified in terms of the dominant role played by Prussia. Imperial Germany was in fact the creation and creature of Prussian policy; its policy was determined by Prussian interests; its offices were filled by Prussian officials. One may well doubt whether it was truly federal. It did, of course, have several federal features, but these features were illusory and were designed to conceal the power structure that lay behind the institutional facade. The states were allotted certain functions under the constitution and were separately represented in the Bundesrat, which was the principal legislative organ of the central government; but these features of federalism were far outweighed by the preponderance of Prussia in all imperial matters.

The Bundesrat was a unique institution of great importance and of great interest to students of politics and government. Its functions were partly legislative, partly administrative, and partly judicial. It quite overshadowed the popularly elected Lower House in importance. Moreover, it constituted a real instrumentality of federalism in that the component units were represented in it, not equally it is true, but in such a way that the state and not the population group was the basis of representation. The state delegations in the Bundesrat were appointed and paid by the state governments; and, what is much more significant, they were required to cast their votes in state blocks at the instructions of the state governments. Thus the states were truly and adequately represented in the organs of the central government and, had the states been anywhere near equal in size and influence, there would have been much less doubt of the federal quality of the imperial constitution. But the tremendous variations in the size and strength of the states made imperial federalism a mockery.

This fact is perhaps most clearly seen in the provisions for amending the constitution. According to Article 78 amendments could be initiated by either of the two legislative Houses, but the role of the Reichstag (the Lower House) was quite negligible. Policy decisions on these as on other matters were made in the Bundesrat. Constitutional amendments were accomplished by legislative processes subject to two conditions that had to be met. The first of these was that no amendment took effect if it was opposed by fourteen votes in the Bundesrat.[1] Prussia possessed in that body a total of seventeen votes, three more than enough to block any amendment; hence she had an absolute veto over any proposed amendment. It may be noted also that other combinations of states could by agreement accomplish the same thing, but no other state had as many as fourteen votes[2] and only one combination of even three states had that many. The second condition on constitutional amendments was that no state could be deprived of any of the rights guaranteed to it by the constitution without its own consent being given thereto.[3] This was certainly an instrumentality of federalism, but it afforded no very significant protection to the states, since the constitution guaranteed very few things of importance to them. Moreover, the questions whether a law was merely an ordinary law or an amendment to the constitution and whether it was contrary to the privileges of a particular state were decided by an ordinary majority in the Bundesrat.[4]

It will be seen that the states as such had no role in the process of constitutional amendment, and this led many German jurists to conclude that the Reich possessed *Kompetenz-Kompetenz*, or the ability to change the constitution so as to control the extent of its own competences.[5] This was certainly true, for the Bundesrat was an organ of the central government. But the jurists largely ignored the fact that the state delegations in the Bundesrat constituted federal instrumentalities of a most decided kind. State selected, state paid, state instructed, they provided as adequate participation for

[1] Article 78, clause 1.

[2] Bavaria had the next largest delegation with six votes.

[3] Article 78, clause 2.

[4] See Fritz-Konrad Krüger, *The Government and Politics of the German Empire*, Yonkers, New York, 1915, p. 25.

[5] The endless debates on the subject are ably summarized by Rupert Emerson, *State and Sovereignty in Modern Germany*, New Haven, 1928.

the states as could have been achieved by a requirement that the states themselves must concur in the amendments to the constitution (unless, of course, the inequality of the states' voting strength were to have been abolished).

But the role of the Bundesrat in the ordinary course of affairs can easily be exaggerated. Policy was determined not so much by the votes in that body as by the government of Prussia, which was in turn largely subject to the will of the King-Emperor. It is true that Prussia did not possess a majority in the Bundesrat, but she needed no such majority. Her size and prestige and above all her military strength were such that she could dictate her decisions to the rest of the empire. Indeed, it was these very factors that had created the empire in the first place; there had been no pronounced desire on the part of the other states to be united under such a system.[1] The government of Germany under the imperial constitution was nothing less than a dictatorship of the Prussian monarch exercised through the institutional structure of a semi-federal constitution. The constitution 'was supposed to be federal but its federalism was fraudulent, window dressing to make the dictatorship of Prussia more respectable . . . the fate of Germany was determined by the King-Emperor's absolute will, influenced in Bismarck's time by good advice, influenced after his time by bad advice or by none at all'.[2]

### *Weimar Germany*

The same question—whether or not the constitution was federal—was raised with regard to the system of government established at Weimar in 1919.[3] Despite efforts to install in Germany a wholly unitary system of government, many federal elements were retained; the Weimar assembly refused to abolish the old *Länder*. The principal stronghold of federalism in Germany has long been in the larger provinces of the south where differences of religious faith, historic traditions, local pride, and the natural desire of the local bureaucracies to maintain themselves in the face of the expansion of Prussia

[1] A. J. P. Taylor, *The Course of German History*, New York, 1946, pp. 115 ff.

[2] Ibid., pp. 117–19.

[3] See Herbert Kraus, *The Crisis of German Democracy*, Princeton, 1932, chap. vii, 'The Reich and its member states'.

and the Reich have strengthened the desire for the continued autonomy of the states.[1]

As a result of these forces the states were continued in much the same form as under the imperial constitution, although some consolidations and border changes were made. As before, the states possessed certain specified powers, but the enumerated powers of the central government were so extensive that little was left for the states.[2] Moreover, in a large area of concurrent powers the principle of Reich supremacy prevailed; any national statute in this sphere invalidated a conflicting state statute.[3]

The principal federal instrumentality in the new constitution was the representation of the states in the Upper House of the legislature, now called the Reichsrat. Though equality of representation was not attempted because of the extreme differences in the size of the states, each state had at least one vote and Prussia was restricted to two-fifths of the membership. Other states were represented roughly in accordance with their populations. Members still voted in state blocks as in the old Bundesrat and, had the influence of the Reichsrat been greater, the states might have been able to exercise through it a strong control over the government of the Reich. As it was, however, the Reichsrat soon assumed a subordinate position and was easily overshadowed by the popularly elected Reichstag. Moreover, the spirit of federalism was not strong enough in Germany to enable the federal structure of the Upper House to be employed to the best advantage. On very few occasions did it serve to articulate the desires of the states at the national level. Its members were appointed and instructed by the state governments; but they were mostly permanent and, since they worked closely with the Reich Government, 'they were better suited to advise their governments at home than *vice versa*'.[4] The feeling for federalism that had made necessary the perpetuation of the *Länder* was not strong enough to make them effective federal units.

[1] Arnold J. Zurcher, *The Experiment with Democracy in Central Europe*, New York, 1933, p. 50.

[2] Articles 6–13.

[3] Article 13.

[4] Karl Loewenstein, in Shotwell, ed. *Governments of Continental Europe*, rev. edn., New York, 1952, p. 407.

The unitary features of the Weimar constitution were much more striking than the federal features. The Reichsrat failed to serve any marked federal purpose and legislative power was concentrated in the Reichstag, which was popularly elected on a nation-wide population franchise not based on the states. The states, moreover, according to the principle of 'mobility of frontiers',[1] could be altered, merged, or wholly abolished by Reich legislation without their consent; and this was done on more than one occasion. The *Länder* were almost wholly subordinated to the Reich; their powers were greatly limited and those of the Reich much extended. Moreover, the division of powers had a characteristic substantially different from that of federations in the English-speaking world. Instead of allotting powers, both in their legislative and administrative aspects, to one government or the other, the Weimar system assigned the function of legislation largely to the Reich and that of administration largely to the states. The Reich administered through its own agencies only a small portion of its own laws; the rest were carried out by the administrative agencies of the states. This 'vertical' division of powers contrasts sharply with the ordinary 'horizontal' division that appears in most federal systems.[2] It becomes even more significant when viewed in the light of Articles 14, 15, and 48 of the constitution, which empowered the Reich to supervise the administration of federal laws by the states and if necessary to take over the state governments in order to ensure their execution. Such powers in the central government hardly comport with the co-ordinate and mutually independent status of central and component governments ordinarily expected in states which we call federal. Though the component units were still called by the old name *Länder*, and though in some of them, especially in the South, the old particularisms persisted, the government of Weimar Germany functioned very much the same as that of a unitary state.

This is clearly shown in the provisions for constitutional amendment. Proposals to amend the constitution required the consent of two-thirds of those voting in the Reichstag, two-thirds of the membership being present, as well as two-thirds of those present and voting in the Reichsrat.[3] If the Reichstag

[1] Article 18. [2] Zurcher, op. cit., p. 41. [3] Article 76.

insisted upon an amendment to which the Reichsrat refused its assent, the amendment became law unless the latter within two weeks requested a popular referendum. In such a referendum the amendment could be defeated only if a majority of the electorate voted and if a majority of those voting disapproved.[1] Amendments could also be proposed by a popular initiative of one-tenth of the electorate, in which case they were to be submitted to a referendum in which the approval of an absolute majority of the electorate was necessary for their adoption.

There is very little that is federal in these procedures. In the referenda only the total vote was considered; whether the majorities were distributed among the states or concentrated in a few states made no difference; the state governments as such had no part in the process. It is true that the states were represented in the Reichsrat, which did play a part in the process; but the record of the Reichsrat was one of co-operation with the Reichstag, and in any case the opposition of the Reichsrat could be overridden.

In practice, from 1919 to 1929 Germany added seven major amendments and sixteen minor ones to her constitution.[2] But these figures include only the amendments that directly and formally changed specific sections of the constitution. In addition to this there grew up at once the practice of amending the constitution 'informally' without making specific changes in the constitutional instrument. When the Reichstag desired legislation that was in apparent conflict with the provisions of the constitution, the desired law was considered to be effective if it was passed by two-thirds majorities in each House. This practice rendered the actual meaning of the constitution at any one time highly obscure, for these changes did not alter its exterior form in any way. This procedure was employed on something like sixty occasions[3] and became almost a routine method of legislation. It became very nearly impossible to tell what was and what was not a part of the constitution.

After 1930 it became apparent that constitutional reform on a large scale would be necessary to save the republic; but by

[1] Article 75.

[2] Zurcher, op. cit., p. 35. It may be added that no amendments were ever made through the use of the popular initiative.

[3] Loewenstein, op. cit., p. 433.

this time the anti-republican parties were in a position to block any attempt at such reform since they could prevent the necessary two-thirds majorities in the two Houses. This was one of the reasons for the extensive use of the extraordinary powers of Article 48 after that time. By 1930 democratic government in Germany was fast disappearing; it had existed only as long as the Allied Powers were willing to insist on its continuation, and it began to collapse when this insistence was abandoned. Weimar had never been a federal constitution, but whatever federal elements there were in it were immediately destroyed when the National Socialists came to power.

### *The Bonn Constitution*

The constitution adopted by the constituent assembly at Bonn in 1949 also proclaims a federal republic. The federal elements in this constitution are perhaps more clearly marked than under the Weimar system, but the two constitutions are very similar and it is difficult to conclude that the new one is truly federal according to the customary criteria of federalism. The constitution embraces the eleven states of the three western zones of military occupation, though it takes account of the possibility of incorporating the rest of Germany into the system.

The federal legislature is again bicameral; the Lower House, now called the Bundestag, is elected directly according to population; the Upper House (Bundesrat) again displays a federal principle in that its membership is based on state representation. In the Bundesrat the states are assigned three, four, or five votes roughly according to their population. Members of the Upper House are also members of the governments of the *Länder*; each *Land* has as many members as it has votes and these votes must again be cast in solid state blocks. The Bundesrat has only a delaying function in ordinary legislation, but in a few specified matters, one of which is constitutional amendment, its consent is necessary.

The federal government is assigned a short list of exclusive powers upon which the states may legislate only if directly so empowered by the federal government. Both states and national government may legislate upon a longer list of concurrent powers, but in this sphere the states may act only when the federal government has not acted.[1] A further provision declares that 'Federal law shall supersede *Land* law'.[2] Residuary powers are reserved to the states,[3] but these are likely to be of slight importance in view of the scope of the powers assigned to the federation. The dominant role of the federation is further pointed up by the provisions for the compulsion of states in the administration of federal law, which are reminiscent of the 'federal execution' of Article 48 of the Weimar constitution. If states fail in their duty to administer federal law or in their obligations to the federation, the federal government may send commissioners into the states to secure the execution of the law and these representatives may use whatever force is necessary to carry out their tasks.[4]

Constitutional amendments may be passed by a two-thirds vote in each of the two Houses of the national legislature. The constitution states that 'such law shall require approval of two-thirds of the members of the Bundestag and two-thirds of the votes of the Bundesrat'.[5] This would seem to require two-thirds of all the members of the Lower House but only two-thirds of those voting in the Upper. No ratification by the states is required, but in an Upper House of this kind the states are represented as states, since the members are members of the state governments and must vote in state blocks. Whether this will become a real instrumentality of federalism in the amending process, however, will depend largely on the nature of the party system. No provision for popular initiative or referendum is made; the decision of the two Houses is final.

Three limitations are imposed, however, upon the power to amend.[6] No amendment may affect (*a*) 'the organization of the federation into *Länder*', (*b*) 'the basic cooperation of the *Länder* in legislation', or (*c*) the 'basic principles laid down in Articles one and twenty'. Of the specially protected articles, the first provides for the inviolability of human rights and the dignity of man; the twentieth states that the constitution rests upon the principles of constitutionalism and popular sovereignty

[1] This distribution of powers is found in Articles 71–74.
[2] Article 31.
[3] Articles 30, 70.
[4] Articles 37, 84, 85.
[5] Article 79, Section 2.
[6] Article 79, Section 3.

and that it constitutes a 'democratic and social federal state'. This attempt to entrench certain clauses is open to the same objection that has been raised before, namely, that there is nothing to prevent the legislature from abolishing the protection in one Act and immediately invading the protected clauses in the next. In this instance, however, the question is largely academic, for the entrenched clauses are of a general kind that would be most difficult to interpret or enforce with any precision. Although these are clearly federal instrumentalities, one may cast doubt upon their effectiveness.

## F. LATIN AMERICA

In the first half of the nineteenth century Central and South America were swept by a revolutionary movement that resulted in the establishment of some twenty independent republics whose constitutions were modelled in large part upon that of the United States. Four of these constitutions—those of Argentina, Brazil, Venezuela, and Mexico—were federal in nature, but the federalism that was established in these countries was in many respects artificial. The constitution of the United States was employed as a model and it was a federal constitution. Thus it happened that in several instances the federal parts of that constitution were included in the new instruments of Latin America even when there was no real need for such an arrangement. In many cases the states that were incorporated into the new federal polities were created from nothing in order to balance out a federal system. It is true that many of the states had been administrative units under the old unitary systems and that a few, such as Buenos Aires in Argentina and São Paulo in Brazil, had something of an historic tradition behind them; but for the most part the states of the new federations were artificial creations, designed to satisfy the requirement that a federation must be composed of states.

But this was not the only explanation. There was a widespread feeling among the Latin American revolutionaries that centralism implied autocracy, and this feeling produced a desire for some kind of federal decentralization. Moreover, some of the new countries, particularly Brazil and Argentina, were so large that their administration as unitary states would have been difficult. But the important point is that the component units of the new states, or most of them, had no background as separate associations, and their establishment was the result of a prior decision to create a federal constitution.

The second point to be made is that although these constitutions were constructed adequately and properly according to the federal plan, they have remained largely a statement of ideals rather than practical guides to the organization and processes of government.[1] The federal constitutions were imposed upon societies that had been accustomed to the autocratic administration of a unitary monarchical state; there was no background of popular government and the democratic institutions of the new constitutions were put into effect before the populations they were designed to serve had been prepared for them. The result is well known. Government in Latin America has been dictatorial, not democratic; and dictatorial government seldom suits the needs of a federal system.

Of the four federal constitutions now in force, Mexico's is the oldest, dating from 1917; the other three are all post-Second World War: Brazil's was adopted in 1946, Venezuela's in 1947, and Argentina's in 1949. There is no need here to describe the four constitutions in detail, but we may examine briefly their provisions for constitutional amendments.[2]

The amending clauses of the constitutions of Argentina and Brazil can hardly be said to display any federal element at all, except the provision that the Upper House of the national legislature must consent to amendments.[3] In all four constitutions the Upper House is composed according to the

[1] See J. Lloyd Mecham, 'Mexican Federalism, Fact or Fiction?', in *Annals of the American Academy*, vol. 208, Mar. 1940, p. 23.

[2] The documents and brief analyses may be found in the appropriate volumes of Amos J. Peaslee, *Constitutions of Nations*, Concord, N.H., 1950. Constitutions change in Latin America with bewildering rapidity. Until 1949 Argentina's was the oldest, dating from 1853. Brazil has had new constitutions in 1891, 1934, 1937, and 1946. Mexico had a series of early constitutions culminating in that of 1857, which was replaced by the present one of 1917. Venezuela has had more than twenty constitutions since 1830; the present one replaced that of 1936. None of the three post-war constitutions mentioned makes any significant change in the amending procedure or in the arrangements for the federal system.

[3] Professor Wheare is led to disqualify the Brazilian constitution as federal on this ground, though not that of Argentina. See *Federal Government*, 3rd edn., 1953, p. 23.

principle of state representation, following ordinary federal practice. In Argentina amendments may be initiated by two-thirds of both Houses of Congress but must be adopted by a 'convention called for the purpose'.[1] The constitution does not specify how the convention is to be organized, but practice has empowered the Congress to provide for these details.[2] It has not been based on state representation, but has been elected on the same popular basis as that of the Lower House of the legislature. Amendments of a formal nature have not been frequent.

In Brazil amendments may be proposed by either one-fourth of the membership of either House of the national legislature or by petitions from one-half of the state legislatures, if assembled within a period of two years. In either case ratification is accomplished by a two-thirds vote in both Houses of the national legislature in two consecutive sessions.[3] The states here may play a part in the initiation of amendments but not in the ratification process.

In the Mexican constitution the provision for amendment[4] most nearly resembles that of the United States, though the requirements were deliberately made easier to satisfy. Initiation of amendments is by a two-thirds vote in both Houses of the national Congress and ratification is by a majority of the state legislatures. In this process the federal element is clearly seen; the states as such must approve the amendment before it can take effect.

The Venezuelan constitution, if the provisions of the amending clause be a proper criterion, is probably the most rigid since the Polish *plenum veto*. A triple procedure is provided. Amendments may be initiated in either of two ways: by one-fourth of the total membership of either House of the Congress, or by two-thirds of the state legislatures, voting by absolute majorities. In either case the proposal is submitted to the two Houses of Congress, which must approve it by ordinary majorities; then finally it is submitted to the state legislatures, two-thirds of which must approve it by absolute majorities.[5]

[1] Article 21.

[2] Santos P. Amadeo, *Argentine Constitutional Law*, New York, 1944, p. 45.

[3] Article 217.

[4] Article 135.

[5] Article 248.

But in the practical operation of government in Latin America the provisions of constitutions have been very largely subordinated to the exigencies of presidential dictatorships. With large illiterate Indian populations, a nearly complete absence of democratic traditions, and little experience with the complexities of federal government, the Latin American federations have been unable to prevent the centralization of government into the hands of those who, by the use of military force, have been able to control the agencies of the national administration.[1] Changes in the political regime take place not so much by the process of election as by the process of revolution. The officers of the state governments are by and large the lieutenants of the president in power at the time, and the officers of the federal government seldom encounter difficulty in securing the consent of the states to either general policies or amendments to the constitution.

Constitutional amendments usually do take place in accordance with the provisions of the constitutions, but so long as the processes of constitutional government are employed merely as channels for the exercise of dictatorial authority, the observance of constitutional requirements is of little significance. What is significant is the nature and function of the dictatorship itself. Constitutions in Latin America have been notoriously shortlived; and this is as true in the federal as in the unitary states. It is the military authority of the dictator-president that determines whether a constitution will be replaced or not, or whether amendments will be incorporated into it; it is this same authority that compels the observance or non-observance of all constitutional forms.

In Latin America there are four ostensible federal systems. But federalism in each of them has been confined to the constitution; it has had little effect on the processes of government.[2] So long as the government is subordinated to the will of a dictator, centralization in fact if not in form must result. In

[1] See J. Lloyd Mecham, 'The Origins of Federalism in Mexico', in Conyers Read, ed. *The Constitution Re-considered*, New York, 1938; also P. A. Martin, 'Federalism in Brazil', in the same volume; K. C. Wheare, op. cit., pp. 22 ff.

[2] In some countries—Uruguay and Mexico, for example—recent developments are somewhat more encouraging to the advocates of constitutional government. But the general pattern of Latin American government over a period of years has been the same.

two of these federations the states are given a role in the amending process; in two they are not. But in all four constitutional amendments have been adopted at the will of and in the manner prescribed by the current military authority. Constitutional forms are used, but in such a way that extra-constitutional purposes are achieved.

In Britain and South Africa we observed that constitutions which are normally considered unitary may be amended by processes that are frequently federal in character. In Latin America just the opposite may be seen. Here are constitutions that are federal in structure but which are amended by processes that are essentially unitary. The formal provisions for amendment carry little significance in view of the fact that they do not affect the result. If we are justified in calling South Africa federal in some respects because its unitary institutions function on occasion as though they were federal, we are to the same extent justified in calling the Latin American countries unitary because their federal institutions function in many respects as though they were unitary. It is not the form of the institution or the pattern of the prescribed procedures that determines the nature of a political society, but rather the way in which those institutions and procedures are employed. And even more significant for the study of politics and government is the task of determining *why* they function as they do.

# 7

# FEDERALISM AND CONSTITUTIONAL CHANGE

THAT constitutions change in many ways, both formally and informally, is as true of federations as of unitary systems, as true of democracies as autocracies; formal amendment is only one of these ways. In each of the federal systems we have examined the constitution is altered in several different fashions. Customs and conventions are slowly transformed to produce new constitutional practices; the interpretative agencies create new meanings of old clauses; new statutes compel new applications of old principles. All these things produce changes in the constitutional structure. Our present concern with formal amendment should not be permitted to obscure the other, and frequently more significant, means by which changes are brought about. Frequently also considerations that are wholly extraconstitutional may produce such far-reaching changes in the processes of government that the constitution loses much of its importance and effectiveness as a guide to the real pattern of politics. Mussolini's Italy, for example, maintained the fiction of the *Statuto* of 1848 long after it had become apparent that it had lost its force.

But among the various means of constitutional change, the formal amendment of the constitution stands alone. For this is a higher authority than any of the rest. If any question of conflict should arise, formal amendment is of greater significance than the others because it can override any of the others. Whatever changes may be brought about through the other processes, formal amendment can reverse them all; it constitutes the ultimate authority in the state and the one within whose ambit all others must operate.

We speak here not of federal states alone but of all states; that which controls the power to amend the constitution controls the framework that contains and determines all political processes.

## *Amendment in Federal and Unitary States*

The procedure of formal amendment constitutes the classical distinction between the 'flexible' and the 'rigid' constitution. A rigid constitution, according to the traditional definition, is one in which amendments can be made only by a procedure different from that employed for ordinary legislation. Most writers, as we have seen, have argued that federalism requires not only a written but also a rigid constitution. It must be written in order that the powers and functions assigned to the central government and to the states may be set out clearly and thus provide a common frame of reference within which all questions concerning their exercise may be decided. It must be rigid so that the states may be secured, to some extent at least, in the functions assigned to them by the distribution. Logically there would seem to be no reason why a federation could not employ a flexible constitution, but historically all federal constitutions have been rigid.

But the rigid constitution is not confined to the federal state; unitary governments also make use of its devices; indeed it may be said that most written constitutions are in some way rigid; that is, the procedure by which they may be amended differs in some way, however slight, from that of ordinary legislation. This differentiation of procedures that constitutes the difference between rigid and flexible constitutions may take one or more of several different forms. Among unitary states three different methods may be observed:

1. The constitution may require that the legislature when making formal changes must function with a fixed quorum or approve such amendments by fixed majorities. Without a requirement either of a special quorum or a special majority the constitution would be not rigid but flexible, since there would then be no difference between constitutional amendment and ordinary legislation. The requirements on these two matters vary considerably. An ordinary quorum is a majority of the members of a body; the special quorum required in this case is usually two-thirds; Belgium and Germany have both used this scheme. The requirement that the legislature must approve an amendment by special majorities also takes several forms. Many constitutions (e.g. the French Third

Republic, post-war Italy) require an absolute majority of all members; others require two-thirds, as in Austria, Norway, and the U.S.S.R.; in Czechoslovakia a majority of three-fifths was required. The quorum and required majority may differ between the two Houses or between two sessions of the same House; thus in Italy a simple majority is required the first time an amendment is passed but an absolute majority for the required second vote; the French Fourth Republic requires a referendum unless the Lower House passes the amendment by a two-thirds vote or both Houses pass it by a three-fifths vote.

2. A second provision frequently found in unitary constitutions is the requirement that the Parliament shall be dissolved and a new one elected whenever an amendment is proposed. This is found, for example, in Belgium and in the pre-war Yugoslav constitution.

3. A third technique is to require a joint session of the two Houses of the legislature at which either ordinary or special majorities may be required. The French Third Republic required an absolute majority of a joint session; for certain purposes the South African constitution requires a two-thirds majority of such a session. Finally, it should be noted that any of these methods may be used in combination and that modern constitutions have produced from such combinations an endless variety of amending clauses.

We have spoken of the foregoing techniques as features of unitary constitutions. But any of them may be employed by federal constitutions as well. The United States requires a two-thirds majority of both Houses of Congress; Australia requires absolute majorities. A total revision in Switzerland requires the dissolution and re-election of both Houses when a referendum indicates a desire for such a revision. But the more characteristic feature of amendment in federal constitutions is the requirement that the component units must give consent to the alteration. This consent is elicited in several different ways and more than one of these may be included in the same constitution. The United States constitution permits the Congress to choose between ratification by state legislatures and conventions held in the states; Mexico employs only the state legislatures. Australia and Switzerland utilize a popular referendum in which majorities must be returned within a given number of the component units. The solicitation of consent in Canada takes place through an informal process of consultation.

Moreover, the number of states of a federal country that must consent varies greatly. In Australia and Switzerland a mere majority is required, although in Australia this majority results in a requirement equivalent to two-thirds, since there are but six states. In Brazil a majority of the state legislatures must approve an amendment. In Venezuela two-thirds of the states must consent; in the United States three-fourths. In the German Empire fourteen votes in the Bundesrat could forestall an amendment.[1] In Canada, though the situation is far from clear, it would seem that certain kinds of amendments would require the consent of all the provinces.

The constitutional referendum may be classed as a supplementary device which is essential in neither federal nor unitary constitutions but is usable in both. Among the unitary states that have employed it are the French Fourth Republic, Eire, Denmark, and Italy; Australia and Switzerland employ it as a federal mechanism. The efforts to secure its adoption in the United States for the ratification of amendments to the national constitution have been discussed in Chapter 5. All of the American states, save Delaware, employ it for the amendment of the state constitutions. The referendum provides a convenient way of differentiating the amendment procedure from that of ordinary legislation as well as affording a popular sanction for changes in the fundamental law. In federations it serves also as a device for securing the consent of the people of the states to such changes.

### *The Necessity of a Particular Procedure of Amendment in a Federal State*

Many writers on federalism have suggested that one of its features, even one of its defining characteristics, is the requirement that constitutional changes be made only with the consent of the component units. Furthermore, federations are frequently distinguished from confederations on the

[1] The total number in the Bundesrat varied from fifty-eight to sixty-two at different times. The required majority was thus from 70 to 75 per cent.

ground that in the latter the consent of all the component units is necessary, whereas in the former only a certain portion need consent although all must be consulted. What light has been shed upon this matter in the course of the present investigation? Can it properly be said that a federal system requires a special, even a particular procedure of constitutional amendment? Conversely, does a particular amendment procedure identify a particular state as federal?

We may observe first of all that no two of the federations we have examined have procedures in all respects identical. Clearly no precise form is necessary. But our interest lies not in the precise form but in the principle of state consultation. Here there is great similarity; but even so the procedures differ. Australia employs a popular referendum in which a majority of the total population must approve the proposed amendment and in addition majorities in four of the six states must approve. In Switzerland a majority of the whole must approve as well as majorities in eleven and a half of the twenty-two cantons. These two procedures of ratification are essentially identical. In the United States, however, not a mere majority but three-fourths of the states are required and their approval must be given either by the state legislatures or by conventions in the states, as one or the other method may be chosen by the Congress. Clearly there is a significant difference in application here, but it can hardly be said that the principle of state consultation has been violated; the requirement has merely been increased from a majority to three-fourths and the manner in which the approval is expressed has been changed. Another important difference exists, however. In Switzerland and Australia the mechanics of the popular referendum produce an expression of public opinion in every state or canton at precisely the same time; in the United States the consent of the states is given whenever the state agency (almost invariably the legislature) decides to give it. Ratification is thus spread out over a longer period and it is frequently impossible to say that the states approved a proposed amendment at a given time; ratifications accumulate until the necessary number is reached. Even so, in America as in the other two countries, the principle of state consultation is maintained; amendments take place only by the consent of a given number of the component units; and this process of eliciting their consent is institutionalized in the constitution.

In Canada, however, a very different situation exists. Not only is the amendment procedure not institutionalized in the constitution, it is not formalized or standardized at all. Canada differs from the others not so much in the fact that her constitution for so long contained no provision for amendment but in the fact that the political process by which decisions on proposed amendments are made has never acquired a pattern that stands as a guide for action. Even in the unwritten constitution of Canada there is no standard amendment procedure. It is true that certain precedents have been established, but the precedents conflict. If one poses the simple question, 'is it necessary to consult the provinces before amending the constitution?' there is no clear answer. On some occasions it has been done but on others it has not. On at least one occasion the constitution was amended over the strong objection of the province of Quebec.

Is this an indication that Canada is not federal? Such a conclusion is difficult to reach, in view of the numerous other features of federal government that appear in the Canadian constitution. The issue at this point becomes unrealistic. One can define federal government in a number of different ways, and definitions can be devised to fit almost any circumstances. If we define federal government merely in terms of a distribution of powers we could include a number of countries that are not ordinarily thought to have federal governments; Italy would be such a country under its 1948 constitution; South Africa, Germany, Canada, and even Britain might be included. If we define it in terms of representation in the Upper House, the list would be different; if in terms of a rigid amending procedure employing some formal device for consultation with the component units, then a different and much smaller list of countries would be included and Canada would not be federal. Canada and all other countries are federal or not according to the way federalism is defined. Such exercises are interesting but of little worth. Canada, by most of the criteria that have been applied to the subject by its students, is a federal state. And certainly if we go beyond the constitutional form to observe the make-up of the society and the operation of the institutions, there can be no doubt whatever.

Moreover, in some of the countries that have been labelled federal in accordance with various definitions of federalism, the procedure of amendment has been wholly different. In New Zealand, in Soviet Russia, in Austria, in Germany under Weimar and Bonn, and in certain of the Latin American countries, constitutions otherwise ostensibly federal have made no provision at all for consulting the component units in the process of amending the constitution. In others, such as Mexico and Venezuela, the constitution takes cognizance of the need for consulting the states but extraconstitutional considerations have rendered these provisions largely meaningless.

Furthermore, in certain unitary states such as South Africa and Great Britain, the procedure by which the constitution is altered takes the federal diversities of those societies into account even though this is not legally necessary. Certain unitary states, in other words, have operated their constitutions on occasion as though they were federal even though formally they were not.

Clearly then the formal procedure of amendment is not an accurate index of the federal character of the constitution, and even less is it a reliable indication of the nature of the society that subtends the institutions of government.

Let us refer again to the analogy of the spectrum, which was employed in the first chapter. According to the degree of territorial diversity within the society, the several nations fall into places in a spectrum which extends from the highly unified society on the one hand to the highly diversified on the other. Societies well over towards the latter end of this spectrum are so heterogeneous in their composition as to require a number of instrumentalities for the articulation and protection of the diversities within them. One of these instrumentalities will almost inevitably be found in the nature of the amending process, since it is the control of this element that ultimately determines the nature of the constitutional structure. But the instrumentality may not appear as a clause in the constitution; it may be only a manner of doing things or an attitude towards political questions.

Every country that is far enough over in this spectrum, every federal society if you will, has a special federalized amending process, whether it be institutionalized in a formal amending procedure or not. In Canada, Britain, and South Africa the process is not institutionalized; in Canada, indeed, it is not even standardized. In Australia, Switzerland, and the United States it is made into a formal constitutional provision requiring special extraordinary majorities and so on. The forms differ greatly, but in fact the several countries work through processes that are similar.

When we say, therefore, that every federal government has a special amending process, the emphasis is placed on the word 'process'. We refer not to the requirements that so many states must consent in order that an amendment may be adopted but to the political process by which such consent is elicited—to the process of consulting the interests of the federal elements in the society itself.

### *Clauses and Cultures*

Still another consideration enters into the matter. Institutions in different cultural environments produce different results, whether the institutions be party systems, a principle of dissolution, or a scheme for constitutional amendment. We ignore political and cultural realities if we insist that a constitution in order to be federal must include a particular kind of provision for amendment; we reduce federalism to absurdity if we insist that exactly the same procedures must be employed. A procedure which produces one result in one country may produce one that is wholly different in another.

We have observed that the procedures employed in Australia and Switzerland are very similar in nature but have produced very different results. This procedure in Switzerland has resulted in a great number of successful amendments; in Australia it has produced very few. The general nature of political attitudes, the content of the respective cultural traditions, is vastly different in the two countries. And the results produced by nearly identical institutional devices are different. Whether this is the whole explanation I do not know; certainly it helps to understand the differences. By way of contrast we may observe that Australia and the United States have cultural and especially historical backgrounds that are much more nearly alike. In these two countries procedures of amendment that differ greatly in form have produced very similar results.

Although the procedures are dissimilar, neither has amended its constitution on many occasions, even though proposals for amendments have been numerous in both countries.[1] Consider too the fact that the amendment provisions in the Mexican constitution are very similar to those in that of the United States. That these two have operated in vastly different ways requires no comment.

Students of federalism have been too much concerned with the documentary constitution and too little concerned with the processes of government which it presumably determines. A wiser conception embraces both. The constitution cannot be the ultimate determinant, for the constitution itself is the creature of politics. It is true that it also helps determine the course of political decisions and may even more frequently provide the forms those decisions must take. But this is derivative and secondary; the primary explanations must be pursued farther. What determines the nature of political institutions in a federal state is the cultural and sociological and psychological make-up of the people whom they are intended to serve. If the diversities in the society are great enough to make necessary a system of federal instrumentalities of a certain kind, and if this system includes a certain type of amending process, then we may say that federalism makes necessary a special kind of process of amendment. But this is not the same thing as saying that all federal constitutions must have an amending procedure of this or that sort. Such a definition is, of course, weak and of little use in the classification of constitutions, but this is because it makes no effort to assist such a classification. What gives body and meaning to it is the process itself, and the process is a function not solely of the formal provisions of the constitution but of the diversities within that complex of psychological and sociological habits and values that makes men act as they do.

### *The Institutionalization of the Federal Amending Process*

In Australia, Switzerland, and the United States the process by which amendments are adopted is channelled through, and

[1] This suggestion carries a meaning for the charge of excessive rigidity that has so often been levelled at the American constitution. Defenders of the present system may point out that Australia has amended her constitution even less frequently, and if it be objected that her procedure, too, is too difficult, the experience of Switzerland may be cited.

therefore masked by, a formal amending procedure, carefully institutionalized in the constitution itself. In Canada, South Africa, and Britain this is not true. In these latter countries, therefore, the process is more flexible and can take different forms on different occasions. In the course of the adoption of some amendments in these countries the component units have not been consulted as such; this cannot happen in those countries with formal and rigid procedures, for there no amendment, whatever its purposes, can be effected without using the formal procedure that is established for all amendments.

In any country there are many amendments of such a nature that the component units are not directly concerned in them, so far as the subject-matter is concerned. In countries where the process is not institutionalized it has not ordinarily been considered necessary to consult the federal entities regarding such amendments. In these countries the question whether the federal elements should be consulted in the process depends upon the nature of the amendment itself. But the question is a delicate one. Who must decide whether they should be consulted? It would seem reasonable that the component units themselves ought to have the right to answer such a question. Since the process is informal, the federal elements merely by voicing opinions and objections take part in the process. This is not a situation in which some official of the central government asks himself or his colleagues whether it is advisable to ask for opinions from all the provinces. The project is introduced; public discussion takes place; the provincial governments, if they are concerned in the matter, express opinions in whatever way seems best. Ergo, the states are consulted. It may be objected that there is no guarantee that their opinions will be effective. This is quite true. But we are discussing not the ability of the individual units to *control* amendments, but their ability to take part in the political process that produces the decisions. The sanction lies not in the law or even in the constitution, but in the habitual practices, the conventional attitudes, and the respect with which one group of citizens entertains the views of another. Ultimately the decision may be made in spite of fierce opposition from one unit or from a group of units, and in a country that is formally unitary such a decision will be made by the officers of the central government. But this does not mean that the federal entities had no part in the process; it only means that the decision went against some of them. Not everyone can be satisfied with the decisions that constitute public policy, least of all in a federal society.

In the state where the process is not institutionalized some amendments are adopted after consulting the component elements and some are adopted without consulting them. This suggests the hypothesis that a country may be federal for certain purposes and not federal for others. We are speaking now not of the formal provisions of constitutions but of the complexities and diversities in the society itself. Now in both kinds of state, i.e. where the process is institutionalized and where it is not, some questions arise in which the states have a decided interest *qua* states; some arise in which they do not have such an interest. In states where the process is institutionalized both kinds of questions must be referred to the federated elements through the formal procedure which embraces them; the states must be consulted whether they desire it or not. In states where the process is not so institutionalized, only the questions in which the states have an interest *qua* states are resolved federally. Since the procedure is not formalized but may be adapted to suit the need of the matter at hand, other questions, in which the states have no direct concern, need not be referred to them. In these instances the process is not federal but unitary.

### *Federal Instrumentalities in the Amending Process*

We have employed the term 'instrumentality' to signify any procedure, institution, concept, convention, or attitude that serves to articulate and protect the diversities that constitute the psycho-sociological basis of the federal community. Where the process of constitutional amendment is institutionalized several such instrumentalities are to be found.

The first and most obvious of these is the requirement that a certain number of the component elements must consent to the adoption of the amendment before it can become a part of the constitution. This has already been adequately discussed and requires no further mention here.

A second federal instrumentality is the representation of

the states in the second chamber of the national legislature. We have observed that this representation has not in most cases served as an adequate protective device for the states, since the members of the Upper House tend to be elected and to vote according to the fortunes and policies of the political parties with which they are associated rather than according to the interests of the federal unit which they represent. But in some cases, Imperial Germany for example, these representatives have served their purpose well. In Switzerland and the United States the federal units are represented by two members each in the second chamber; in Australia each has ten; in all three countries the principle is maintained. Some writers have held that equality in the Upper House is an essential element of a federal constitution. But in some countries this is clearly absurd; if the states vary greatly in size and population, it is most difficult to persuade the large state to accept parity of representation with the small. In the German Empire the largest state comprised three-fifths of the population while the smallest comprised only one twenty-five hundredth. In Canada the largest province contains one-third of the population while the smallest contains less than one-hundredth. Clearly in such cases it would be unreasonable to insist on parity.[1] The principle need not be equality but merely an assured, and perhaps disproportionate, representation for the small states. In both these instances the small states were considerably over-represented, despite a lack of strict equality. In Canada the country is divided into four regions, each represented by twenty-four senators. Ontario and Quebec each constitute a region; the maritime and the western provinces each divide a region among themselves. Newfoundland, in addition, is represented by six senators.[2] For the present discussion the significance of the representation of the states in the upper chamber is that that body is required to consent to amendments in all four of the federations to which our principal study has been devoted. In other countries that have been called federal this is frequently the only federal element

[1] In the United States the variety extends from New York, with about one sixteenth of the population, to Nevada, with about one thousandth; the reader may judge whether equality of representation here is reasonable.

[2] British North America Act, 1949; schedule, Section 4.

in the amending process. This has been the case in Brazil, Austria, South Africa, and New Zealand.

A third instrumentality of federalism that appears in some amending procedures is the provision by which the states may initiate amendments to the constitution. In the United States two-thirds of the states may petition the Congress to call a constitutional convention for the purpose of submitting amendments for ratification. In Brazil amendments may be proposed by petitions of a majority of the states, provided they are assembled within a two-year period. We have already observed the difficulties inherent in such provisions as these. The states find it difficult to agree on a proposal when each must act on its separate initiative, and the result has been that such provisions have been little used. The presence of such a device in some constitutions, however, does constitute a federal instrumentality and, though it is seldom put to use, it is available should the need arise.

The fourth instrumentality that may be mentioned is the provision in several constitutions limiting the use to which the amending power itself may be put. This device is not necessarily a federal instrumentality but it may be employed as such. It appears in unitary constitutions as well; the constitution of the French Third Republic, for example, forbade any amendment that would introduce a form of government other than the republican. In federal states such provisions usually have to do with the protection of the federal entities. The United States constitution prohibits the impairment of a state's equality of representation in the Senate without the state's consent; two other limitations of a temporary nature expired in 1808. No such limitations were found in Canada before 1949, since no provision was made in the constitution for amendments; but the Act of that year did provide several limitations of this kind, to which reference has been made. In Switzerland the amending power is unrestricted, since the constitution declares that it may be amended 'wholly or partially'. In Australia a rather complicated clause is included forbidding any alteration diminishing a state's representation in either House or a change in its boundaries without the state's consent.[1]

[1] See the discussion above, pp. 157 ff.

Whether these limitations are effective has never been put to the test. It has been argued by some writers[1] that all that is required is a series of two amendments, the first abolishing the guarantee and the second attacking the protected clause. Doubtless this is legally true, although there would seem to be some doubt about the question in Australia. There the prohibitions in the amending clause are followed by the phrase 'or in any manner affecting the provisions of the constitution in relation thereto'; if the amending clause itself is one of the provisions relating 'thereto', then it may be (and has been) argued that the amending clause, or the appropriate part of it, may not be amended by the ordinary process but would require the consent of all the states to its alteration.

The only instance[2] in which the limitations of this kind have been called into operation was in South Africa in 1936, when the entrenched clause relating to the Cape native franchise was repealed. Here a special procedure was employed in which a joint session and a two-thirds vote was necessary to change the clause. Although the Statute of Westminster had seemingly given the parliament plenary power so that the restriction was no longer legally binding, the procedure was followed anyway; and this in a state that was not federal but unitary. The same problem was more clearly posed in 1952, when the Court denied to the Government the power to evade these restrictions.

### *Federalism and Popular Government*

Federal government is suitable only to those polities that are organized upon a democratic or republican foundation. By this is meant merely that it is incompatible with any form of dictatorship or absolutism. Federal government presupposes a desire and an ability to secure the component units against encroachment by the central government. If the latter is an authoritarian dictatorship, it is difficult to see how the safeguards of the federal structure can be worth much; the states would continue perhaps to exercise their functions, but only on the sufferance of the central government. Of course, this would not immediately destroy the diversification within the society that originally required a federal scheme of govern-

[1] See W. F. Willoughby, *The Government of Modern States*, New York, 1924, p. 143.

[2] But see above, p. 239, note 1.

ment, but so far as the scheme itself is concerned it would be at the mercy of the dictator. Logically the two are not incompatible, but practically one would contradict the other.

This, indeed, has been the case in Latin America, where dictatorial regimes in the central governments of federal states have reduced the federal elements of the constitutions to nullities; much the same thing can be said of Soviet Russia. In such a situation, if Russian or Latin American experience be a valid criterion, it appears that the central dictatorship in order to maintain itself must place in the positions of authority in the states officials who are subservient to the regime. The states thus become mere agencies of the ruling group in the central government and the independent and co-ordinate status that characterizes the relation of states to central government in a true federation becomes meaningless. The unlimited power of an autocratic central government necessarily subverts or threatens at all times to subvert the federal principle.[1] It may also be argued that the states themselves cannot be autocratic in character[2] else the nature of federalism is completely altered. The crucial question becomes that of the manner of choosing the central legislature. How are the states controlled by autocratic governments to be represented? Dictatorship means the abolition of free elections, the deprivation of the right of criticism, and the end of popular government. Can it be supposed that states controlled in this manner will participate equitably and peacefully alongside those founded on democratic principles? This question has long troubled the advocates of federalism in India, where the prospective federal states have long shown great variations in the degree of self rule or autocracy to which they have been accustomed.[3]

[1] The example of the Nazis' destruction of the German federal states may also be cited. See Roger H. Wells, 'The Liquidation of the German Laender', *Amer. Pol. Sci. Rev.*, vol. 30, 1936, p. 350. The problem is also discussed by K. C. Wheare, *Federal Government*, pp. 47 f.; Roscoe Pound in *Federalism as a Democratic Process*, New Brunswick, N.J., 1942, p. 12; and Herman Finer, *The Theory and Practice of Modern Government*, vol. 1, p. 55.

[2] See Wheare, loc. cit., and William P. Maddox, 'The Political Basis of Federation', *Amer. Pol. Sci. Rev.*, vol. 35, 1941, p. 1125.

[3] The component states under the Indian constitution of 1950 are divided into three classes. One of these consists of the old princely states (or unions of such states) in which the head of state is still the maharajah. Each has an elected

Federalism as a form of government cannot harbour among the component states diversities so great that no common foundation exists for uniting the separate entities into one federal system. Federalism presupposes both unity and diversity and constitutes a device for compromising these opposite tendencies. It demands at the very least a mutual respect among the federated units, and this respect can only be built out of certain common features in the historical background and common acceptance of certain political attitudes and institutions. If some of the uniting units possess a democratic background and others a heritage of autocracy, the success of the federation will be at least questionable. Of all the factors that go into the matrix out of which federations are produced, similarity of social and political traditions is probably the most important. Dictatorship and democracy seem clearly incompatible in a federal scheme of government.

### *Federalism and Majority Rule*

It seems equally clear that federalism is inconsistent with a doctrine of strict majority rule if applied to the whole of the federal community. If federal government is incompatible with the absolute rule of a dictator, it follows that it is similarly incompatible with the absolute rule of an oligarchy and that it is incompatible with the absolute rule of a majority.[1] It is not the nature of the central government that produces the incompatibility but the fact that its powers are absolute.

By its very nature federalism is anti-majoritarian. A federal government is designed to protect and afford a means of articulation for the territorial diversities within the larger community. All the instrumentalities of federal government are devices whose purpose is to prevent the unqualified majority of the whole society from riding unchecked over the interests of any of the federated elements. It is a technique for the protection of a minority within one state or several states

legislature and a responsible executive council. Thus democratic forms have been established in all areas, even those with strong autocratic traditions. How well this will work no one seems prepared to say, but most prognoses are favourable. See Sir Ivor Jennings, *The Commonwealth in Asia*, Oxford, 1951, chap. 7.

[1] The argument is Dean Pound's; see op. cit., pp. 12–13.

against the majority in the rest of the states. Indeed, the written constitution itself, as Lord Bryce suggested, is a device for the checking of majority rule. Such a constitution, he said, 'is a recognition of the truth that majorities are not always right, and need to be protected against themselves by being obliged to recur, at moments of haste or excitement, to maxims they had adopted at times of cool reflection'.[1] If the rigid constitution limits majority rule, how much more so does a federal constitution in which the central government must take counsel with the states in the process of making decisions.

It would seem, however, that there is nothing to prevent the application of the principle of majority rule in the component units themselves. Federalism requires only that the states as states participate in the political process at the national level; it lays down no requirements about how the decision of the state itself is arrived at.[2] Though the determinants of federalism are found in the state communities, its problems are most frequently found in the centre or in the relations of the centre to the components.

Half a century ago J. Allen Smith wrote a book in which he bitterly criticized the undemocratic spirit of the American scheme of government.[3] In it he argued that a true democracy had to embrace the principle of majority rule. One of his principal points of attack was the amending procedure, which required the consent of three-fourths of the states before an amendment to the constitution could be adopted.[4] His criticism was justified, but only within his own frame of reference. It was phrased in the wrong terms. He was in fact criticizing

[1] Bryce, *Modern Democracies*, 1924 edn., vol. ii, p. 11.

[2] This should, of course, be qualified in terms of the argument in regard to autocracy in the preceding section.

[3] *The Spirit of American Government*, New York, 1907.

[4] 'A constitution is in no proper sense the embodiment of the will of the people unless it recognizes the right of the majority to amend' (op. cit., p. 63). Again, 'all democratic constitutions are flexible and easy to amend. This follows from the fact that in a government which the people really control, a constitution is merely the means of securing the supremacy of public opinion and not an instrument for thwarting it. . . . A government is democratic just in proportion as it responds to the will of the people; and since one way of defeating the will of the people is to make it difficult to alter the form of government, it necessarily follows that any constitution which is democratic in spirit must yield readily to changes in public opinion' (p. 40).

a federal system for serving the ends it was intended to serve. The point is not that Smith had forgotten that the framers were not democrats; he points out that fact with glee. What he was suggesting was not that the devices of government were inadequate but that the ends they served were wrong. What he ignored was that even in 1907 the United States was still composed of states.

The amending clause was an excellent spot for his attack and the criticisms he made of it would have been equally applicable to any federation. Nearly all governments that are called federal employ some device in the amending process to *prevent* a mere majority from changing the constitution. We have observed above that federal amending procedures contain several different instrumentalities of federalism. All these instrumentalities are designed to preclude the possibility that a mere majority of the people in the whole nation will impose upon a minority of dissident states an amendment to the constitution to which they are opposed.

Statistical data on such a problem are hard to come by. But experience with amending procedures in certain federations does shed a little light on the question of majority rule. In Australia and Switzerland, and probably in the United States as well, there have been instances in which a majority of the whole people have approved an amendment but have been unable to secure its adoption because of the federal elements in the amending procedure. In Australia the aviation amendment in 1937 received a majority of the total popular vote but was approved in only two states. Similarly, in 1946 two amendments granting the Commonwealth powers over industrial employment and organized marketing received popular majorities but failed for lack of approval in the necessary number of states. In Switzerland a similar instance occurred in 1866, when a proposal concerning the regulation of weights and measures was approved by a slim majority in the general referendum but received support in only nine and one-half cantons. It is surprising that no other instances of this kind have occurred in Switzerland in view of the large number of referenda that have been held on constitutional questions. In 1910, however, the reverse of this situation occurred when a proposal for the employment of proportional representation was approved in a majority of the cantons, but failed to receive a majority in the nation-wide referendum.[1]

In the United States the data are not sufficiently accurate to afford a basis for generalization; but there have been several amendments proposed by the Congress which have been ratified by more than a majority of the states, comprising in each case more than a majority of the population, but which failed since they were not ratified by three-fourths of the states.[2] One of the proposals submitted along with the present bill of rights received the approval of ten out of fourteen states, representing eighty per cent. of the population. The 1810 proposal on titles of nobility was ratified by twelve out of eighteen states, representing 60 per cent. of the population. And finally, the child-labour amendment was approved in twenty-eight out of forty-eight states, the population of which comprised 56 per cent. of the nation.

These data do not display any truths that we have not already known about the nature of the amending process. But they do help validate the proposition that the safeguards of a federal amending procedure serve the purpose of preventing hasty amendments by a mere numerical majority of the population of the whole. In each of the three federations, it seems clear, there have been instances where amendments have been defeated which, though approved by the majority, lacked the support of a sufficient number of the component units. The federal elements in the amending process have been effective in some measure at least. Doubtless, too, they have had indirect effects as well, for which statistical data cannot be obtained.

Does this prove that federalism in undemocratic? Certainly it does, if democracy be defined in terms of majority rule. But there is far from a general agreement that majority rule is the touchstone of democracy. Many democrats would assert that the protection of minorities is equally essential to the democratic form of government, and the federal amending procedure has clearly been more consistent with this principle. Federalism cannot be dismissed as evil because it does not fit into a theory of majoritarian democracy. It is not here

[1] See tables above, pp. 185 and 187.

[2] The point has been discussed more fully above, at pp. 234 f.

suggested that it is a thing of value in itself; but it does satisfy certain important needs in a complex society and enables countries of continental dimensions to conduct their affairs with justice and dispatch without resorting to dictatorships.[1] It solves certain problems that might otherwise remain unsolved and perpetuates diversities that are valuable. So long as these ends are of value, so also is federalism. The meaning of democracy is by no means clear; theorists and others are still arguing about what the term implies. To condemn federalism as undemocratic because it prevents pure majority rule is to assume a definition of democracy that not all men who call themselves democrats would accept.[2] Every federation arrives now and then at the point where the plans of the majority are estopped by a minority employing the federal instrumentalities. In such situations those who happen to be in the majority on that issue complain loudly about the obstinacy of the few. They argue that the will of the majority is being thwarted and suggest by implication at least that this is ethically wrong; the term 'will of the majority' carries with it certain moral overtones in these days of enlightened democracy. But what the *ad hoc* majoritarians forget is that a federal state is a different thing, that it is not intended to operate according to a majority principle.

We cannot apply the standards of unitary government to a federal state. If the opinion of a majority is a sufficient guide for public policy in a community, then it is unlikely that a federal system will have been established in that community. The fact that it has been established is a clear indication that such a majority is not an adequate guide.

## *States' Rights and the Comity of the States*

Federalism demands of its employers a habit of thought towards political questions—a way of approaching the decision-making process—that denies the need or desirability of such

[1] Dean Pound calls attention to the fact that no country of continental extent has ever been ruled otherwise than as an autocracy or a federal state. Op. cit., p. 23.

[2] Nor is federalism the only limitation on majority rule that may be professed and admired by those who consider themselves democrats. Individual rights, the separation of powers, judicial review, and the rigid constitution itself may all serve to restrain the majority.

arithmetical determination of policies. The question whether the majority of the states and the people can coerce the minority of the states and the people is one that ought never to arise in a federal community. When it does, the foundation upon which the federal edifice is erected has been shaken.

In the United States, for example, the North comprises a large majority both of the states and of the people. When the South disinters its claims of states' rights and resorts to a filibuster in the Senate, the North is quick to condemn such action. Since the Second World War southern senators have conducted several filibusters in order to prevent the enactment of a civil rights programme; the North held that this was a morally untenable position, but whether that was true or not was beside the point. What the North forgets is that the United States is still a federal country and that it can only operate on federal principles, among which one of the most inviolable is the division of powers that has assigned such matters to the states. It is probably true, in view of the recent line of decisions in the Supreme Court, that a civil rights programme could be justified in American constitutional law. But federalism is always more than a question of constitutional law. It is a question of the ability of a people that is heterogeneous in regard to traditions, economic interests, and political and social background to live together in harmony and to enjoy the benefits of their co-operative enterprise.

When the Southern states undertake to preserve what they consider their rights by blocking all business in the Senate,[1] the tragedy is not that that dignified body is stultified (though that too is a tragedy) but that the component elements of this federal system are forced into a position where they feel it necessary to resort to such means to preserve their rights. When a filibuster begins in the American Senate, the constitution and the federal system are laid bare.

But the states in a federal system can be too much emphasized. Federalism makes demands both ways. The citizens of the states are the citizens of the whole as well. The logic of state protection can lead easily to the conclusion that the consent of each state should be necessary for any action. Since

[1] See Walter Lippmann in the *New York Herald Tribune*, 17 Mar. 1949.

the purpose of federal government is to afford security to the diversities of the components, this would be a logical doctrine; otherwise the constitution could be amended to deprive any state of particularities which it cherishes. This would indeed be ideal, but it would cripple federal governments as it crippled America under the Articles, and it would make meaningless any distinction between *Bundesstaat* and *Staatenbund*.[1]

It is equally necessary to recognize that the states, when they enter into a federation, contribute to the formation of a wholly new legal and political entity. Their entry into such a scheme involves their undertaking a certain risk that their own prerogatives may be subverted by a majority or some other proportion of the rest of the states through whatever procedures of constitutional amendment are agreed upon. There are responsibilities on both sides. The whole community must take care lest the desires and rights of some of the states are needlessly overridden. The states must take care lest, by undue insistence upon those rights and wants, they destroy the comity that is essential to federal government.[2]

The spirit of co-operative enterprise and mutual respect which is essential to the proper operation of a federal system is demanded from both majorities and minorities, from the former so that they may not override the rights of the latter, and from the latter so that they may not unreasonably hold

[1] Professor MacIver would seem to place most of the responsibility for maintaining the comity of the federal society upon the majorities that may threaten the states: '. . . in a true federation each constituent has *ex hypothesi* a certain autonomy, recognized in the articles of union. This would seem to imply that no change in its relation to the whole or to the others can legitimately be forced upon it by a majority outside itself, or, more strictly, that *apart from the conditions it has accepted in entering the federation or at any later time* it remains in the position of a free state. The fact that a state resigns certain powers should not logically prejudice the powers that it retains. Its tenacity in respect of these powers may impede the development of the federal state of which it is a member and may seriously interfere with projects of a national character. But this is a difficulty inherent in the very form of federation.' Robert M. MacIver, *The Modern State*, Oxford, 1926, p. 379. But one of the conditions it accepts upon entering the federation is that the constitution may be amended by something less than the unanimous approval of the states.

[2] 'The success of the system in the great things which it can accomplish depends on the completeness with which the local unit is relieved of all fear that outside forces and outside majorities are going to interfere with its peculiarities or impose regulations upon it which it considers to be unjust.' G. B. Adams, *Federal Government, Its Function and Method*, New York, 1919, p. 111.

up the progress of the former or of the whole. By way of illustration, such a spirit of co-operation should prevent the North from trying to put through a civil rights programme over the vigorous protests of the South, and it should militate against the possibility that essential changes in the Canadian constitution be made against the opposition of Quebec. But at the same time it should bring about a proper expectation that neither the South nor Quebec will hold up changes in their respective constitutions for minor reasons. Every federal system has on occasion been embarrassed by members that have been too zealous in the defence of their rights.

The difficulty is that this spirit of co-operation is a necessary antecedent to any conciliatory attitude on the part of, say, Quebec in a particular situation. But a conciliatory attitude in a series of situations is necessary before the proper spirit of co-operation can be developed. The development of the two is concomitant and circular. Quebec is so conscious of her rights that she is too anxious to protect them; hence she blocks changes that really do her no harm. This is because the necessary spirit of respect and confidence has not grown up. But one of the reasons it has not grown up is that Quebec has been too anxious to protect herself.

## *Forms and Process*

We have insisted throughout, first, that it is more important to observe how an institution operates than to examine the constitutional provisions concerning the institution itself, and, second, that the way it operates depends upon the nature of the diversities in the society and the attitudes of the people towards the value of those diversities. But this must not blind us to the fact that the institution itself is of importance too. We may argue that federalism demands for its proper functioning an attitude of mutual respect and co-operation; but this attitude or spirit is not always present. Indeed, if it were perfectly developed there would be little need for a federal system and little likelihood that it would be established. So far as this spirit of co-operative enterprise is concerned, federalism is always operating at less than maximum efficiency and in something less than the most desirable fashion. Since this is true, the institution and its legal attributes do have significance. If the desired attitudes are lacking and government must be by conflict instead of compromise and integration, then it makes a great deal of difference what kind of institution is provided in the constitution. It is quite willingly conceded that it is more difficult to adopt constitutional amendments when three-fourths of the states must consent than when only a majority is required.

But the words of the clause are by no means a conclusive indication of how the procedure is likely to work. The political process that operates behind the words is of much greater significance. It is the process that determines whether the constitution will be rigid or flexible. And the process is the function of the complex of diversities in the society and the attitudes of the people towards them.

The form and the process can never be separated. Each affects the other and together they produce an entity which we have called the instrumentality. The form, once adopted and employed, enters into the psycho-sociological framework and colours the attitudes and the process. Federalism is the product of both and of the integrating interaction between them.

# APPENDIX A

## AMENDMENT PROVISIONS IN SELECTED CONSTITUTIONS

### 1. *The Commonwealth of Australia*

CHAPTER VIII

ALTERATION OF THE CONSTITUTION

128. This Constitution shall not be altered except in the following manner:—

The proposed law for the alteration thereof must be passed by an absolute majority of each House of the Parliament, and not less than two nor more than six months after its passage through both Houses the proposed law shall be submitted in each State to the electors qualified to vote for the election of members of the House of Representatives.

But if either House passes any such proposed law by an absolute majority, and the other House rejects or fails to pass it or passes it with any amendment to which the first-mentioned House will not agree, and if after an interval of three months the first-mentioned House in the same or the next session again passes the proposed law by an absolute majority with or without any amendment which has been made or agreed to by the other House, and such other House rejects or fails to pass it or passes it with any amendment to which the first-mentioned House will not agree, the Governor-General may submit the proposed law as last proposed by the first-mentioned House, and either with or without any amendments subsequently agreed to by both Houses, to the electors in each State qualified to vote for the election of the House of Representatives.

When a proposed law is submitted to the electors the vote shall be taken in such manner as the Parliament prescribes. But until the qualification of electors of members of the House of Representatives becomes uniform throughout the Commonwealth, only one-half the electors voting for and against the proposed law shall be counted in any State in which adult suffrage prevails.

And if in a majority of the States a majority of the electors voting approve the proposed law, and if a majority of all the electors voting also approve the proposed law, it shall be presented to the Governor-General for the Queen's assent.

No alteration diminishing the proportionate representation of any State in either House of the Parliament, or the minimum number of representatives of a State in the House of Representatives, or increasing, diminishing, or otherwise altering the limits of a State, or in any manner affecting the provisions of the Constitution in relation thereto, shall become law unless the majority of the electors voting in that State approve the proposed law.

## 2. *The Swiss Confederation*

[Since the amending clause of the Swiss constitution has undergone significant changes since the adoption of the constitution of 1848 the original provision is given below, followed by the new provisions as they appeared after the revisions of 1874 and 1891. In each case the whole of chapter iii is reproduced.]

### *Constitution of 1848*

#### CHAPTER III

#### REVISION OF THE FEDERAL CONSTITUTION

Art. 111. The federal Constitution may be revised at any time.

Art. 112. The revision shall take place according to the forms fixed by federal legislation.

Art. 113. Whenever one section of the Federal Assembly proposes a revision of the federal Constitution and the other section does not consent to it, or, whenever fifty thousand qualified Swiss voters request a revision, the question whether the federal Constitution ought to be revised shall be in either case submitted to the vote of the Swiss people, who shall vote yes or no.

If in either case the majority of the Swiss citizens taking part in the vote reply affirmatively, the two Councils shall be dissolved and re-elected for the purpose of preparing the revision.

Art. 114 (and last). The revised federal Constitution shall take effect when it has been accepted by a majority of the Swiss citizens taking part in the vote and by a majority of the cantons.

### *Constitution of 1874*

#### CHAPTER III

#### REVISION OF THE FEDERAL CONSTITUTION

Art. 118. The federal Constitution may be revised at any time.

Art. 119. The revision shall take place according to the forms fixed by federal legislation.

Art. 120. Whenever one section of the Federal Assembly proposes a revision of the federal Constitution and the other section does not consent to it, or, whenever fifty thousand qualified Swiss voters request a revision, the question whether the federal Constitution ought to be revised shall be in either case submitted to the vote of the Swiss people, who shall vote yes or no.

If in either case the majority of the Swiss citizens taking part in the vote reply affirmatively, the Councils shall be dissolved and re-elected for the purpose of preparing the revision.

Art. 121. The revised federal Constitution shall take effect when it has been accepted by a majority of the Swiss citizens taking part in the vote and by a majority of the cantons.

In determining the majority of the cantons the vote of a half canton shall be counted as half a vote.

The result of the popular vote in each canton shall be considered to be the vote of the canton.

## *Revised Amending Clause of 1891*

### CHAPTER III

### REVISION OF THE FEDERAL CONSTITUTION

*Article 118.* The Federal Constitution may at any time be wholly or partially amended.

*Article 119.* A total revision is effected through the forms fixed for federal legislation.

*Article 120.* When either division of the Federal Assembly passes a resolution for the total revision of the Constitution, and the other division does not agree, or when 50,000 Swiss voters demand a total revision, the question whether the Constitution ought to be revised is in either case submitted to the people, who vote Yes or No.

If in either case a majority of the Swiss citizens who vote pronounce in the affirmative, there shall be a new election of both Councils for the purpose of undertaking the revision.

*Article 121.* A partial revision may take place by means of the popular initiative, or through the forms prescribed by federal law.

The popular initiative consists of a request by fifty thousand qualified Swiss voters for the adoption of a new article in the Constitution or for the repeal or amendment of specified articles in the Constitution already in force.

If by means of a popular initiative several different provisions are presented for revision or for introduction into the Federal Constitution, each shall comprise the subject of a separate initiative demand.

The initiative demand may take the form of a proposal in general terms or of a draft proposal complete in all details.

When the initiative is couched in general terms, the two chambers, if they approve of it, will undertake the partial revision in the sense indicated, and will submit it for the approval or rejection of the people and the cantons. If, on the contrary, they do not approve, the question whether there shall be a partial revision will be submitted to a vote of the people; if a majority of the Swiss citizens taking part in the vote reply in the affirmative, the Federal Assembly will proceed to undertake the revision in conformity with the decision of the people.

When the demand takes the form of a draft proposal complete in all details, and the Federal Assembly approves of it, the proposal shall be submitted for adoption or rejection by the people and the cantons. If the Federal Assembly does not approve, it may draft a proposal of its own or may recommend to the people that the proposed draft be rejected and it may submit its counter-proposal or recommendation of rejection to vote at the same time as the measure presented by the popular initiative.

*Article 122.* A federal law shall determine the formalities to be observed in regard to popular initiative demands and in regard to the balloting on the revision of the federal Constitution.

*Article 123.* The revised federal Constitution, or the revised part thereof, shall take effect when it has been accepted by a majority of the Swiss citizens taking part in the vote and by a majority of the cantons.

In determining the majority of the cantons the vote of a half-canton shall be counted as half a vote.

The result of the popular vote in each canton shall be considered to be the vote of the canton.

## 3. *The United States of America*

### Article V

The Congress, whenever two thirds of both Houses shall deem it necessary, shall propose Amendments to this Constitution, or, on the Application of the Legislatures of two thirds of the several States, shall call a convention for proposing Amendments, which, in either case, shall be valid to all Intents and Purposes, as Part of this Constitution, when ratified by the Legislatures of three fourths of the several States, or by Conventions in three fourths thereof, as the one or the other Mode of Ratification may be proposed by the Congress; provided that no Amendment which may be made prior to the Year One thousand eight hundred and eight shall in any Manner affect the first and fourth Clauses in the Ninth Section of the first Article; and that no State, without its Consent, shall be deprived of its equal Suffrage in the Senate.

[Note: The temporarily protected provisions referred to are as follows:

Article I, Section 9:

Clause 1. The Migration or Importation of such Persons as any of the States now existing shall think proper to admit, shall not be prohibited by the Congress prior to the Year One thousand eight hundred and eight, but a Tax or duty may be imposed on such Importation, not exceeding ten dollars for each Person.

Clause 4. No Capitation, or other direct, Tax shall be laid, unless in Proportion to the Census or Enumeration hereinbefore directed to be taken.]

## 4. *The Union of South Africa*

### PART X

### AMENDMENT OF THE ACT

152. Parliament may by law repeal or alter any of the provisions of this Act: Provided that no provision thereof, for the operation of which a definite period of time is prescribed, shall during such period be repealed or altered: And provided further that no repeal or alteration of the provisions contained in this section, or in sections *thirty-three* and *thirty-four* (until the number of members of the House of Assembly has reached the limit therein prescribed, or until a period of ten years has elapsed after the establishment of the Union, whichever is the longer period), or in sections *thirty-five* and *one hundred and thirty-seven*, shall be valid unless the Bill embodying such repeal or alteration shall be passed by both Houses of Parliament sitting together, and at the third reading be agreed to by not less than two-thirds of the total number of members of both Houses. A Bill so passed at such joint sitting shall be taken to have been duly passed by both Houses of Parliament.

[Note: The protected or 'entrenched' clauses are as follows:

Section 33: Establishes the number of members of the House of Assembly for each province; permits their increase and prohibits their diminution.

Section 34: Prescribes the manner in which representation of the provinces in the House of Assembly may be increased.

Section 35: Authorizes Parliament to prescribe qualifications for voting, but prohibits any interference, for reasons of colour, with the franchise of those who possessed it in the Cape of Good Hope at the time of Union.

Section 137: Establishes English and Dutch languages as the official languages of the Union and requires that all Parliamentary records, etc., shall be published in both.]

## 5. *Imperial Germany*

### 14. General Stipulations

LXXVIII. Alterations in the Constitution take place by way of legislation. They are considered as rejected if they have 14 votes in the Council of the Confederation against them.

Those provisions of the Constitution of the Empire, by which certain rights are established for separate States of the Confederation in their relation to the community, can only be altered with the consent of the State of the Confederation entitled to those rights.

## 6. *Weimar Germany*

Article 75.—A decision of the Reichstag can be annulled by the decision of the people only when a majority of those entitled to the franchise take part in the vote.

Article 76.—The constitution may be amended by legislation. But decisions of the Reichstag as to such amendments come into effect only if two-thirds of the legal total of members be present, and if at least two-thirds of those present have given their consent. Decisions of the Reichsrat in favour of amendments of the Constitution also require a majority of two-thirds of the votes cast. Where an amendment of the Constitution is decided by an appeal to the people as the result of a Popular Initiative, the consent of the majority of the voters is necessary.

Should the Reichstag have decided upon an alteration of the Constitution in spite of the objection of the Reichsrat, the President of the Reich shall not promulgate the law if the Reichsrat, within two weeks, demands an appeal to the people.

## 7. *Federal Republic of Germany* (*Bonn*)

### Article 79

1. The Basic Law may be amended only by a law which expressly alters or adds to the text of the Basic Law.

2. Such a law shall require the approval of two-thirds of the members of the Bundestag and two-thirds of the votes of the Bundesrat.

3. An amendment to this Basic Law by which the organization of the Federation into Laender, the basic co-operation of the Laender in legislation or the basic principles laid down in Articles 1 and 20 are affected, shall be inadmissible.

[Note: The articles specially protected by para. 3 are as follows:

*Art. 1.* 1. The dignity of man shall be inviolable. To respect and protect it shall be the duty of all state authority.

2. The German people therefore acknowledges inviolable and inalienable human rights as the basis of every human community, of peace and of justice in the world.

3. The following basic rights shall be binding as directly valid law on legislation, administration and judiciary. . . .

*Art. 20.* 1. The Federal Republic of Germany is a democratic and social federal state.

2. All state authority emanates from the people. It shall be exercised by the people in elections and plebiscites and by means of separate legislative, executive and judicial organs.

3. Legislation shall be limited by the constitution, the executive and the administration of justice by legislation and the law.]

## 8. *India*

### *Constitution of 1950*

PART XX

AMENDMENT OF THE CONSTITUTION

368. An amendment of this Constitution may be initiated only by the introduction of a Bill for the purpose in either House of Parliament, and when the Bill is passed in each House by a majority of the total membership of that House and by a majority of not less than two-thirds of the members of that House present and voting, it shall be presented to the President for his assent and upon such assent being given to the Bill, the Constitution shall stand amended in accordance with the terms of the Bill:

Provided that if such amendment seeks to make any change in—

(*a*) article 54, article 55, article 73, article 162 or article 241,[1] or
(*b*) Chapter IV of Part V, Chapter V of Part VI, or Chapter I of Part XI,[2] or
(*c*) any of the Lists in the Seventh Schedule,[3] or
(*d*) the representation of States in Parliament, or
(*e*) the provisions of this article,

the amendment shall also require to be ratified by the Legislatures of not less than one-half of the States specified in Parts A and B of the

[1] These concern the election of the President (54 and 55), national–state relations in the execution of law (73 and 162), and the establishment by Parliament of High Courts in the States (241).

[2] These concern respectively the union judiciary, high courts in the states, and the distribution of powers.

[3] These are lists of the exclusive powers of the national and state governments and of the concurrent powers shared by both.

First Schedule by resolutions to that effect passed by those Legislatures before the Bill making provision for such amendment is presented to the President for assent.

## 9. *Argentina*

*Constitution of 1949*

PART FIRST

CHAPTER I

Art. 21. The Constitution may be amended entirely or in any of its parts. The necessity for a reform must by declared by Congress with the vote of two-thirds of its members present; but it shall not be effected except by a convention called for the purpose.

## 10. *Brazil*

*Constitution of 1946*

TITLE NINE

Art. 217. The Constitution may be amended.

1. An amendment shall be considered proposed, if presented by at least one-fourth of the members of the Chamber of Deputies or of the Federal Senate, or by more than one-half of the legislative assemblies of the states, in the course of two years, each of these manifesting itself by majority of its members.

2. An amendment shall be considered accepted it if be approved in two discussions by an absolute majority of the Chamber of Deputies and of the Federal Senate, in two ordinary, consecutive legislative sessions.

3. If the amendment shall obtain in one of the chambers, in two discussions, the vote of two-thirds of its members, it shall immediately be submitted to the other; and if approved in this chamber by the same process, and by equal majority, it shall be considered accepted.

4. The amendment shall be promulgated by the executive committees of the Chamber of Deputies and of the Federal Senate. After publication, over the signatures of the members of both committees, it shall be appended, with its respective sequence number, to the text of the Constitution.

5. The Constitution shall not be modified while a state of siege is in force.

6. Bills tending to abolish the Federation and the Republic shall not be admitted to consideration.

## 11. *Mexico*

### *Constitution of 1917*

TITLE VIII

CONCERNING AMENDMENTS TO THE CONSTITUTION

Art. 135. The present Constitution may be extended or amended. In order that the additions or amendments may become part of the same, it shall be necessary that the Congress of the Union, by a vote of two-thirds of the individuals present, agree to the amendments or additions and that they be approved by a majority of the legislatures of the States. The Congress of the Union shall count the votes of the legislatures and shall make announcement of the additions or amendments approved.

## 12. *Venezuela*

### *Constitution of 1947*

TITLE VIII

CONCERNING CONSTITUTIONAL AMENDMENTS

Art. 248. This Constitution may be amended, wholly or partially, on the initiative of the legislative assemblies or of the national Congress in either of its Chambers.

Art. 249. When the initiative comes from the legislative assemblies, the national Congress will declare it according to law if two-thirds of the former, assembled in regular sessions, have considered an amendment necessary or appropriate, by means of resolutions approved in each assembly by an absolute majority of the whole of its members. The initiative being declared according to law, the Chambers will discuss the amendment by the system established in this Constitution for the discussion of ordinary laws. Amendments or additions being approved, the president of the Congress will submit them to the legislative assemblies for their ratification, which will be given by the same procedure provided for the initiative.

Art. 250. When the initiative comes from either of the Chambers of the Congress, it must be proposed by a fourth part of the whole of its members, following the system established in this Constitution for the discussion of ordinary laws. Amendments or additions being approved, the president of the Congress will submit them to the legislative assemblies in their regular sessions of the following year for their ratification, which will be considered valid when it is approved by two-thirds of them, in their regular sessions and by means of the vote of an absolute majority of the whole of the members of each assembly.

Art. 251. Amendments or additions may not be made except on the points on which the previously indicated majority of legislative assemblies agree.

Art. 252. In any case, the definitive vote of the legislative assemblies will be returned to the Congress for its final scrutiny, which being made, if it results that the amendments or reforms have been legally ratified by the legislative assemblies, the Constitution thus amended or reformed will enter into force on the same day of its publication in the *Gaceta oficial de los Estados Unidos de Venezuela.*

# APPENDIX B

## THE BRITISH NORTH AMERICA (NO. 2) ACT, 1949

An Act to amend the British North America Act, 1867, as respects the amendment of the Constitution of Canada.

(12, 13 & 14 Geo. VI, chap. 81) (16 Dec. 1949)

Whereas the Senate and the House of Commons of Canada in Parliament assembled have submitted an Address to His Majesty praying that His Majesty may graciously be pleased to cause a measure to be laid before the Parliament of the United Kingdom for the enactment of the provisions hereinafter set forth:

Be it therefore enacted by the King's most Excellent Majesty, by and with the advice and consent of the Lords Spiritual and Temporal, and Commons, in this present Parliament assembled, and by the authority of the same, as follows:—

1. Section ninety-one of the British North America Act, 1867 is hereby amended by renumbering Class 1 thereof as Class 1A and by inserting therein immediately before that Class the following as Class 1:—

> '1. The amendment from time to time of the Constitution of Canada, except as regards matters coming within the classes of subjects by this Act assigned exclusively to the Legislatures of the provinces, or as regards rights or privileges by this or any other Constitutional Act granted or secured to the Legislature or the Government of a province, or to any class of persons with respect to schools or as regards the use of the English or the French language or as regards the requirements that there shall be a session of the Parliament of Canada at least once each year, and that no House of Commons shall continue for more than five years from the day of the return of the Writs for choosing the House; provided, however, that a House of Commons may in time of real or apprehended war, invasion or insurrection be continued by the Parliament of Canada if such continuation is not opposed by the votes of more than one-third of the members of such House.'

2. This Act may be cited as the British North America (No. 2) Act, 1949 and shall be included among the Acts which may be cited as the British North America Acts, 1867 to 1949.

# APPENDIX C

## THE STATUTE OF WESTMINSTER, 1931

An Act to give effect to certain resolutions passed by Imperial Conferences held in the years 1926 and 1930.

(22 Geo. V, chap. 4) (11 Dec. 1931)

Whereas the delegates of His Majesty's Governments in the United Kingdom, the Dominion of Canada, the Commonwealth of Australia, the Dominion of New Zealand, the Union of South Africa, the Irish Free State and Newfoundland, at Imperial Conferences holden at Westminster in the years of our Lord nineteen hundred and twenty-six and nineteen hundred and thirty did concur in making the declarations and resolutions set forth in the Reports of the said Conferences:

And whereas it is meet and proper to set out by way of preamble to this Act, that inasmuch as the Crown is the symbol of the free association of the members of the British Commonwealth of Nations, and as they are united by a common allegiance to the Crown, it would be in accord with the established constitutional position of all the members of the Commonwealth in relation to one another that any alteration in the law touching the Succession to the Throne or the Royal Style and Titles shall hereafter require the assent as well of the Parliaments of all the Dominions as of the Parliament of the United Kingdom:

And whereas it is in accord with the established constitutional position that no law hereafter made by the Parliament of the United Kingdom shall extend to any of the said Dominions as part of the law of that Dominion otherwise than at the request and with the consent of that Dominion:

And whereas it is necessary for the ratifying, confirming and establishing of certain of the said declarations and resolutions of the said Conferences that a law be made and enacted in due form by authority of the Parliament of the United Kingdom:

And whereas the Dominion of Canada, the Commonwealth of Australia, the Dominion of New Zealand, the Union of South Africa, the Irish Free State and Newfoundland have severally requested and consented to the submission of a measure to the Parliament of the United Kingdom for making such provision with regard to the matters aforesaid as is hereafter in this Act contained:

Now, therefore, be it enacted by the King's most Excellent Majesty by and with the advice and consent of the Lords Spiritual and Temporal, and Commons, in this present Parliament assembled, and by the authority of the same, as follows:—

1. In this Act the expression 'Dominion' means any of the following Dominions, that is to say, the Dominion of Canada, the Commonwealth of Australia, the Dominion of New Zealand, the Union of South Africa, the Irish Free State and Newfoundland.

2.—(1) The Colonial Laws Validity Act, 1865, shall not apply to any law made after the commencement of this Act by the Parliament of a Dominion.

(2) No law and no provision of any law made after the commencement of this Act by the Parliament of a Dominion shall be void or inoperative on the ground that it is repugnant to the law of England, or to the provisions of any existing or future Act of Parliament of the United Kingdom, or to any order, rule or regulation made under any such Act, and the powers of the Parliament of a Dominion shall include the power to repeal or amend any such Act, order, rule or regulation in so far as the same is part of the law of the Dominion.

3. It is hereby declared and enacted that the Parliament of a Dominion has full power to make laws having extra-territorial operation.

4. No Act of Parliament of the United Kingdom passed after the commencement of this Act shall extend, or be deemed to extend, to a Dominion as part of the law of that Dominion, unless it is expressly declared in that Act that that Dominion has requested, and consented to, the enactment thereof.

5. Without prejudice to the generality of the foregoing provisions of this Act, sections seven hundred and thirty-five and seven hundred and thirty-six of the Merchant Shipping Act, 1894, shall be construed as though reference therein to the Legislature of a British possession did not include reference to the Parliament of a Dominion.

6. Without prejudice to the generality of the foregoing provisions of this Act, section four of the Colonial Courts of Admiralty Act, 1890 (which requires certain laws to be reserved for the signification of His Majesty's pleasure or to contain a suspending clause), and so much of section seven of that Act as requires the approval of His Majesty in Council to any rules of Court for regulating the practice and procedure of a Colonial Court of Admiralty, shall cease to have effect in any Dominion as from the commencement of this Act.

7.—(1) Nothing in this Act shall be deemed to apply to the repeal, amendment or alteration of the British North America Acts, 1867 to 1930, or to any order, rule or regulation made thereunder.

(2) The provision of section two of this Act shall extend to laws made by any of the Provinces of Canada and to the powers of the legislatures of such Provinces.

(3) The powers conferred by this Act upon the Parliament of Canada or upon the legislatures of the Provinces shall be restricted to the

enactment of laws in relation to matters within the competence of the Parliament of Canada or of any of the legislatures of the Provinces respectively.

8. Nothing in this Act shall be deemed to confer any power to repeal or alter the Constitution or the Constitution Act of the Commonwealth of Australia or the Constitution Act of the Dominion of New Zealand otherwise than in accordance with the law existing before the commencement of this Act.

9.—(1) Nothing in this Act shall be deemed to authorise the Parliament of the Commonwealth of Australia to make laws on any matter within the authority of the States of Australia, not being a matter within the authority of the Parliament or Government of the Commonwealth of Australia.

(2) Nothing in this Act shall be deemed to require the concurrence of the Parliament or Government of the Commonwealth of Australia in any law made by the Parliament of the United Kingdom with respect to any matter within the authority of the States of Australia, not being a matter within the authority of the Parliament or Government of the Commonwealth of Australia, in any case where it would have been in accordance with the constitutional practice existing before the commencement of this Act that the Parliament of the United Kingdom should make that law without such concurrence.

(3) In the application of this Act to the Commonwealth of Australia the request and consent referred to in section four shall mean the request and consent of the Parliament and Government of the Commonwealth.

10.—(1) None of the following sections of this Act, that is to say, sections two, three, four, five and six, shall extend to a Dominion to which this section applies as part of the law of that Dominion unless that section is adopted by the Parliament of the Dominion, and any Act of that Parliament adopting any section of this Act may provide that the adoption shall have effect either from the commencement of this Act or from such later date as is specified in the adopting Act.

(2) The Parliament of any such Dominion as aforesaid may at any time revoke the adoption of any section referred to in subsection (1) of this section.

(3) The Dominions to which this section applies are the Commonwealth of Australia, the Dominion of New Zealand and Newfoundland.

11. Notwithstanding anything in the Interpretation Act, 1889, the expression 'Colony', shall not, in any Act of the Parliament of the United Kingdom passed after the commencement of this Act, include a Dominion or any Province or State forming part of a Dominion.

12. This Act may be cited as the Statute of Westminster, 1931.

# APPENDIX D

## BIBLIOGRAPHY

THE works listed in the bibliography below are divided into nine categories. It will be appreciated that many books fall into two or more of these categories and that the assignment to one or the other has been in some cases quite arbitrary. It is hoped, however, that the classification will be of assistance to those who seek references to a more limited portion of the field than that covered by the bibliography as a whole.

Certain items that have been used in the preparation of the book are not included in the bibliography. Their use has been general throughout the treatment of each country and references to specific points are found in the footnotes. These items include debates, journals, and sessional papers of the several legislatures; collected laws and statutes of the several countries; reports of the courts of the several countries; newspapers and certain other periodicals.

The nine categories of the bibliography are as follows:



### 1. GENERAL WORKS

#### *Books*

ADAMS, GEORGE BURTON, *Federal Government, Its Function and Method,* New York, 1919.

BLUNTSCHLI, J. K., *The Theory of the State,* tr. Ritchie *et al.*, London, 1885; 3rd edn., 1898.

BORGEAUD, CHARLES, *Adoption and Amendment of Constitutions in Europe and America,* tr. Hazen, New York and London, 1895.

BOWIE, ROBERT R. and FRIEDRICH, CARL J., eds. *Studies in Federalism,* Boston, 1954.

BRIE, SIEGFRIED, *Der Bundesstaat,* Leipzig, 1874.

—— *Theorie der Staatenverbindungen,* Stuttgart, 1886.

BRYCE, JAMES (VISCOUNT BRYCE), *Modern Democracies,* 2 vols., New York, 1921.

—— *Studies in History and Jurisprudence,* 2 vols., Oxford, 1901.

BURGESS, JOHN W., *Political Science and Comparative Constitutional Law*, 2 vols., Boston, 1890.

DICEY, ALBERT VENN, *Introduction to the Study of the Law of the Constitution*, London, 1885; 9th edn. by E. C. S. Wade, 1939.

FINER, HERMAN, *The Theory and Practice of Modern Government*, 2 vols., London, 1932; 1 vol. edn., 1934, 2nd edn., New York, 1949.

FOLLETT, MARY P., *The New State*, New York, 1918.

FREEMAN, EDWARD A., *History of Federal Government in Greece and Italy*, London, 1863; 2nd edn. by J. B. Bury, 1893.

FRIEDRICH, CARL J., *Constitutional Government and Democracy*, Boston, 1937; 3rd edn., 1950.

HART, ALBERT BUSHNELL, *Introduction to the Study of Federal Government*, Harvard Historical Monographs No. 2, Boston, 1891.

JAMESON, JOHN ALEXANDER, *The Constitutional Convention; Its History, Powers and Modes of Proceeding*, Chicago, 1867; 4th edn. entitled *A Treatise on Constitutional Conventions*, Chicago, 1887.

JELLINEK, GEORG, *Allgemeine Staatslehre*, Berlin, 1900; 3rd edn., 1914.

KARVE, D. G., *Federations: A Study in Comparative Politics*, London, 1932.

KEITH, ARTHUR BERRIEDALE, *Federation: Its Nature and Conditions*, London, 1942.

LASKI, HAROLD J., *Studies in the Problem of Sovereignty*, New Haven, 1917.

MACIVER, ROBERT M., *The Modern State*, Oxford, 1926.

MAIER, HEDWIG, *Deutscher und Europäischer Föderalismus*, Stuttgart, 1948.

MARRIOTT, SIR JOHN A. R., *The Mechanism of the Modern State*, 2 vols., Oxford, 1927.

MOGI, SOBEI, *The Problem of Federalism: A Study in the History of Political Theory*, 2 vols., London, 1931.

MOUSKHELICHVILI, M., *La Théorie juridique de l'état fédéral*, Paris, 1931.

NEWTON, ARTHUR P., *Federal and Unified Constitutions*, London, 1923.

PEASLEE, AMOS J., *Constitutions of Nations*, 3 vols., Concord, N.H., 1950.

POLEY, ARTHUR P., *The Federal Systems of the United States and the British Empire*, London, 1913.

READ, CONYERS, ed. *The Constitution Re-considered*, New York, 1938.

SAIT, EDWARD MCCHESNEY, *Political Institutions: A Preface*, New York, 1938.

SCHLESINGER, RUDOLF, *Federalism in Central and Eastern Europe*, London, 1945.

SHOTWELL, JAMES T., ed. *Governments of Continental Europe*, New York, 1942; rev. edn., 1952.

SIDGWICK, HENRY, *The Development of European Polity*, London, 1903.

—— *The Elements of Politics*, London, 1891; 4th edn., 1929.

SMITH, HERBERT A., *Federalism in North America: A Comparative Study of Institutions in the United States and Canada*, Boston, 1923.

WHEARE, KENNETH C., *Federal Government*, Oxford, 1946; 3rd edn., 1953.

—— *Modern Constitutions*, Oxford, 1951.

WILLOUGHBY, W. F., *The Government of Modern States*, New York, 1924.

WILSON, WOODROW, *The State*, Boston, 1889.

ZURCHER, ARNOLD J., *The Experiment with Democracy in Central Europe*, New York, 1933.

## *Articles*

ARON, RAYMOND, 'A Suggested Scheme for a Study of Federalism', 4 *International Soc. Sci. Bulletin* 45 (1952).

BOEHM, MAX H., 'Federalism', *Encyclopedia of the Social Sciences*, New York, 1931.

FREUND, PAUL A., 'A Supreme Court in a Federation: Some Lessons from Legal History', 53 *Columbia Law Rev.* 597 (1953).

KIRCHHEIMER, OTTO, 'The Decline of Intra-state Federalism in Western Europe', 3 *World Politics* 281 (1951).

LANDECKER, W. S., 'The Dynamics of Political Integration in Federal Systems', 4 *International Soc. Sci. Bulletin* 55 (1952).

LASKI, HAROLD J., 'The Obsolescence of Federalism', 98 *New Republic* 367 (1939).

LEACOCK, STEPHEN, 'Limitations on Federal Government', 5 *Procs. Amer. Pol. Sci. Assn.* 37 (1908).

LIVINGSTON, WILLIAM S., 'A Note on the Nature of Federalism', 67 *Pol. Sci. Quar.* 81 (1952).

MADDOX, WILLIAM P., ' The Political Basis of Federation', 35 *Amer. Pol. Sci. Rev.* 1125 (1941).

MARRIOTT, SIR JOHN A. R., 'Nationalism and Federalism', 274 *Quar. Rev.* 339 (1940).

—— 'Problems of Federalism', 277 *Quar. Rev.* 27 (1941).

NAWIASKY, HANS, 'Notes sur le concept fédéralisme', *Politeia*, vol. 1, Fasc. 1, 1948–9, p. 7.

RIVERO, J., 'Introduction to a Study of the Development of Federal Societies', 4 *International Soc. Sci. Bulletin* 5 (1952).

ROGERS, NORMAN McL., 'The Political Principles of Federalism', 1 *Canadian Journ. of Ec. and Pol. Sci.* 337 (1935).

SAMUEL, HERBERT (VISCOUNT SAMUEL), 'Federal Government', 72 *Nineteenth Century* 676 (1912).

SEYDEL, MAX VON, 'Der Bundesstaatsbegriff', 28 *Zeitschrift für die gesammte Staatswissenschaft* 185 (1872).

## 2. CANADA

### *Government Documents*

Canada, *The British North America Act and Amendments 1867–1927*, Ottawa, 1928.

Canada, *The British North America Act and Amendments*, ed. Ollivier, Ottawa, 1943.

Canada, *The British North America Acts and Selected Statutes, 1867–1948*, ed. Ollivier, Ottawa, 1949.

Canada, Bureau of Statistics, *Canada—An Official Handbook of Present Conditions and Recent Progress* (issued annually).

Canada, Bureau of Statistics, *The Canada Year-Book* (issued annually).

Canada, Dominion-Provincial Conference, 1935, *Record of Proceedings*, Ottawa, 1936.

Canada, *Dominion-Provincial Conference, Ottawa, 1941, Plenary Session, January 14–15, 1941*, Ottawa, 1941.

Canada, *Dominion-Provincial and Interprovincial Conferences from 1887 to 1926*, Ottawa, 1951.

Canada, Parliament, *Précis of Discussions, Dominion-Provincial Conference, November 3–10, 1927*, Sessional Papers, 1928, No. 69.

Canada, Parliament, House of Commons, Special Committee on the British North America Act, 1935, *Proceedings and Evidence and Report*, Ottawa, 1935.

Canada, *Proceedings of the Conference of Federal and Provincial Governments, Ottawa, December 4–7, 1950*, Ottawa, 1951.

Canada, *Proceedings of the Constitutional Conference of Federal and Provincial Governments, January 10–12, 1950*, Ottawa, 1950.

Canada, *Proceedings of the Constitutional Conference of Federal and Provincial Governments (Second Session), Quebec, September 25–28, 1950*, Ottawa, 1950.

Canada, Royal Commission on Dominion-Provincial Relations, Alberta, *The Case for Alberta*, Edmonton, 1938.

Canada, Royal Commission on Dominion-Provincial Relations, British Columbia, *The Governments of Canada Before the Rowell Commission*, Vancouver, 1938.

Canada, Royal Commission on Dominion-Provincial Relations, British Columbia, *British Columbia in the Canadian Federation: A Submission Presented to the Royal Commission on Dominion-Provincial Relations by the Government of British Columbia*, Victoria, 1938.

Canada, Royal Commission on Dominion-Provincial Relations, *Evidence*, Ottawa, 1940.

Canada, Royal Commission on Dominion-Provincial Relations, Manitoba, *Manitoba's Case: A Submission to the Royal Commission on Dominion-Provincial Relations*, Winnipeg, 1937.

Canada, Royal Commission on Dominion-Provincial Relations, New Brunswick, *Submission by the Government of the Province of New Brunswick to the Royal Commission on Dominion-Provincial Relations*, Fredericton, 1938.

Canada, Royal Commission on Dominion-Provincial Relations, Nova Scotia, *Submission by the Government of the Province of Nova Scotia to the Royal Commission on Dominion-Provincial Relations*, 2 vols., Halifax, 1938.

Canada, Royal Commission on Dominion-Provincial Relations, Quebec, *Statement of the Government of the Province of Quebec*, English text, Quebec, 1938.

Canada, Royal Commission on Dominion-Provincial Relations, *Report*, 3 vols., 1940.

Canada, Royal Commission on Dominion-Provincial Relations, Saskatchewan, *A Submission by the Government of Saskatchewan to the Royal Commission on Dominion-Provincial Relations*, Regina, 1937.

Canada, Senate, *Report on the British North America Act by Parliamentary Counsel of the Senate*, Ottawa, 1939.

Canada, Senate, Special Committee on the Machinery of Government, *Report*, Ottawa, 1919.

Province of Canada, Parliament, 1865, *Parliamentary Debates on the Subject of the Confederation of the British North American Provinces, 3rd sess., 8th Provincial Parliament of Canada*, Quebec, 1865 (usually cited as 'Confederation Debates').

## *Books*

BOURINOT, SIR JOHN, *Federal Government in Canada*, Johns Hopkins Studies in Hist. and Pol. Sci., Baltimore, 1889.

BRACQ, J. C., *The Evolution of French Canada*, New York, 1924.

BRADY, ALEXANDER, *Canada*, London, 1932.

—— ed. *Canada After the War*, Toronto, 1943.

*Cambridge History of the British Empire*, vol. vi, *Canada*, 1930.

*Canadian Problems As Seen by Twenty Outstanding Men of Canada*, Toronto, 1933.

CLEMENT, W. H. P., *The Law of the Canadian Constitution*, Toronto, 1904.

CLOKIE, HUGH McD., *Canadian Government and Politics*, Toronto, 1944.

Comité Permanent des Congrès de la Langue Française, *Mémoire*, Montreal, 1938 (submission to the Royal Commission).

DAWSON, ROBERT MACG., *Constitutional Issues in Canada, 1900–1931*, Oxford, 1933.

—— *The Government of Canada*, Toronto, 1947.

EGGLESTON, WILFRID, *The Road to Nationhood: A Chronicle of Dominion-Provincial Relations*, Toronto, 1946.

GÉRIN-LAJOIE, PAUL, *Constitutional Amendment in Canada*, Toronto, 1950.

GROULX, ABBÉ LIONEL, *La Confédération canadienne, ses origines*, Montreal, 1918.

KENNEDY, W. P. M., *The Constitution of Canada*, Oxford, 1922.

—— *Documents of the Canadian Constitution, 1759–1915*, Toronto, 1918.

—— *The Nature of Canadian Federalism*, Toronto, 1921.

—— *Statutes, Treaties and Documents of the Canadian Constitution, 1713–1929*, Toronto, 1930.

LEFROY, A. H. F., *Canada's Federal System*, Toronto, 1913.

MACKAY, ROBERT A., *The Unreformed Senate of Canada*, Oxford, 1926.

MARTIN, CHESTER, ed. *Canada in Peace and War*, Oxford, 1941.

MAXWELL, J. A., *Recent Developments in Dominion-Provincial Fiscal Relations in Canada*, New York, 1948.

MORIN, WILFRID, *Nos droits minoritaires: les minorités françaises au Canada*, Montreal, 1943.

MUNRO, WILLIAM B., *American Influences on Canadian Government*, Toronto, 1929.

NELSON, JOHN, *The Canadian Provinces, Their Problems and Policies*, Toronto, 1924.

OLLIVIER, MAURICE, *Problems of Canadian Sovereignty from the B.N.A. Act, 1867, to the Statute of Westminster, 1931*, Toronto, 1945.

POPE, SIR JOSEPH, *Confederation: being a series of hitherto unpublished documents bearing on the British North America Act*, Toronto, 1895.

RICHER, LÉOPOLD, *Notre problème politique*, Montreal, 1938.

RIDDELL, WILLIAM R., *The Canadian Constitution in Form and in Fact*, New York, 1923.

ROSS, SIR GEORGE, *The Senate of Canada, its Constitution, Powers and Duties, Historically Considered*, Toronto, 1914.

SIEGFRIED, ANDRÉ, *The Race Question in Canada*, London, 1907.

Société Saint-Jean-Baptiste de Montréal, *Le Canada, pays anglo-français* (*Mémoire presenté à la commission royale des relations entre le dominion et les provinces*), Montreal, 1938.

WARD, NORMAN, *The Canadian House of Commons: Representation*, Toronto, 1950.

## *Articles*

BALLEM, JOHN B., 'Delegation—the Approach of the Supreme Court of Canada to the British North America Act', 29 *Canadian Bar Rev.* 79 (1951).

BASTEDO, F. L., 'Amending the British North America Act', 12 *Canadian Bar Rev.* 209 (1934).

BRADY, ALEXANDER, 'The Critical Problems of Canadian Federalism', 32 *Amer. Pol. Sci. Rev.* 957 (1938).

—— 'Report of the Royal Commission on Dominion-Provincial Relations', 21 *Canadian Hist. Rev.* 245 (1940).

BROSSARD, ROGER, 'The Working of Confederation: A French Canadian View', 3 *Canadian Journ. of Ec. and Pol. Sci.* 333 (1937).

CARON, REV. FR. ARTHUR, 'Notre constitution nationale', 5 *Revue de l'Université d'Ottawa* 277 (1935).

CLOKIE, HUGH MCD., 'Basic Problems of the Canadian Constitution', 8 *Canadian Journ. of Ec. and Pol. Sci.* 1 (1942).

DAFOE, J. W., 'Revising the Constitution', 37 *Queen's Quar.* 1 (1930).

DONNELLY, M. S., 'Constitutional Amendment in Canada', 4 *Parliamentary Affairs* 443 (1951).

EGGLESTON, WILFRID, 'Amending the Canadian Constitution', 56 *Queen's Quar.* 576 (1949–50).

—— 'Dominion-Provincial Relations', 253 *Annals Amer. Acad. of Pol. and Soc. Sci.* 40 (1947).

FITZGERALD, GERALD F., 'The Compact Theory and the Consent of Provinces to Amendments', 13 *Revue de l'Université d'Ottawa* 456 (1943).

GÉRIN-LAJOIE, PAUL, 'Du pouvoir d'amendement constitutionnel au Canada', 29 *Canadian Bar Rev.* 1136 (1951).

—— 'Réflexions sur la constitution canadienne', *Institut Social Populaire, Publication Mensuelle, No. 455*, Montreal, June 1952.

JENNINGS, SIR IVOR, 'Constitutional Interpretation: the Experience of Canada', 51 *Harvard Law Rev.* 1 (1937).

KENNEDY, GILBERT D., 'Amendment of the British North America Acts in Relation to British Columbia, Prince Edward Island, and Newfoundland', 8 *Univ. of Toronto Law Journ.* 208 (1949–50).

LEACOCK, STEPHEN, 'The Nine Sovereignties of Canada: How a Royal Commission Keeps Trouble Asleep', 17 *Barron's* 13 December 1937, p. 12.

LIVINGSTON, WILLIAM S., 'The Amending Power of the Canadian Parliament', 45 *Amer. Pol. Sci. Rev.* 437 (1951).

MALLORY, J. R., 'The "Compact" Theory of Confederation', 21 *Dalhousie Rev.* 342 (1941–2).

MAXWELL, J. A., 'Petitions to London by Provincial Governments', 14 *Canadian Bar Rev.* 738 (1936).

ROGERS, NORMAN McL., 'The Compact Theory of Confederation', *Proc. Canad. Pol. Sci. Assoc.*, 1931, p. 205.

—— 'The Constitutional Impasse', 41 *Queen's Quar.* 475 (1934).

—— 'Genesis of Provincial Rights', 14 *Canadian Hist. Rev.* 9 (1933).

ROWAT, D. C., 'Recent Developments in Canadian Federalism', 18 *Canadian Journ. of Ec. and Pol. Sci.* 1 (1952).

SCOTT, F. R., 'The British North America (No. 2) Act, 1949', 8 *Univ. of Toronto Law Journ.* 201 (1950).

—— 'Centralization and Decentralization in Canadian Federalism', 29 *Canadian Bar Rev.* 1094 (1951).

—— 'Constitutional Adaptations to Changing Functions of Governments', 11 *Canadian Journ. of Ec. and Pol. Sci.* 329 (1945).

—— 'Forgotten Amendments to the Canadian Constitution', 20 *Canadian Bar Rev.* 339 (1942).

—— 'The Special Nature of Canadian Federalism', 13 *Canadian Journ. of Ec. and Pol. Sci.* 13 (1947).

## 3. AUSTRALIA

### *Government Documents*

Australia, Bureau of Census and Statistics, *Local Government in Australia*, Melbourne (1919 ?).

Australia, Commonwealth Grants Commission, *Report* (issued annually).

Australia, Conference of Commonwealth and State Ministers, 1926, *Report on Debates*, Melbourne, 1926.

Australia, Conference of Commonwealth and State Ministers, 1929, *Proceedings and Decisions of Conference*, Canberra, 1929.

Australia, Conference of Commonwealth and State Ministers, Melbourne, 8–14 June 1933, *Proceedings and Decisions of Conference with Appendices*, Canberra, 1933.

Australia, Conference of Commonwealth and State Ministers, *Proceedings and Decisions of Conference held in Adelaide, August 26–28, 1938*, Canberra, 1936.

Australia, Conference of Commonwealth and State Ministers on Constitutional Matters, Melbourne, 16–28 February 1934, *Proceedings and Decisions*, Canberra, 1935.

Australia, *Convention of the Representatives of the Commonwealth and State Parliaments to Consider the Reference of Powers by the States to the Parliament of the Commonwealth*, Canberra, 1942.

Australia, Home Affairs Department, Electoral Branch, *Amendment of the Constitution: federal referendum: The Case For and Against* (published for each referendum).

Australia, *The Official Year Book of the Commonwealth of Australia* (issued annually).

Australia, Prime Minister's Department, *The Federal Guide* (issued irregularly).

Australia, Royal Commission on the Constitution, *Report*, Canberra, 1929.

Australia, Royal Commission on the Constitution, *Report of Proceedings and Minutes of Evidence*, Canberra, 1929.

Australia, Royal Commission on the Finances of South Australia, *Report*, Canberra, 1929.

Australia, Royal Commission on the Finances of Western Australia, as Affected by Federation, *Report*, Canberra, 1925.

### *Books*

BLAND, F. A., *Government in Australia: Selected Readings*, Sydney, 1939; rev. edn., 1944.

BRENNAN, T. C., *Interpreting the Australian Constitution*, Melbourne, 1938.

*Cambridge History of the British Empire*, vol. vii, part 1, *Australia*, 1933.

CAMPBELL, D. A. S., ed. *Post-War Reconstruction in Australia*, Australian Institute of Pol. Sci., Sydney, 1944.

CANAWAY, ARTHUR P., *The Failure of Federalism in Australia*, London, 1930.

COCKBURN, SIR JOHN, *Australian Federation*, London, 1901.

*Constitutional Revision in Australia*, Australian Institute of Pol. Sci., Sydney, 1944.

CRISP, L. F., *Parliamentary Government of the Australian Commonwealth*, New Haven, 1949.

DEAKIN, ALFRED, *The Federal Story: the Inner History of the Federal Cause*, Melbourne, 1944 (written in 1900).

*Decentralization*, Australian Institute of Pol. Sci., Sydney, 1948.

DRUMMOND, DAVID HENRY, *Australia's Changing Constitution: No States or New States*, Sydney, 1943.

DUNCAN, WALTER G. K., ed. *Trends in Australian Politics*, Australian Institute of Pol. Sci., Sydney, 1935.

*Federalism in Australia*, Australian Institute of Pol. Sci., Melbourne, 1949.

GRATTAN, C. HARTLEY, ed. *Australia*, Berkeley, Calif., 1947.

GREENWOOD, GORDON, *The Future of Australian Federalism: A Commentary on the Working of the Constitution*, Melbourne, 1946.

HANCOCK, SIR KEITH, *Australia*, London, 1930.

HIGGINS, H. B., *Essays and Addresses on the Australian Commonwealth Bill*, Melbourne, 1900.

HOLMAN, WILLIAM A., *Three Lectures on the Australian Constitution*, Sydney, 1928.

HUNT, ERLING M., *American Precedents in Australian Federation*, New York, 1930.

KERR, D., *The Law of the Australian Constitution*, Sydney, 1925.

MOORE, W. HARRISON, *The Constitution of the Commonwealth of Australia*, London, 1902.

NICHOLAS, H. S., *The Australian Constitution*, Sydney, 1948.

OVERACKER, LOUISE, *The Australian Party System*, New Haven, 1952.

PATON, G. W., ed. *The Commonwealth of Australia*, London, 1952.

PORTUS, GARNET V., ed. *Studies in the Australian Constitution*, Australian Institute of Pol. Sci., Sydney, 1933.

QUICK, SIR JOHN and GARRAN, SIR ROBERT, *The Annotated Constitution of the Australian Commonwealth*, Sydney, 1901.

REEVES, W. PEMBER, *State Experiments in Australia and New Zealand*, London, 1902.

SAWER, GEOFFREY, *Cases on the Constitution of the Commonwealth of Australia*, Sydney, 1948.

—— ed. *Federalism; An Australian Jubilee Study*, Melbourne, 1952.

SWEETMAN, EDWARD, *Australian Constitutional Development*, Melbourne, 1925.

WARNER, KENNETH O., *An Introduction to Some Problems of Australian Federalism*, Seattle, Wash., 1933.

WYNES, WILLIAM A., *Legislative and Executive Powers in Australia*, Sydney, 1936.

## *Articles*

BAILEY, KENNETH H., 'The Constitution of the Commonwealth: the Report of the Royal Commission on the Constitution of the Commonwealth', 5 *Economic Record* 289 (1929).

—— 'The Reform of the Commonwealth Constitution', 11 *Australian Quar.* 5 (Mar. 1939).

BEASLEY, F. R., 'Problems of Federalism in Australia', 13 *Foreign Affairs* 328 (1935).

—— 'The Secession Movement in Western Australia', 8 *Australian Quar.* 31 (Mar. 1936).

BLAND, F. A., 'Revising the Australian Constitution', 7 *New York Univ. Law Quar. Rev.* 595 (1930).

BROADBENT, J. E., 'Constitutional Amendments in Australia', 25 *Journ. of Comp. Legis. and Int. Law* 1 (Nov. 1943).

CANAWAY, ARTHUR P., 'The By-Pass of Constitutional Reform', 13 *Australian Law Journ.* 394 (1940).

—— 'The Safety Valve of the Commonwealth Constitution', 12 *Australian Law Journ.* 108 (1938).

DIXON, SIR OWEN, 'Aspects of Australian Federalism', 5 *Univ. of Toronto Law Journ.* 241 (1944).

EVATT, HERBERT V., 'Alteration of the Constitution', 16 *Australian Law Journ.* 160 (1942).

—— 'Constitutional Interpretation in Australia', 3 *Univ. of Toronto Law Journ.* 1 (1939).

FRIEDMANN, W., 'Trethowan's Case, Parliamentary Sovereignty, and Limits of Legal Change', 24 *Australian Law Journ.* 103 (1950).

GARRAN, SIR ROBERT, 'The Development of the Australian Constitution', 40 *Law Quar. Rev.* 202 (1924).
HOLMAN, W. A., 'Constitutional Relations in Australia: Commonwealth and States', 46 *Law Quar. Rev.* 502 (1930).
KIRWAN, SIR JOHN, 'Western Australia and Australian Federation', 109 *Nineteenth Century* 169 (1931).
MACDONNELL, W. A., 'Western Australia's Plea for Secession', 15 *Dalhousie Rev.* 315 (1935).
MILLS, STEPHEN, 'Thirty Years' Working of the Australian Constitution', 15 *Journ. of Comp. Legis. and Int. Law* 1 (Feb. 1933).
PIESSE, E. L., 'Federation and Western Australia', 10 *Economic Record* 7 (1934).
WARNER, KENNETH O., 'Australian Federalism at the Crossroads', 4 *Pacific Affairs* 120 (1931).

## 4. SWITZERLAND

### *Government Documents*

Switzerland, *Bundesblatt der Schweizerischen Eidgenossenschaft* (*Feuille fédérale de la confédération suisse*).
Switzerland, *Statistisches Jahrbuch der Schweiz* (*Annuaire statistique de la Suisse*).

### *Books*

BROOKS, ROBERT C., *The Government and Politics of Switzerland*, Yonkers, New York, 1920.
BURCKHARDT, W., *Le Droit Fédéral suisse: Jurisprudence du conseil fédéral et de l'assemblée fédérale en matière de droit public et de droit administratif depuis 1903*, Paris, 1933.
—— *Kommentar der schweizerischen Bundesverfassung*, 7 vols., Berne, 1904–5; 3rd edn., 1931.
COSTE-FLORET, ANDRÉE, *Les Votations populaires fédérales en Suisse de 1874 à 1935*, Montpellier, 1938.
DEPLOIGE, SIMON, *The Referendum in Switzerland*, tr. Trevelyan, London, 1894.
FLEINER, F., *Schweizerisches Bundesstaatsrecht*, Tübingen, 1923.
HILTY, KARL, *Les Constitutions fédérales de la confédération suisse*, Neuchâtel, 1891.
HUGHES, CHRISTOPHER, *The Federal Constitution of Switzerland*, Oxford, 1954.
LEVY-ULLMAN, H. and MIRKINE-GUETZÉVITCH, B., *Suisse*, vol. 6 in the series *La Vie juridique des peuples*, Paris, 1935.
LLOYD, HENRY D., *A Sovereign People: A Study of Swiss Democracy*, New York, 1907.
MOSES, BERNARD, *The Federal Government of Switzerland*, New York, 1889.

PRIVAT, EDMOND, *Trois expériences fédéralistes, États-Unis d'Amérique, Confédération Suisse, Société des Nations*, Neuchâtel, 1942.

RAPPARD, WILLIAM E., *La Constitution fédérale de la Suisse, 1848–1948*, Neuchâtel, 1948.

—— *The Government of Switzerland*, New York, 1936.

—— *L'Individu et l'état dans l'évolution constitutionnel de la Suisse*, Zurich, 1936.

TRIPP, MYRON L., *The Swiss and United States Federal Constitutional Systems: A Comparative Study*, Paris, 1940.

VINCENT, JOHN M., *Government in Switzerland*, New York, 1913.

—— *State and Federal Government in Switzerland*, Baltimore, 1891.

## *Articles*

LLOYD, ROGER, 'Switzerland—"Union in Partition"', 143 *Nineteenth Century* 104 (1948).

PILLER, JOSEPH, 'Le Fédéralisme suisse', *Politeia*, vol. 1, Fasc. 1, 1948–9, p. 94.

ROUGEMONT, DENIS DE (tr. Maisel), 'Idea of a Federation: Lessons to be Derived from Switzerland', 17 *Virginia Quar. Rev.* 491 (1941).

## 5. UNITED STATES

### *Government Documents*

U.S., Department of State, Memorandum, *The Child Labor Amendment*, mimeo., no date.

U.S., Department of State, *Ratification of the Twenty-First Amendment to the Constitution of the United States*, Publ. No. 573, Washington, 1934.

U.S., House of Representatives, *Documents Illustrative of the Formation of the Union of the American States*, ed. C. C. Tansill, 69th Cong., 1st sess., House Doc. No. 398, Washington, 1927.

U.S., Library of Congress, Legislative Reference Service, *Legislative History of Amendments to the Constitution of the United States: Amendment the 20th*, ed. Myrtis Jarrell, Washington, 1934.

U.S., Library of Congress, Legislative Reference Service, *Proposed Amendments to the Constitution*, 70th Cong., 2nd sess., 1929, House Doc. No. 551, ed. Michael A. Musmanno, Washington, 1929.

U.S., Library of Congress, Legislative Reference Service, *Recent State Action on Calling Constitutional Conventions and Constitutional Revisions*, ed. M. H. Pendleton, Washington, 1935.

U.S., Senate, Committee on Judiciary, *Hearings Before a Sub-Committee on S.J.R. 134 proposing an amendment to the U.S. Constitution relative to the ratification of constitutional amendments by popular vote*, 75th Cong., 3rd sess., Washington, 1938.

U.S., Senate, *Applications of State Legislatures for a National Constitutional Convention*, ed. Senator Millard F. Tydings, 71st Cong., 2nd sess., Sen. Doc. No. 78, Washington, 1930.

U.S., Senate, *Proposed Amendments to the Constitution of the United States, 1889–1926*, ed. C. C. Tansill, 69th Cong., 1st sess., Sen. Docs. vol. viii, Washington, 1926.

U.S., Senate, Secretary of the Senate, *Proposed Amendments to the Constitution of the United States introduced in Congress Dec. 6, 1926 to Jan. 4, 1941*, ed. Edwin A. Halsey, Washington, 1941.

U.S., Senate, Secretary of the Senate, *Proposed Amendments to the Constitution of the United States Introduced in Congress from the 69th Congress, 2nd sess., through the 79th Congress, December 6, 1926 to January 3, 1947*, ed. Carl A. Loeffler, Washington, 1947.

[Note: other Congressional documents may be found in the bibliography below under the name of the author or editor.]

## *Books*

AMES, HERMAN V., *see* Articles.

BLAND, JULIA M., *Georgia and the Federal Constitution*, Department of State Publ. No. 1078, Washington, 1937.

BRAXTON, A. C., *The 15th Amendment: An Account of its Enactment*, Staunton, Va., 1933.

BROWN, EVERETT S., *Ratification of the Twenty-First Amendment of the Constitution of the United States: State Conventions and Laws*, Ann Arbor, Mich., 1938.

BRYCE, JAMES (VISCOUNT BRYCE), *The American Commonwealth*, 3 vols., London and New York, 1888; rev. edn., 2 vols., 1931–3.

CAHILL, FRED V., *Judicial Legislation*, New York, 1952.

CALHOUN, JOHN C., *Disquisition on Government and Discourse on the Constitution and Government of the United States*, ed. Kralle, Columbia, S.C., 1851.

CLARK, JANE PERRY, *The Rise of a New Federalism*, New York, 1938.

DODD, WALTER F., *The Revision and Amendment of State Constitutions*, Baltimore, 1910.

ELLIOTT, JONATHAN, *Debates in the Several State Conventions on the Adoption of the Federal Constitution . . .*, 5 vols., Philadelphia, 1836–45; 2nd edn., Washington, 1854.

ELLIOTT, WILLIAM Y., *The Need for Constitutional Reform*, New York, 1935.

*Federalism as a Democratic Process*, essays by ROSCOE POUND, CHARLES HOWARD MCILWAIN, ROY F. NICHOLS, with commentaries by EDWARD S. CORWIN and FRANCIS W. COKER, New Brunswick, N.J., 1942.

*The Federalist*, by ALEXANDER HAMILTON, JAMES MADISON, and JOHN JAY, (written in 1787–88; various editions).

FLACK, HORACE E., *The Adoption of the Fourteenth Amendment*, Baltimore, 1908.

HAZLITT, HENRY, *A New Constitution Now*, New York, 1947.

HOCKETT, HOMER C., *The Constitutional History of the United States*, 2 vols., New York, 1939.

HORWILL, H. W., *The Usages of the American Constitution*, Oxford, 1925.
KING, JUDSON, *American Principles and the Wadsworth Amendment*, Washington, 1925.
LE DUC, THOMAS, *Connecticut and the First Ten Amendments to the Federal Constitution*, Sen. Doc. No. 96, 75th Cong., 1st sess., 1937.
MATHEWS, JOHN M., *Legislative and Judicial History of the 15th Amendment*, Baltimore, 1909.
McLAUGHLIN, ANDREW C., *A Constitutional History of the United States*, New York, 1935.
MERRIAM, CHARLES E., *American Political Theories*, New York, 1903.
—— *American Political Ideas, 1865–1917*, New York, 1920.
MYERS, DENIS P., *Massachusetts and the First Ten Amendments to the Constitution*, Sen. Doc. No. 181, 74th Cong., 2nd sess., Washington, 1936.
—— *The Process of Constitutional Amendment*, Sen. Doc. No. 314, 76th Cong., 3rd sess., Washington, 1940.
ORFIELD, LESTER B., *The Amending of the Federal Constitution*, Ann Arbor, Mich., 1942.
POORE, BENJAMIN P., *Federal and State Constitutions, Colonial Charters, and Other Organic Laws of the United States*, Philadelphia, 1877.
SMITH, JAMES ALLEN, *The Spirit of American Government*, New York, 1907.
SWISHER, CARL B., *The Growth of Constitutional Power in the United States*, Chicago, 1946.
WILSON, WOODROW, *Congressional Government*, Boston, 1885.
—— *Constitutional Government in the United States*, New York, 1908.

## *Articles*

AMES, HERMAN V., 'The Amending Provision of the Federal Constitution in Practice', 63 *Procs. of Amer. Phil. Soc.* 62 (1924).
—— 'The Proposed Amendments to the Constitution of the United States During the First Century of its History', *Amer. Hist. Assoc., Annual Report*, 1896, vol. 2, p. 1.
—— 'Recent Development of the Amending Power as Applied to the Federal Constitution', 72(2) *Procs. of Amer. Phil. Soc.* 87 (1933).
ARNESON, BEN A., 'Is it Easy to Amend the Constitution?', 60 *Amer. Law Rev.* 600 (1926).
BACON, SELDEN, 'How the Tenth Amendment Affected the Fifth Article of the Constitution', 16 *Virginia Law Rev.* 771 (1930).
BROWN, EVERETT S., 'Procedure of Amendment', 185 *Annals Amer. Acad. of Pol. and Soc. Sci.* 85 (1936).
—— 'The Ratification of the Twenty-First Amendment', 29 *Amer. Pol. Sci. Rev.* 1008 (1935).
BROWN, GEORGE S., 'The People Should be Consulted as to Constitutional Changes', 16 *Amer. Bar Assoc. Journ.* 404 (1930).
BURGESS, JOHN W., 'American Commonwealth', 1 *Pol. Sci. Quar.* 9 (1886).
CARMAN, ERNEST C., 'Why and How the Present Method of Amending

the Federal Constitution Should be Changed', 17 *Oregon Law Rev.* 102 (1938).

CLARK, HOMER, 'The Supreme Court and the Amending Process', 39 *Virginia Law Rev.* 621 (1953).

CORWIN, EDWARD S., and RAMSEY, M. L., 'The Constitutional Law of Constitutional Amendment', 26 *Notre Dame Lawyer* 185 (1951).

CUMMINGS, HOMER S., 'The Nature of the Amending Process', 6 *George Washington Law Rev.* 247 (1938).

DODD, WALTER F., 'Amending the Federal Constitution', 30 *Yale Law Journ.* 321 (1921).

DOWLING, NOEL T., 'Clarifying the Amending Process', 1 *Washington and Lee Law Rev.* 215 (1940).

—— 'A New Experiment in Ratification', 19 *Amer. Bar Assoc. Journ.* 383 (1933).

ELDRIDGE, SEBA, 'Need for a More Democratic Procedure of Amending the Constitution', 10 *Amer. Pol. Sci. Rev.* 683 (1916).

FEIBELMAN, H. U., 'The Evolution of Article V', 38 *Commercial Law Journ.* 197 (1933).

FRIERSON, WILLIAM L., 'Amending the Constitution of the United States', 33 *Harvard Law Rev.* 659 (1920).

GARRETT, FINIS J., 'Amending the Federal Constitution', 7 *Tennessee Law Rev.* 286 (1929).

GRINNELL, FRANK W., 'Finality of State's Ratification of a Constitutional Amendment', 11 *Amer. Bar Assoc. Journ.* 192 (1925).

HOLDING, A. M., 'Perils to be Apprehended from Amending the Constitution', 57 *Amer. Law Rev.* 481 (1923).

JAMESON, JAMES F., 'Studies in the History of the Federal Convention of 1787', *Amer. Hist. Assoc., Annual Report*, 1902, vol. 1, p. 157.

JOHNSTONE, FREDERIC B., 'An Eighteenth Century Constitution', 7 *Illinois Law Rev.* 265 (1912).

LEE, BLEWETT, 'Abolishing the Senate By Amendment', 16 *Virginia Law Rev.* 364 (1930).

LINCOLN, ALEXANDER, 'Ratification by Conventions', 18 *Massachusetts Law Quar.* 287 (1933).

LIVINGSTON, WILLIAM S., 'The Legal and Political Determinants of American Federalism', 34 *Southwestern Soc. Sci. Quar.* 40 (1953).

MACHEN, ARTHUR W., JR., 'Is the Fifteenth Amendment Void?', 23 *Harvard Law Rev.* 168 (1910).

MARBURY, WILLIAM L., 'The Limitations Upon the Amending Power', 33 *Harvard Law Rev.* 223 (1919).

MARTIG, RALPH R., 'Amending the Constitution', 35 *Michigan Law Rev.* 1253 (1937).

MARTIN, W. L., 'The Amending Power: the Background of the Income Tax Amendment', 39 *Amer. Bar Assn. Journ.* 21; 124 (1953).

MCBAIN, HOWARD L., 'Amending the Federal Constitution', 31 *Amer. Mercury* 204 (1934).

—— 'Or By Conventions', *New York Times*, 11 December 1932, Sec. 4, p. 1.

McGovney, D. O., 'Is the Eighteenth Amendment Void Because of its Contents?', 20 *Columbia Law Rev.* 499 (1920).

Miller, Justin, 'Amendment of the Federal Constitution: Should It be Made More Difficult?', 10 *Minnesota Law Rev.* 185 (1926).

Mitchell, William D., 'Methods of Amending the Constitution', 25 *Lawyer and Banker* 265 (1932).

Musmanno, Michael A., 'The Difficulty of Amending Our Federal Constitution, Defect or Asset?', 15 *Amer. Bar Assoc. Journ.* 505 (1929).

—— 'Is the Amendment Process Too Difficult?', 57 *Amer. Law Rev.* 694 (1923).

Needham, Charles W., 'Changing the Fundamental Law', 69 *Univ. of Pennsylvania Law Rev.* 223 (1921).

Platz, W. A., 'Article Five of the Federal Constitution', 3 *George Washington Law Rev.* 17 (1934).

Putney, Bryant, 'Revision of the Constitution', 1 *Editorial Research Reports* 287 (1937).

Radin, Max, 'The Intermittent Sovereign', 39 *Yale Law Journ.* 514 (1930).

Robinson, W. A., 'Advisory Referendum in Massachusetts on the Child Labor Amendment', 19 *Amer. Pol. Sci. Rev.* 69 (1925).

Skinner, George D., 'Intrinsic Limitations on the Power of Constitutional Amendment', 18 *Michigan Law Rev.* 213 (1920).

Smith, J. Hopkinson, 'Is Prohibition Constitutional?', 4 *Plain Talk* 415 (1929).

Smith, Munroe, 'Shall We Make Our Constitution Flexible?', 194 *North Amer. Rev.* 657 (1911).

Stevens, D. N., 'Ratification of Proposed Federal Amendment After Prior Rejection', 11 *Southern California Law Rev.* 472 (1938).

Taft, Henry W., 'Amendment of the Federal Constitution. Is the Power Conferred by Article Five Limited by the Tenth Amendment?', 16 *Virginia Law Rev.* 647 (1930).

Taft, William Howard, 'Can Ratification of an Amendment to the Constitution be Made to Depend Upon a Referendum?', 29 *Yale Law Journ.* 821 (1920).

Thompson, J. David, 'The Amendment of the Federal Constitution', 3 *Procs. Acad. Pol. Sci.* 65 (1912).

Uhl, Raymond, 'Sovereignty and the Fifth Article', 16 *Southwestern Soc. Sci. Quar.* 1 (1936).

Wechsler, Herbert, 'The Political Safeguards of Federalism: the Role of the States in the Composition and Selection of the National Government', 54 *Columbia Law Rev.* 543 (1954).

Weinfeld, Abraham C., 'Power of Congress Over State Ratifying Conventions', 51 *Harvard Law Rev.* 473 (1938).

Westervelt, G. N., 'Amend Article V', 24 *Lawyer and Banker* 166 (1931).

Wheeler, Wayne B., 'Is a Constitutional Convention Impending?', 21 *Illinois Law Rev.* 782 (1927).

White, Justin D., 'Is There an Eighteenth Amendment?', 5 *Cornell Law Quar.* 113 (1920).

WILLIAMS, GEORGE W., 'Are There Any Limitations on the Power to Amend the United States Constitution?', 5 *Temple Law Quar.* 554 (1931).

WILLIS, HUGH E., 'The Doctrine of the Amendability of the United States Constitution', 7 *Indiana Law Journ.* 457 (1932).

—— 'The Doctrine of Sovereignty Under the United States Constitution', 15 *Virginia Law Rev.* 437 (1929).

WILLIS, PAUL G. and WILLIS, GEORGE L., 'The Politics of the Twenty-Second Amendment', 5 *Western Political Quar.* 469 (1952).

WILTSE, C. M., 'Calhoun's Democracy: Problems of the Sovereign State and the Autonomy of its Component Elements', 3 *Journal of Politics* 210 (1941).

## 6. UNION OF SOUTH AFRICA

### *Books*

BRAND, R. H., *The Union of South Africa*, Oxford, 1909.

*Cambridge History of the British Empire*, vol. vii, *South Africa*, 1936.

COWEN, DENNIS V., *Parliamentary Sovereignty and the Entrenched Sections of the South Africa Act*, Cape Town and Johannesburg, 1951.

HOFMEYR, JAN H., *South Africa*, 1930; 2nd edn. by J. C. Cope, New York, 1952.

KENNEDY, W. P. M. and SCHLOSBERG, H. J., *The Law and Custom of the South African Constitution*, Oxford, 1935.

MARQUARD, LEO, *The People and Policies of South Africa*, Oxford, 1952.

MAY, HENRY JOHN, *The South African Constitution*, Cape Town and Johannesburg, 1949. (A revised edition of Kennedy and Schlosberg listed above.)

NATHAN, MANFRED, *The South African Commonwealth*, Johannesburg, 1919.

### *Articles*

COWEN, DENNIS V., 'The Entrenched Sections of the South Africa Act', 70 *South African Law Journ.* 238 (1953).

—— 'Legislature and Judiciary: Reflections on the Constitutional Issue in South Africa, Part I', 15 *Modern Law Rev.* 282 (1952).

—— Ibid., Part II, 16 *Modern Law Rev.* 273 (1953).

GRISWOLD, E. N., 'The Demise of the High Court of Parliament in South Africa', 66 *Harvard Law Rev.* 864 (1953).

KOVALSKY, S., 'Federal Elements in the Union Constitution', 49 *South African Law Journ.* 479 (1932).

LEACOCK, STEPHEN, 'The Union of South Africa', 4 *Amer. Pol. Sci. Rev.* 498 (1910).

MAY, HENRY JOHN, 'The Union of South Africa, the Provinces and the Central Government', 18 *State Government* 115 (1945).

MCWHINNEY, EDWARD, 'The Union Parliament, the Supreme Court, and the Entrenched Clauses of the South Africa Act', 30 *Canadian Bar Rev.* 692–722; 734–41 (1952).

POLLOK, WALTER, 'The Legislative Competence of the Union Parliament', 48 *South African Law Journ.* 269 (1931).

WOOLSEY, LESTER H., 'A Comparative Study of the South African Constitution', 4 *Amer. Journ. of Int. Law* 1 (1910).

## 7. GERMANY

### *Books*

BORNHAK, KONRAD, *Grundriß des Deutschen Staatsrechts*, Leipzig, 1907.

BRECHT, ARNOLD, *Federalism and Regionalism in Germany*, New York, 1945.

EMERSON, RUPERT, *State and Sovereignty in Modern Germany*, New Haven, 1928.

HAENEL, ALBERT, *Deutsches Staatsrecht*, Leipzig, 1892.

KRAUS, HERBERT, *The Crisis of German Democracy: A Study of the Spirit of the Constitution of Weimar*, Princeton, 1932.

KRÜGER, FRITZ-KONRAD, *The Government and Politics of the German Empire*, Yonkers, N.Y., 1915.

LABAND, PAUL, *Das Staatsrecht des Deutschen Reiches*, 3 vols., Tübingen and Leipzig, 1876–82; 4th edn., 4 vols., 1901.

LITCHFIELD, EDWARD H. and associates, *Governing Postwar Germany*, Ithaca, N.Y., 1953.

MEYER, GEORG, *Lehrbuch des Deutschen Staatsrechtes*, Leipzig, 1879; 5th edn., 1899.

NAWIASKY, HANS, *Die Grundgedanken des Grundgesetzes für die Bundesrepublik Deutschland*, Stuttgart, 1950.

PREUSS, HUGO, *Deutschlands republikanische Reichsverfassung*, Berlin, 1923; 2nd edn., 1924.

REHM, HERMANN, *Unitarismus und Föderalismus in der Deutschen Reichsverfassung*, Dresden, 1898.

TAYLOR, A. J. P., *The Course of German History*, New York, 1946.

WEBER, WERNER, *Spannungen und Kräfte im westdeutschen Verfassungssystem*, Stuttgart, 1951.

### *Articles*

FRIEDRICH, CARL J., 'Rebuilding the German Constitution, Part I', 43 *Amer. Pol. Sci. Rev.* 461 (1949).

—— Ibid., Part II, 43 *Amer. Pol. Sci. Rev.* 677 (1949).

HAUSMANN, JOSEF, 'Das deutsche Reich als Bundesstaat', 33 *Archiv des öffentlichen Rechts* 82 (1914).

HELBOK, A., 'Deutschland und Frankreich, Länderstaat, Einheitstaat', 227 *Deutsche Rundschau* 14 (1931).

MASON, J. B., 'Federalism—the Bonn Model', in *Constitutions and Constitutional Trends Since World War Two*, ed. by Arnold J. Zurcher, New York, 1951

TREIPEL, HEINRICH, 'Der Föderalismus und die Revision der Weimarer Reichsverfassung', 14 *Zeitschrift für Politik* 193 (1924–5).

WELLS, ROGER H., 'The Liquidation of the German Laender', 30 *Amer. Pol. Sci. Rev.* 350 (1936).

## 8. BRITISH COMMONWEALTH AND EMPIRE

### *Government Documents*

United Kingdom, Conference on Devolution, *Letter from Mr. Speaker to the Prime Minister (with appendices), Cmd. 692* (1920).

United Kingdom, Foreign Office, *Constitutions of All Countries*, vol. 1, *The British Empire*, 1938.

United Kingdom, *Report of the Conference on the Operation of Dominion Legislation and Merchant Shipping Legislation, 1929*, Cmd. 3479 (1930).

### *Books*

ADAMS, RANDOLPH G., *Political Ideas of the American Revolution*, Durham, N.C., 1922.

BEAGLEHOLE, JOHN C., ed. *New Zealand and the Statute of Westminster*, Wellington, 1944.

BECKER, CARL L., *The Declaration of Independence*, New York, 1922; rev. edn., 1948.

BRADY, ALEXANDER, *Democracy in the Dominions*, Toronto, 1947; 2nd edn., 1952.

*Cambridge History of the British Empire*, vol. vii, part 2, *New Zealand*, 1933.

DAWSON, ROBERT MACG., *The Development of Dominion Status, 1900–1936*, Oxford, 1936.

EGERTON, HUGH E., *Federations and Unions Within the British Empire*, Oxford, 1911; 2nd edn., 1924.

EVATT, HERBERT V., *The King and His Dominion Governors*, Oxford, 1936.

HIGHT, J. and BAMFORD, H. D., *The Constitutional History and Law of New Zealand*, Christchurch, 1914.

JENNINGS, SIR IVOR, *The Commonwealth in Asia*, Oxford, 1951.

—— *Some Characteristics of the Indian Constitution*, Madras, 1953.

—— and YOUNG, C. M., *Constitutional Laws of the Commonwealth*, Oxford, 1952.

KEITH, ARTHUR BERRIEDALE, *Constitutional Law of the British Dominions*, London, 1933.

—— *The Dominions as Sovereign States: Their Constitutions and Governments*, London, 1938.

—— *Responsible Government in the Dominions*, 3 vols., 1908; 2nd edn., 2 vols., Oxford, 1928.

LABILLIERE, F. P. de, *Federal Britain*, London, 1894.

LIPSON, LESLIE, *The Politics of Equality*, Chicago, 1948.

MANSERGH, NICHOLAS, *The Government of Northern Ireland*, London, 1936.

MORRELL, W. P., *New Zealand*, London, 1935.

—— *The Provincial System in New Zealand, 1852–1876*, London, 1932.

'PACIFICUS', *Federalism and Home Rule*, London, 1910.
SIEGFRIED, ANDRÉ, *Democracy in New Zealand*, tr. Burns, London, 1914.
TARRING, C. J., *Chapters on the Law Relating to the Colonies*, London, 1887; 4th edn., 1913.
WHEARE, KENNETH C., *The Statute of Westminster and Dominion Status*, Oxford, 1938; 5th edn., 1953.

### *Articles*

APPADORAI, A., 'The Indian Constitution: Underlying Principles', 45 *Asiatic Rev.* 483 (1949).
FURBER, HOLDEN, 'Constitution-Making in India', 18 *Far East. Surv.* 85 (1949).
LIPSON, LESLIE, 'Centralization in New Zealand', 18 *State Govt.* 208 (1945).
PRASAD, RAJENDRA, 'The New Indian Constitution', 3 *Parliamentary Affairs* 420 (1950).
SENGUPTA, N. C., 'First Amendment of the Constitution', 5 *Indian Law Rev.* 135 (1951).
WALLACE, D. D., 'The Indian Constitution of 1949', 13 *Journal of Politics* 269 (1951).
WHEARE, KENNETH C., 'The Impact of Federalism upon Parliamentary Government in the Commonwealth', 4 *Parliamentary Affairs* 163 (1950).

## 9. LATIN AMERICA

### *Books*

AMADEO, SANTOS P., *Argentine Constitutional Law*, New York, 1944.
BLANKSTEN, GEORGE I., *Peron's Argentina*, Chicago, 1953.
FITZGIBBON, RUSSELL H., ed. *The Constitutions of the Americas*, Chicago, 1948.
JAMES, HERMAN G. and MARTIN, PERCY A., *The Republics of Latin America*, New York, 1923.
MACDONALD, AUSTIN F., *Latin American Politics and Government*, New York, 1949.
ROWE, LEO STANTON, *The Federal System of the Argentine Republic*, Washington, 1921.

### *Articles*

ILSEY, L. L., 'The Argentine Constitutional Revision of 1949', 14 *Journal of Politics* 224 (1952).
MARTIN, PERCY A., 'Federalism in Brazil', 18 *Hisp. Amer. Hist. Rev.* 143 (1938).
MASUR, GERHARD, 'Democracy in Eclipse', 26 *Virginia Quar. Rev.* 336 (1950).
MECHAM, J. LLOYD, 'Mexican Federalism, Fact or Fiction?', 208 *Annals Amer. Acad. of Pol. and Soc. Sci.* 23 (Mar. 1940).

MECHAM, J. LLOYD, 'The Origins of Federalism in Mexico', 18 *Hisp. Amer. Hist. Rev.* 164 (1938).

PIERSON, W. W., ed. 'Pathology of Democracy in Latin America', 44 *Amer. Pol. Sci. Rev.* 100 (1950).

SCOTT, R. E., 'Argentina's New Constitution: Social Democracy or Social Authoritarianism?', 4 *Western Pol. Quar.* 567 (1951).

WALKER, HARVEY, 'Federalism in Brazil', 18 *State Government* 43 (1945).

WYLER, MARCUS, 'The Development of the Brazilian Constitution, 1891–1946', 31 *Journ. of Comp. Leg. and Int. Law*, Nov. 1949, p. 53.

# INDEX